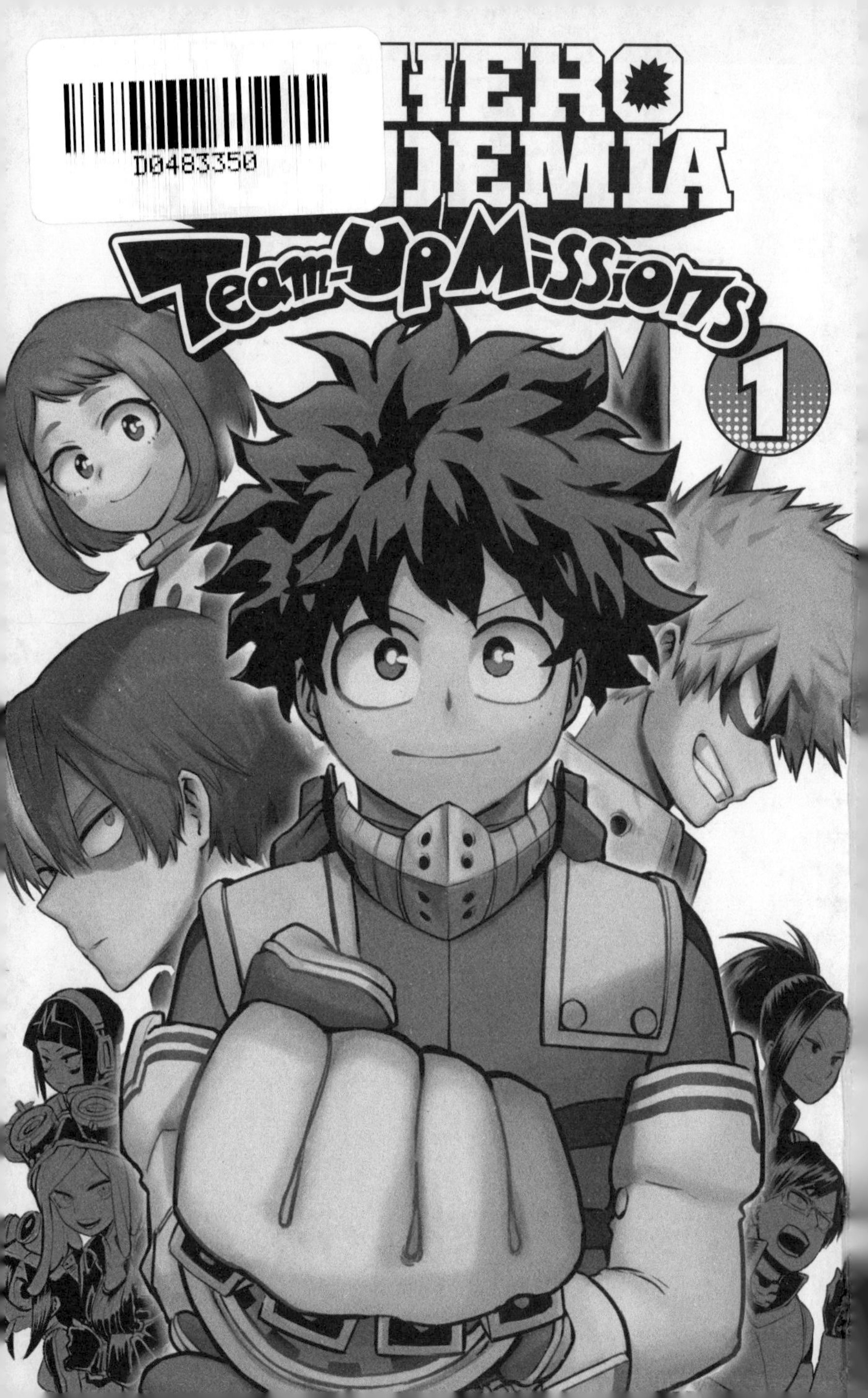
HERO
Team-Up Missions
1

MY HERO ACADEMIA Team-Up Missions

1

SHONEN JUMP Manga Edition

STORY & ART BY
YOKO AKIYAMA

ORIGINAL CONCEPT BY
KOHEI HORIKOSHI

TRANSLATION **Caleb Cook**
TOUCH-UP ART & LETTERING **John Hunt**
DESIGNER **Julian [JR] Robinson**
EDITOR **Hope Donovan**

BOKU NO HERO ACADEMIA TEAM UP MISSION © 2019
by Kohei Horikoshi, Yoko Akiyama
All rights reserved.
First published in Japan in 2019 by SHUEISHA Inc., Tokyo.
English translation rights arranged by SHUEISHA Inc.

Printed in the U.S.A.

Published by VIZ Media, LLC
P.O. Box 77010
San Francisco, CA 94107

10 9 8 7 6 5 4 3 2 1
First printing, March 2021

viz.com

MY HERO ACADEMIA Team-Up Missions 1

Team-Up Missions Begin

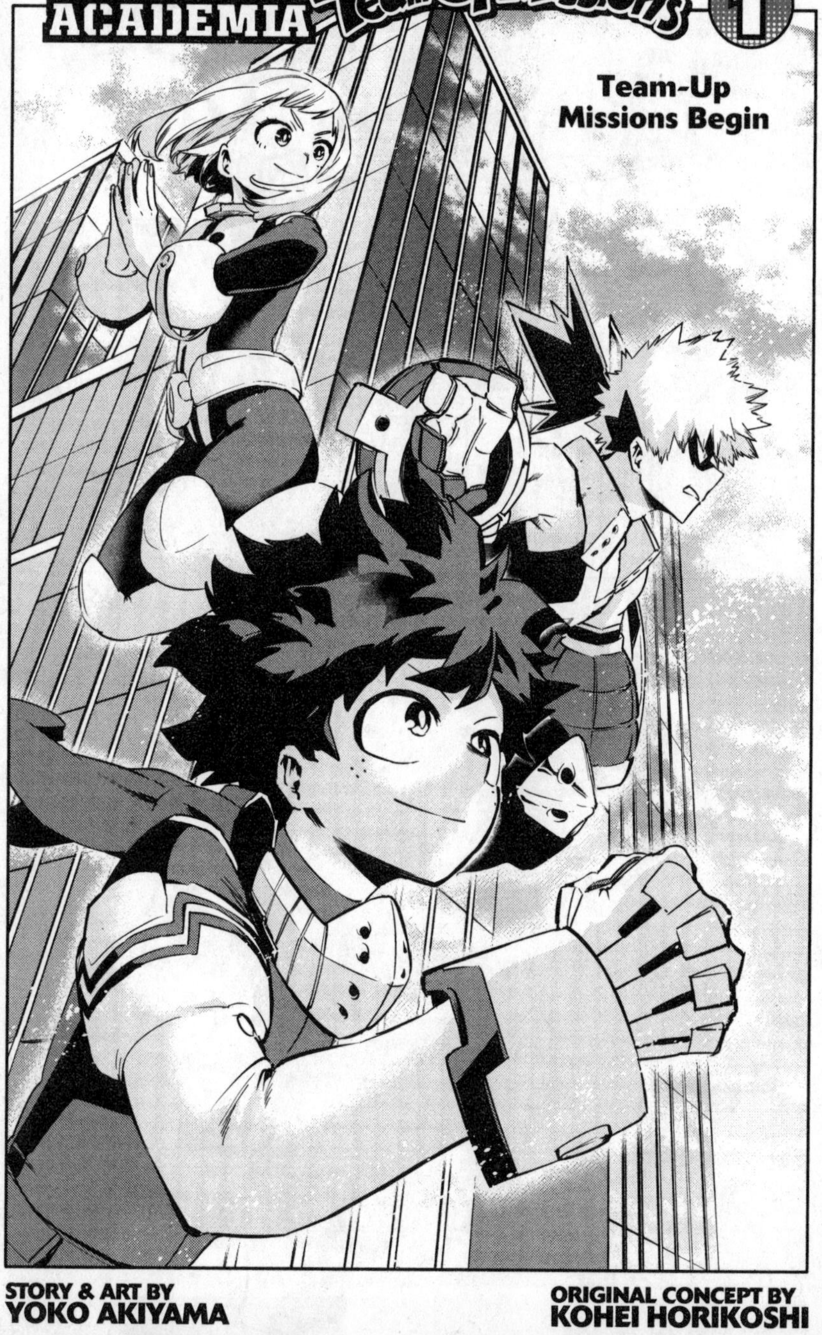

STORY & ART BY
YOKO AKIYAMA

ORIGINAL CONCEPT BY
KOHEI HORIKOSHI

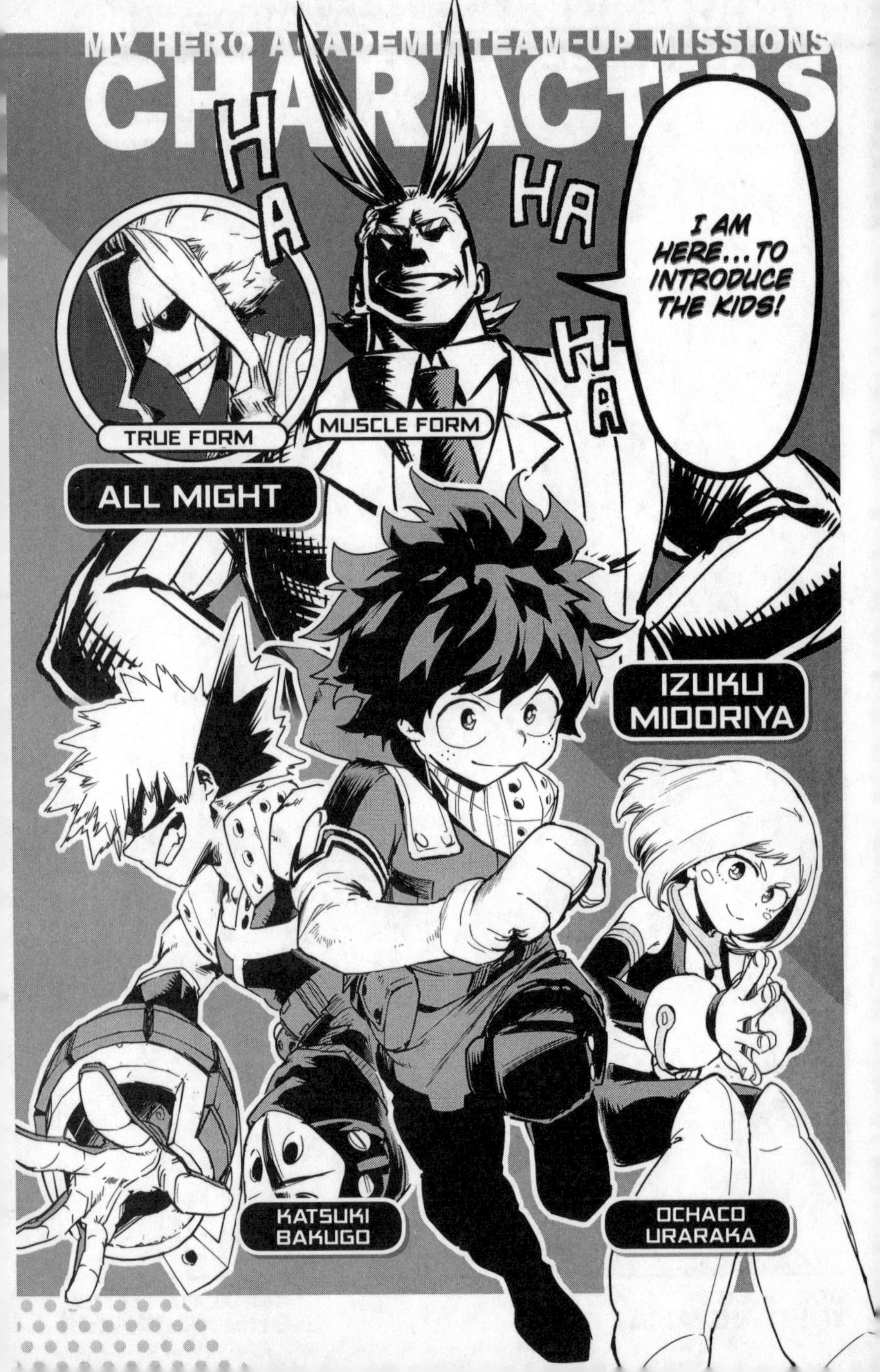
MY HERO ACADEMIA TEAM-UP MISSIONS
CHARACTERS
HA HA HA HA
I AM HERE...TO INTRODUCE THE KIDS!
TRUE FORM
MUSCLE FORM
ALL MIGHT
IZUKU MIDORIYA
KATSUKI BAKUGO
OCHACO URARAKA

STORY

MY HERO ACADEMIA

One day, people began manifesting special abilities that came to be known as "Quirks," and before long, the world was full of superpowered humans. The world then saw an uptick in crime, perpetrated by villains armed with new abilities. But heroes emerged to protect society and are now officially authorized to fight crime in the name of peace.

WHAT'S A TEAM-UP MISSION?

For many years, All Might was known as "the Symbol of Peace," and his mere presence was enough to deter crime. With his retirement from public duty, people are clamoring for the next generation of heroes to rise up, which has led to the creation of a new program—centered around hero students—called Team-Up Missions. By pairing students all over the country with pro heroes, these heroes in training get a chance to improve their teamwork!

U.A. HIGH SCHOOL

SHOTO TODOROKI

TENYA IDA

MOMO YAOYOROZU

TSUYU ASUI

MINORU MINETA

SHOTA AIZAWA
CLASS 1-A HOMEROOM TEACHER

AND MANY MORE!

HEROES

HAWKS

MIRKO

FAT GUM

MY HERO ACADEMIA 1
Team-Up Missions

CONTENTS

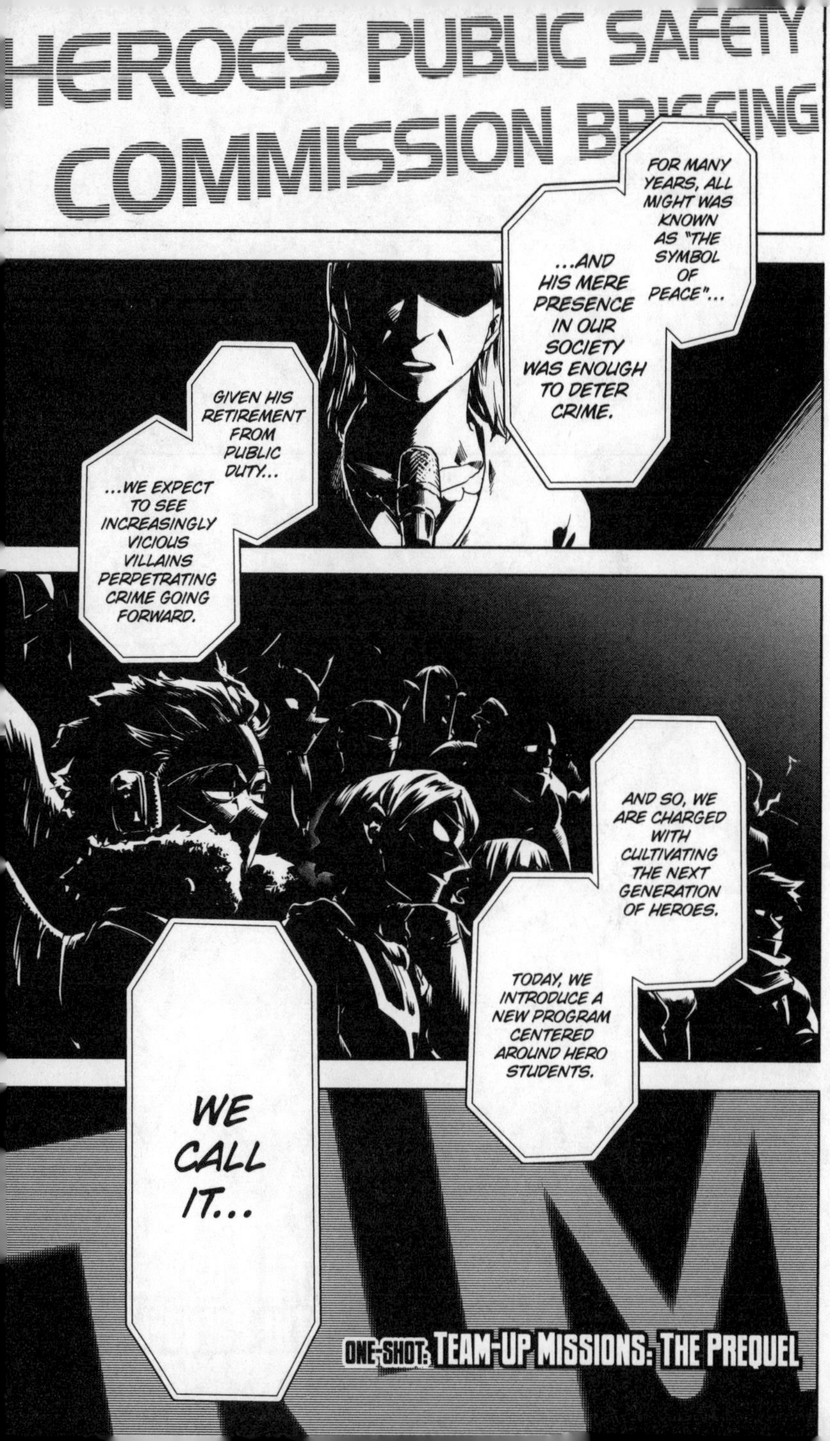
HEROES PUBLIC SAFETY COMMISSION BRIEFING
FOR MANY YEARS, ALL MIGHT WAS KNOWN AS "THE SYMBOL OF PEACE"...
...AND HIS MERE PRESENCE IN OUR SOCIETY WAS ENOUGH TO DETER CRIME.
GIVEN HIS RETIREMENT FROM PUBLIC DUTY...
...WE EXPECT TO SEE INCREASINGLY VICIOUS VILLAINS PERPETRATING CRIME GOING FORWARD.
AND SO, WE ARE CHARGED WITH CULTIVATING THE NEXT GENERATION OF HEROES.
TODAY, WE INTRODUCE A NEW PROGRAM CENTERED AROUND HERO STUDENTS.
WE CALL IT...
ONE-SHOT: TEAM-UP MISSIONS: THE PREQUEL

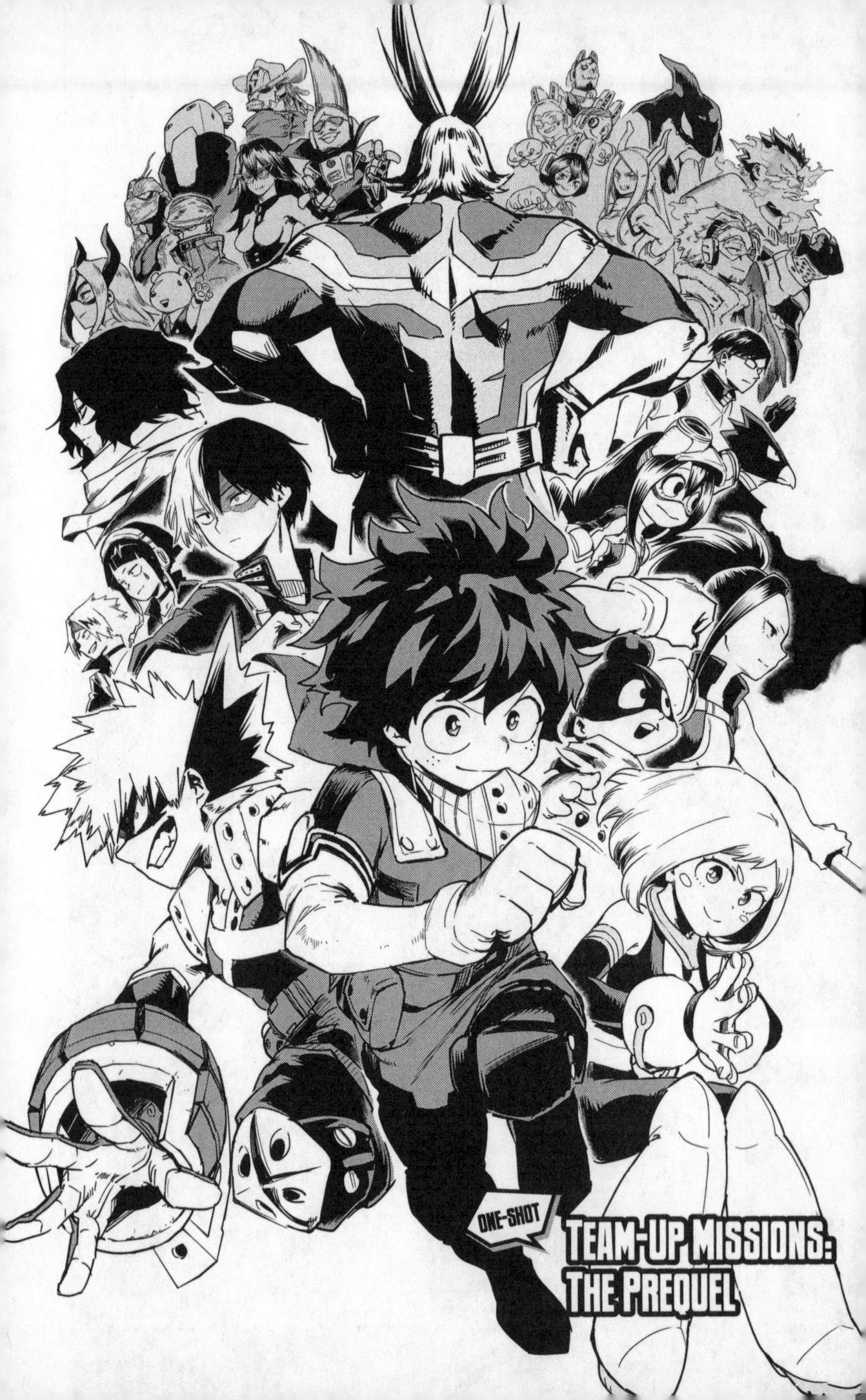
ONE-SHOT
TEAM-UP MISSIONS:
THE PREQUEL

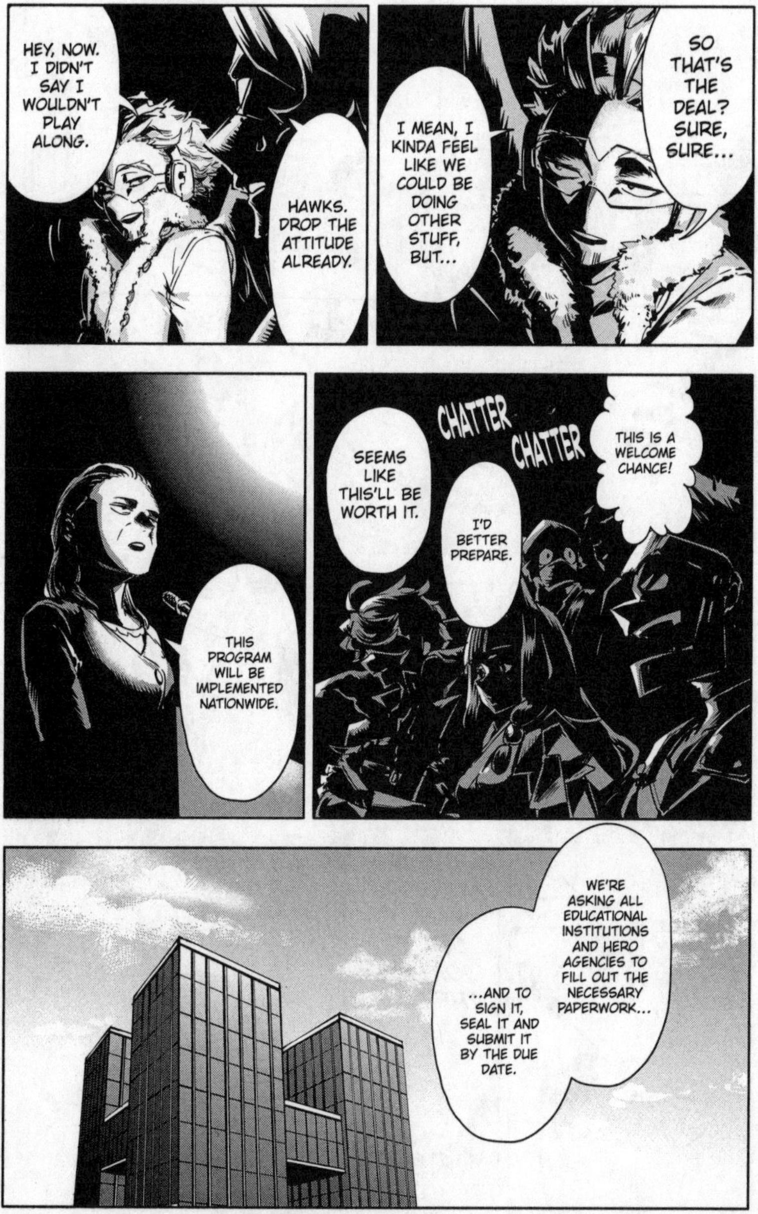
SO THAT'S THE DEAL? SURE, SURE...
I MEAN, I KINDA FEEL LIKE WE COULD BE DOING OTHER STUFF, BUT...
HAWKS. DROP THE ATTITUDE ALREADY.
HEY, NOW. I DIDN'T SAY I WOULDN'T PLAY ALONG.
THIS IS A WELCOME CHANCE!
CHATTER
CHATTER
SEEMS LIKE THIS'LL BE WORTH IT.
I'D BETTER PREPARE.
THIS PROGRAM WILL BE IMPLEMENTED NATIONWIDE.
WE'RE ASKING ALL EDUCATIONAL INSTITUTIONS AND HERO AGENCIES TO FILL OUT THE NECESSARY PAPERWORK...
...AND TO SIGN IT, SEAL IT AND SUBMIT IT BY THE DUE DATE.

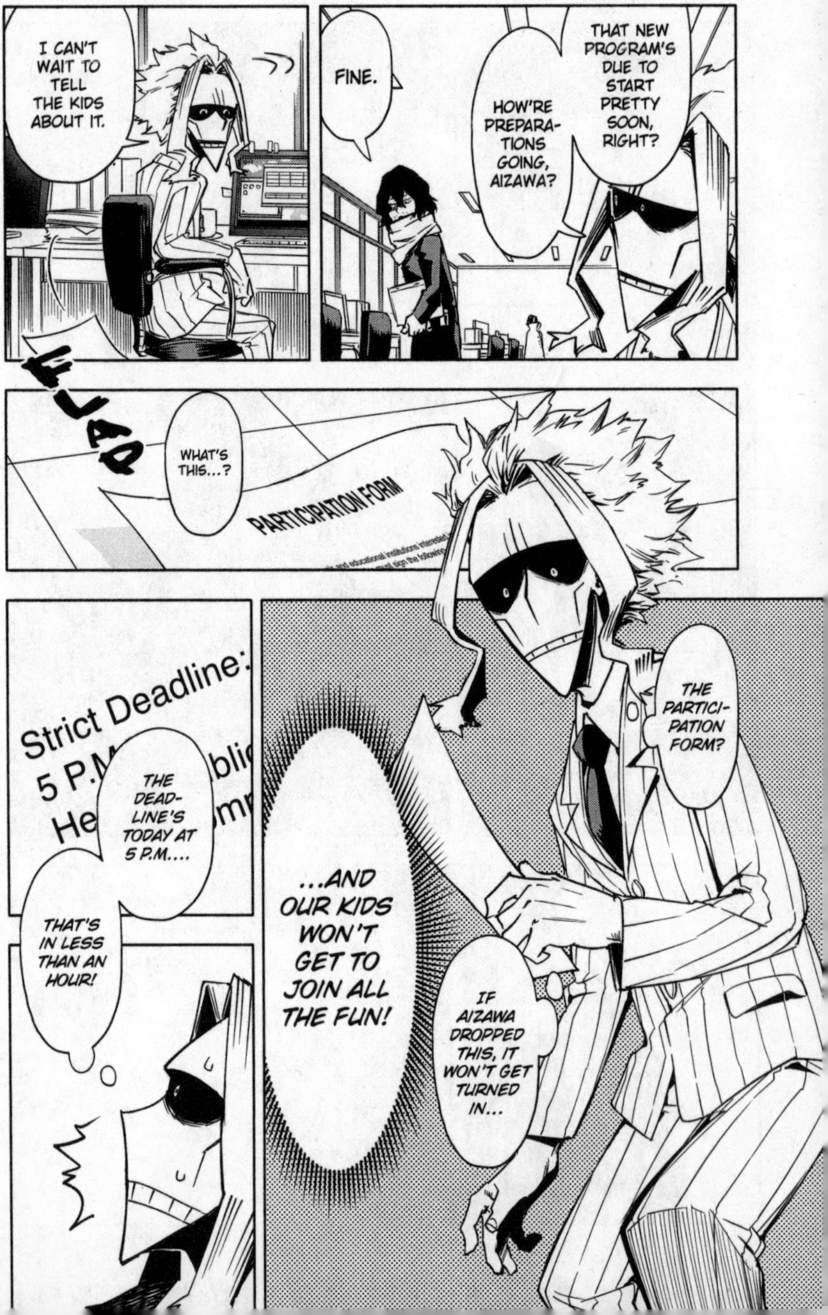
THAT NEW PROGRAM'S DUE TO START PRETTY SOON, RIGHT?
HOW'RE PREPARATIONS GOING, AIZAWA?
FINE.
I CAN'T WAIT TO TELL THE KIDS ABOUT IT.
FLAP
WHAT'S THIS...?
PARTICIPATION FORM
THE PARTICIPATION FORM?
IF AIZAWA DROPPED THIS, IT WON'T GET TURNED IN...
...AND OUR KIDS WON'T GET TO JOIN ALL THE FUN!
Strict Deadline:
THE DEADLINE'S TODAY AT 5 P.M....
THAT'S IN LESS THAN AN HOUR!

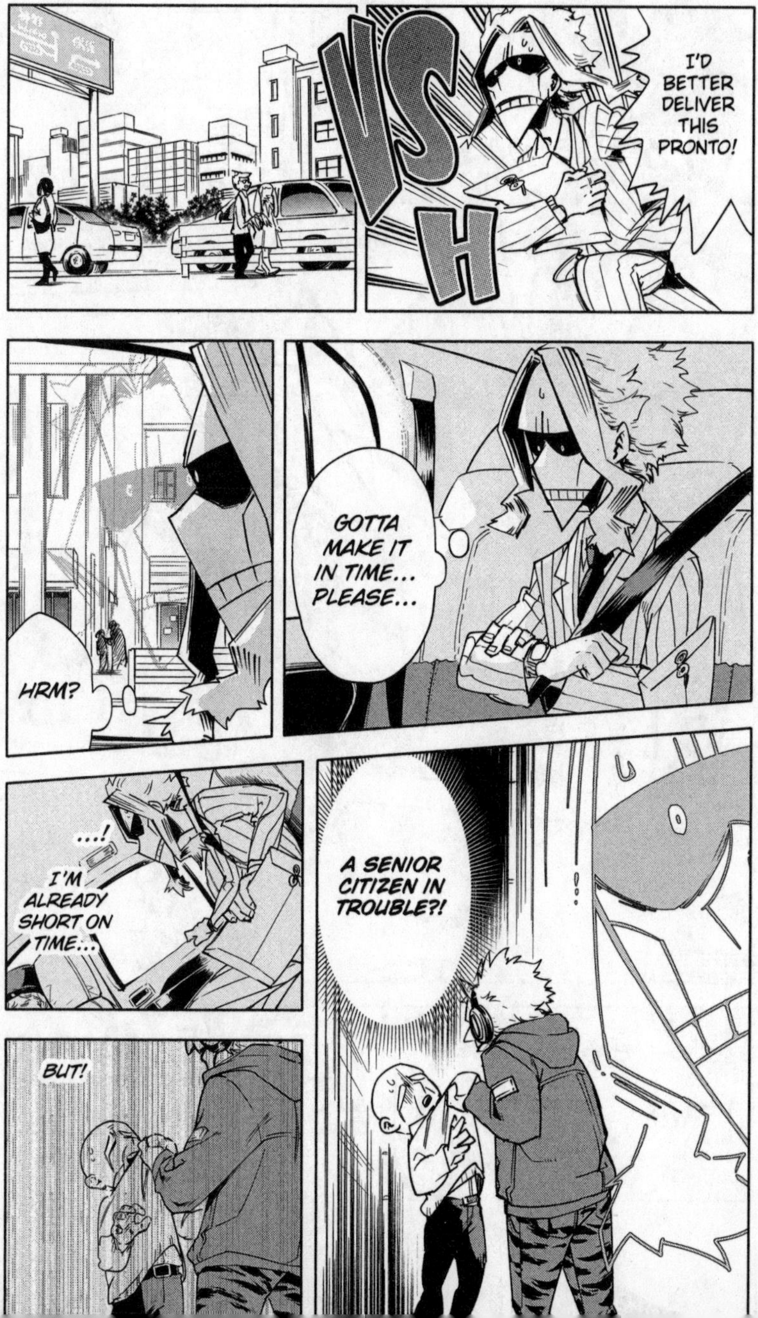
VSH
I'D BETTER DELIVER THIS PRONTO!
GOTTA MAKE IT IN TIME... PLEASE...
HRM?
A SENIOR CITIZEN IN TROUBLE?!
...!
I'M ALREADY SHORT ON TIME...
BUT!

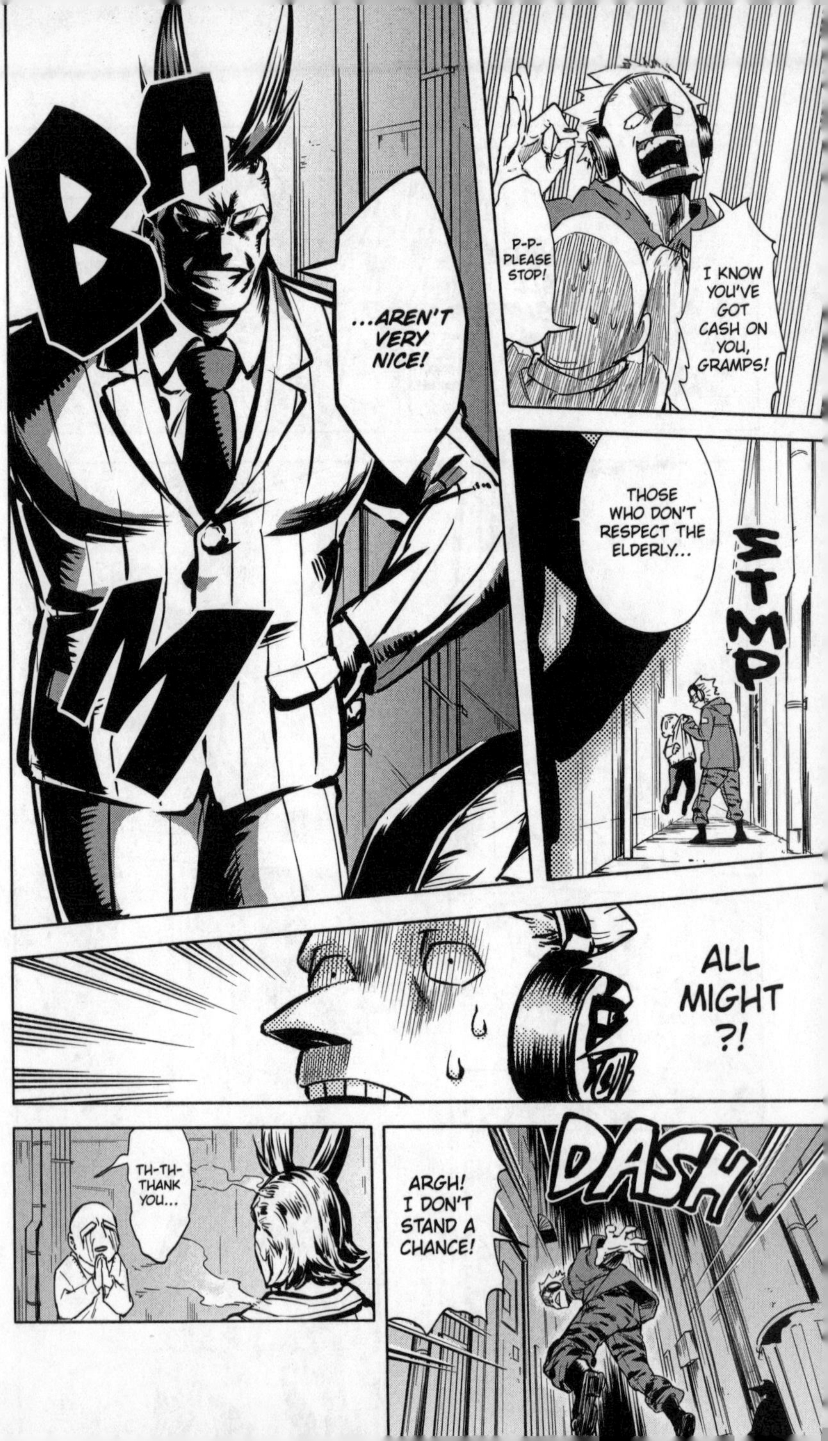
I KNOW YOU'VE GOT CASH ON YOU, GRAMPS!
P-P-PLEASE STOP!
THOSE WHO DON'T RESPECT THE ELDERLY...
STMP
BAM
...AREN'T VERY NICE!
ALL MIGHT ?!
DASH
ARGH! I DON'T STAND A CHANCE!
TH-TH-THANK YOU...

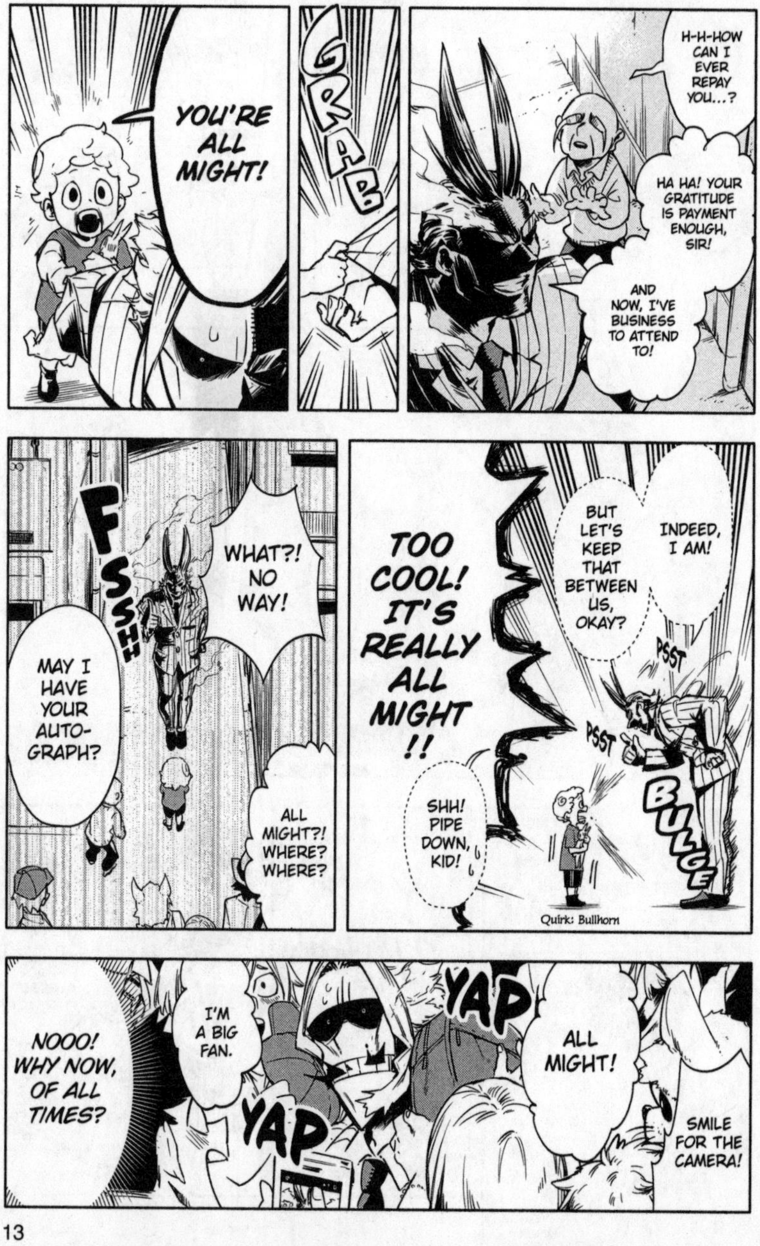
H-H-HOW CAN I EVER REPAY YOU...?
HA HA! YOUR GRATITUDE IS PAYMENT ENOUGH, SIR!
AND NOW, I'VE BUSINESS TO ATTEND TO!
GRAB
YOU'RE ALL MIGHT!
INDEED, I AM!
BUT LET'S KEEP THAT BETWEEN US, OKAY?
PSST
TOO COOL! IT'S REALLY ALL MIGHT !!
PSST
BULGE
SHH! PIPE DOWN, KID!
Quirk: Bullhorn
WHAT?! NO WAY!
FSSHH
MAY I HAVE YOUR AUTO-GRAPH?
ALL MIGHT?! WHERE? WHERE?
SMILE FOR THE CAMERA!
ALL MIGHT!
YAP
I'M A BIG FAN.
YAP
NOOO! WHY NOW, OF ALL TIMES?

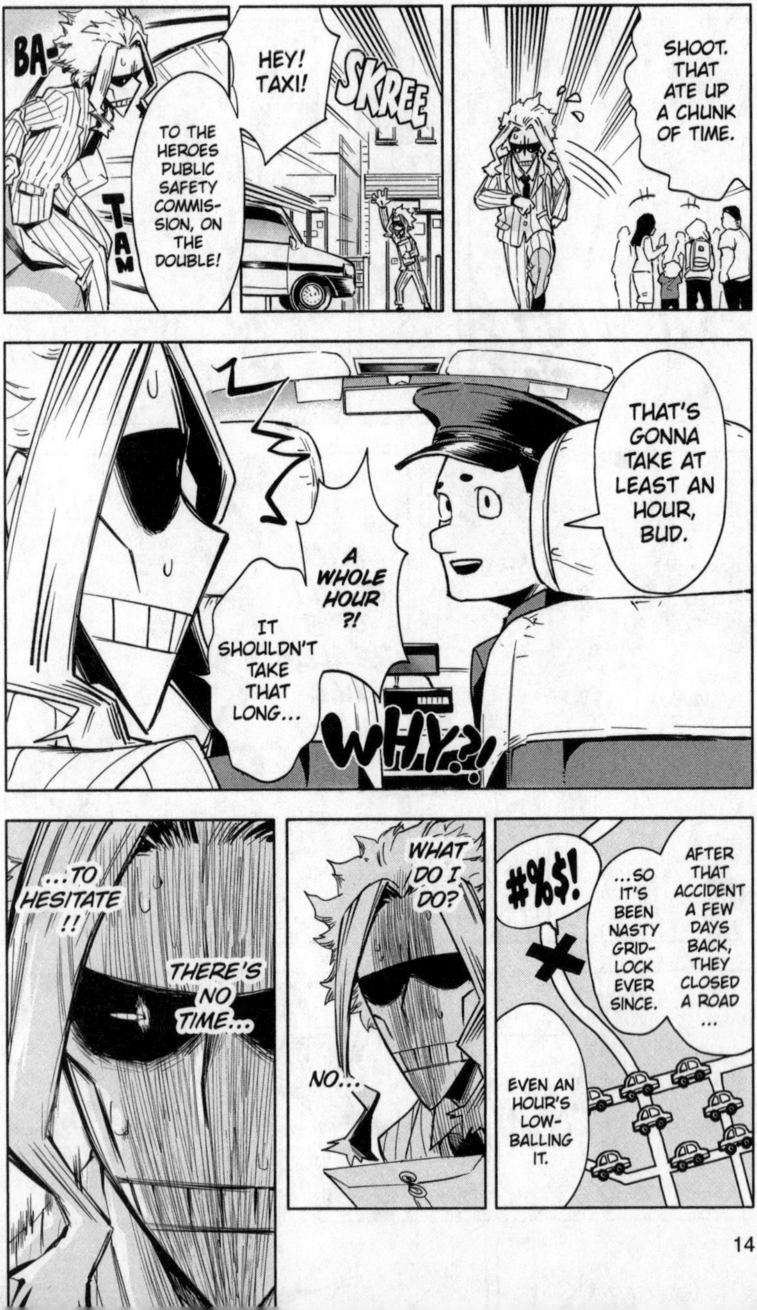
SHOOT. THAT ATE UP A CHUNK OF TIME.
SKREE
HEY! TAXI!
BA-
TO THE HEROES PUBLIC SAFETY COMMIS-SION, ON THE DOUBLE!
TAM
THAT'S GONNA TAKE AT LEAST AN HOUR, BUD.
A WHOLE HOUR?!
IT SHOULDN'T TAKE THAT LONG...
WHY?!
AFTER THAT ACCIDENT A FEW DAYS BACK, THEY CLOSED A ROAD...
...SO IT'S BEEN NASTY GRID-LOCK EVER SINCE.
#%$!
EVEN AN HOUR'S LOW-BALLING IT.
WHAT DO I DO?
NO...
THERE'S NO TIME...
...TO HESITATE!!

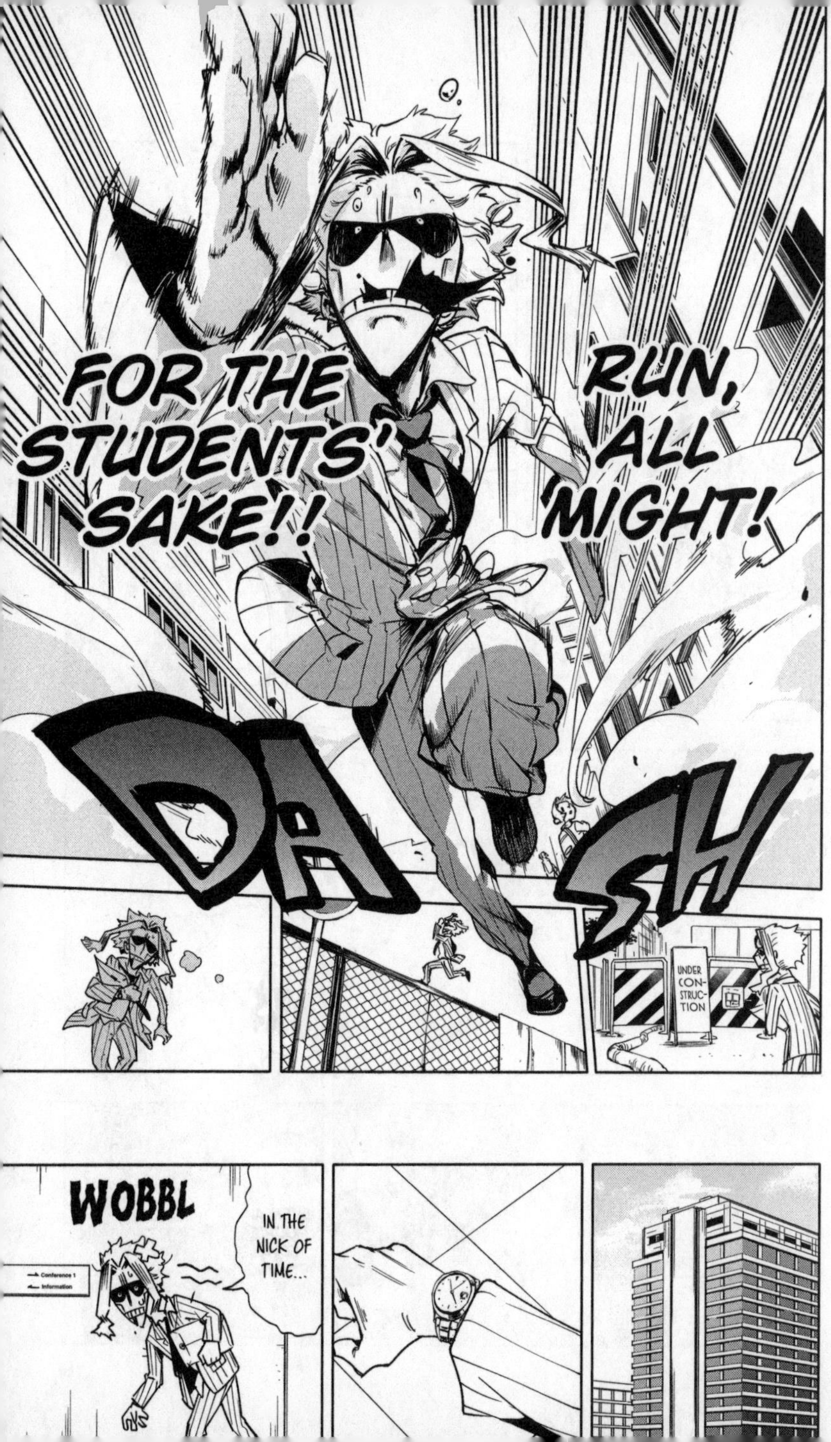
RUN, ALL MIGHT!
FOR THE STUDENTS' SAKE!!
DASH
UNDER CONSTRUCTION
IN THE NICK OF TIME...
WOBBL
Conference 1
Information

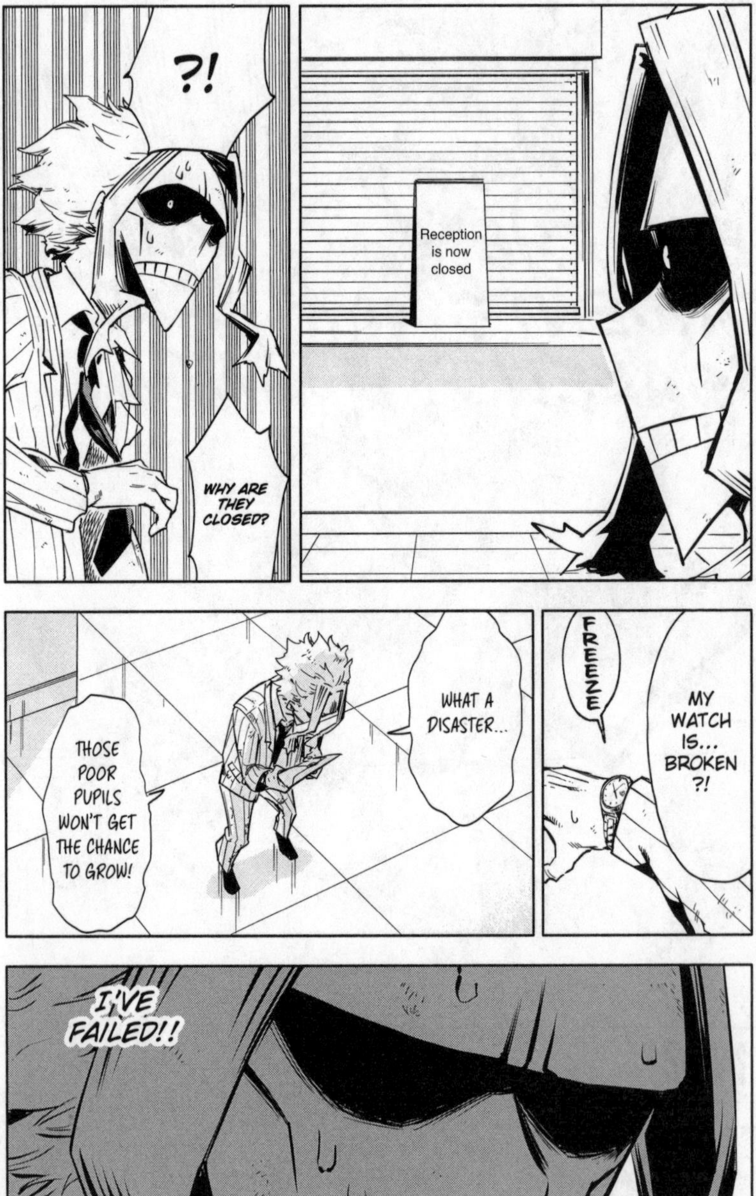
Reception is now closed
?!
WHY ARE THEY CLOSED?
MY WATCH IS... BROKEN ?!
FREEZE
WHAT A DISASTER...
THOSE POOR PUPILS WON'T GET THE CHANCE TO GROW!
I'VE FAILED!!

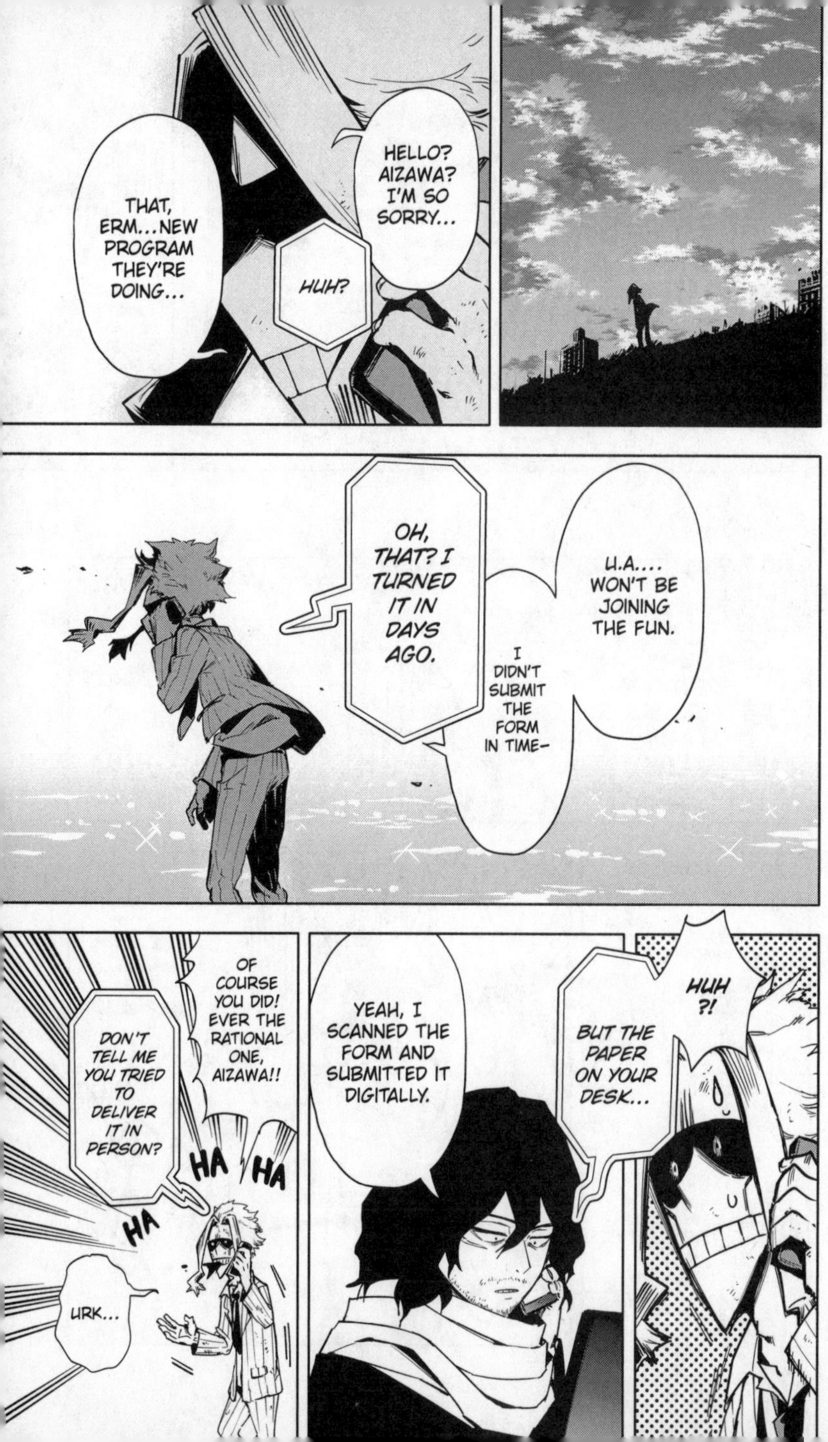
HELLO? AIZAWA? I'M SO SORRY...
HUH?
THAT, ERM...NEW PROGRAM THEY'RE DOING...
U.A.... WON'T BE JOINING THE FUN.
I DIDN'T SUBMIT THE FORM IN TIME—
OH, THAT? I TURNED IT IN DAYS AGO.
HUH ?!
BUT THE PAPER ON YOUR DESK...
YEAH, I SCANNED THE FORM AND SUBMITTED IT DIGITALLY.
OF COURSE YOU DID! EVER THE RATIONAL ONE, AIZAWA!!
DON'T TELL ME YOU TRIED TO DELIVER IT IN PERSON?
HA HA
HA
URK...

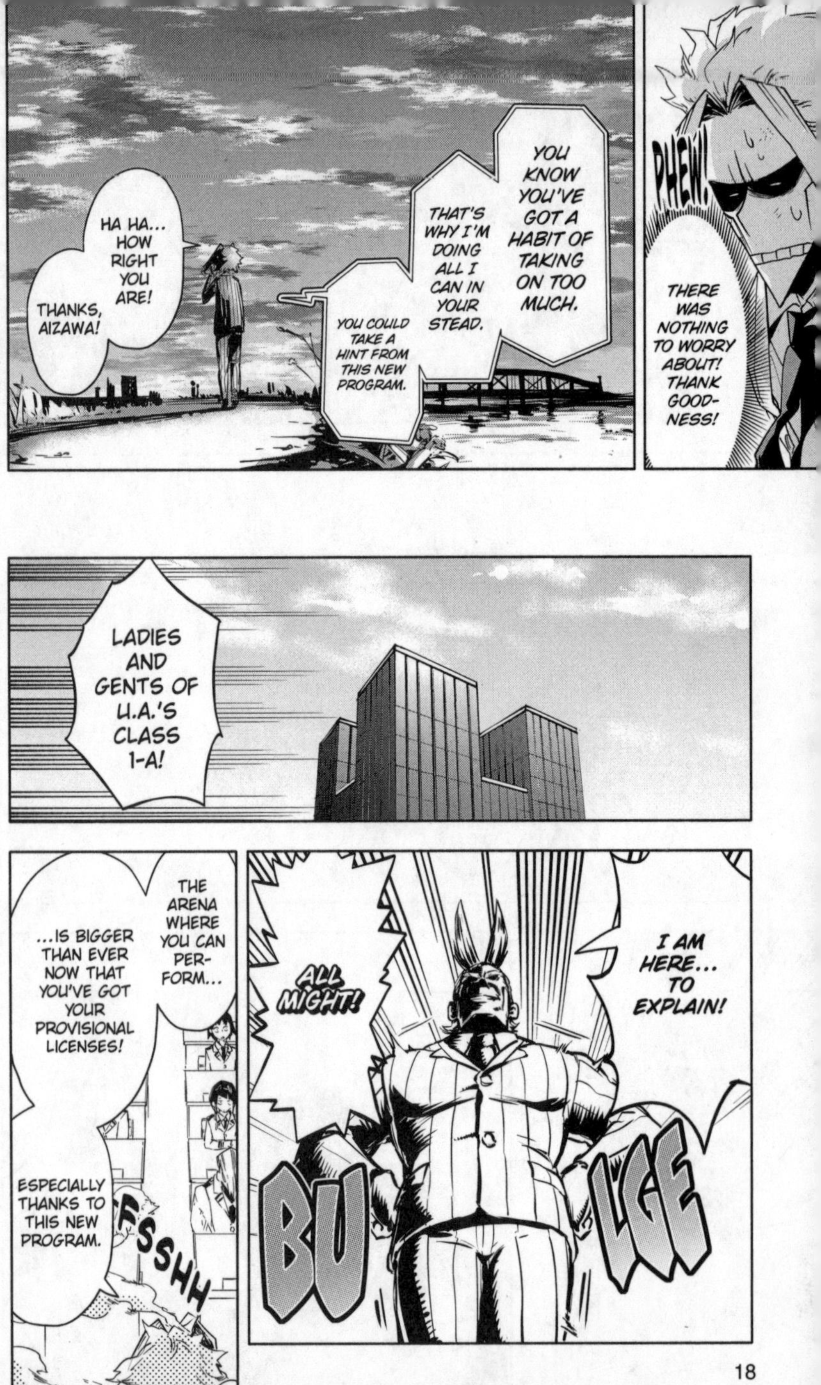
PHEW!
THERE WAS NOTHING TO WORRY ABOUT! THANK GOOD-NESS!
YOU KNOW YOU'VE GOT A HABIT OF TAKING ON TOO MUCH.
THAT'S WHY I'M DOING ALL I CAN IN YOUR STEAD.
YOU COULD TAKE A HINT FROM THIS NEW PROGRAM.
HA HA... HOW RIGHT YOU ARE!
THANKS, AIZAWA!
LADIES AND GENTS OF U.A.'S CLASS 1-A!
I AM HERE... TO EXPLAIN!
ALL MIGHT!
BULGE
THE ARENA WHERE YOU CAN PER-FORM...
...IS BIGGER THAN EVER NOW THAT YOU'VE GOT YOUR PROVISIONAL LICENSES!
ESPECIALLY THANKS TO THIS NEW PROGRAM.
FSSHH

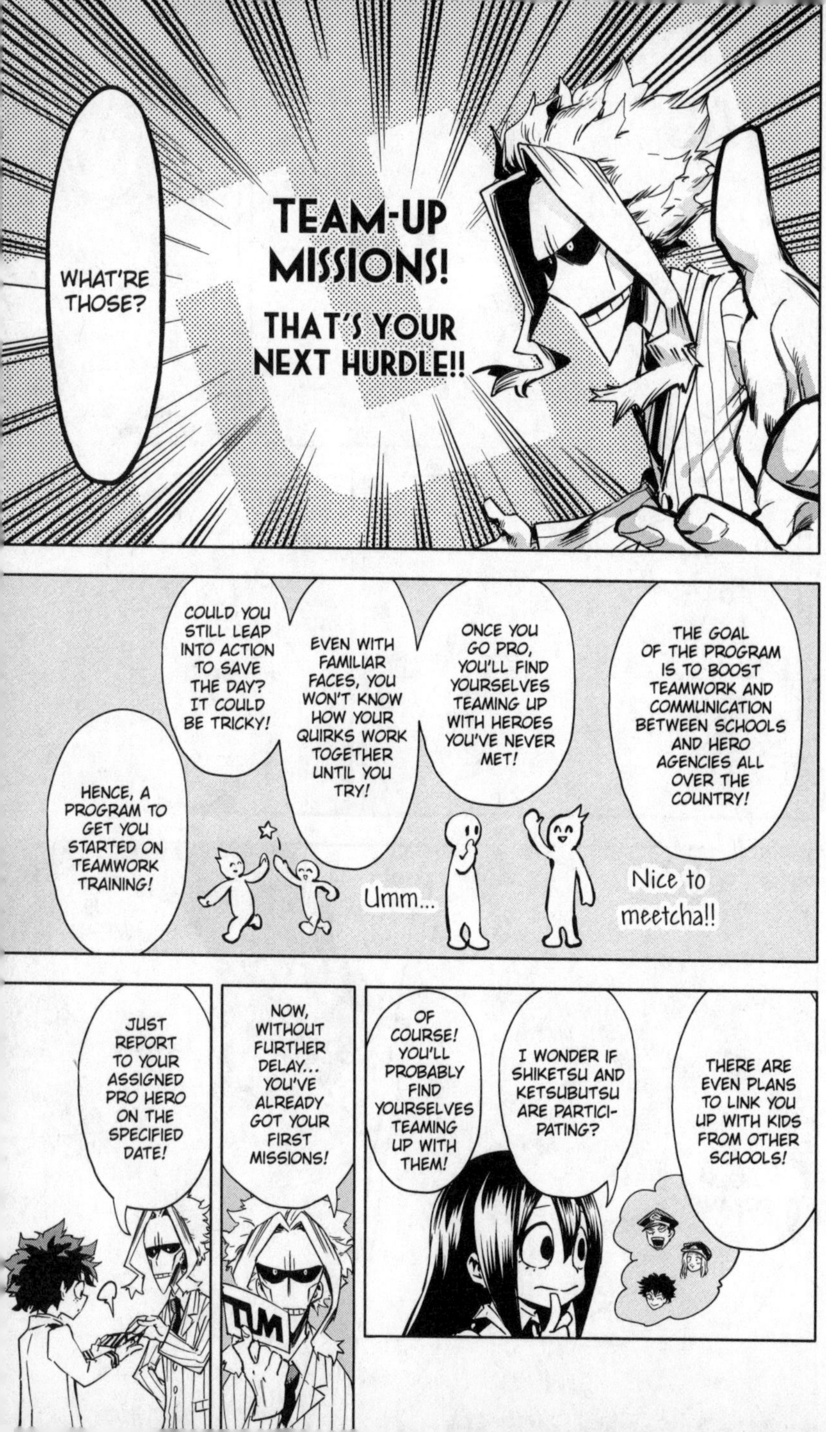
TEAM-UP MISSIONS!
THAT'S YOUR NEXT HURDLE!!
WHAT'RE THOSE?
THE GOAL OF THE PROGRAM IS TO BOOST TEAMWORK AND COMMUNICATION BETWEEN SCHOOLS AND HERO AGENCIES ALL OVER THE COUNTRY!
ONCE YOU GO PRO, YOU'LL FIND YOURSELVES TEAMING UP WITH HEROES YOU'VE NEVER MET!
Nice to meetcha!!
Umm...
EVEN WITH FAMILIAR FACES, YOU WON'T KNOW HOW YOUR QUIRKS WORK TOGETHER UNTIL YOU TRY!
COULD YOU STILL LEAP INTO ACTION TO SAVE THE DAY? IT COULD BE TRICKY!
HENCE, A PROGRAM TO GET YOU STARTED ON TEAMWORK TRAINING!
THERE ARE EVEN PLANS TO LINK YOU UP WITH KIDS FROM OTHER SCHOOLS!
I WONDER IF SHIKETSU AND KETSUBUTSU ARE PARTICI-PATING?
OF COURSE! YOU'LL PROBABLY FIND YOURSELVES TEAMING UP WITH THEM!
NOW, WITHOUT FURTHER DELAY... YOU'VE ALREADY GOT YOUR FIRST MISSIONS!
JUST REPORT TO YOUR ASSIGNED PRO HERO ON THE SPECIFIED DATE!

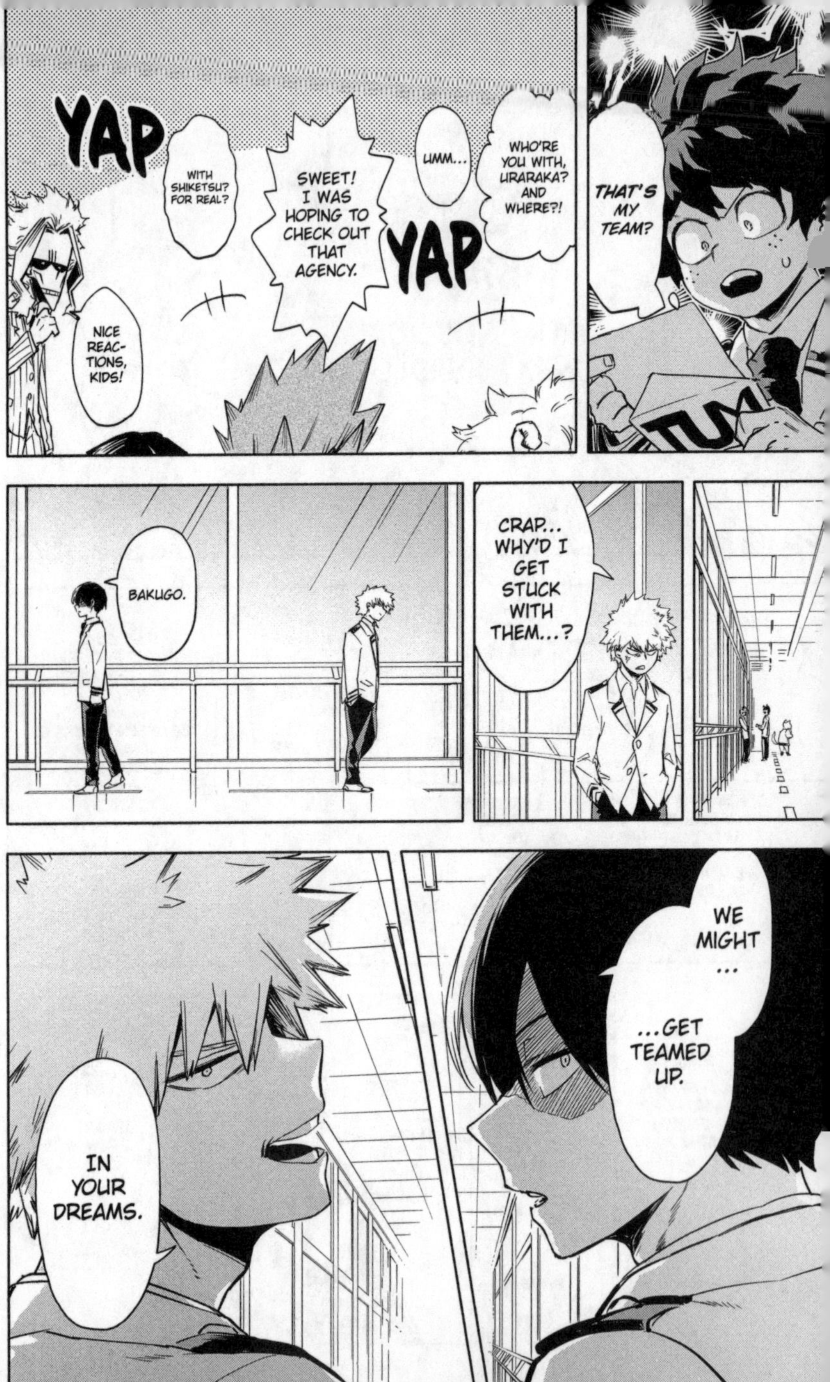
THAT'S MY TEAM?
WHO'RE YOU WITH, URARAKA? AND WHERE?!
UMM...
YAP
SWEET! I WAS HOPING TO CHECK OUT THAT AGENCY.
WITH SHIKETSU? FOR REAL?
YAP
NICE REAC-TIONS, KIDS!
CRAP... WHY'D I GET STUCK WITH THEM...?
BAKUGO.
WE MIGHT...
...GET TEAMED UP.
IN YOUR DREAMS.

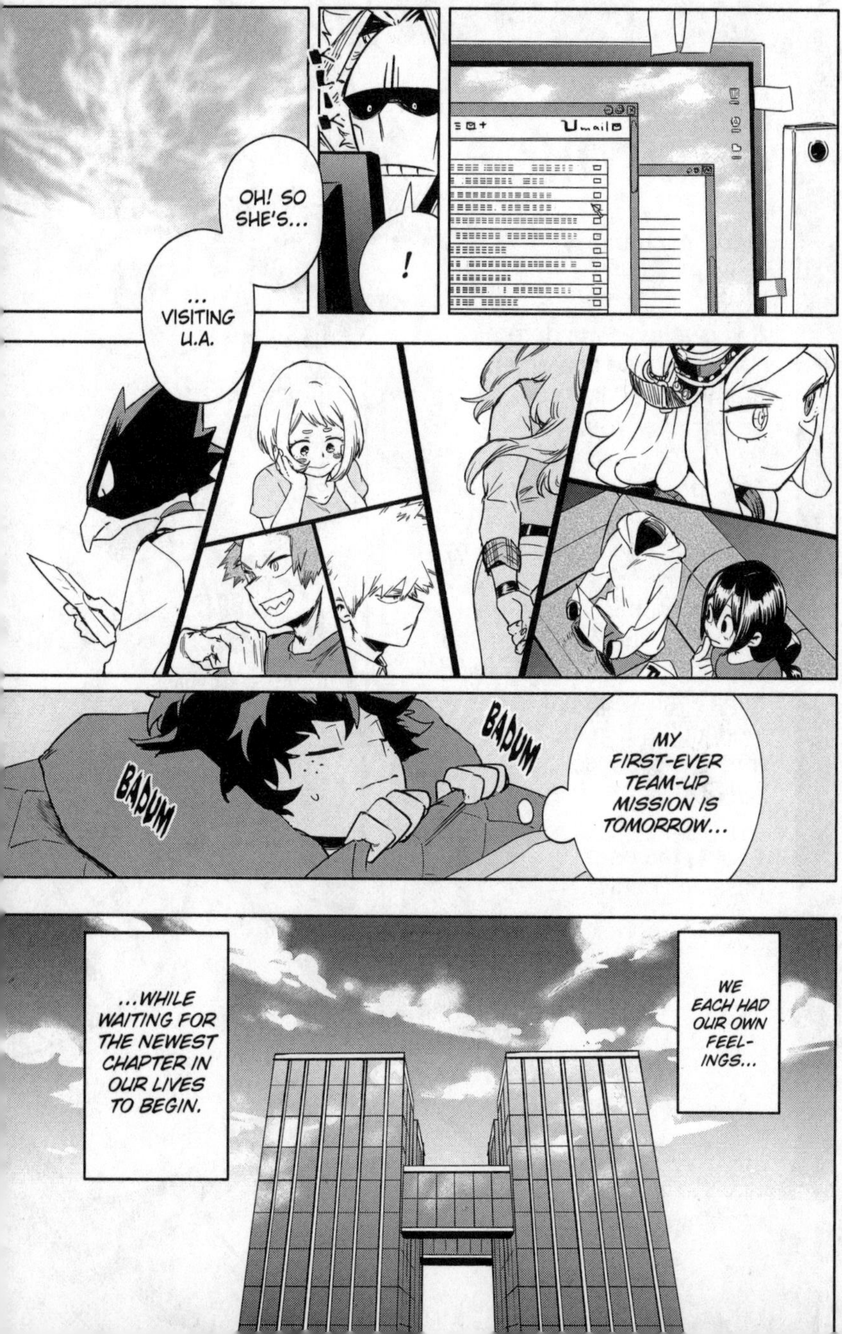
Umail
!
OH! SO SHE'S...
...VISITING U.A.
BADUM
MY FIRST-EVER TEAM-UP MISSION IS TOMORROW...
BADUM
WE EACH HAD OUR OWN FEEL-INGS...
...WHILE WAITING FOR THE NEWEST CHAPTER IN OUR LIVES TO BEGIN.

GREETINGS

Hello, my name is Yoko Akiyama.

If you've ever wondered, "What if these characters teamed up?!" this spin-off series is for you.

My Hero Academia is full of so many awesome and charming characters that my mind ends up racing ahead, wanting nothing more than to draw one, then the next, and sometimes my drawing hand can't even keep up! I'm working hard in the hope that you get a kick out of it!

Let the team-up missions begin!

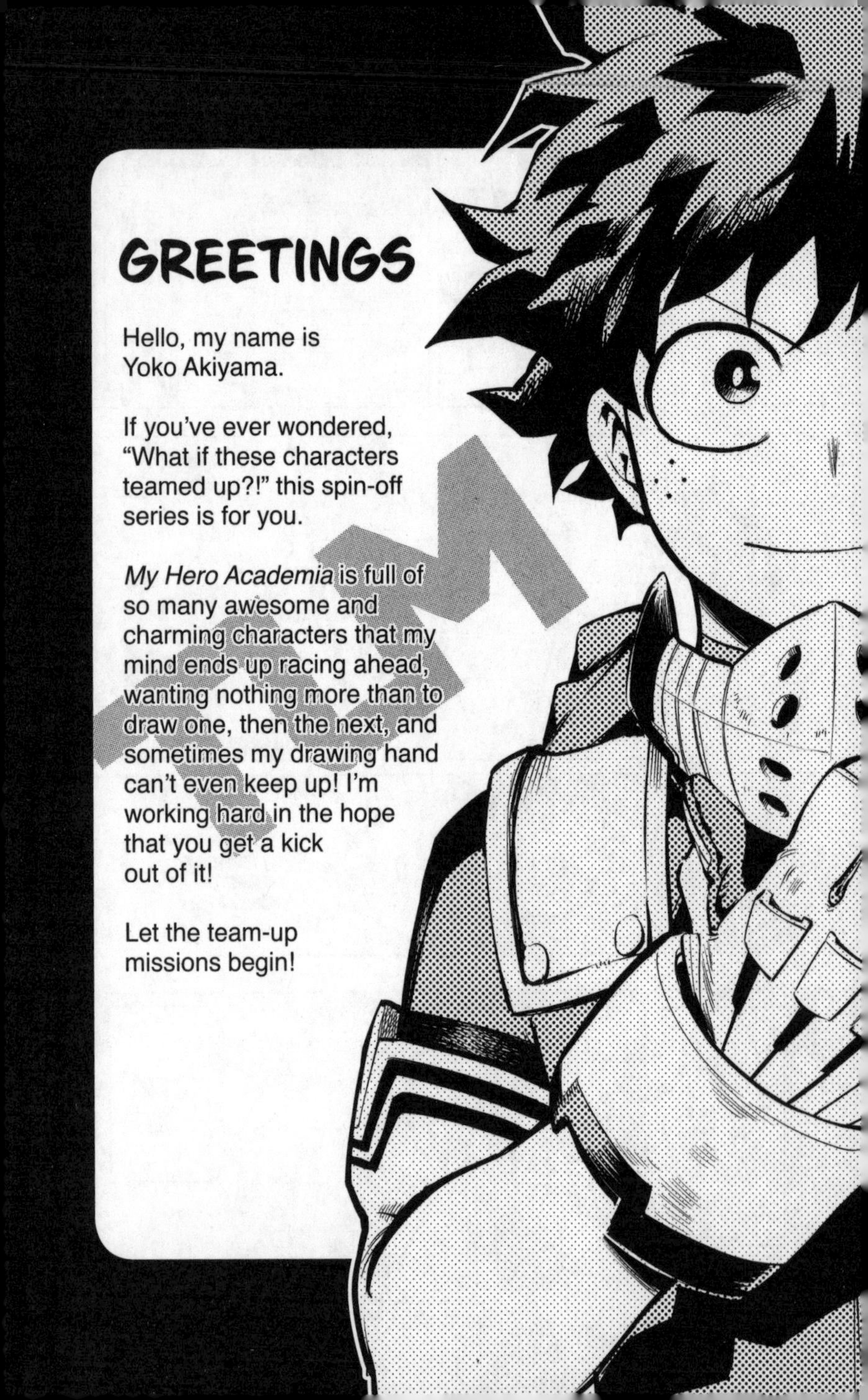

MISSION 1: TEAM-UP MISSIONS BEGIN

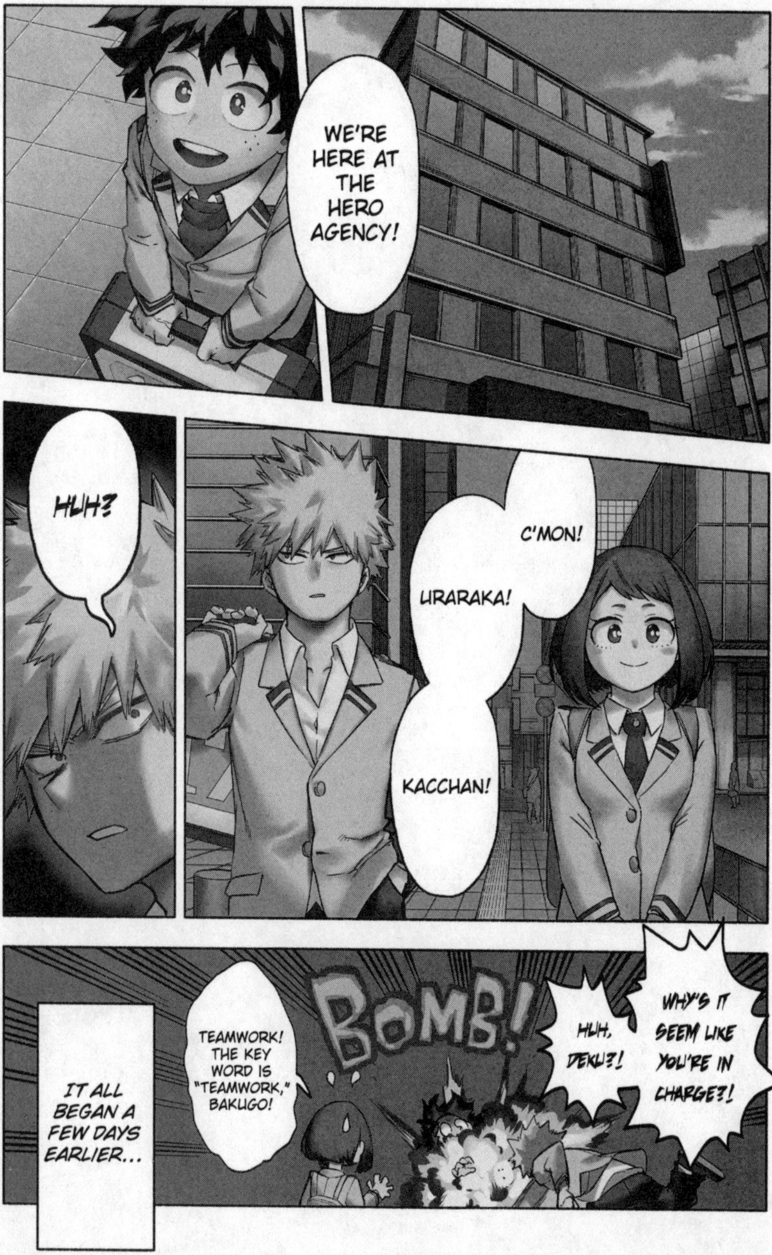
WE'RE HERE AT THE HERO AGENCY!
C'MON!
URARAKA!
KACCHAN!
HUH?
HUH, DEKU?! WHY'S IT SEEM LIKE YOU'RE IN CHARGE?!
BOMB!
TEAMWORK! THE KEY WORD IS "TEAMWORK," BAKUGO!
IT ALL BEGAN A FEW DAYS EARLIER...

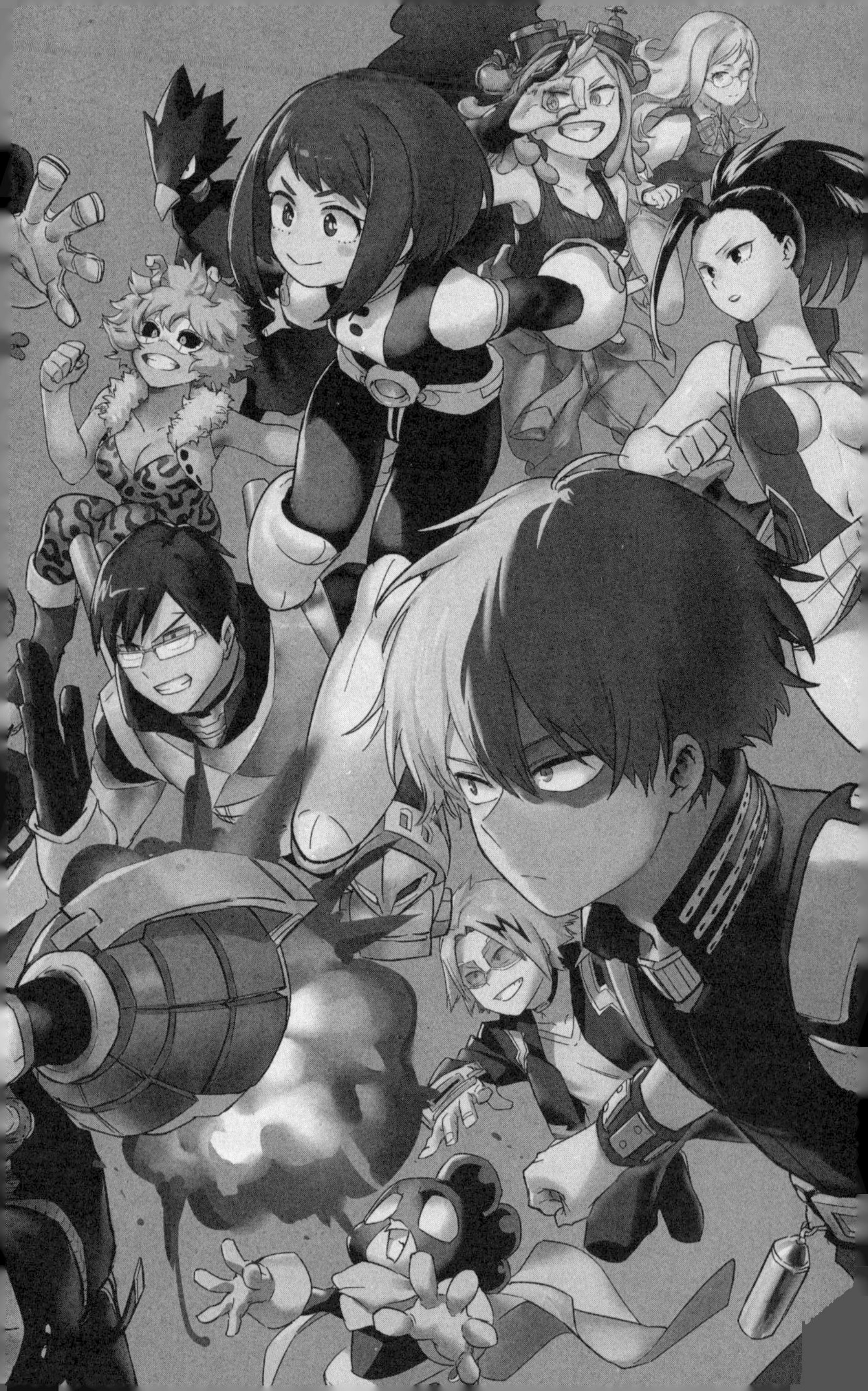

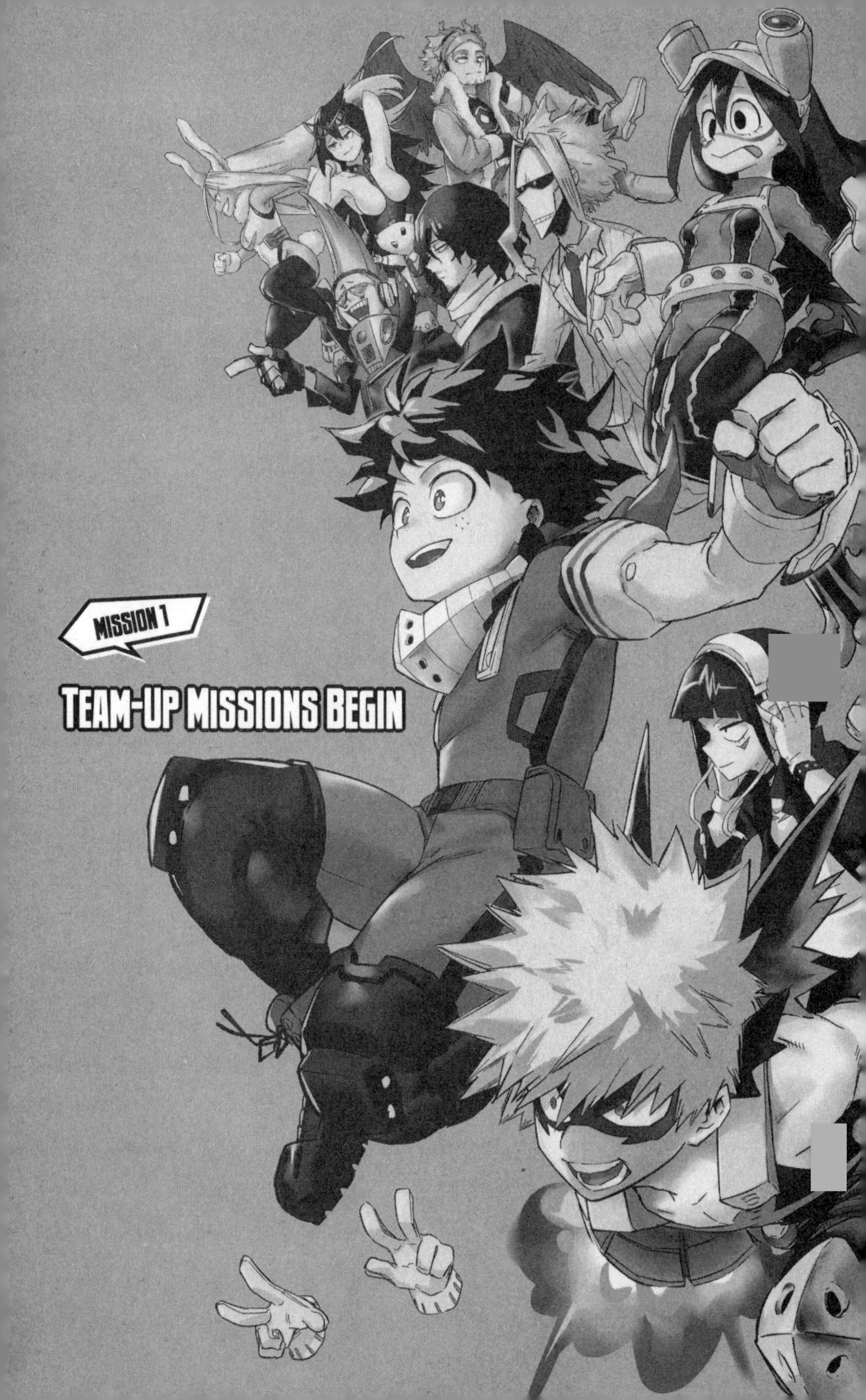
MISSION 1
TEAM-UP MISSIONS BEGIN

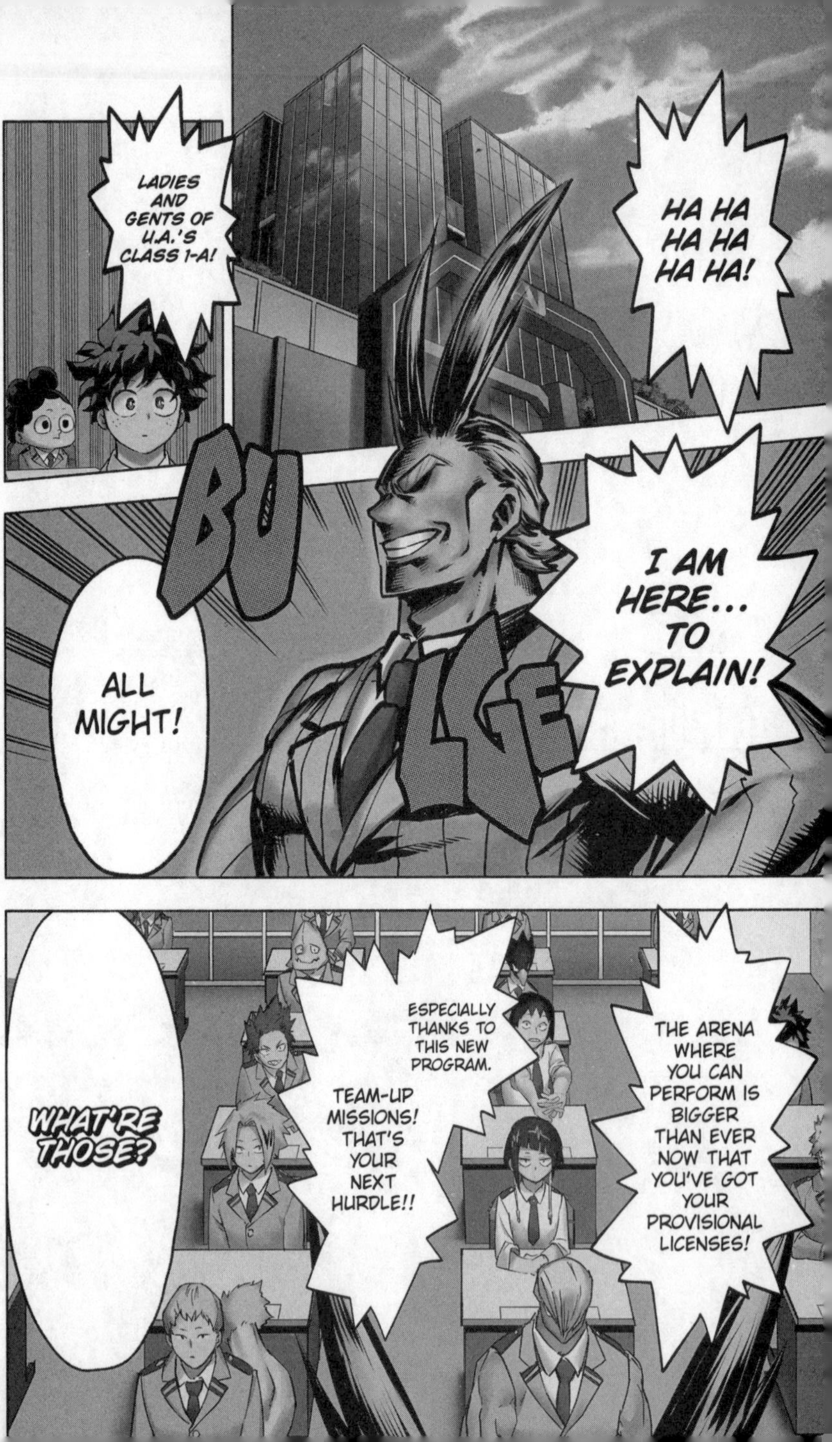
HA HA HA HA HA HA!
LADIES AND GENTS OF U.A.'S CLASS 1-A!
I AM HERE... TO EXPLAIN!
BULGE
ALL MIGHT!
THE ARENA WHERE YOU CAN PERFORM IS BIGGER THAN EVER NOW THAT YOU'VE GOT YOUR PROVISIONAL LICENSES!
ESPECIALLY THANKS TO THIS NEW PROGRAM.
TEAM-UP MISSIONS! THAT'S YOUR NEXT HURDLE!!
WHAT'RE THOSE?

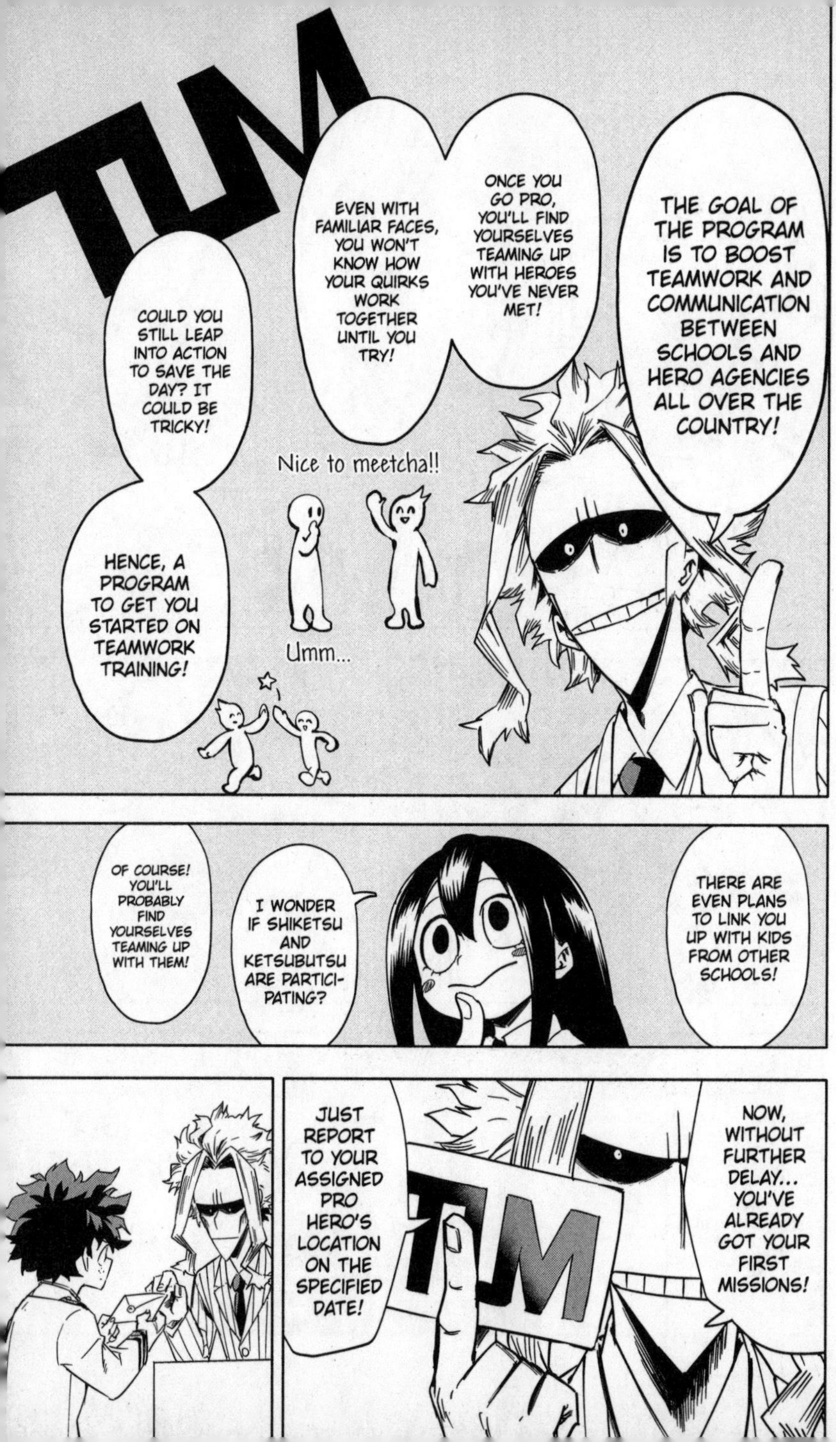
TUM
THE GOAL OF THE PROGRAM IS TO BOOST TEAMWORK AND COMMUNICATION BETWEEN SCHOOLS AND HERO AGENCIES ALL OVER THE COUNTRY!
ONCE YOU GO PRO, YOU'LL FIND YOURSELVES TEAMING UP WITH HEROES YOU'VE NEVER MET!
EVEN WITH FAMILIAR FACES, YOU WON'T KNOW HOW YOUR QUIRKS WORK TOGETHER UNTIL YOU TRY!
COULD YOU STILL LEAP INTO ACTION TO SAVE THE DAY? IT COULD BE TRICKY!
Nice to meetcha!!
Umm...
HENCE, A PROGRAM TO GET YOU STARTED ON TEAMWORK TRAINING!
THERE ARE EVEN PLANS TO LINK YOU UP WITH KIDS FROM OTHER SCHOOLS!
I WONDER IF SHIKETSU AND KETSUBUTSU ARE PARTICI-PATING?
OF COURSE! YOU'LL PROBABLY FIND YOURSELVES TEAMING UP WITH THEM!
NOW, WITHOUT FURTHER DELAY... YOU'VE ALREADY GOT YOUR FIRST MISSIONS!
JUST REPORT TO YOUR ASSIGNED PRO HERO'S LOCATION ON THE SPECIFIED DATE!
TUM

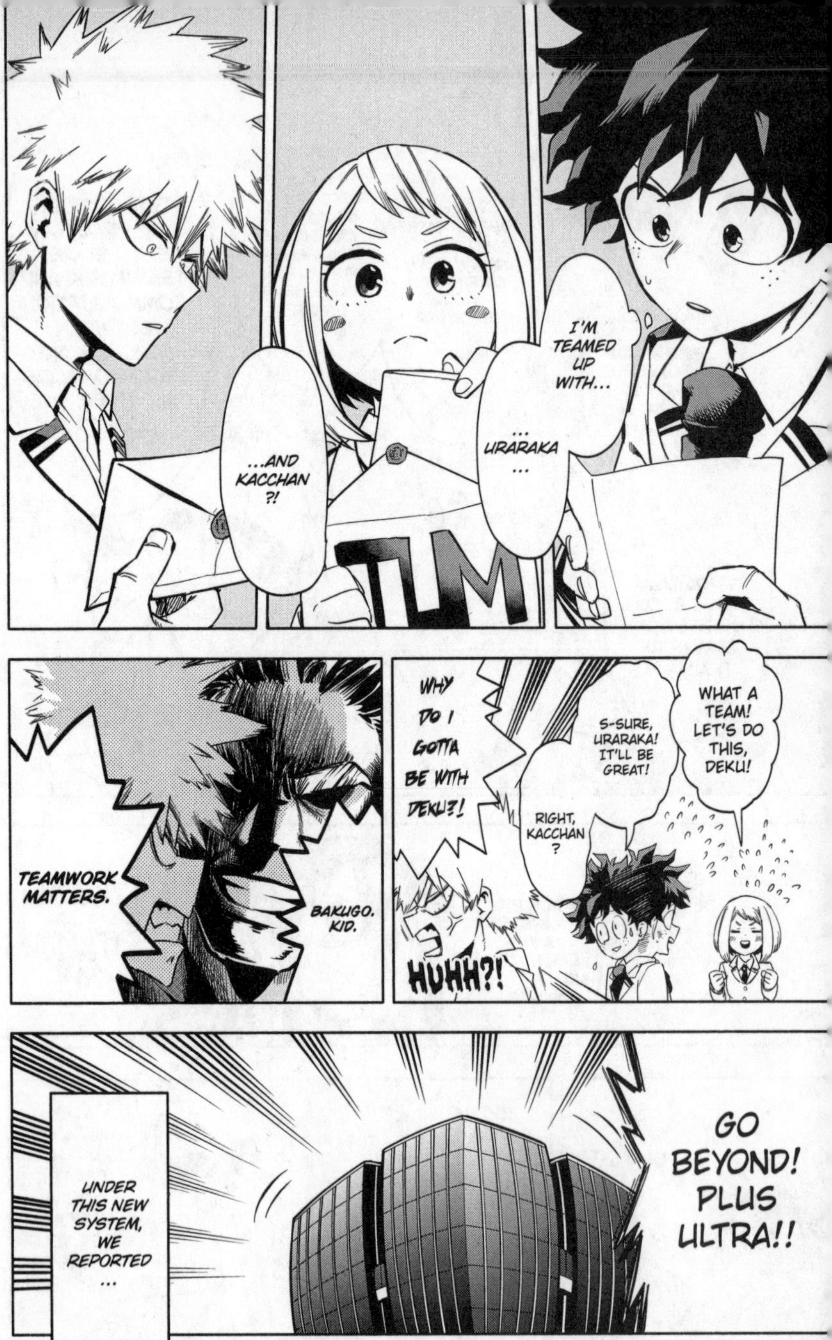
I'M TEAMED UP WITH...
...URARAKA...
...AND KACCHAN?!
WHAT A TEAM! LET'S DO THIS, DEKU!
S-SURE, URARAKA! IT'LL BE GREAT!
RIGHT, KACCHAN?
WHY DO I GOTTA BE WITH DEKU?!
HUHH?!
BAKUGO. KID.
TEAMWORK MATTERS.
GO BEYOND! PLUS ULTRA!!
UNDER THIS NEW SYSTEM, WE REPORTED...

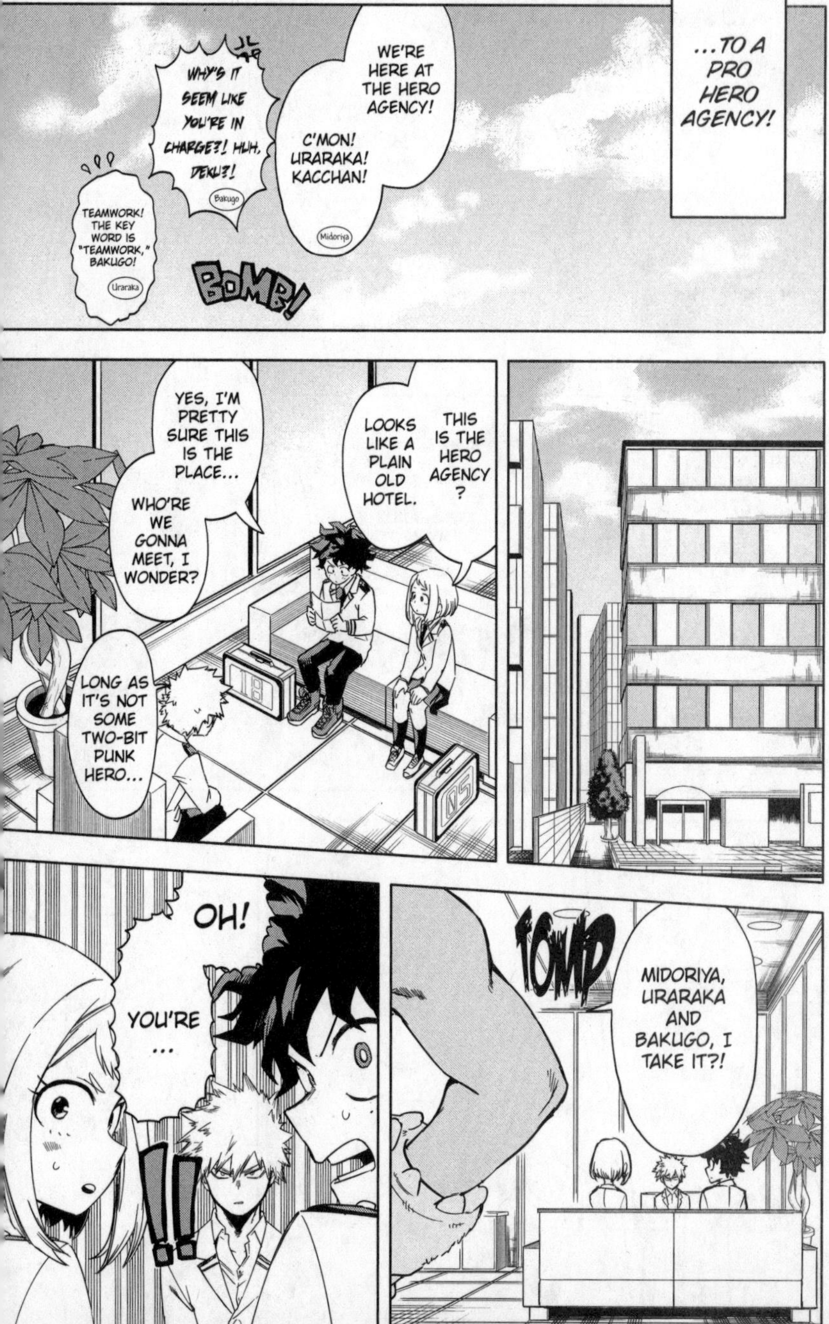
...TO A PRO HERO AGENCY!
WE'RE HERE AT THE HERO AGENCY!
C'MON! URARAKA! KACCHAN!
Midoriya
WHY'S IT SEEM LIKE YOU'RE IN CHARGE?! HUH, DEKU?!
Bakugo
TEAMWORK! THE KEY WORD IS "TEAMWORK," BAKUGO!
Uraraka
BOMB!
THIS IS THE HERO AGENCY?
LOOKS LIKE A PLAIN OLD HOTEL.
YES, I'M PRETTY SURE THIS IS THE PLACE...
WHO'RE WE GONNA MEET, I WONDER?
LONG AS IT'S NOT SOME TWO-BIT PUNK HERO...
TOMP
MIDORIYA, URARAKA AND BAKUGO, I TAKE IT?!
OH!
YOU'RE ...

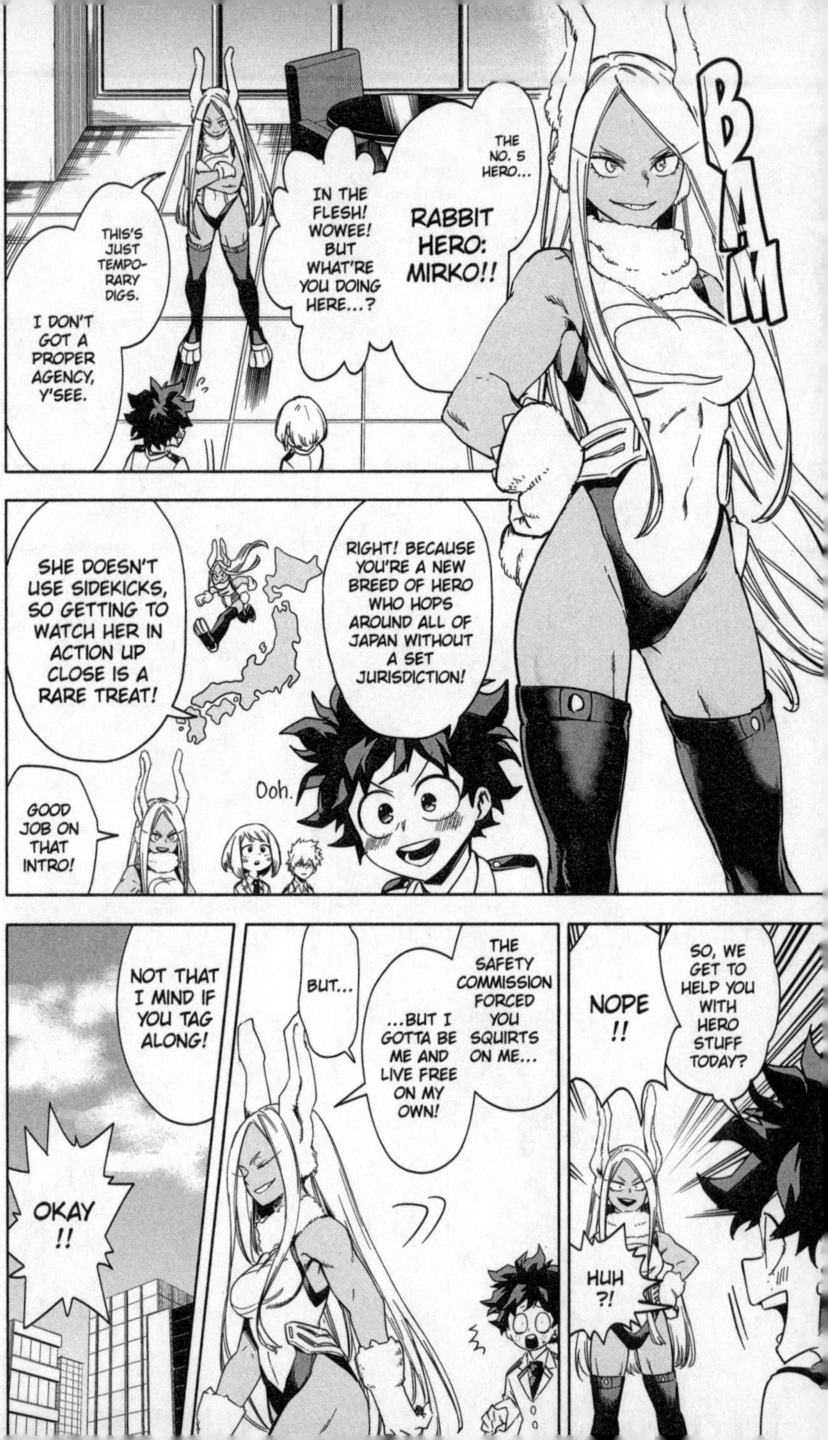
BAM
THE NO. 5 HERO...
RABBIT HERO: MIRKO!!
IN THE FLESH! WOWEE! BUT WHAT'RE YOU DOING HERE...?
THIS'S JUST TEMPORARY DIGS.
I DON'T GOT A PROPER AGENCY, Y'SEE.
RIGHT! BECAUSE YOU'RE A NEW BREED OF HERO WHO HOPS AROUND ALL OF JAPAN WITHOUT A SET JURISDICTION!
SHE DOESN'T USE SIDEKICKS, SO GETTING TO WATCH HER IN ACTION UP CLOSE IS A RARE TREAT!
Ooh.
GOOD JOB ON THAT INTRO!
SO, WE GET TO HELP YOU WITH HERO STUFF TODAY?
NOPE!!
HUH?!
THE SAFETY COMMISSION FORCED YOU SQUIRTS ON ME...
BUT...
...BUT I GOTTA BE ME AND LIVE FREE ON MY OWN!
NOT THAT I MIND IF YOU TAG ALONG!
OKAY!!

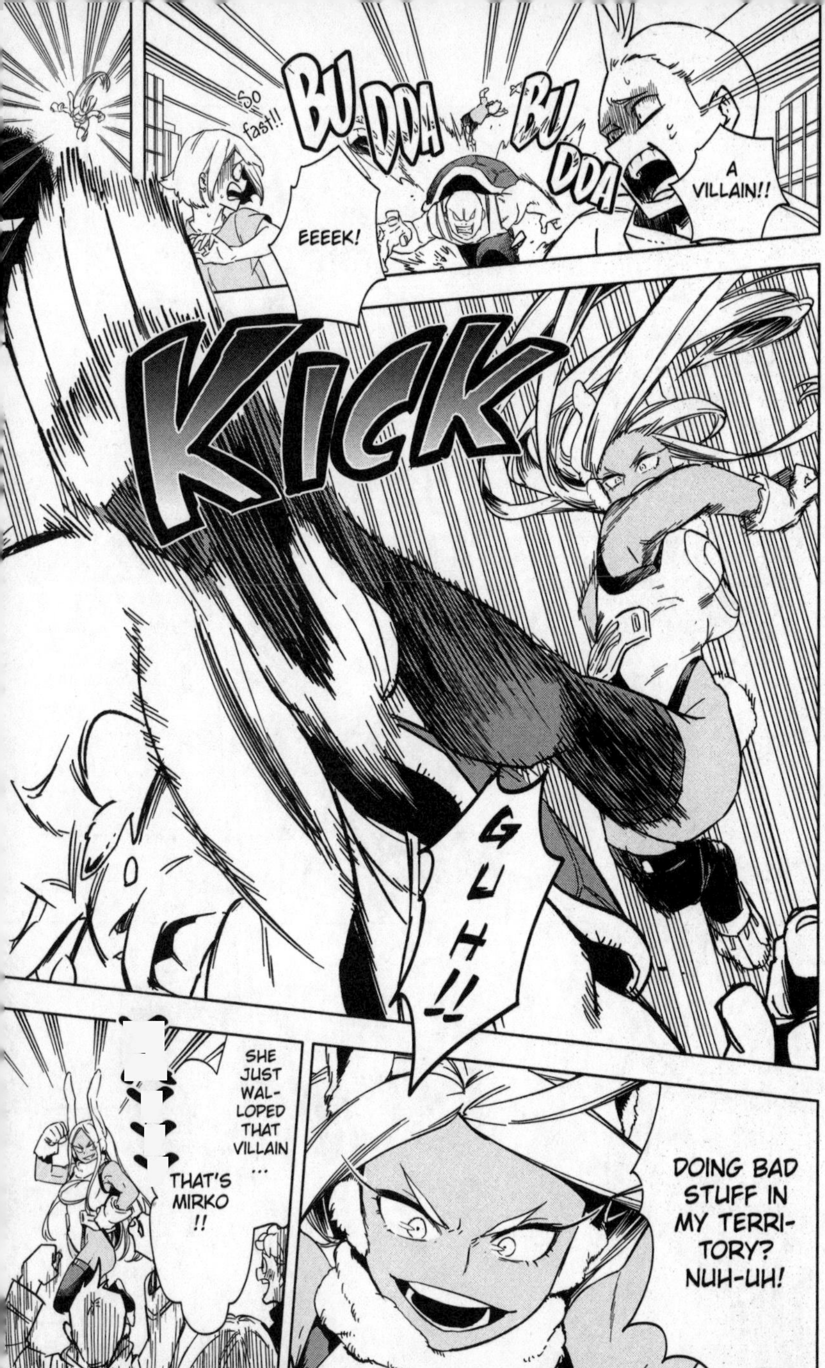
A VILLAIN!!
BU DDA
BU DDA
EEEEK!
So fast!!
KICK
GUH!!
DOING BAD STUFF IN MY TERRITORY? NUH-UH!
SHE JUST WAL-LOPED THAT VILLAIN...
THAT'S MIRKO!!

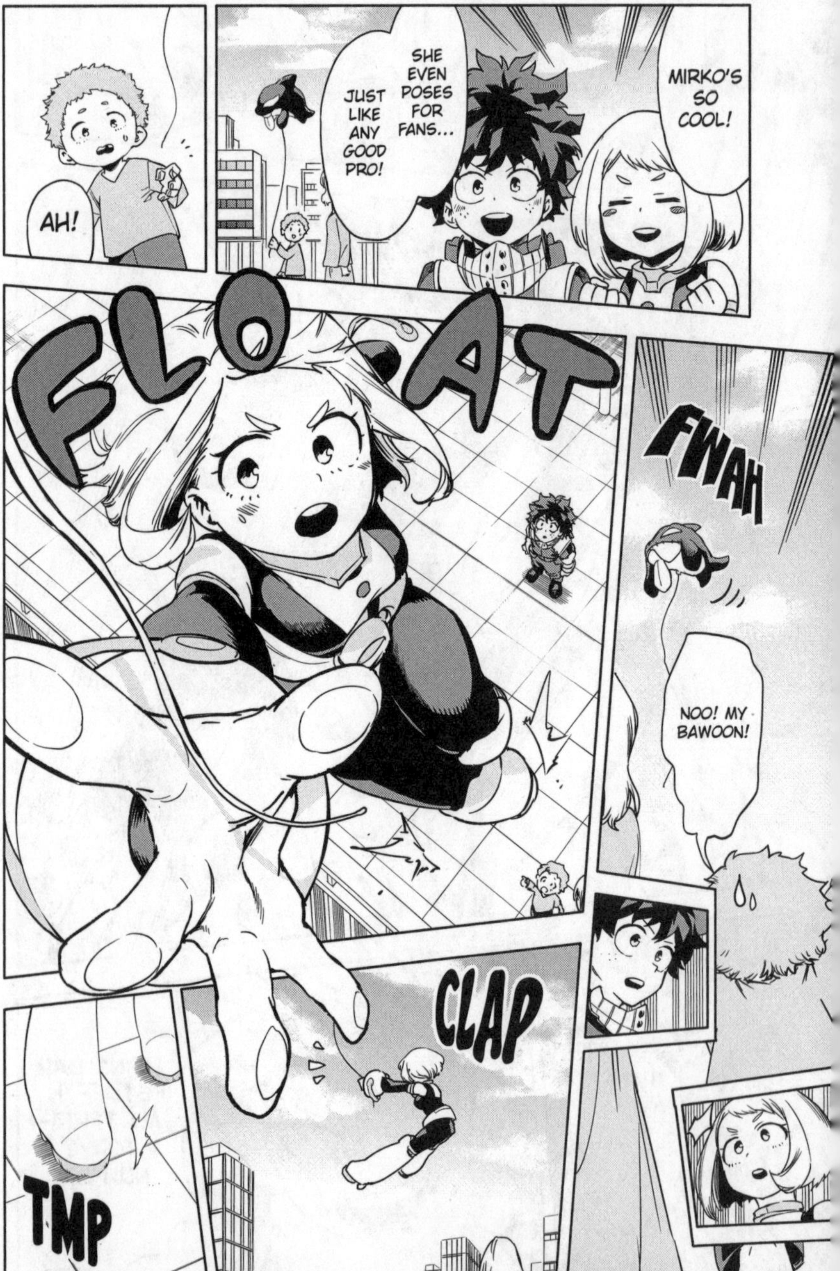
MIRKO'S SO COOL!
SHE EVEN POSES FOR FANS...
JUST LIKE ANY GOOD PRO!
AH!
FWAH
NOO! MY BAWOON!
FLOAT
CLAP
TMP

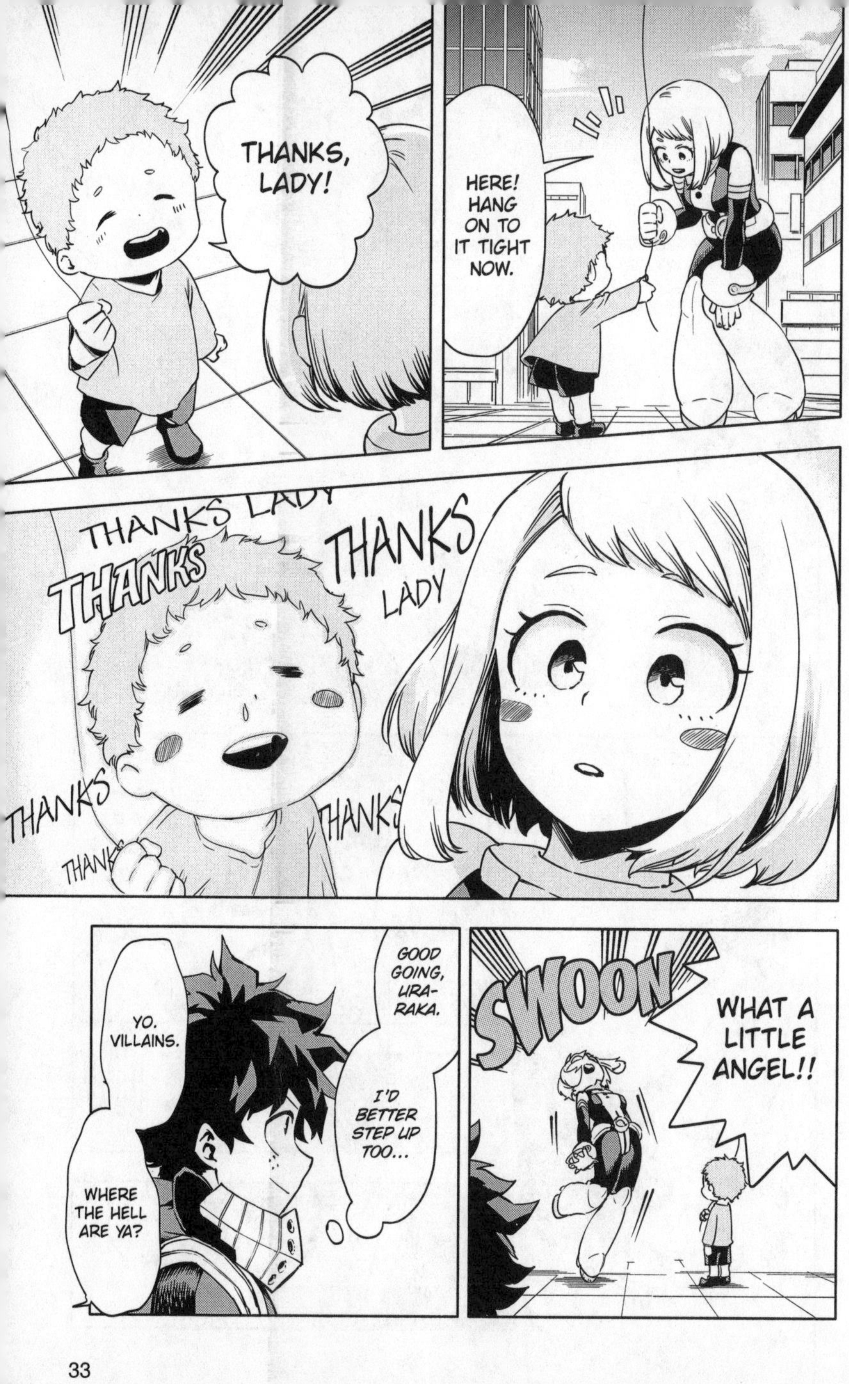
HERE! HANG ON TO IT TIGHT NOW.
THANKS, LADY!
THANKS LADY
THANKS
LADY
THANKS
THANKS
THANKS
THANKS
THANK
SWOON
WHAT A LITTLE ANGEL!!
GOOD GOING, URA-RAKA.
I'D BETTER STEP UP TOO...
YO. VILLAINS.
WHERE THE HELL ARE YA?

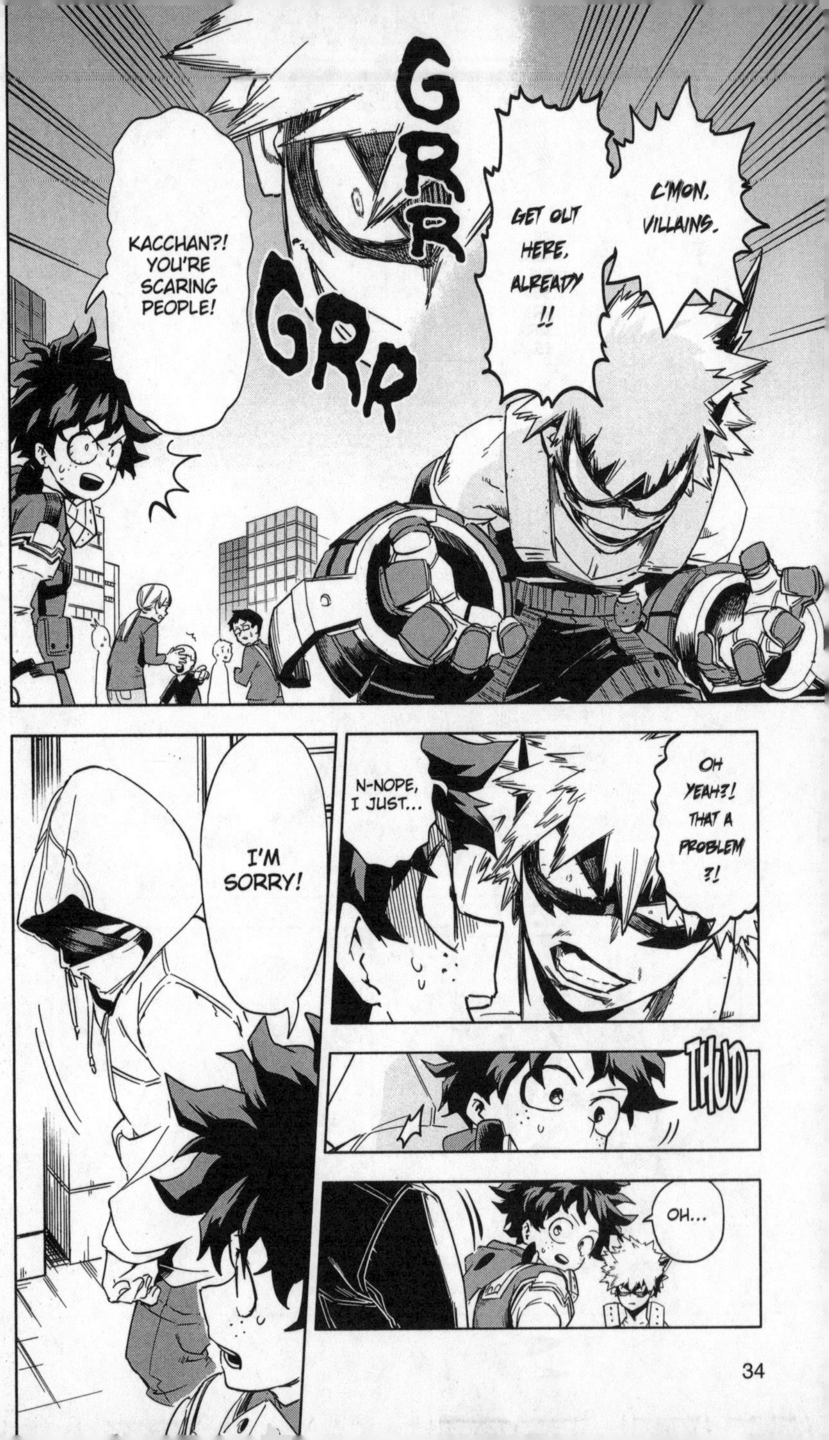
C'MON, VILLAINS.
GET OUT HERE, ALREADY!!
GRR
GRR
KACCHAN?! YOU'RE SCARING PEOPLE!
OH YEAH?! THAT A PROBLEM?!
N-NOPE, I JUST...
THUD
OH...
I'M SORRY!

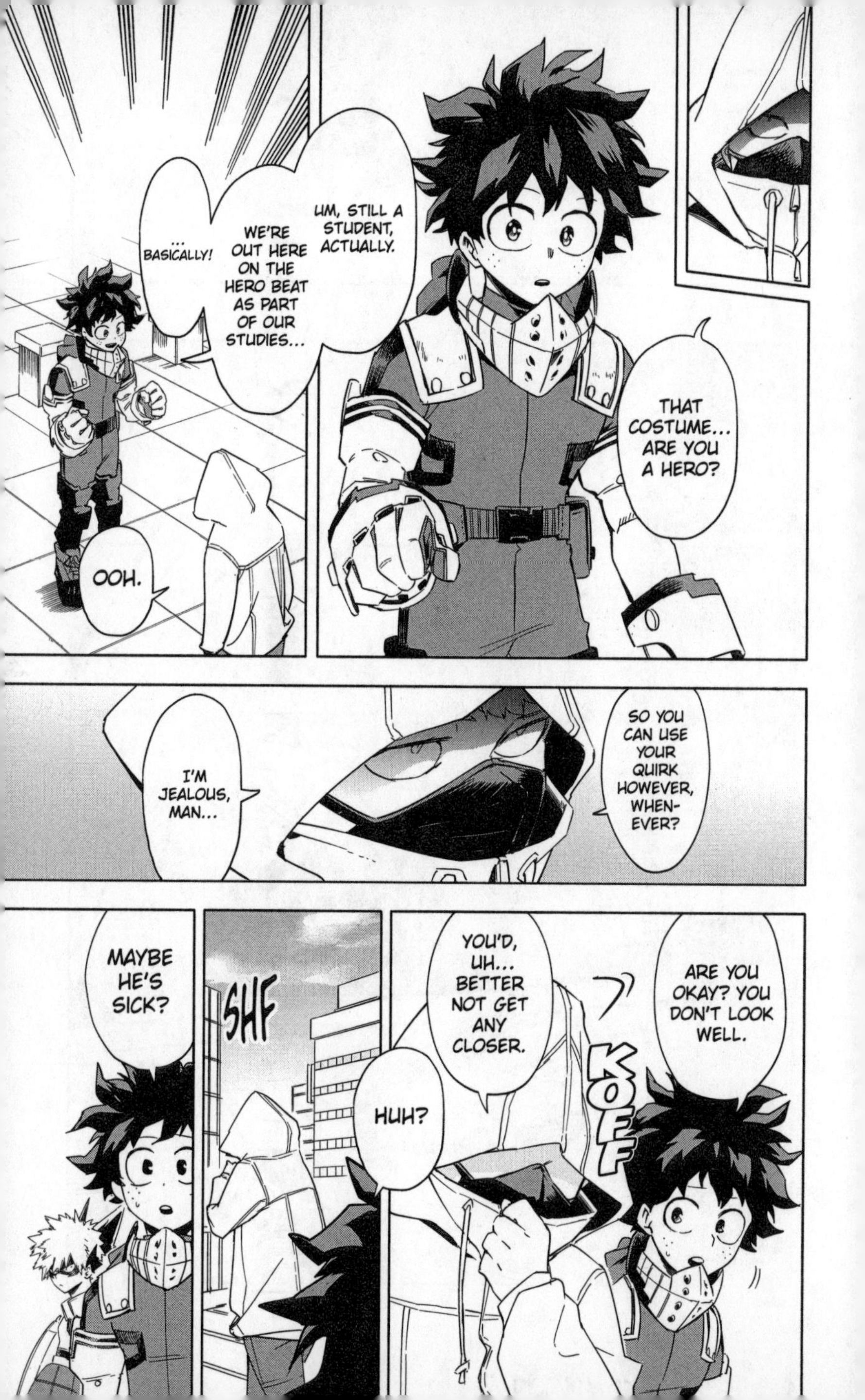
THAT COSTUME... ARE YOU A HERO?
UM, STILL A STUDENT, ACTUALLY.
WE'RE OUT HERE ON THE HERO BEAT AS PART OF OUR STUDIES...
...BASICALLY!
OOH.
SO YOU CAN USE YOUR QUIRK HOWEVER, WHEN-EVER?
I'M JEALOUS, MAN...
ARE YOU OKAY? YOU DON'T LOOK WELL.
KOFF
YOU'D, UH... BETTER NOT GET ANY CLOSER.
HUH?
SHF
MAYBE HE'S SICK?

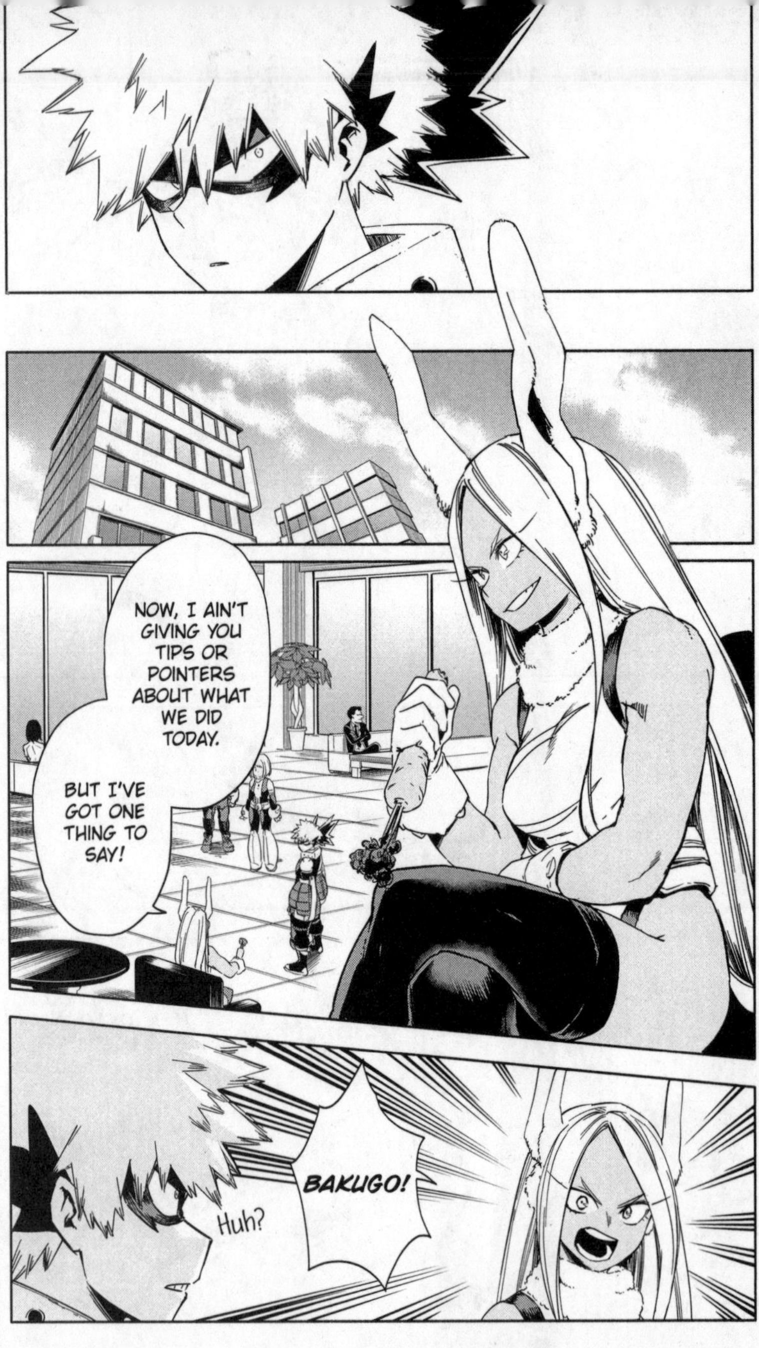
NOW, I AIN'T GIVING YOU TIPS OR POINTERS ABOUT WHAT WE DID TODAY.
BUT I'VE GOT ONE THING TO SAY!
BAKUGO!
Huh?

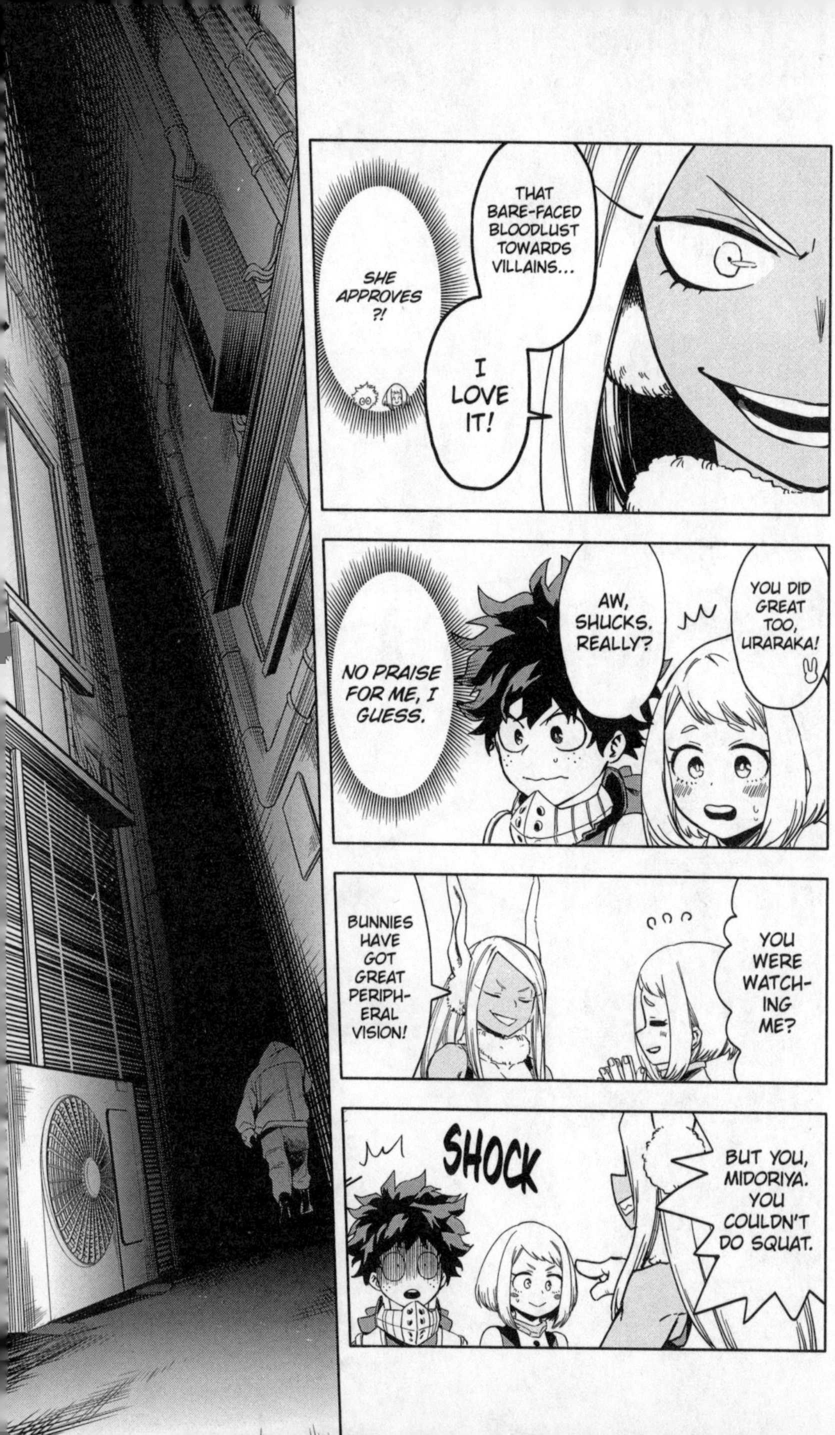
THAT BARE-FACED BLOODLUST TOWARDS VILLAINS...
I LOVE IT!
SHE APPROVES ?!
YOU DID GREAT TOO, URARAKA!
AW, SHUCKS. REALLY?
NO PRAISE FOR ME, I GUESS.
YOU WERE WATCHING-ING ME?
BUNNIES HAVE GOT GREAT PERIPH-ERAL VISION!
BUT YOU, MIDORIYA. YOU COULDN'T DO SQUAT.
SHOCK

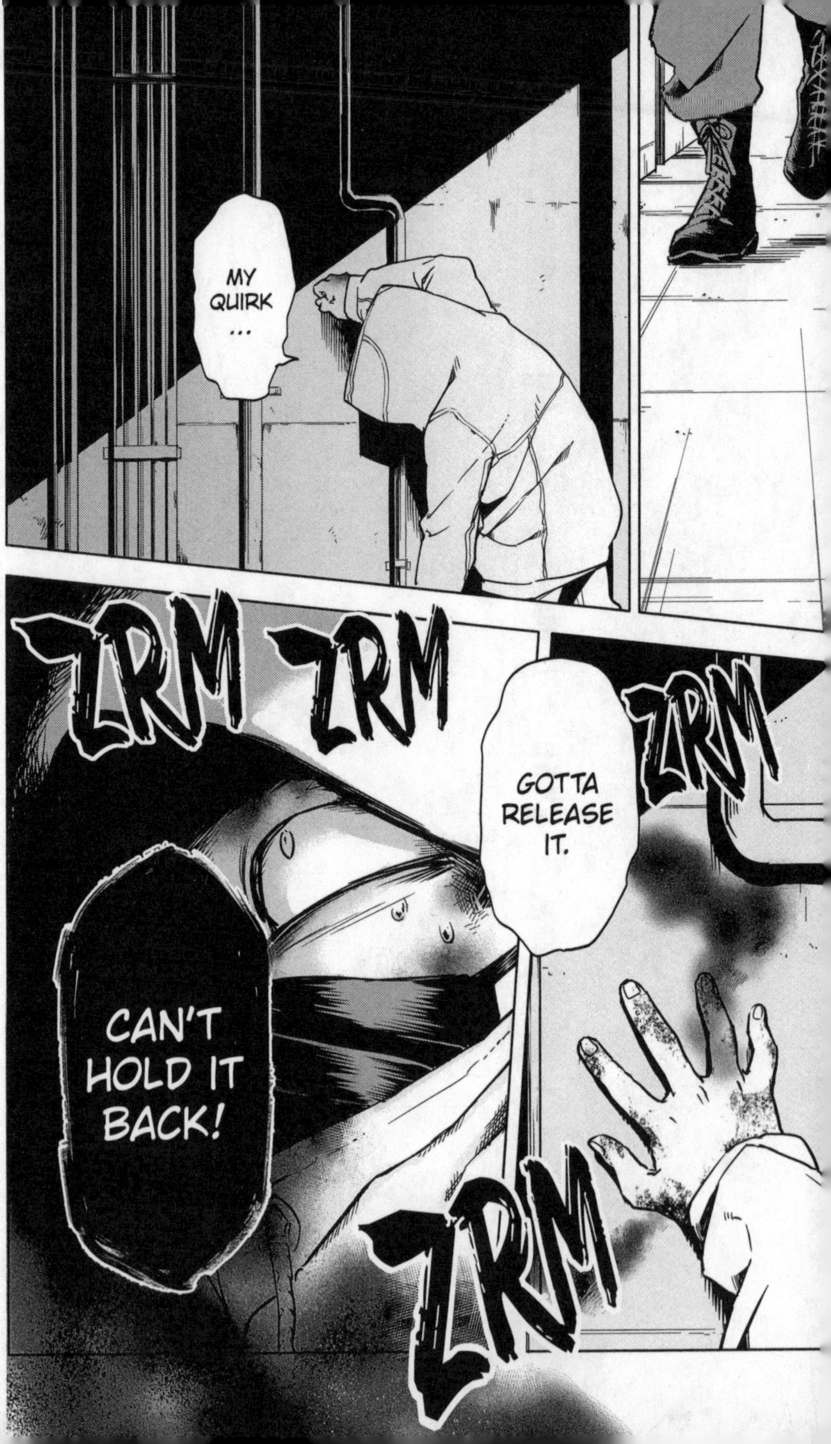
MY QUIRK ...
ZRM
GOTTA RELEASE IT.
ZRM ZRM
CAN'T HOLD IT BACK!
ZRM

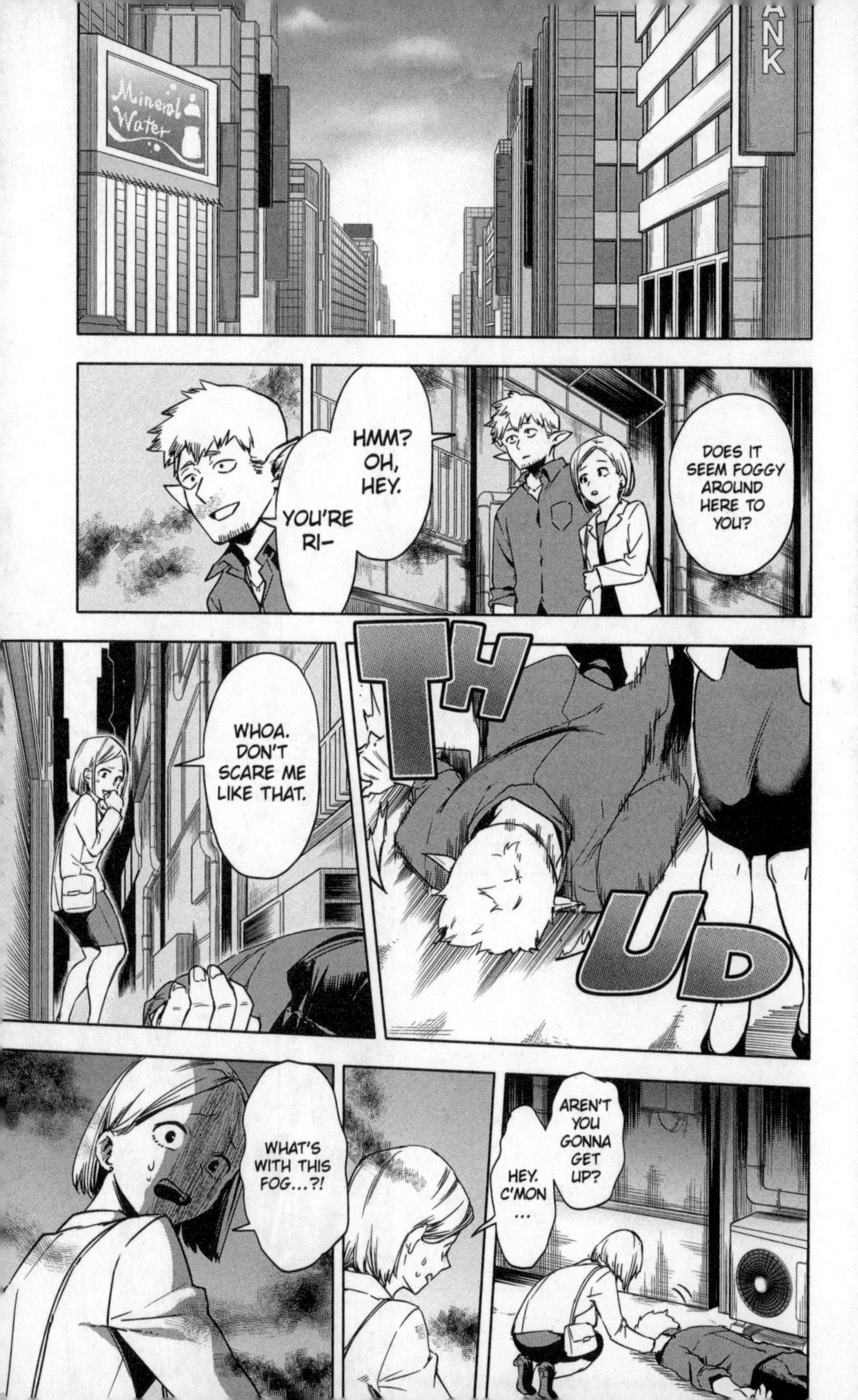
ANK
Mineral Water
DOES IT SEEM FOGGY AROUND HERE TO YOU?
HMM? OH, HEY.
YOU'RE RI–
THUD
WHOA. DON'T SCARE ME LIKE THAT.
AREN'T YOU GONNA GET UP?
HEY. C'MON...
WHAT'S WITH THIS FOG...?!

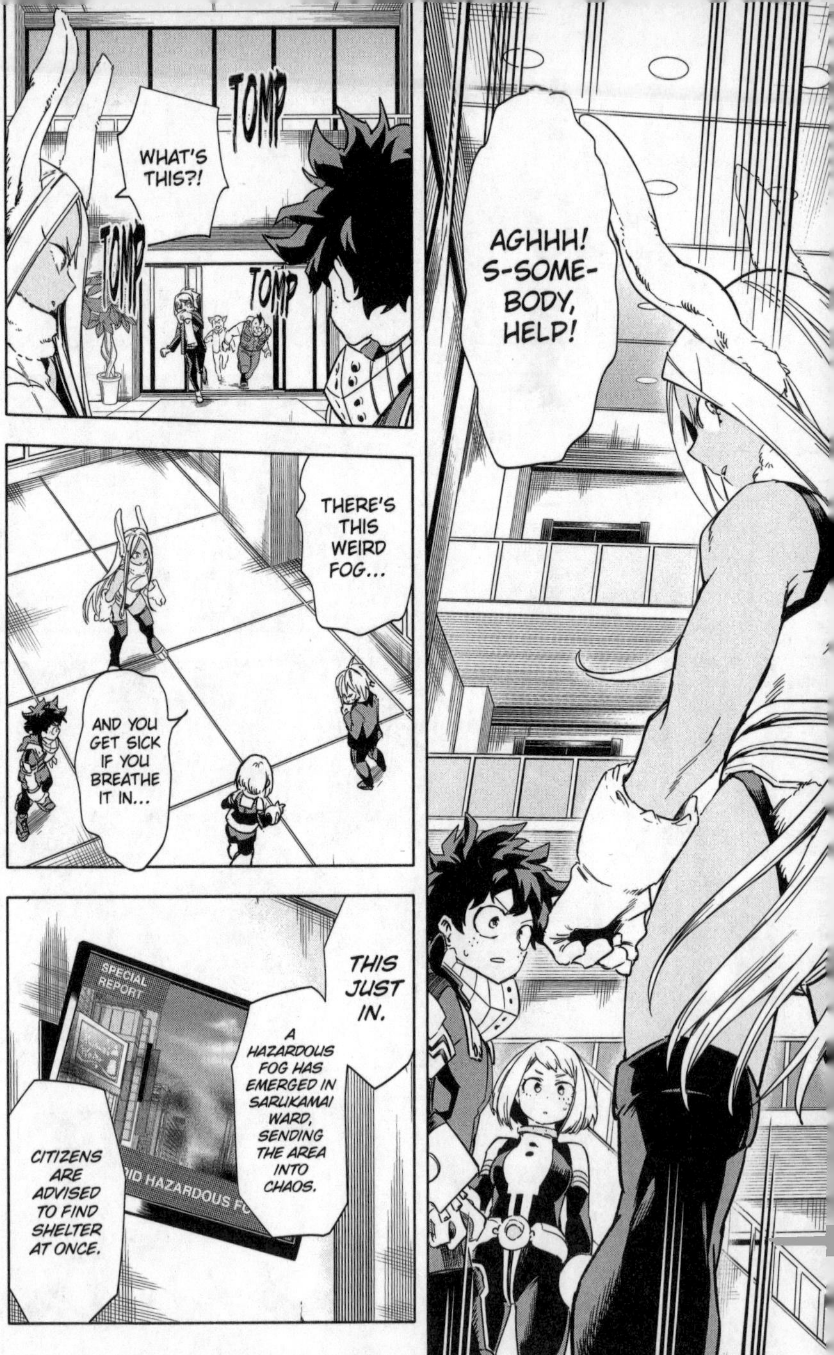
AGHHH! S-SOME-BODY, HELP!
WHAT'S THIS?!
TOMP
TOMP
TOMP
THERE'S THIS WEIRD FOG...
AND YOU GET SICK IF YOU BREATHE IT IN...
THIS JUST IN.
A HAZARDOUS FOG HAS EMERGED IN SARUKAMAI WARD, SENDING THE AREA INTO CHAOS.
CITIZENS ARE ADVISED TO FIND SHELTER AT ONCE.
SPECIAL REPORT
HAZARDOUS FO

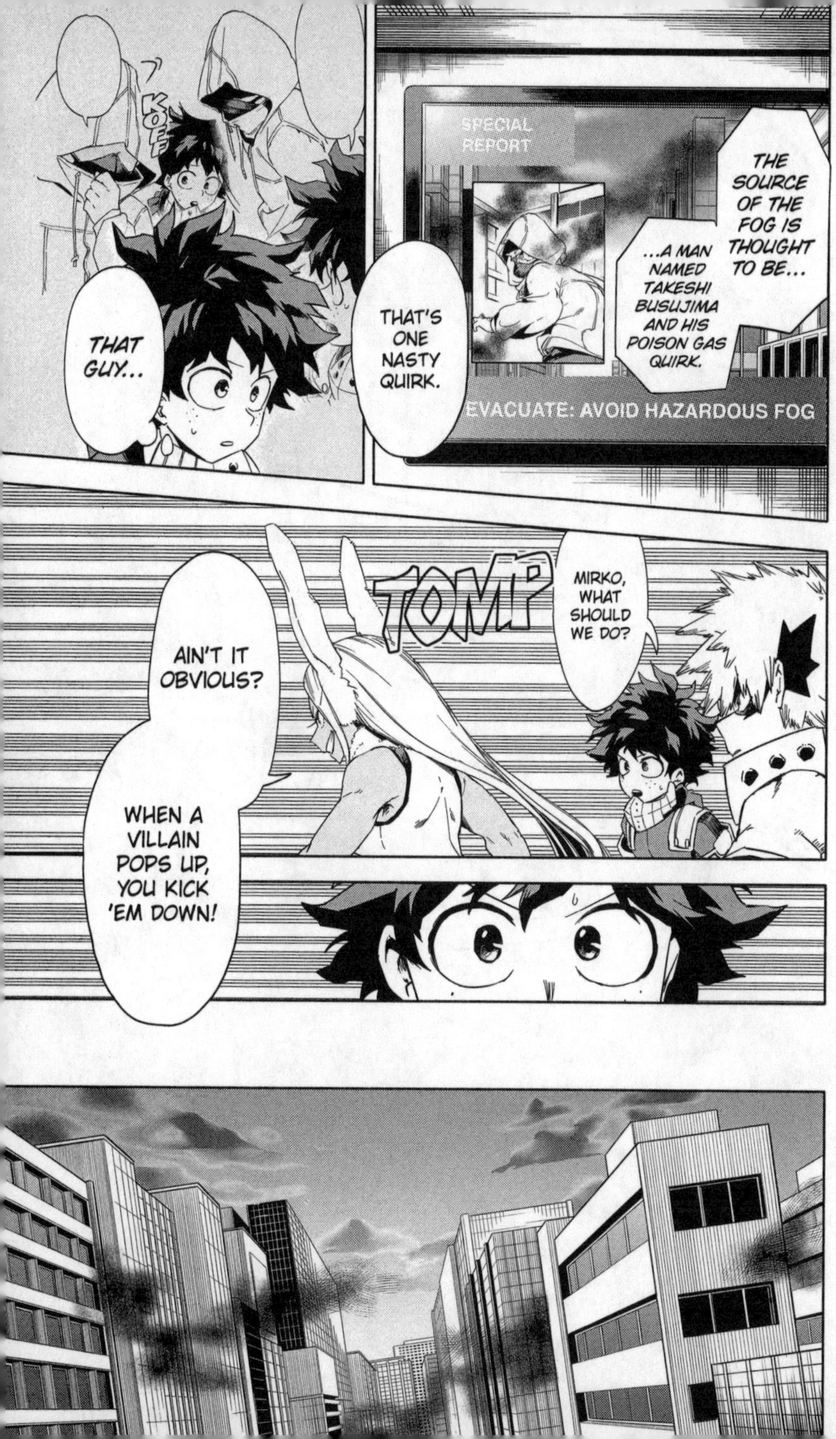
SPECIAL REPORT
THE SOURCE OF THE FOG IS THOUGHT TO BE...
...A MAN NAMED TAKESHI BUSUJIMA AND HIS POISON GAS QUIRK.
EVACUATE: AVOID HAZARDOUS FOG
KOFF
THAT'S ONE NASTY QUIRK.
THAT GUY...
MIRKO, WHAT SHOULD WE DO?
TOMP
AIN'T IT OBVIOUS?
WHEN A VILLAIN POPS UP, YOU KICK 'EM DOWN!

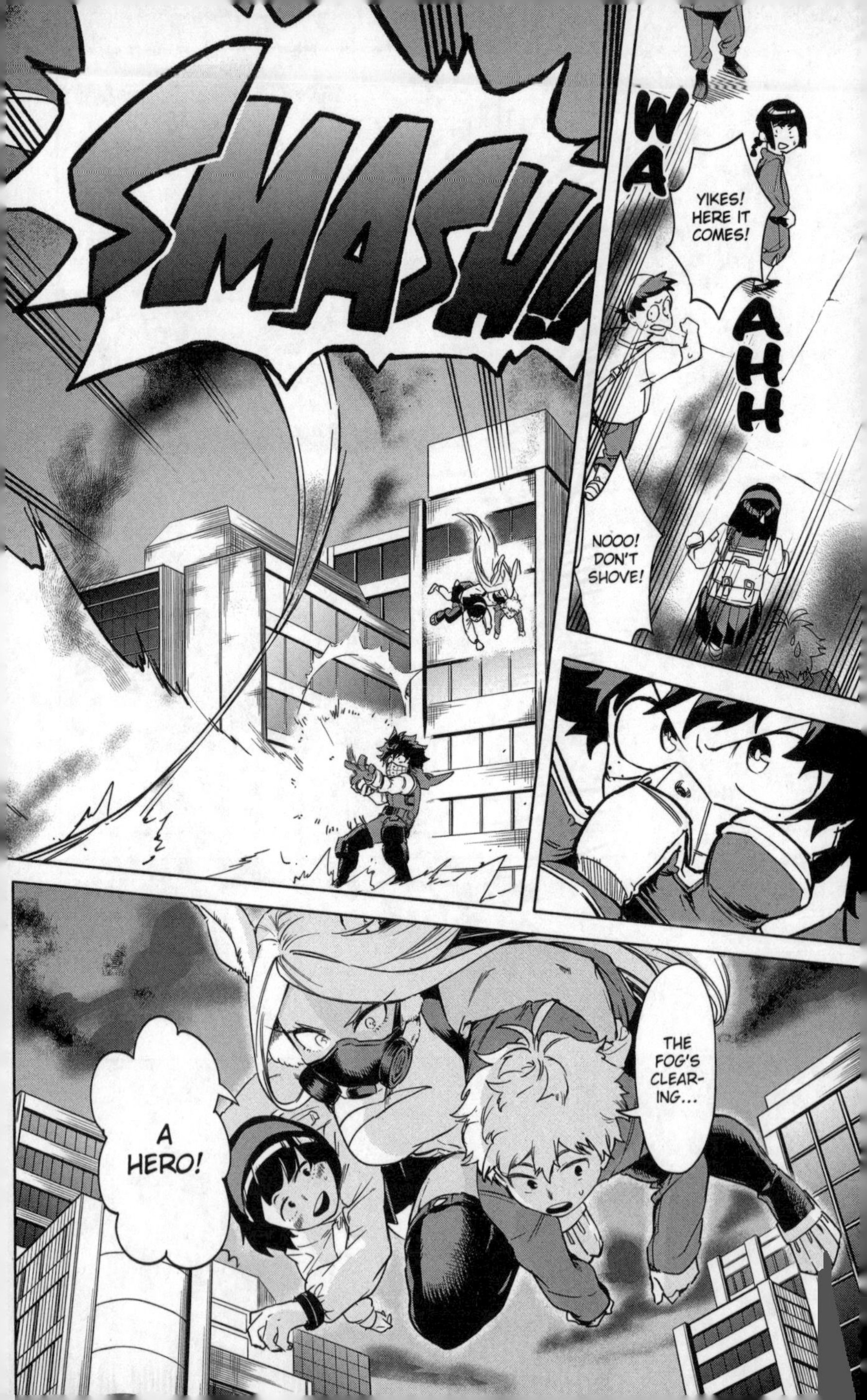
WA
YIKES! HERE IT COMES!
AHH
NOOO! DON'T SHOVE!
SMASH!!
THE FOG'S CLEAR-ING...
A HERO!

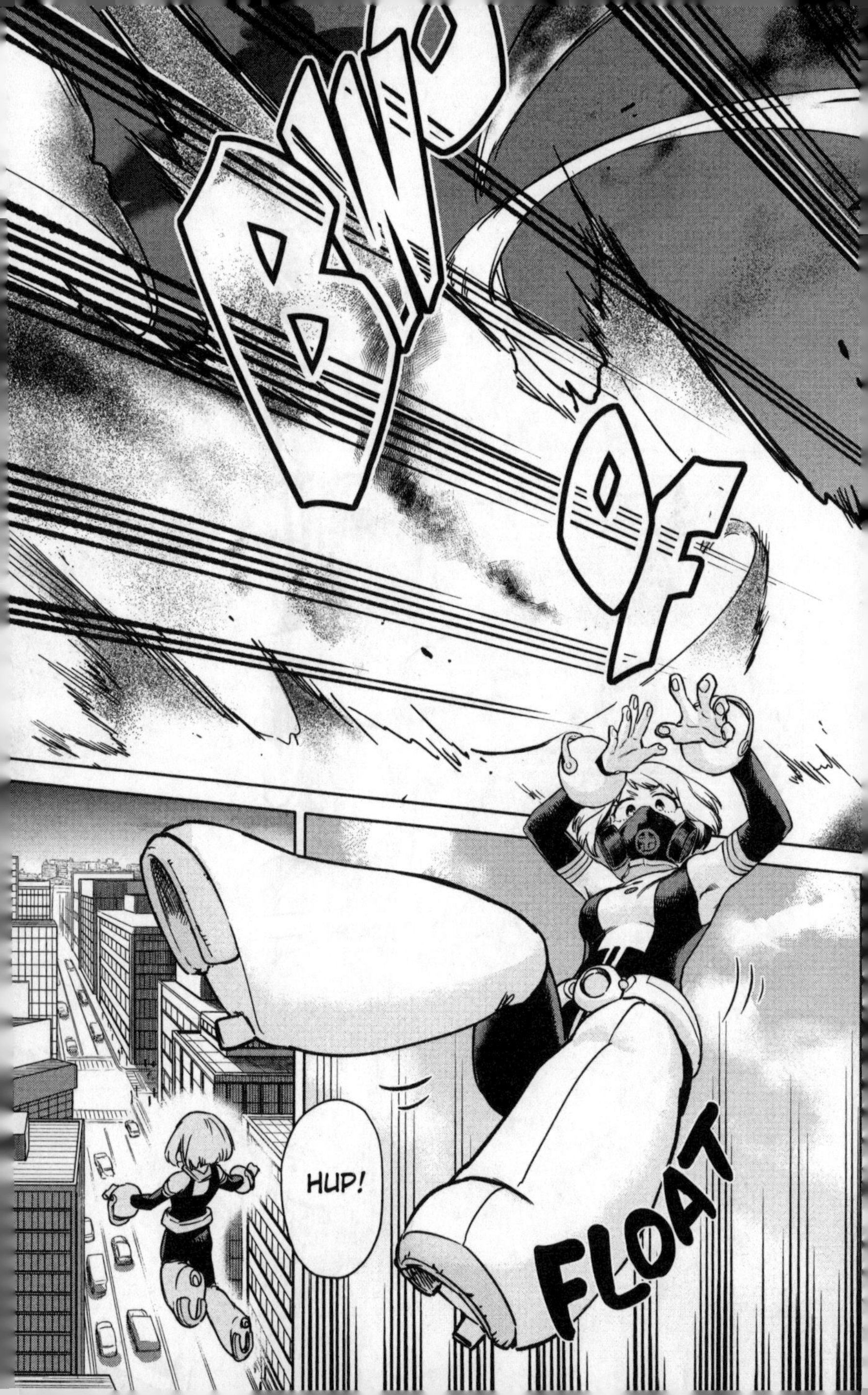
BAM
OOF
HUP!
FLOAT

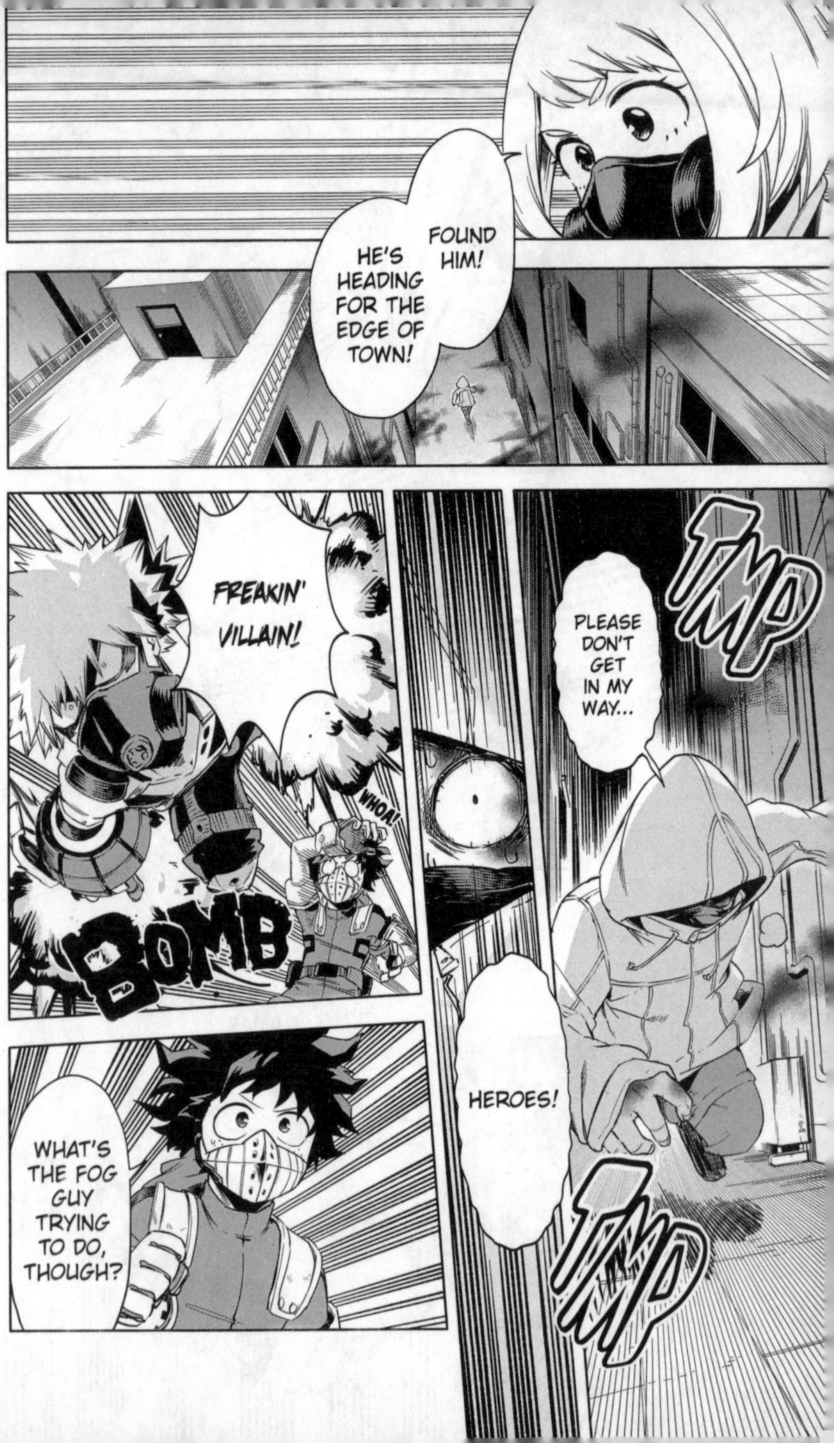
FOUND HIM!
HE'S HEADING FOR THE EDGE OF TOWN!
TMP
PLEASE DON'T GET IN MY WAY...
HEROES!
TMP
FREAKIN' VILLAIN!
WHOA!
BOMB
WHAT'S THE FOG GUY TRYING TO DO, THOUGH?

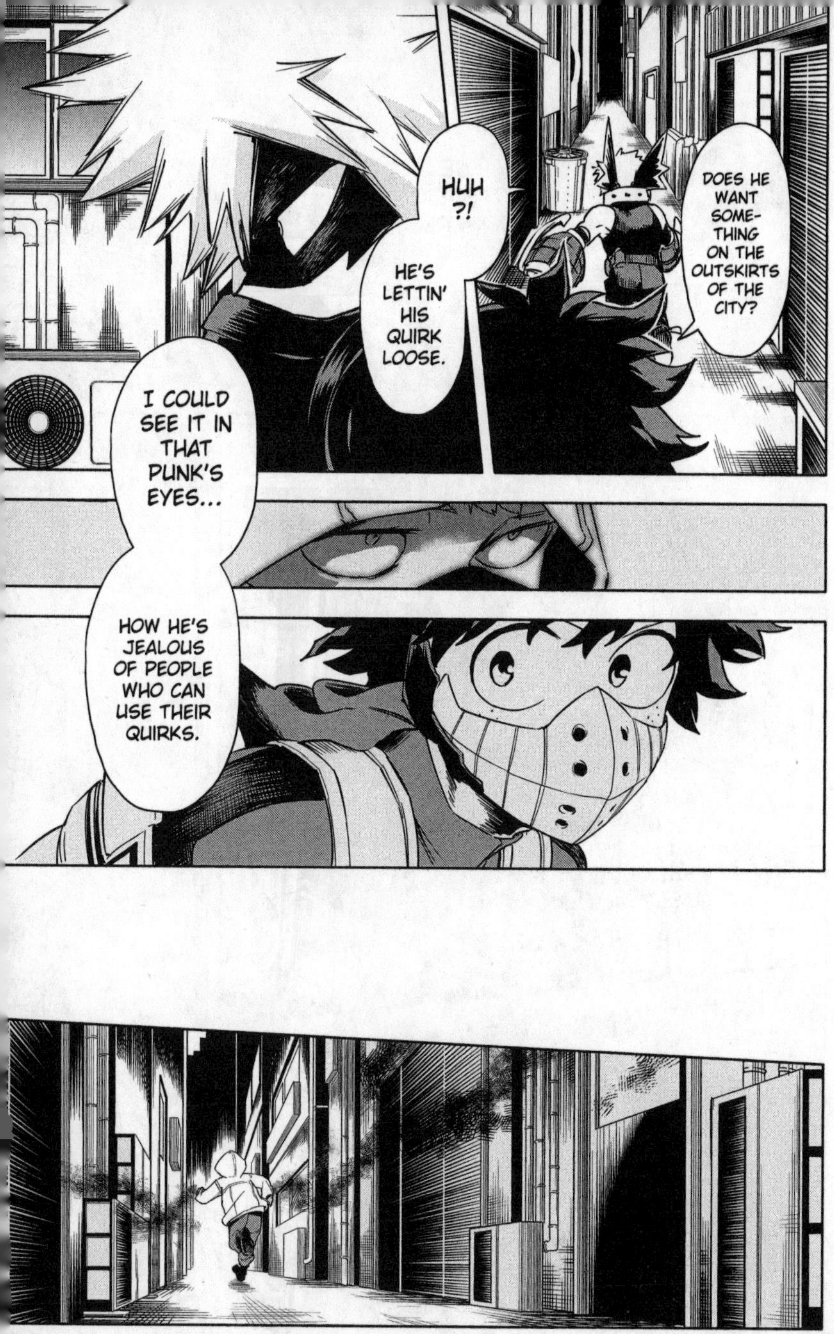
DOES HE WANT SOME-THING ON THE OUTSKIRTS OF THE CITY?
HUH ?!
HE'S LETTIN' HIS QUIRK LOOSE.
I COULD SEE IT IN THAT PUNK'S EYES...
HOW HE'S JEALOUS OF PEOPLE WHO CAN USE THEIR QUIRKS.

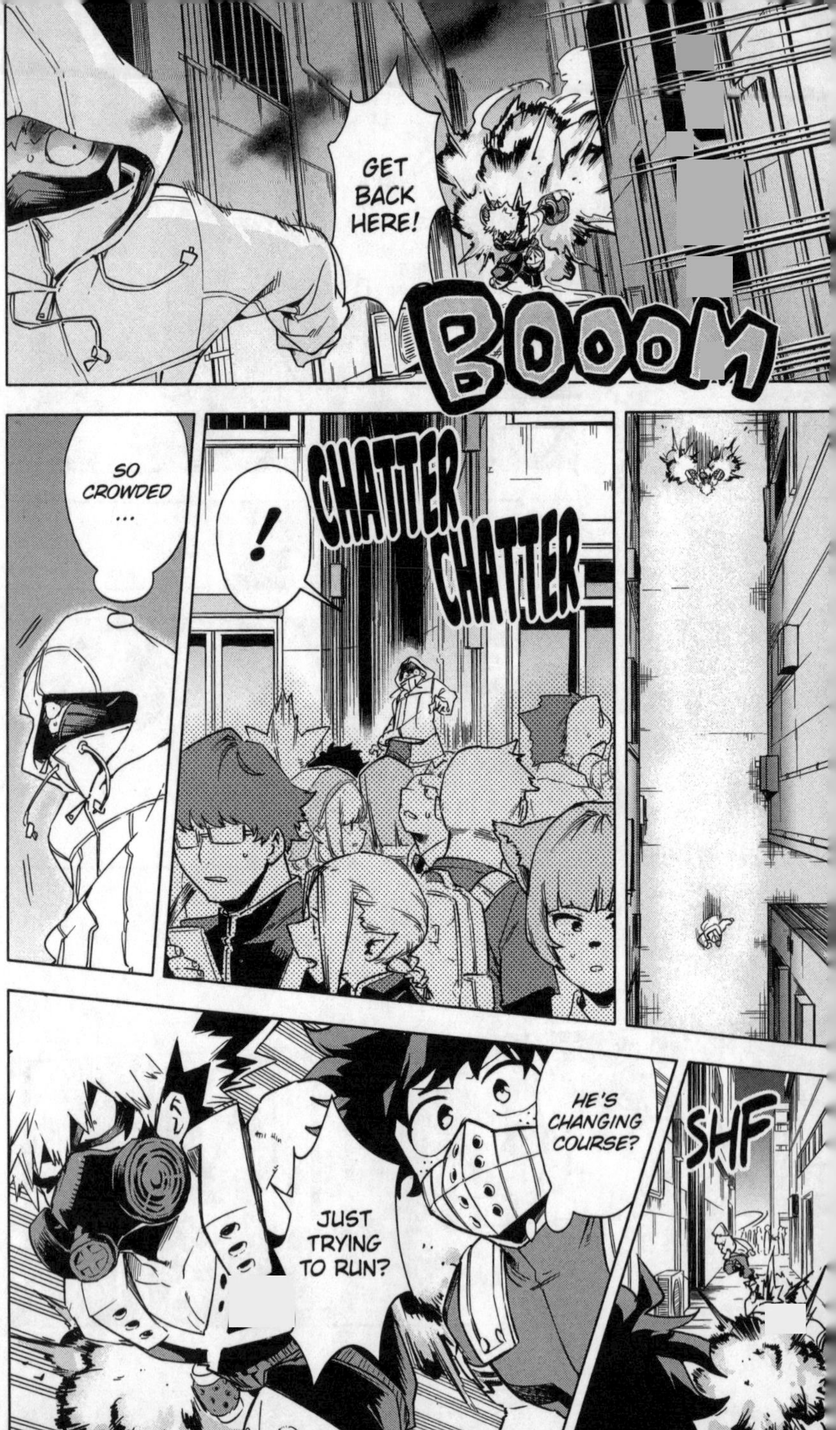
GET BACK HERE!
BOOOM
!
CHATTER CHATTER
SO CROWDED ...
SHF
HE'S CHANGING COURSE?
JUST TRYING TO RUN?

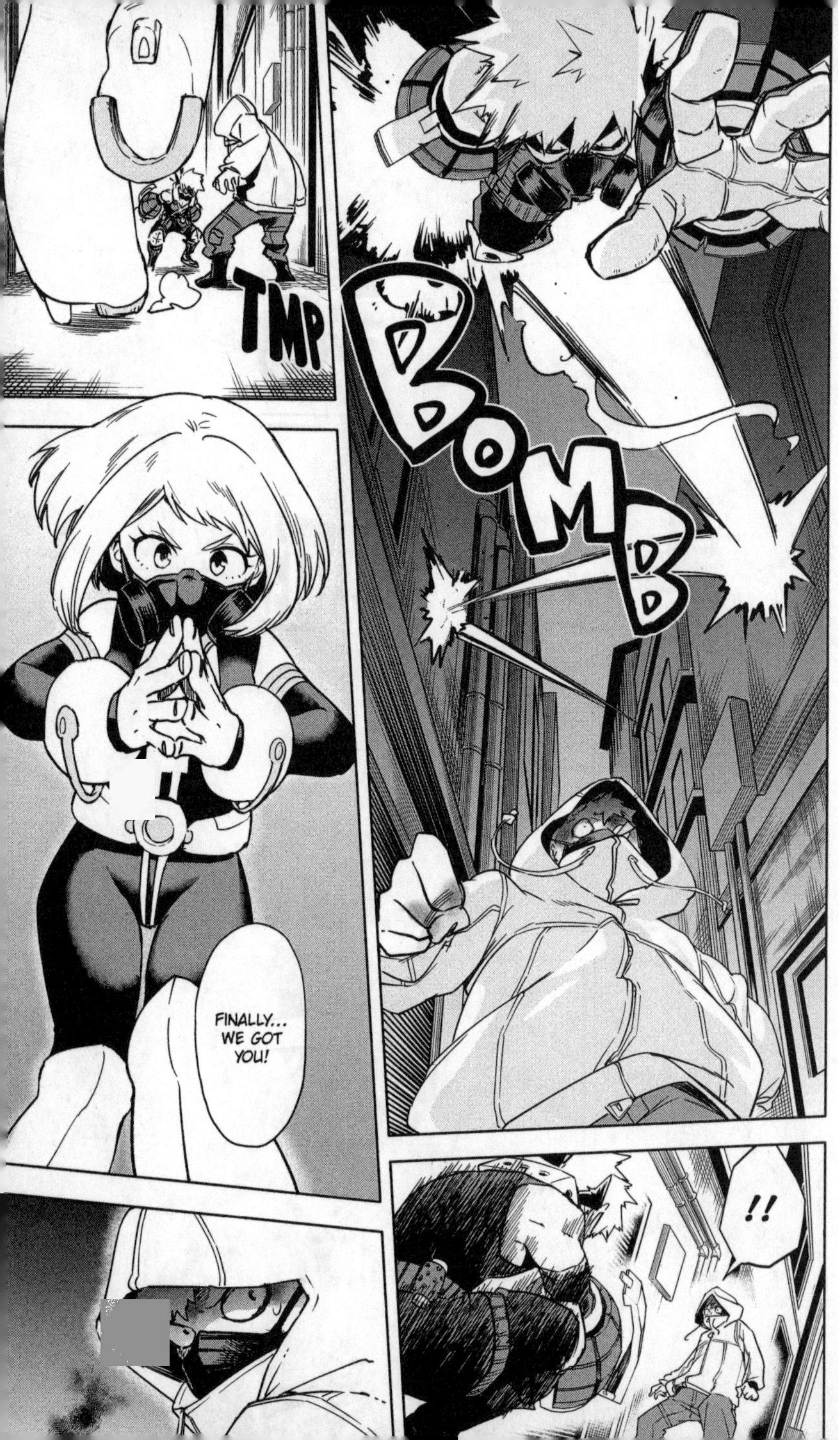
BOMB
TMP
FINALLY... WE GOT YOU!
!!

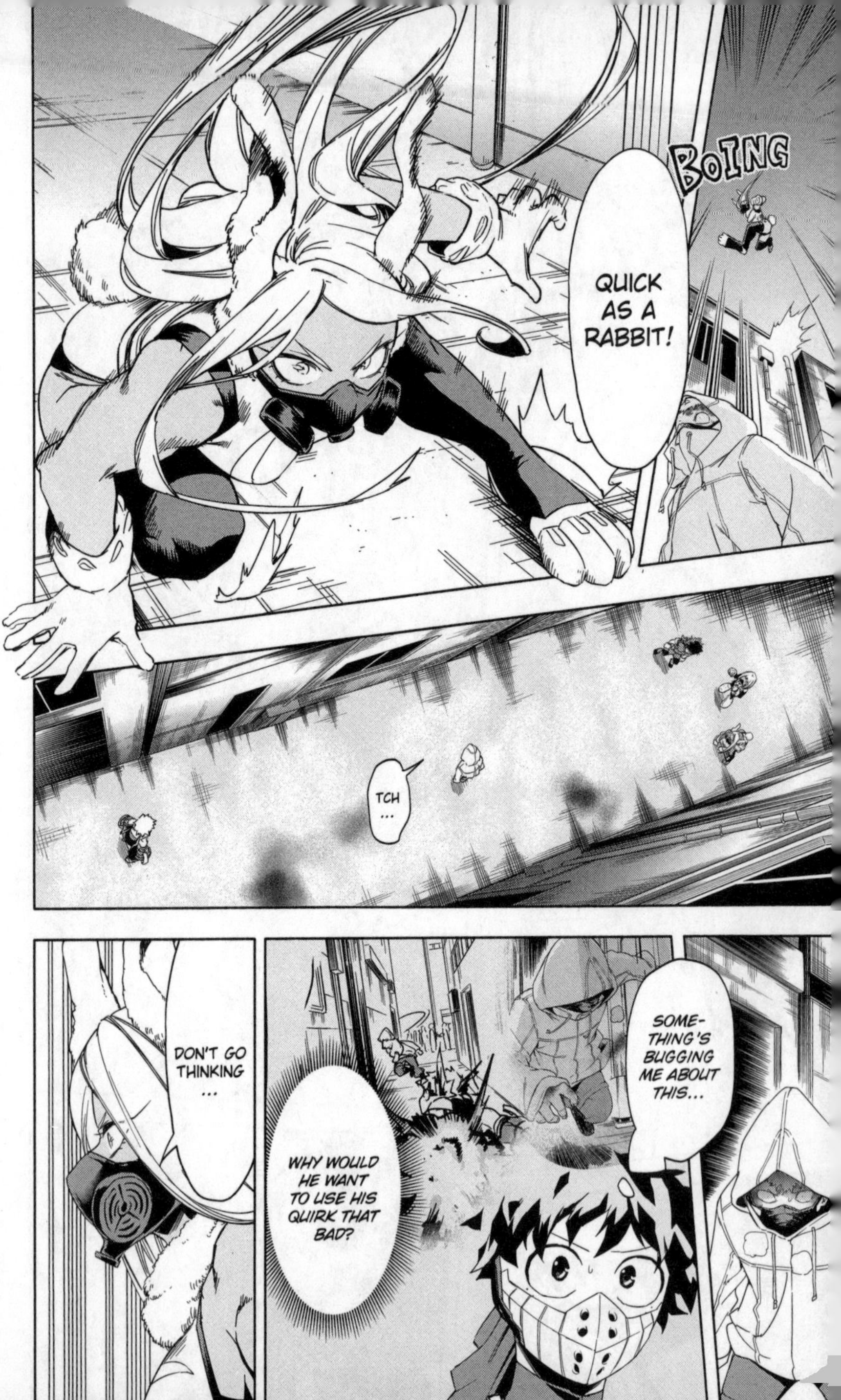
BOING
QUICK AS A RABBIT!
TCH...
SOME-THING'S BUGGING ME ABOUT THIS...
WHY WOULD HE WANT TO USE HIS QUIRK THAT BAD?
DON'T GO THINKING...

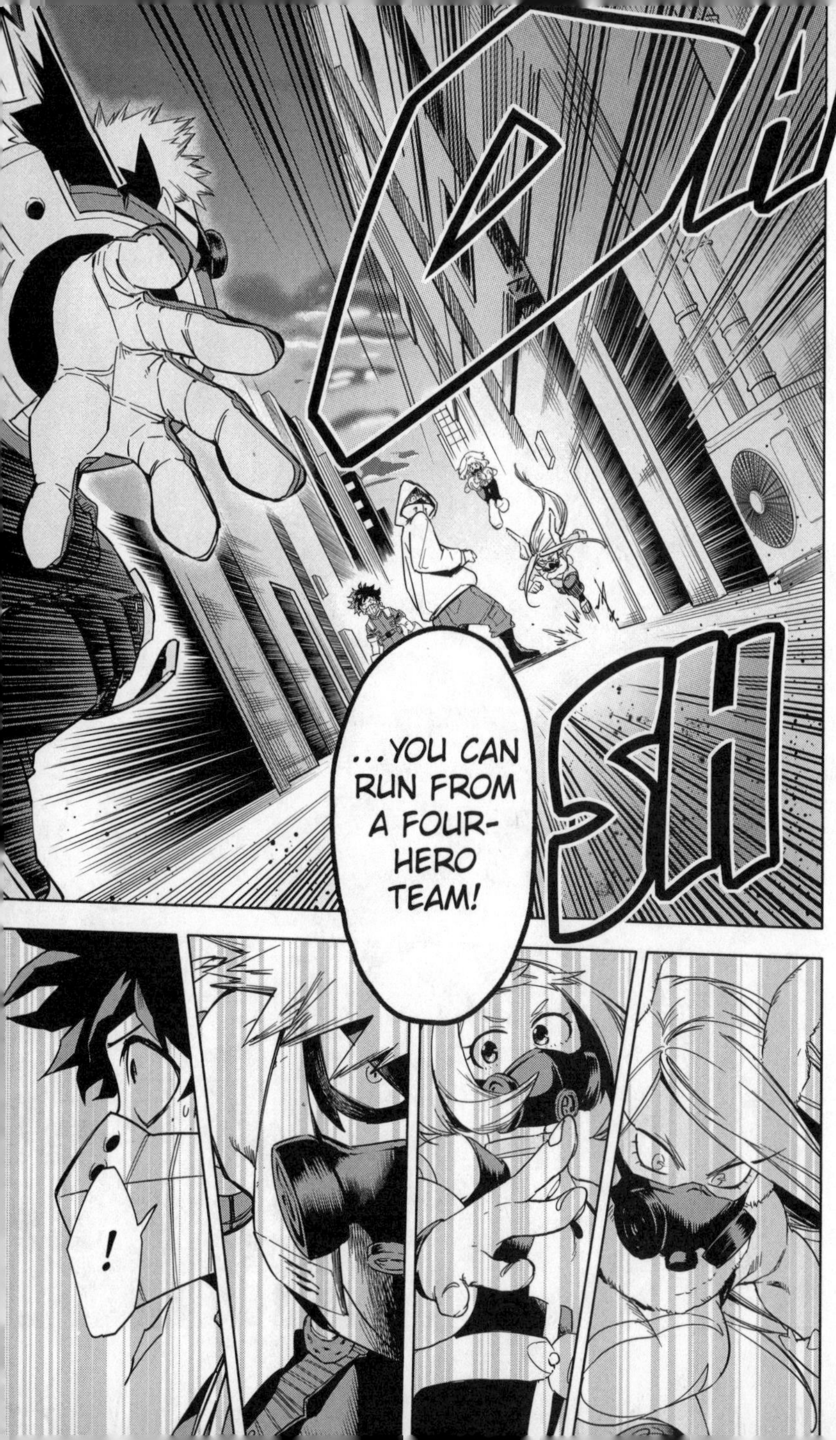

DASH
...YOU CAN RUN FROM A FOUR-HERO TEAM!
!

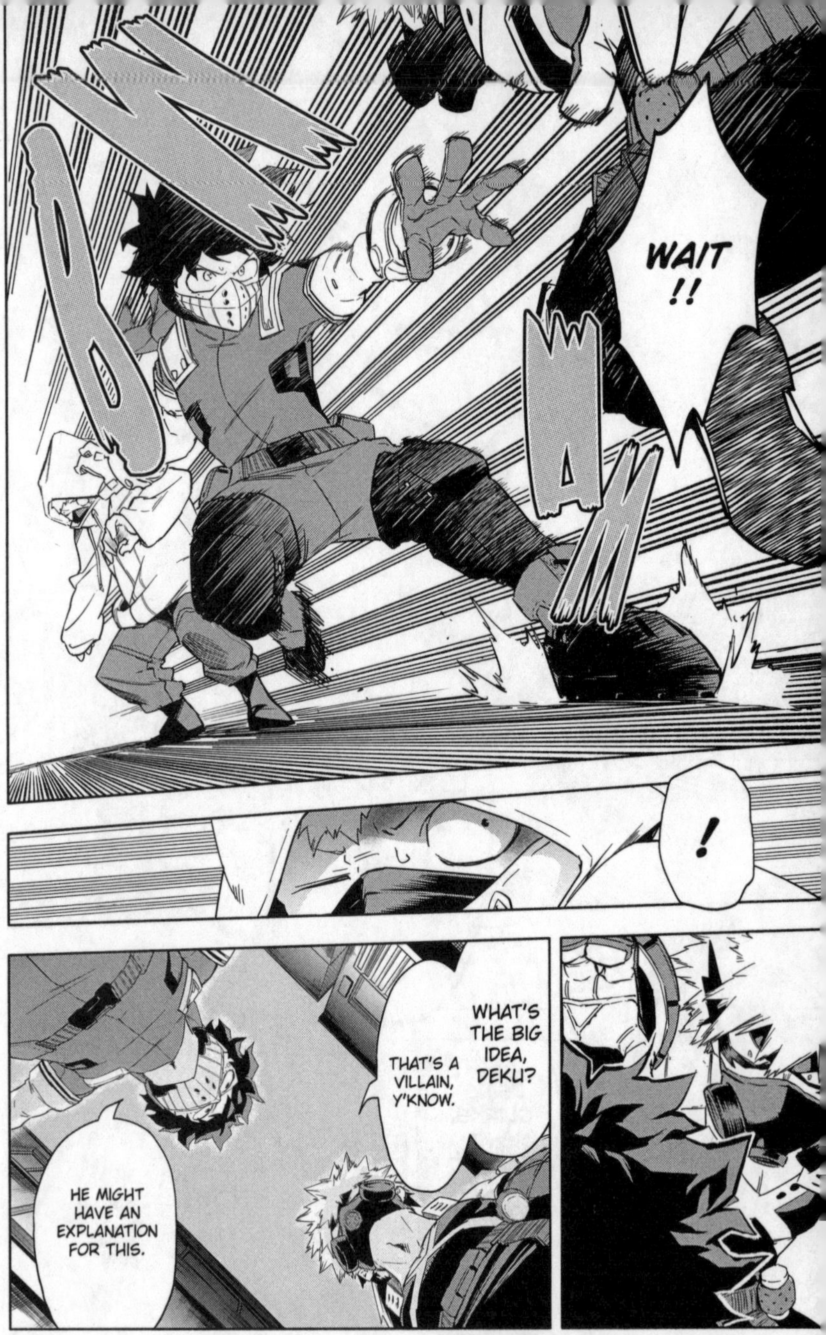
WAIT !!
!
WHAT'S THE BIG IDEA, DEKU?
THAT'S A VILLAIN, Y'KNOW.
HE MIGHT HAVE AN EXPLANATION FOR THIS.

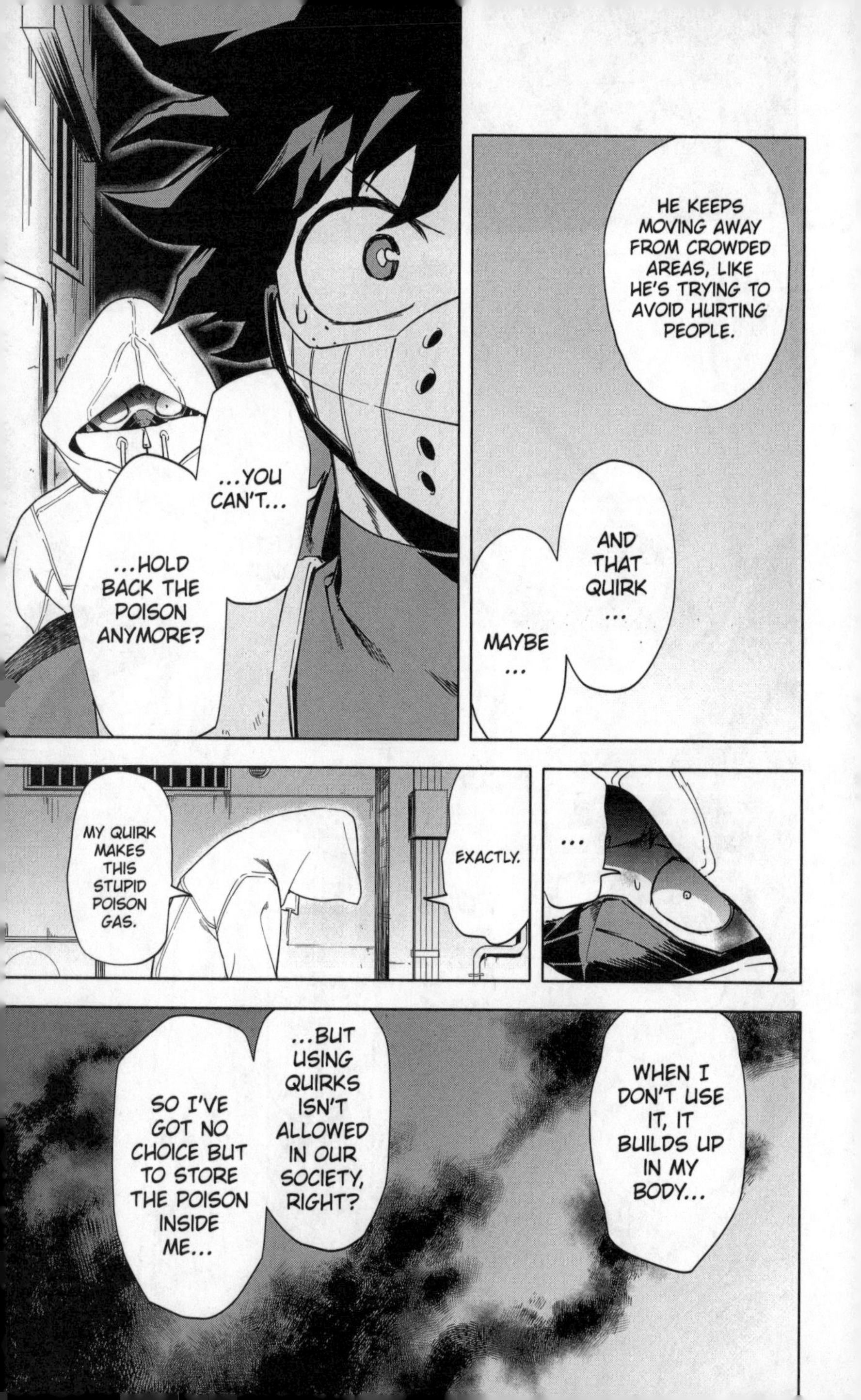
HE KEEPS MOVING AWAY FROM CROWDED AREAS, LIKE HE'S TRYING TO AVOID HURTING PEOPLE.
AND THAT QUIRK...
MAYBE...
...YOU CAN'T...
...HOLD BACK THE POISON ANYMORE?
...
EXACTLY.
MY QUIRK MAKES THIS STUPID POISON GAS.
WHEN I DON'T USE IT, IT BUILDS UP IN MY BODY...
...BUT USING QUIRKS ISN'T ALLOWED IN OUR SOCIETY, RIGHT?
SO I'VE GOT NO CHOICE BUT TO STORE THE POISON INSIDE ME...

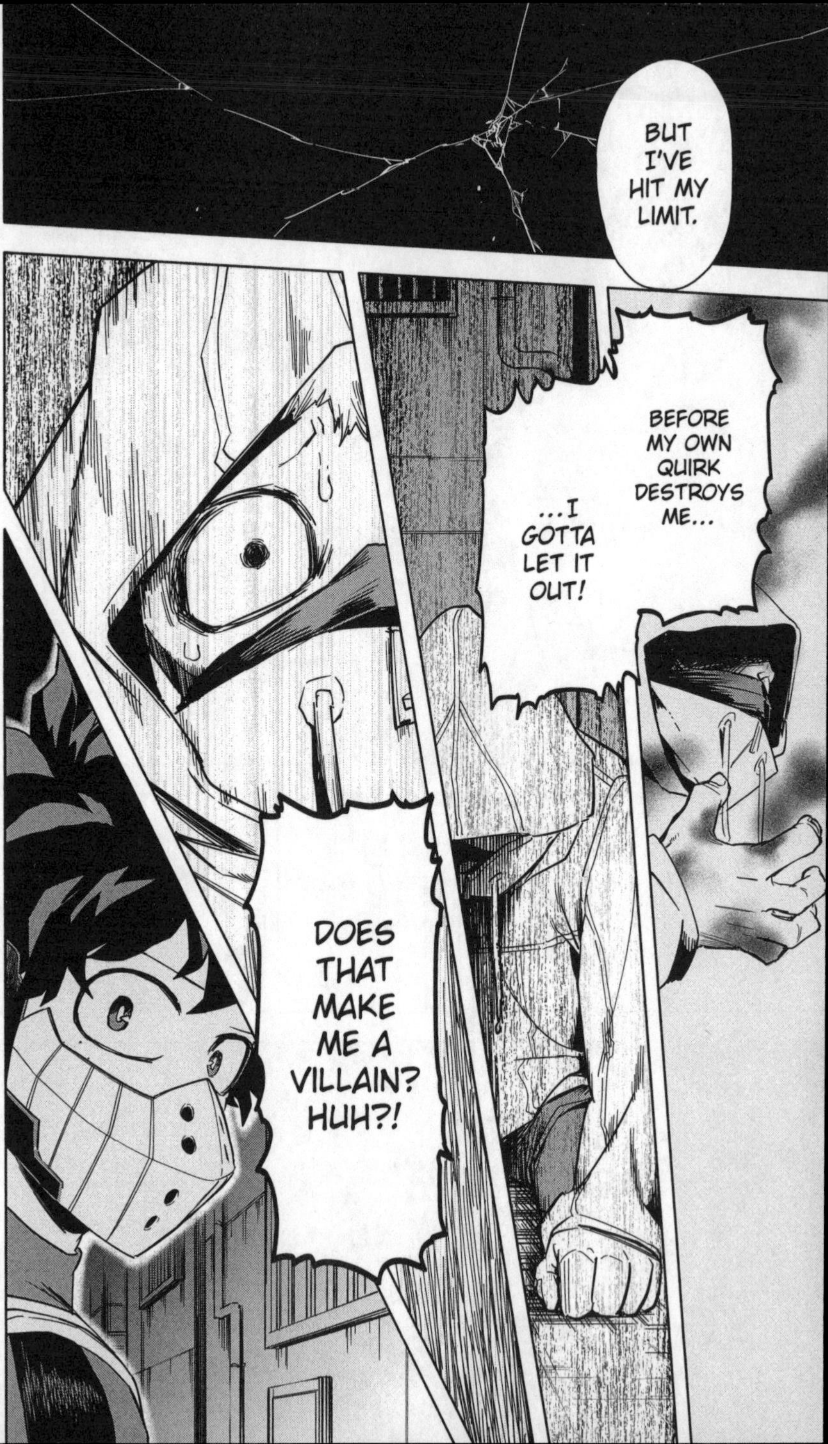
BUT I'VE HIT MY LIMIT.
BEFORE MY OWN QUIRK DESTROYS ME...
...I GOTTA LET IT OUT!
DOES THAT MAKE ME A VILLAIN? HUH?!

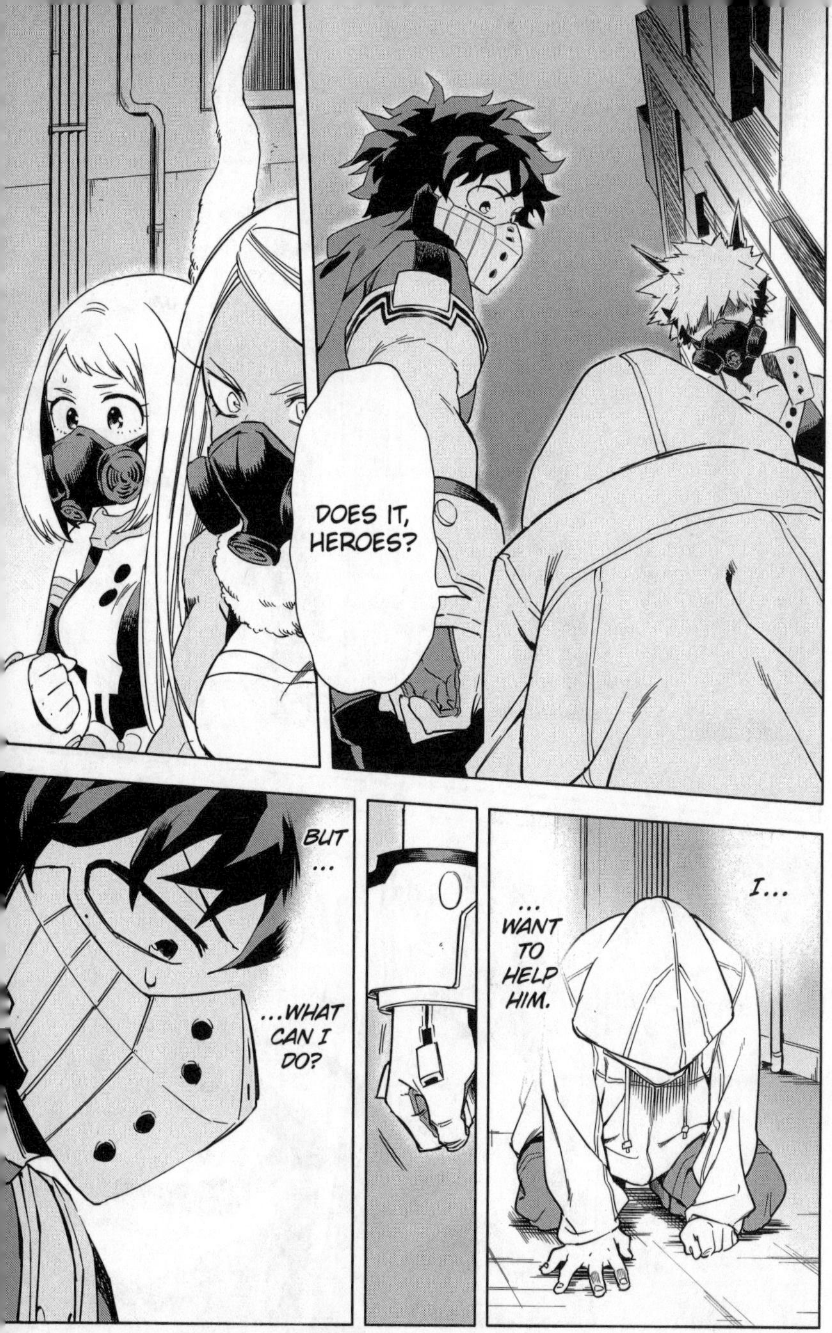
DOES IT, HEROES?
I...
...WANT TO HELP HIM.
BUT ...
...WHAT CAN I DO?

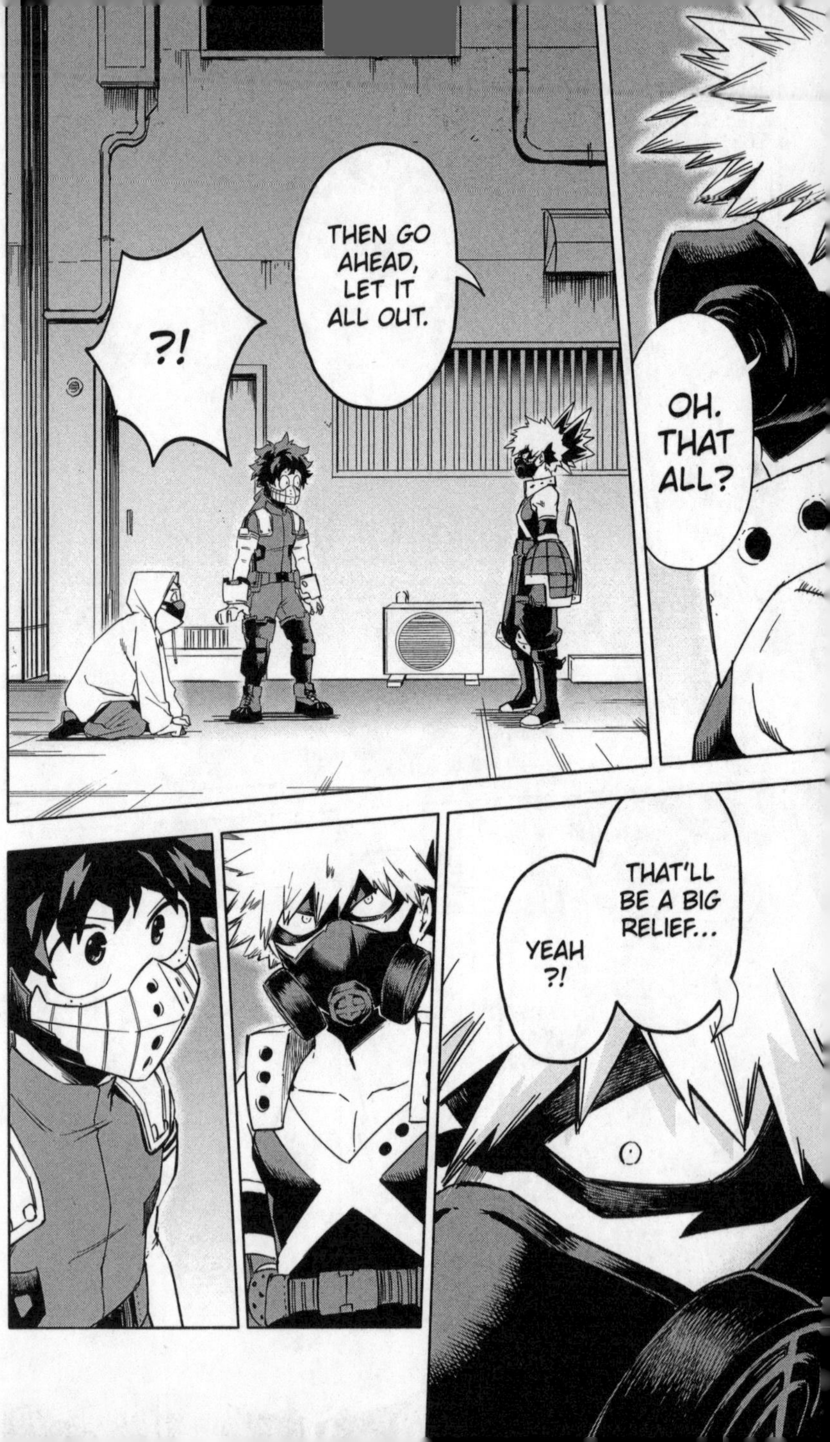
OH. THAT ALL?
THEN GO AHEAD, LET IT ALL OUT.
?!
THAT'LL BE A BIG RELIEF...
YEAH ?!

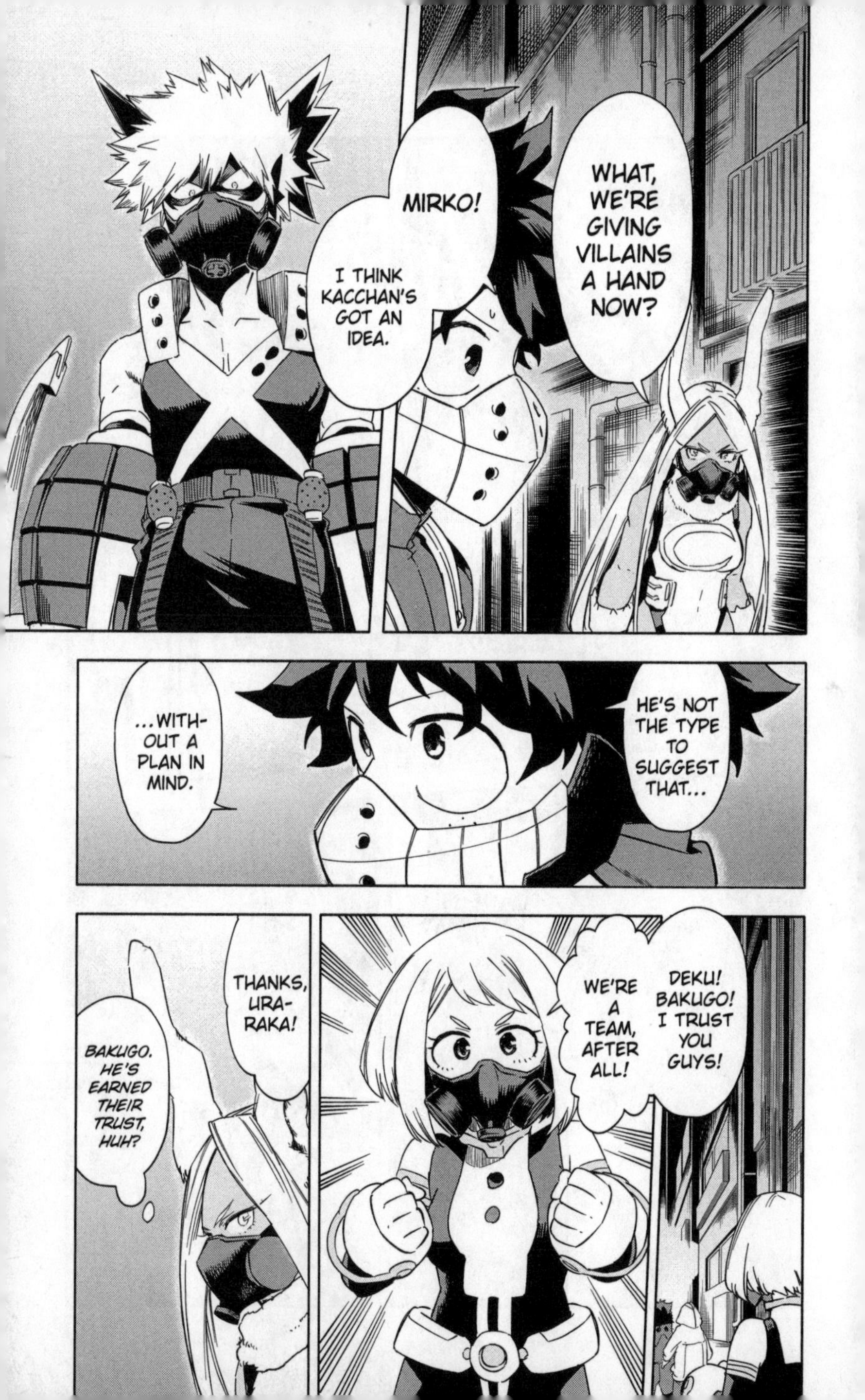
WHAT, WE'RE GIVING VILLAINS A HAND NOW?
MIRKO!
I THINK KACCHAN'S GOT AN IDEA.
HE'S NOT THE TYPE TO SUGGEST THAT...
...WITH-OUT A PLAN IN MIND.
DEKU! BAKUGO! I TRUST YOU GUYS!
WE'RE A TEAM, AFTER ALL!
THANKS, URA-RAKA!
BAKUGO. HE'S EARNED THEIR TRUST, HUH?

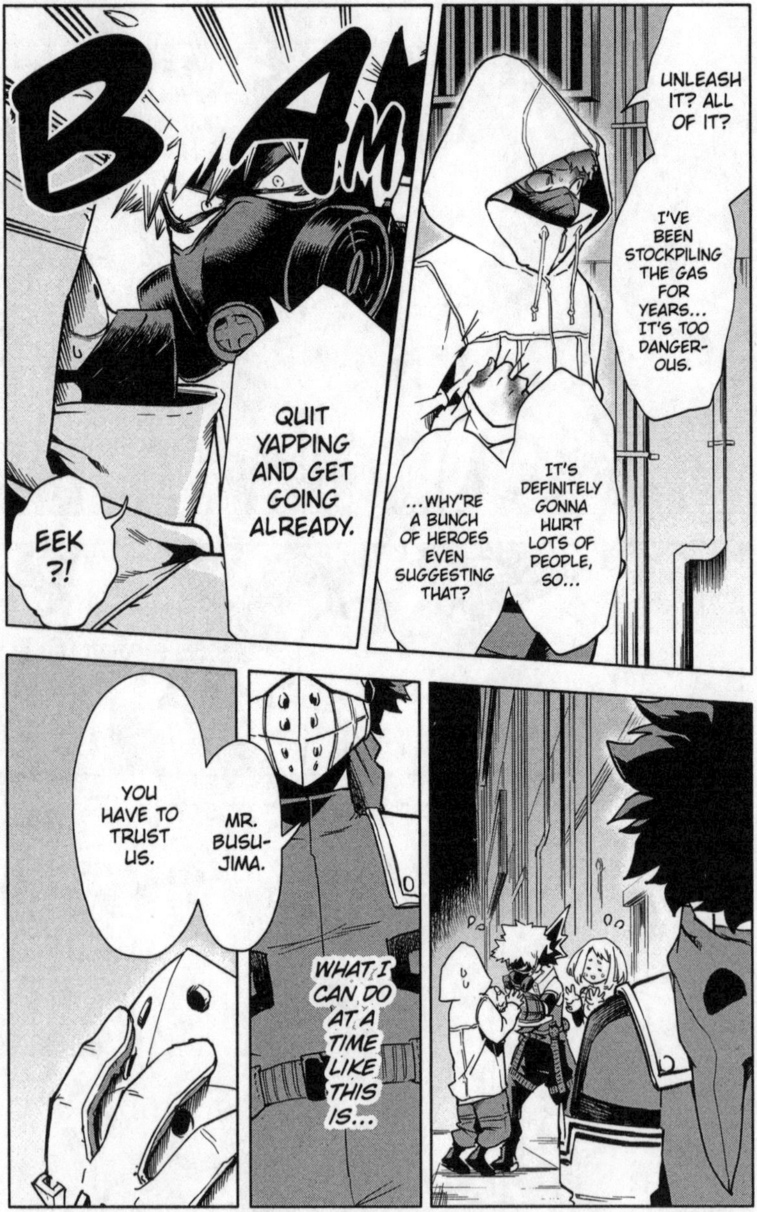
UNLEASH IT? ALL OF IT?
I'VE BEEN STOCKPILING THE GAS FOR YEARS... IT'S TOO DANGEROUS.
IT'S DEFINITELY GONNA HURT LOTS OF PEOPLE, SO...
...WHY'RE A BUNCH OF HEROES EVEN SUGGESTING THAT?
BAM
QUIT YAPPING AND GET GOING ALREADY.
EEK ?!
MR. BUSUJIMA.
YOU HAVE TO TRUST US.
WHAT I CAN DO AT A TIME LIKE THIS IS...

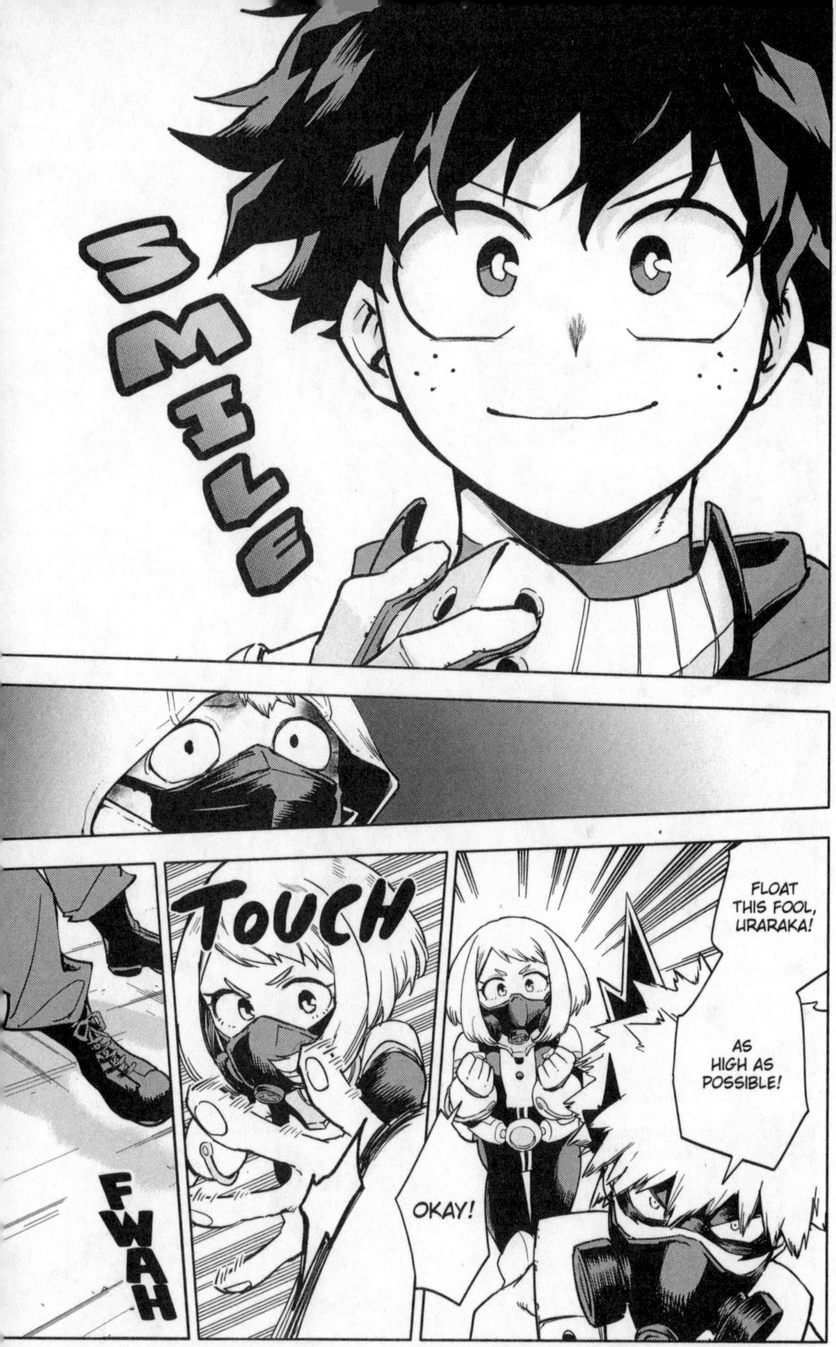
SMILE
FLOAT THIS FOOL, URARAKA!
AS HIGH AS POSSIBLE!
OKAY!
TOUCH
FWAH

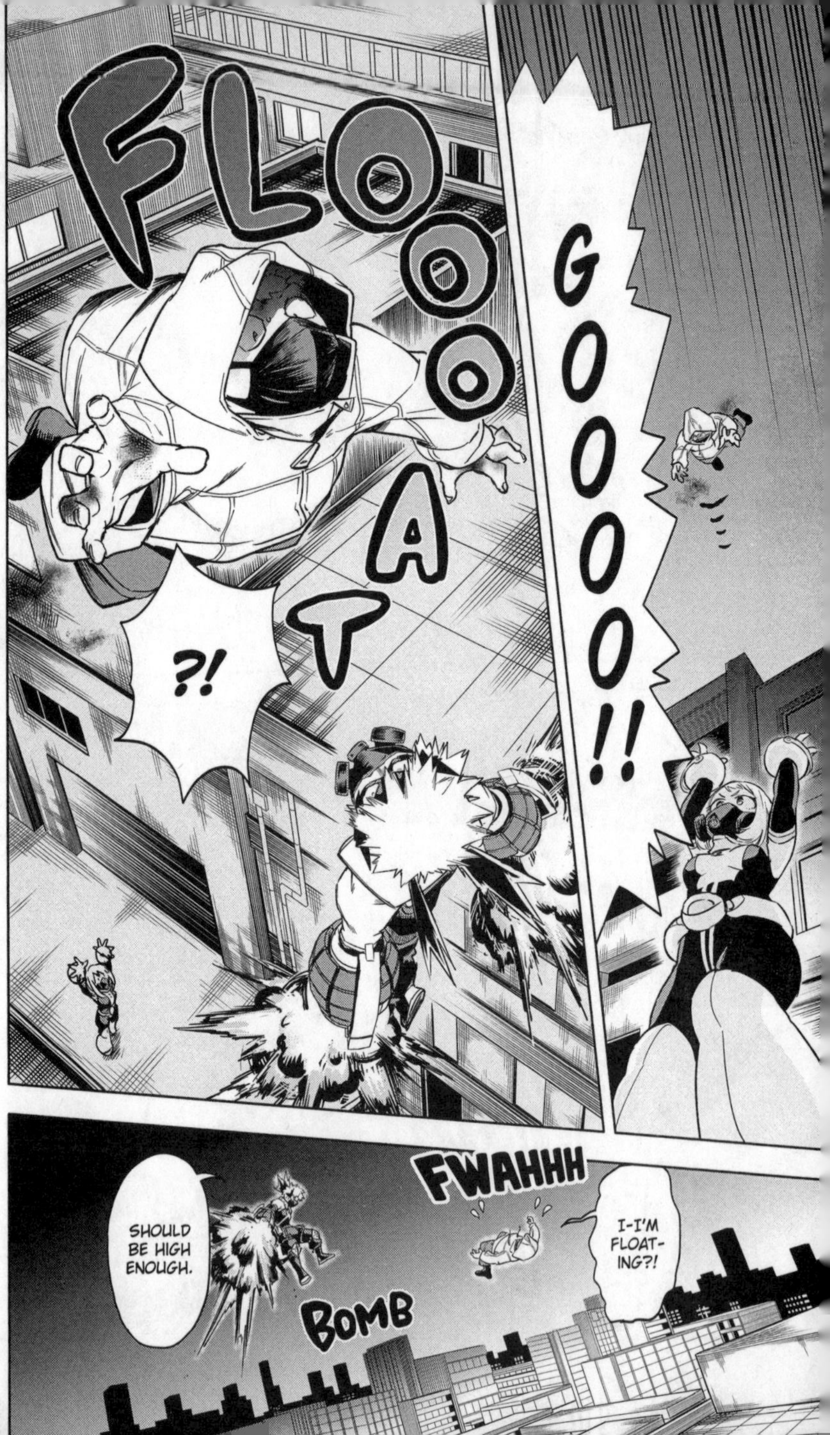
GOOOOOO!!
FLOOOOAT
?!
I-I'M FLOAT-ING?!
FWAHHH
SHOULD BE HIGH ENOUGH.
BOMB

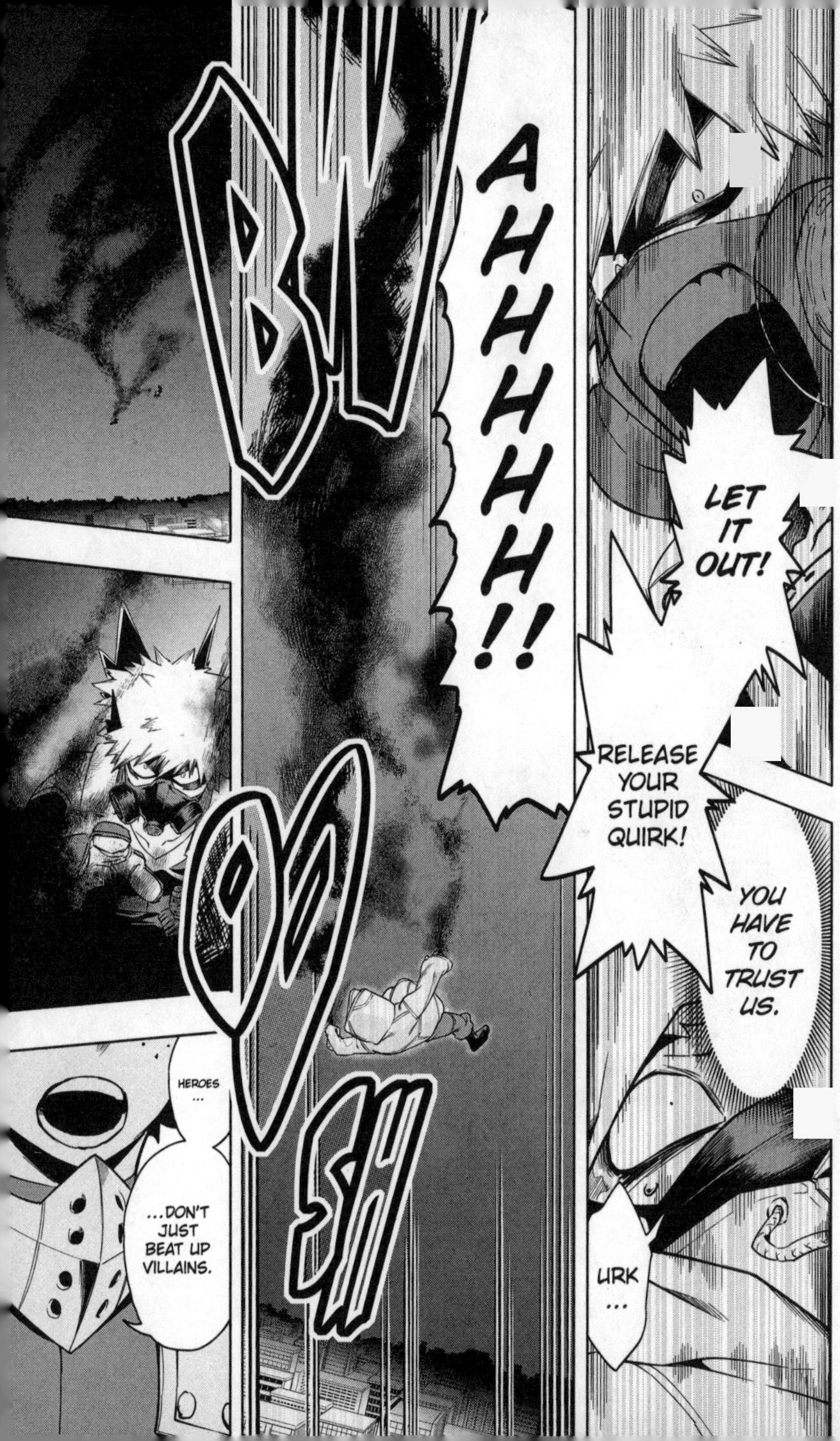
LET IT OUT!
RELEASE YOUR STUPID QUIRK!
YOU HAVE TO TRUST US.
URK...
AHHHHH!!
HEROES...
...DON'T JUST BEAT UP VILLAINS.

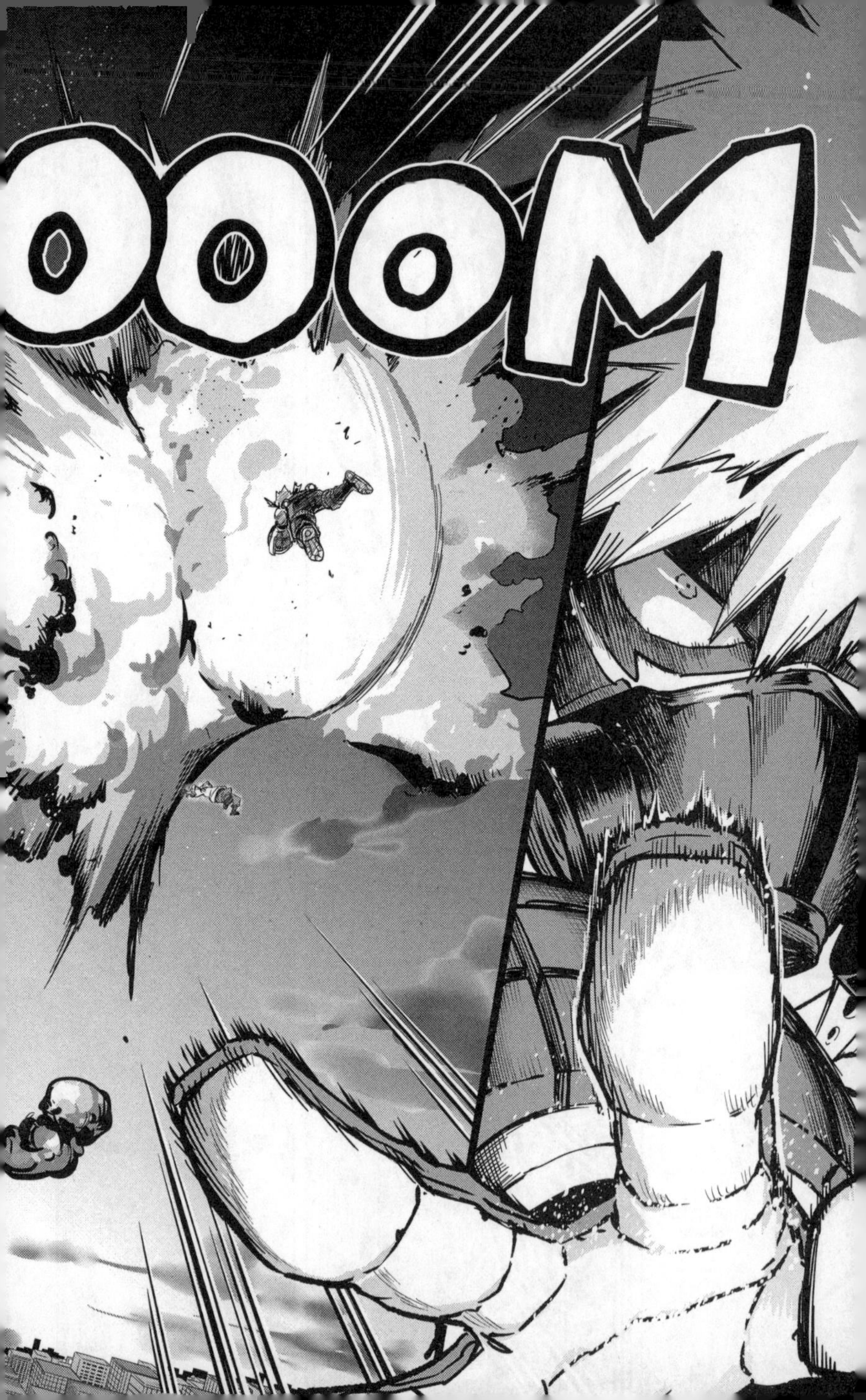
OOOM

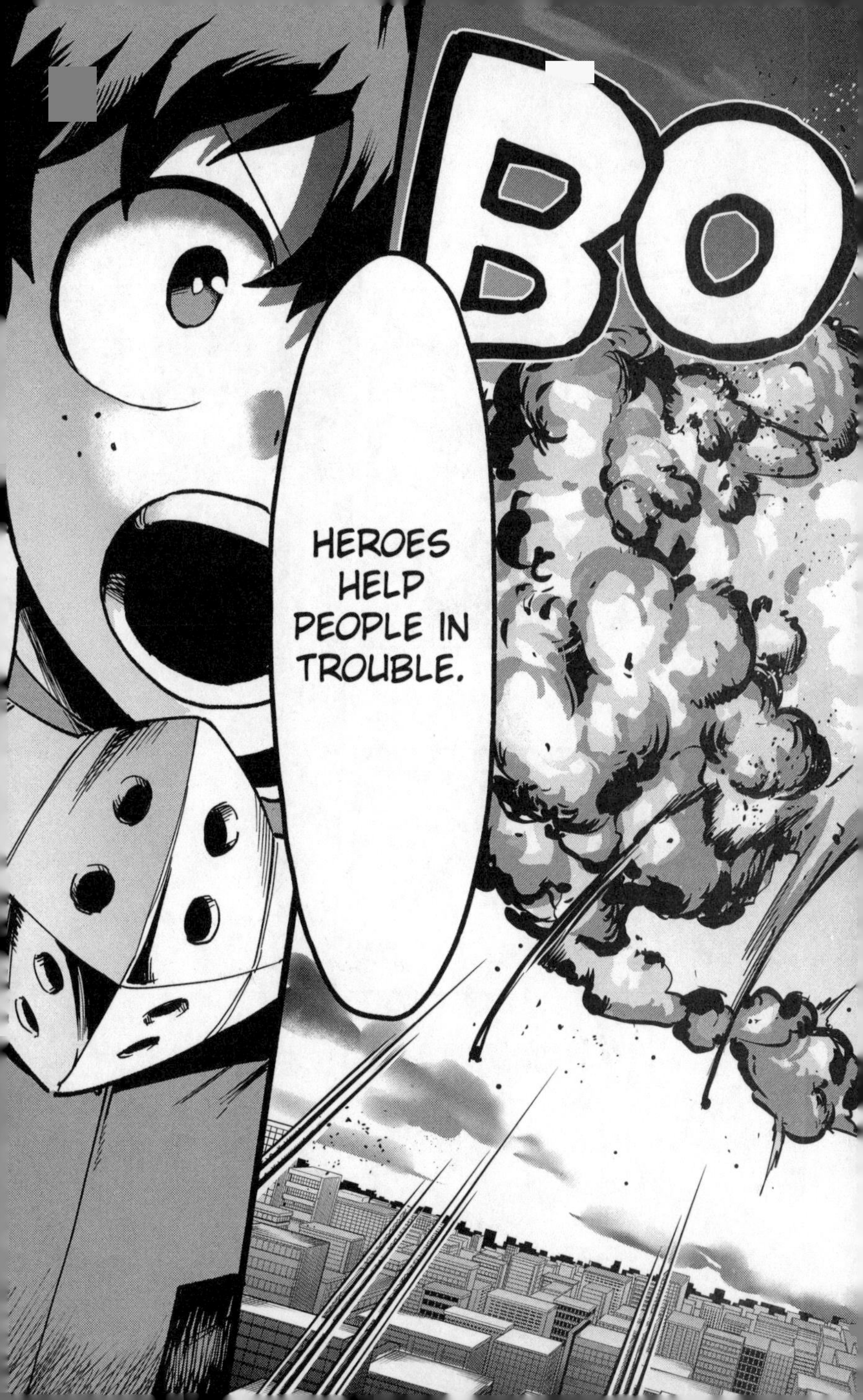
BO
HEROES HELP PEOPLE IN TROUBLE.

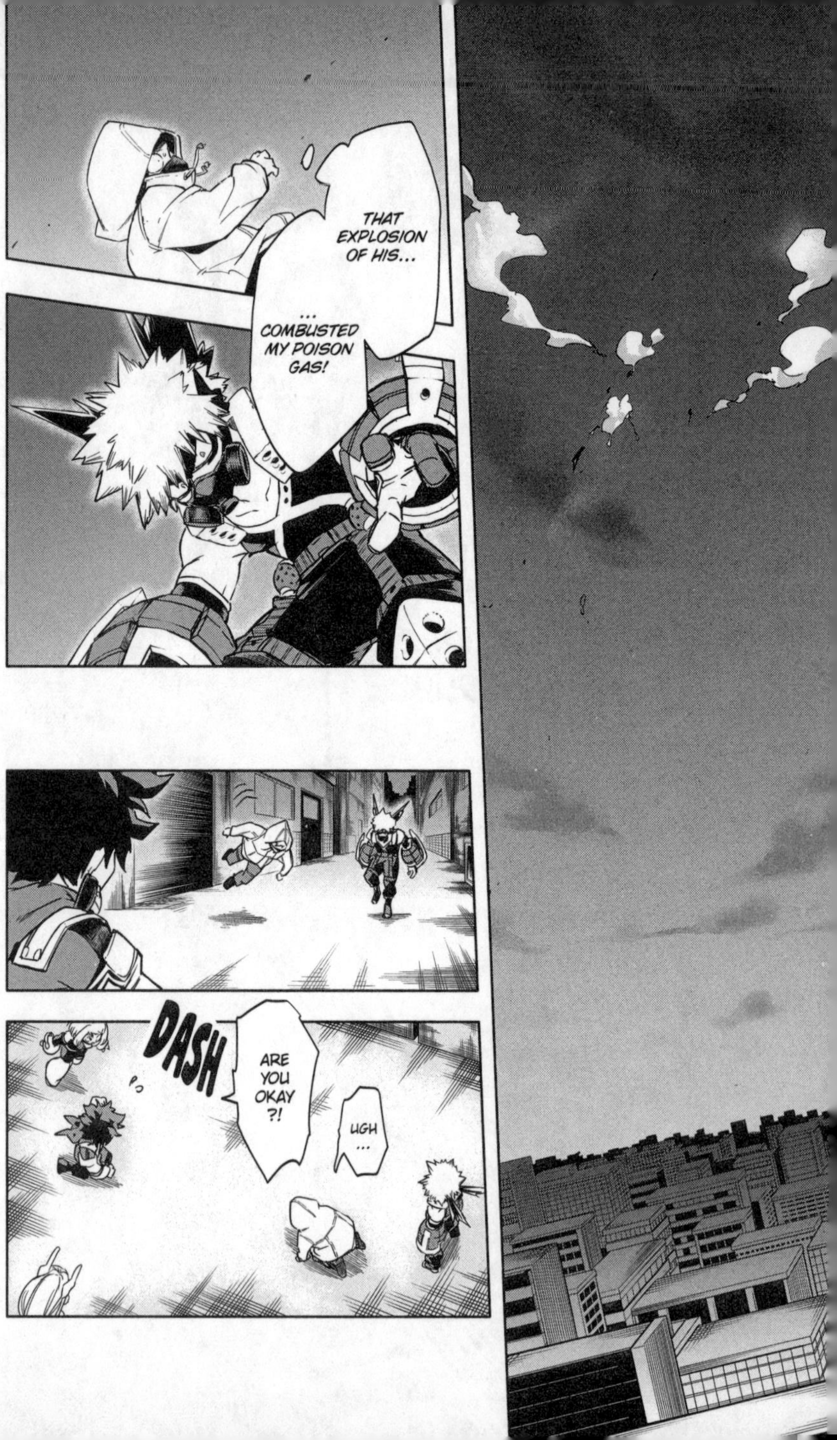
THAT EXPLOSION OF HIS...
...COMBUSTED MY POISON GAS!
DASH
ARE YOU OKAY?!
UGH...

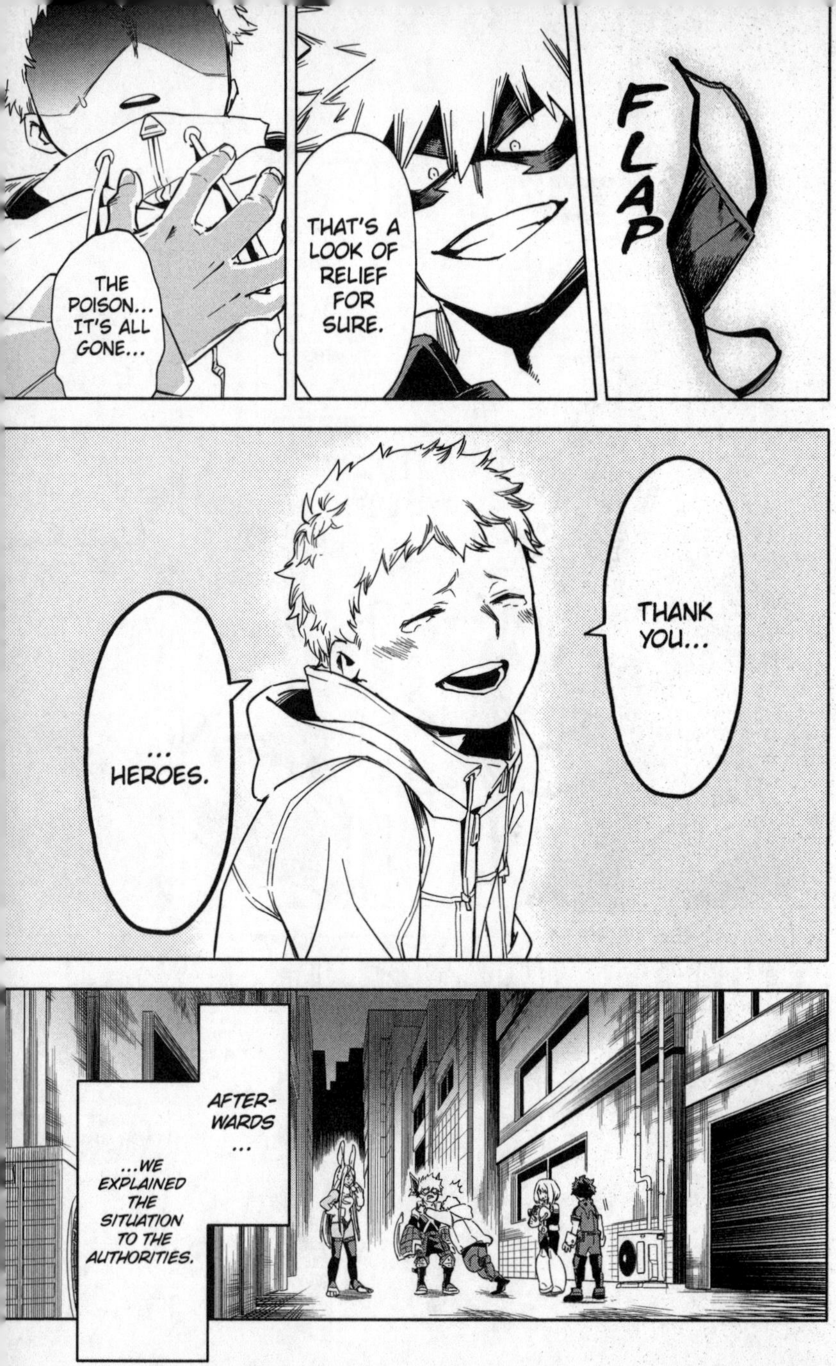
FLAP
THAT'S A LOOK OF RELIEF FOR SURE.
THE POISON... IT'S ALL GONE...
THANK YOU...
... HEROES.
AFTER-WARDS ...
...WE EXPLAINED THE SITUATION TO THE AUTHORITIES.

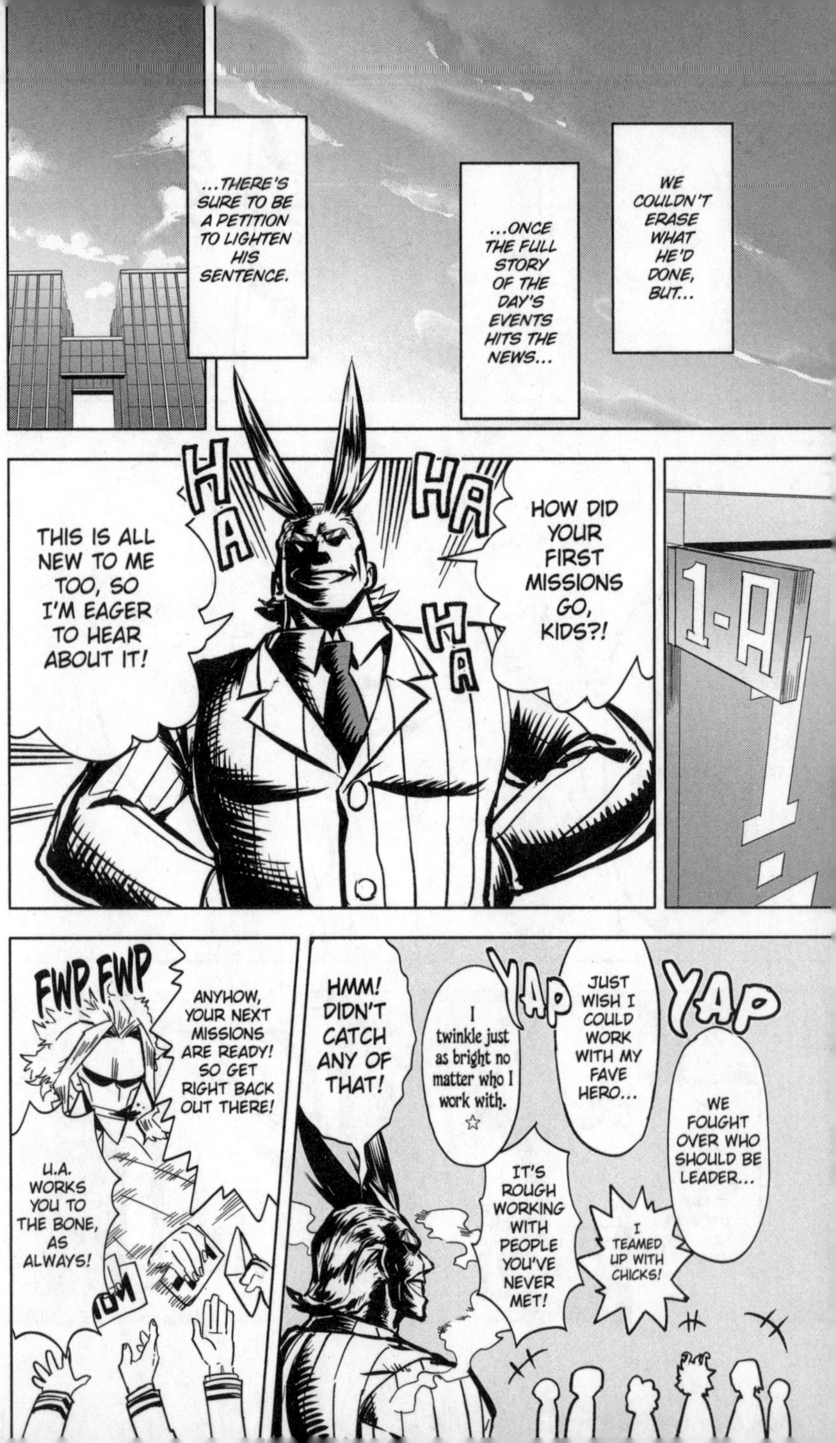
WE COULDN'T ERASE WHAT HE'D DONE, BUT...
...ONCE THE FULL STORY OF THE DAY'S EVENTS HITS THE NEWS...
...THERE'S SURE TO BE A PETITION TO LIGHTEN HIS SENTENCE.
1-A
HA HA HA HA HA HA
HOW DID YOUR FIRST MISSIONS GO, KIDS?!
THIS IS ALL NEW TO ME TOO, SO I'M EAGER TO HEAR ABOUT IT!
YAP YAP
WE FOUGHT OVER WHO SHOULD BE LEADER...
I TEAMED UP WITH CHICKS!
JUST WISH I COULD WORK WITH MY FAVE HERO...
IT'S ROUGH WORKING WITH PEOPLE YOU'VE NEVER MET!
I twinkle just as bright no matter who I work with. ☆
HMM! DIDN'T CATCH ANY OF THAT!
FWP FWP
ANYHOW, YOUR NEXT MISSIONS ARE READY! SO GET RIGHT BACK OUT THERE!
U.A. WORKS YOU TO THE BONE, AS ALWAYS!

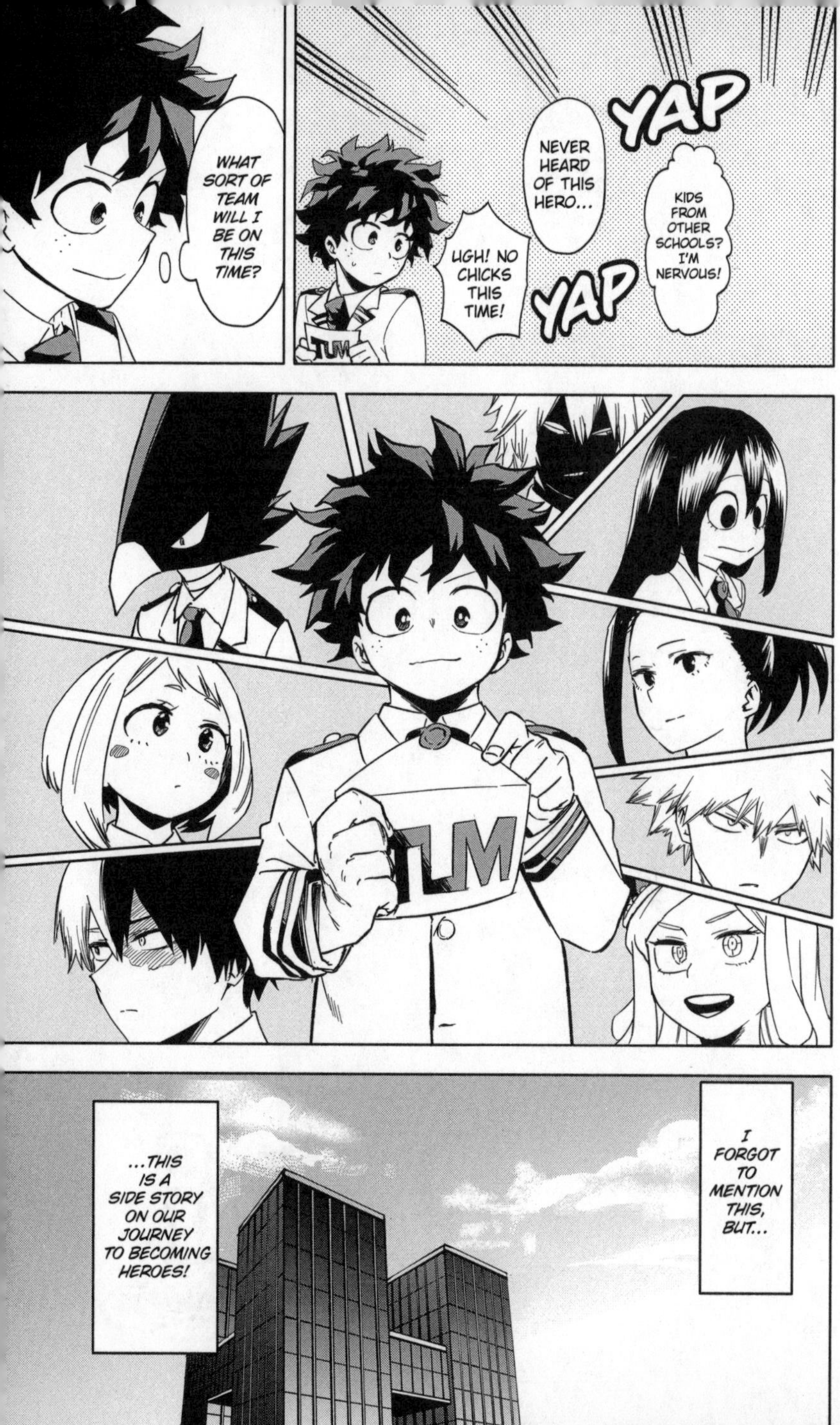
YAP
KIDS FROM OTHER SCHOOLS? I'M NERVOUS!
NEVER HEARD OF THIS HERO...
YAP
UGH! NO CHICKS THIS TIME!
TLM
WHAT SORT OF TEAM WILL I BE ON THIS TIME?
TLM
I FORGOT TO MENTION THIS, BUT...
...THIS IS A SIDE STORY ON OUR JOURNEY TO BECOMING HEROES!

MY HERO ACADEMIA

Team-Up Missions

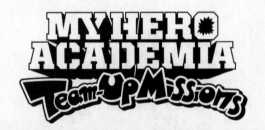

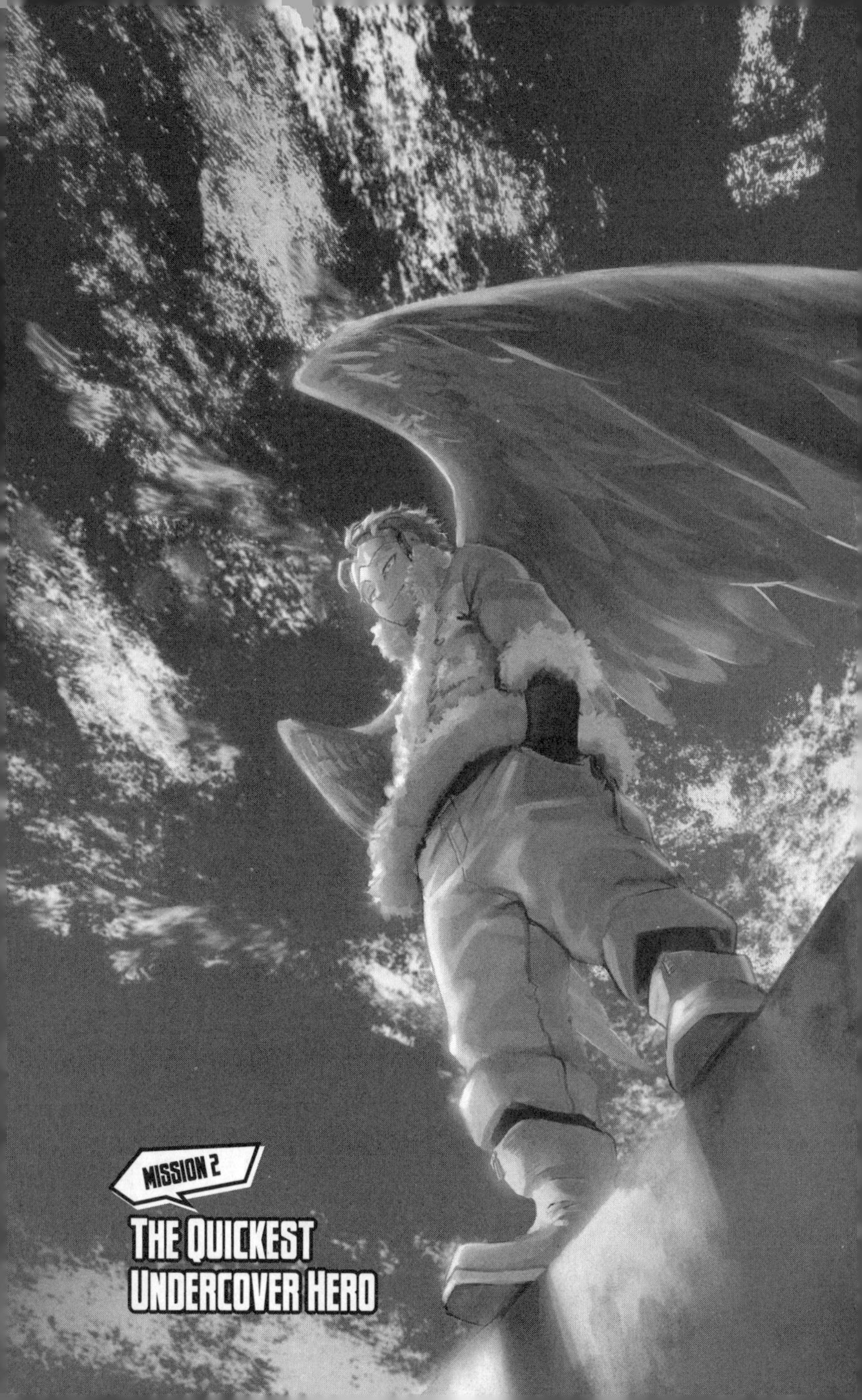
MISSION 2
THE QUICKEST UNDERCOVER HERO

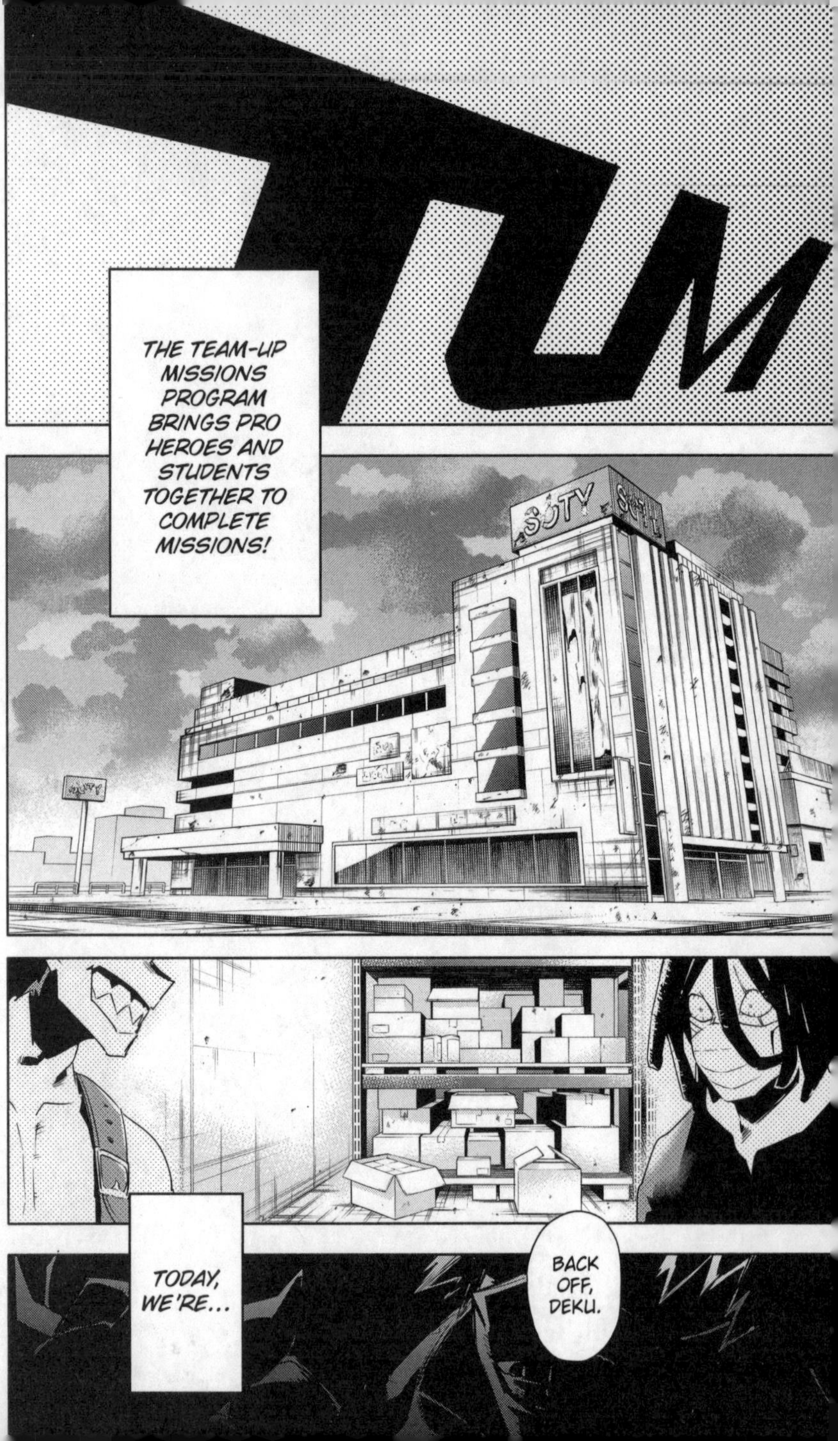
THE TEAM-UP MISSIONS PROGRAM BRINGS PRO HEROES AND STUDENTS TOGETHER TO COMPLETE MISSIONS!
BACK OFF, DEKU.
TODAY, WE'RE...

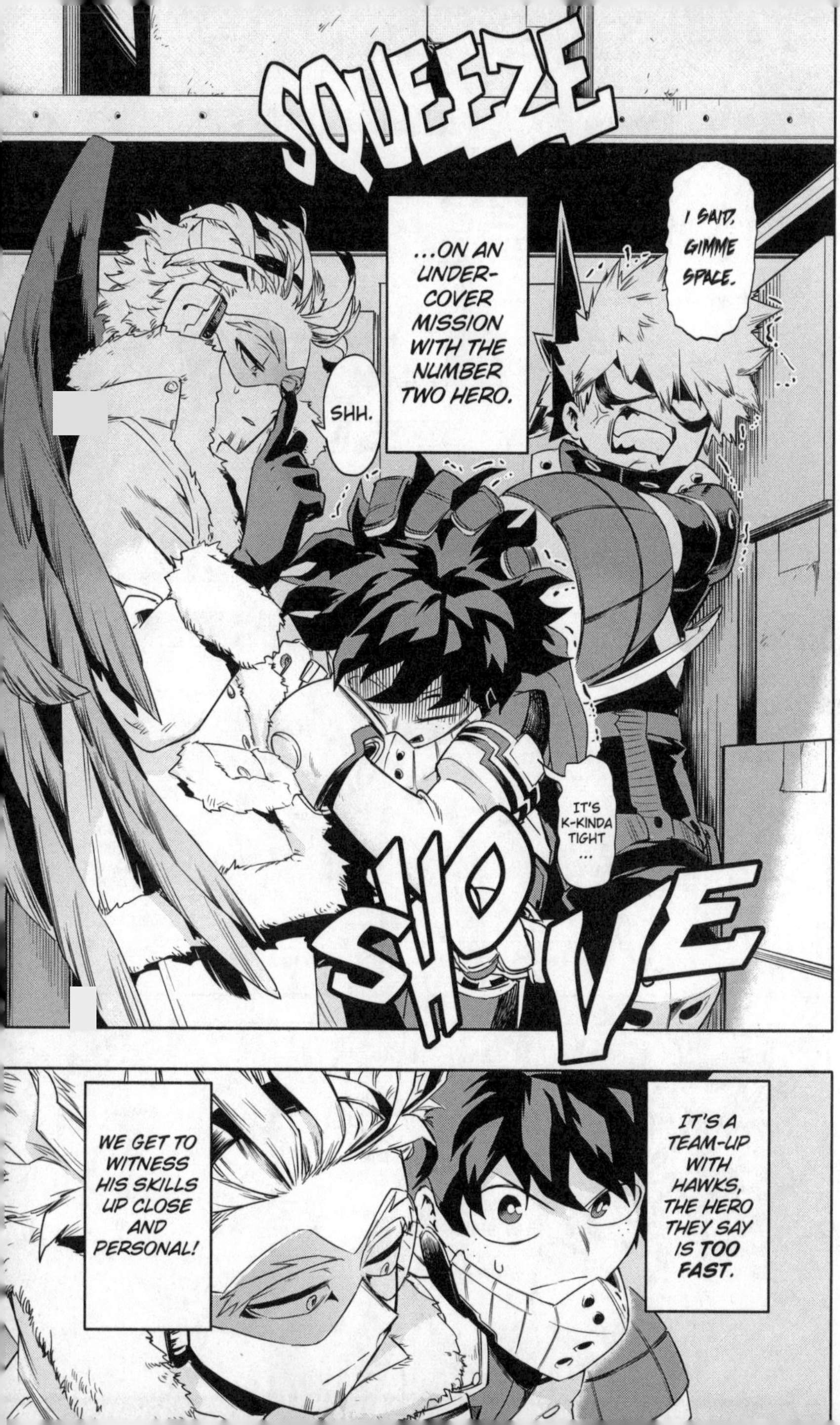
SQUEEZE
I SAID, GIMME SPACE.
...ON AN UNDER-COVER MISSION WITH THE NUMBER TWO HERO.
SHH.
IT'S K-KINDA TIGHT ...
SHOVE
IT'S A TEAM-UP WITH HAWKS, THE HERO THEY SAY IS TOO FAST.
WE GET TO WITNESS HIS SKILLS UP CLOSE AND PERSONAL!

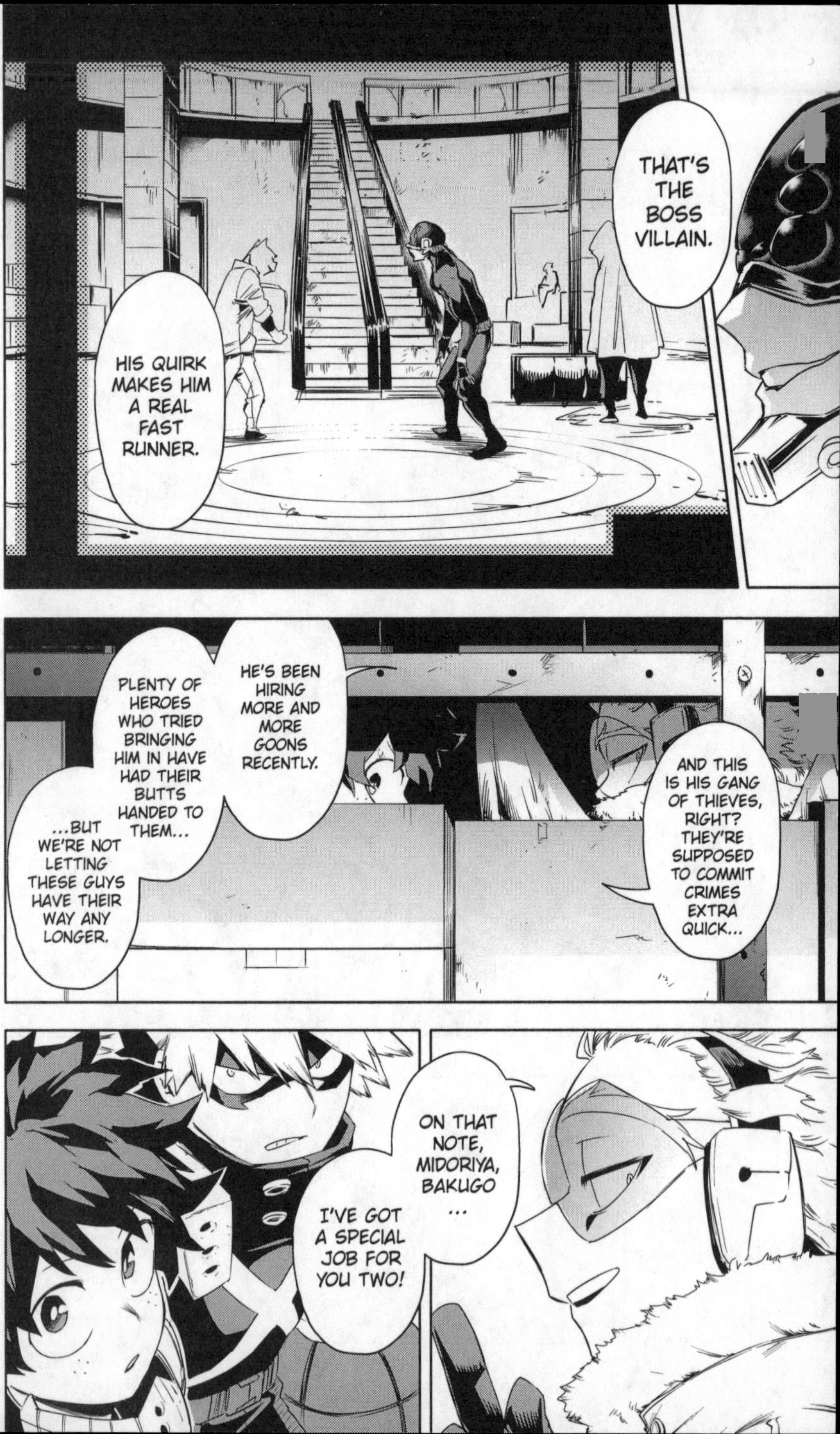
THAT'S THE BOSS VILLAIN.
HIS QUIRK MAKES HIM A REAL FAST RUNNER.
AND THIS IS HIS GANG OF THIEVES, RIGHT? THEY'RE SUPPOSED TO COMMIT CRIMES EXTRA QUICK...
HE'S BEEN HIRING MORE AND MORE GOONS RECENTLY.
PLENTY OF HEROES WHO TRIED BRINGING HIM IN HAVE HAD THEIR BUTTS HANDED TO THEM...
...BUT WE'RE NOT LETTING THESE GUYS HAVE THEIR WAY ANY LONGER.
ON THAT NOTE, MIDORIYA, BAKUGO...
I'VE GOT A SPECIAL JOB FOR YOU TWO!

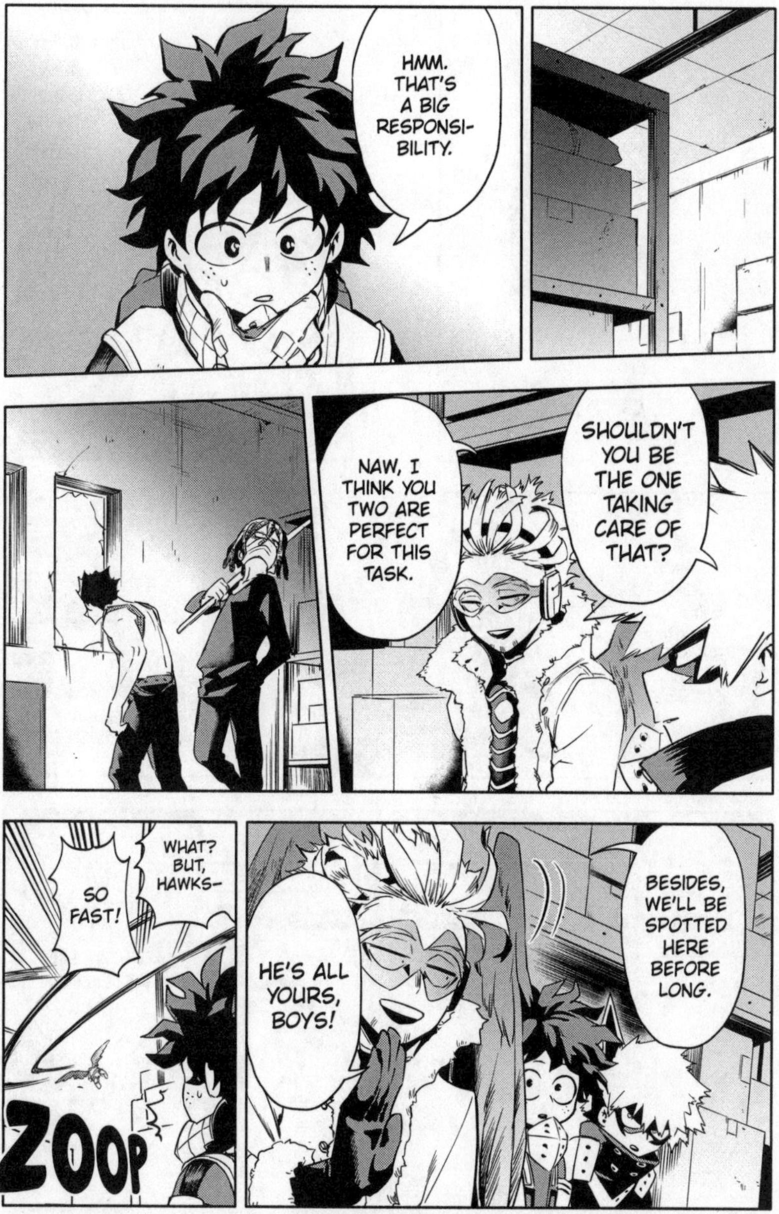
HMM. THAT'S A BIG RESPONSI-BILITY.
SHOULDN'T YOU BE THE ONE TAKING CARE OF THAT?
NAW, I THINK YOU TWO ARE PERFECT FOR THIS TASK.
BESIDES, WE'LL BE SPOTTED HERE BEFORE LONG.
HE'S ALL YOURS, BOYS!
WHAT? BUT, HAWKS–
SO FAST!
ZOOP

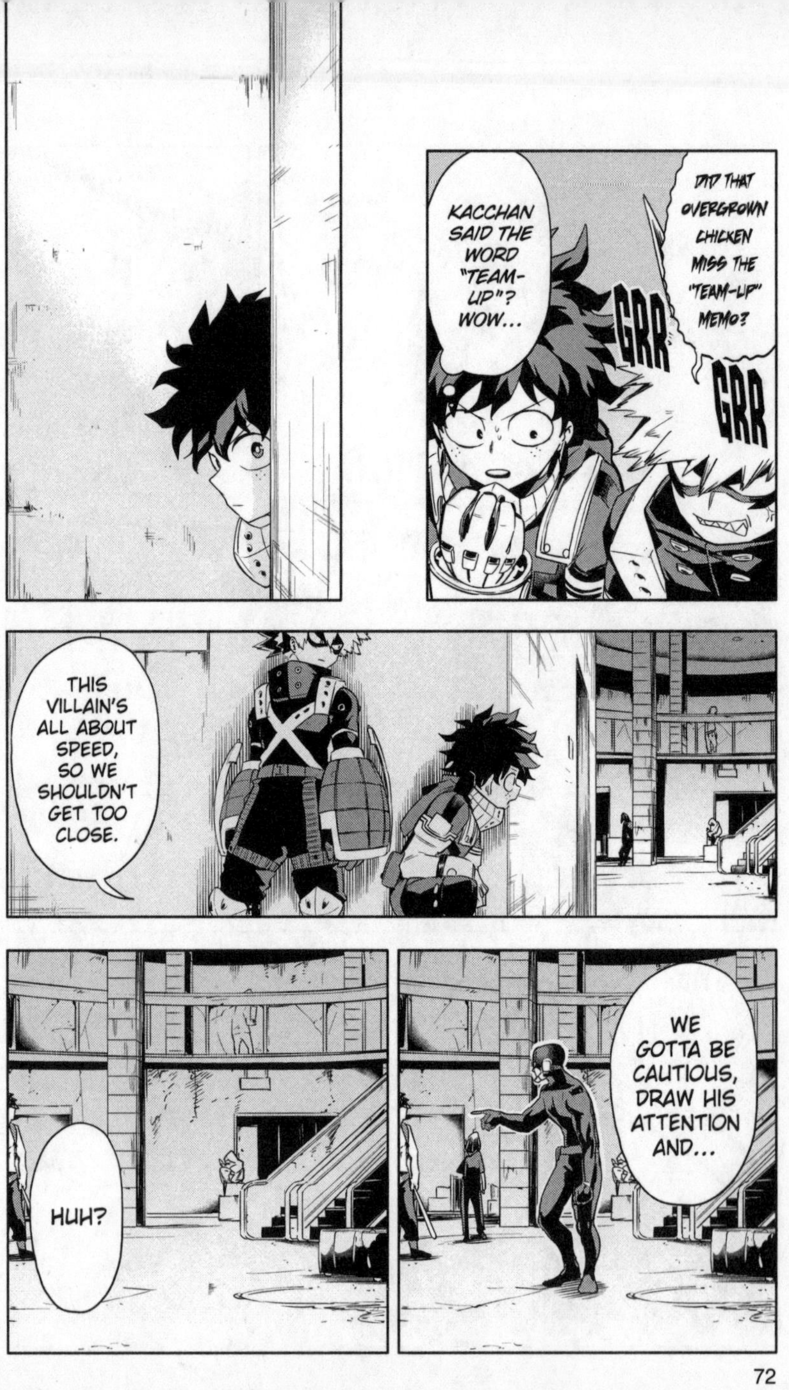
DID THAT OVERGROWN CHICKEN MISS THE "TEAM-UP" MEMO?
KACCHAN SAID THE WORD "TEAM-UP"? WOW...
GRR
GRR
THIS VILLAIN'S ALL ABOUT SPEED, SO WE SHOULDN'T GET TOO CLOSE.
WE GOTTA BE CAUTIOUS, DRAW HIS ATTENTION AND...
HUH?

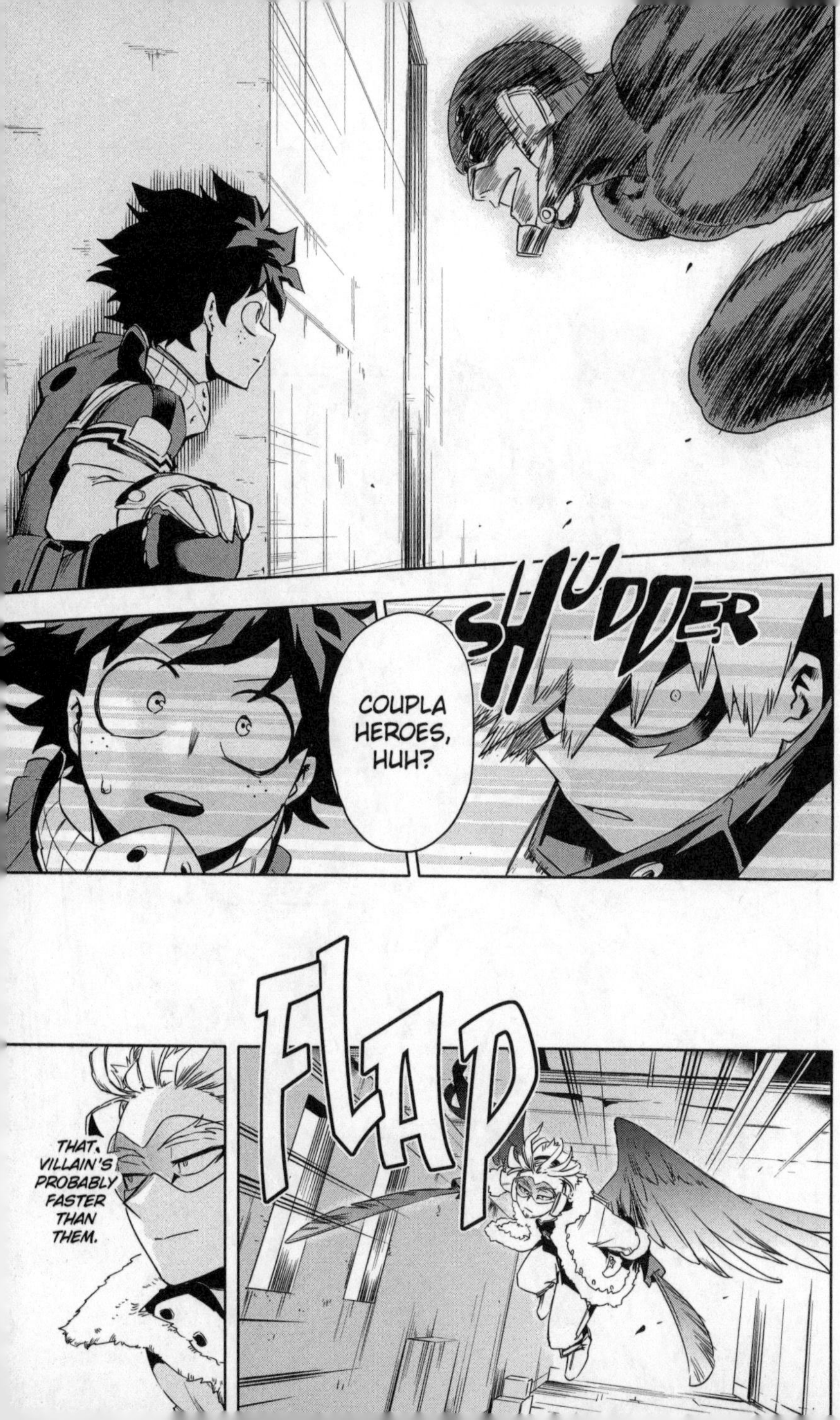
SHUDDER
COUPLA HEROES, HUH?
FLAP
THAT VILLAIN'S PROBABLY FASTER THAN THEM.

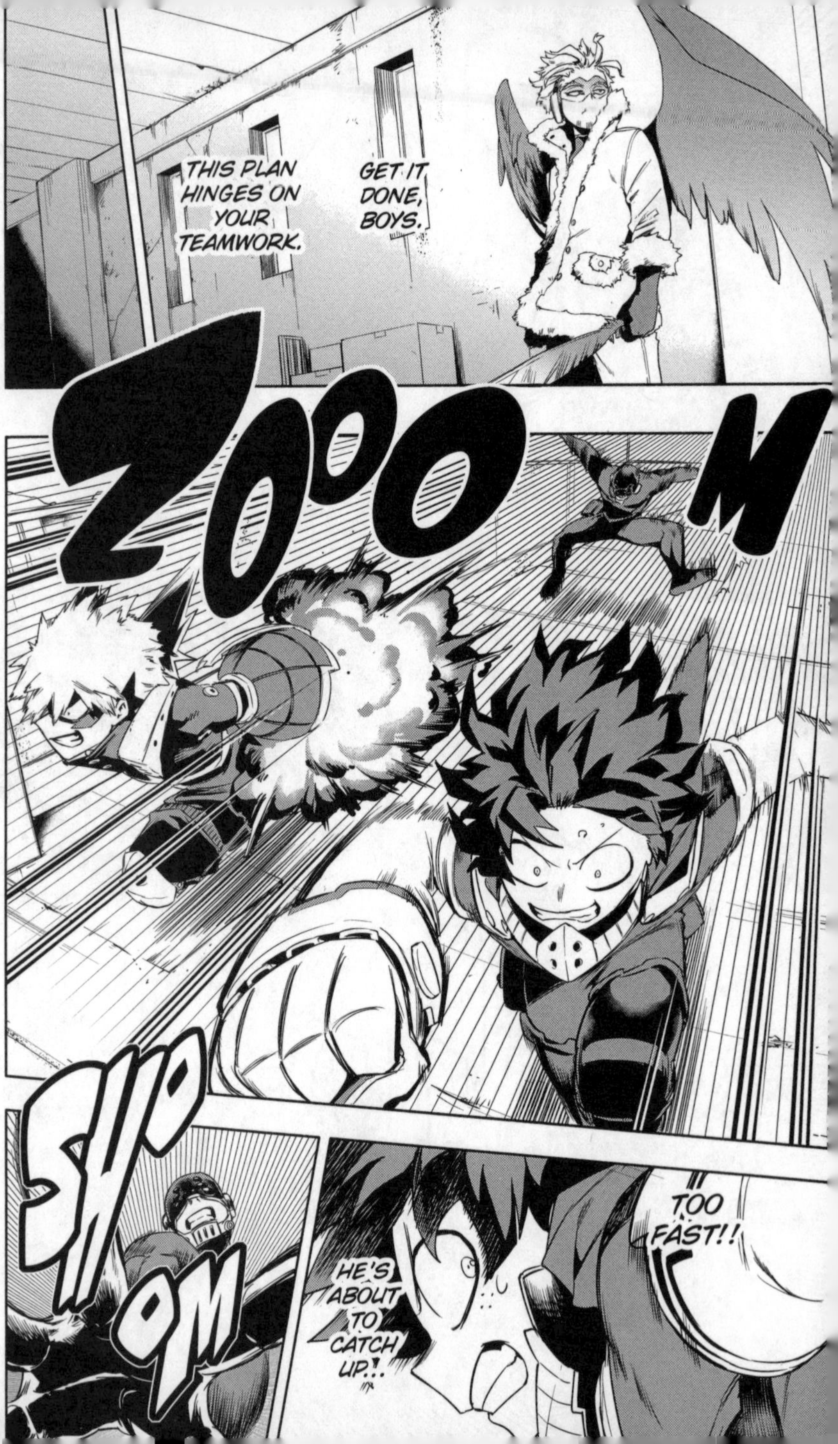
GET IT DONE, BOYS.
THIS PLAN HINGES ON YOUR TEAMWORK.
ZOOOOM
TOO FAST!!
HE'S ABOUT TO CATCH UP...!
SHOOM

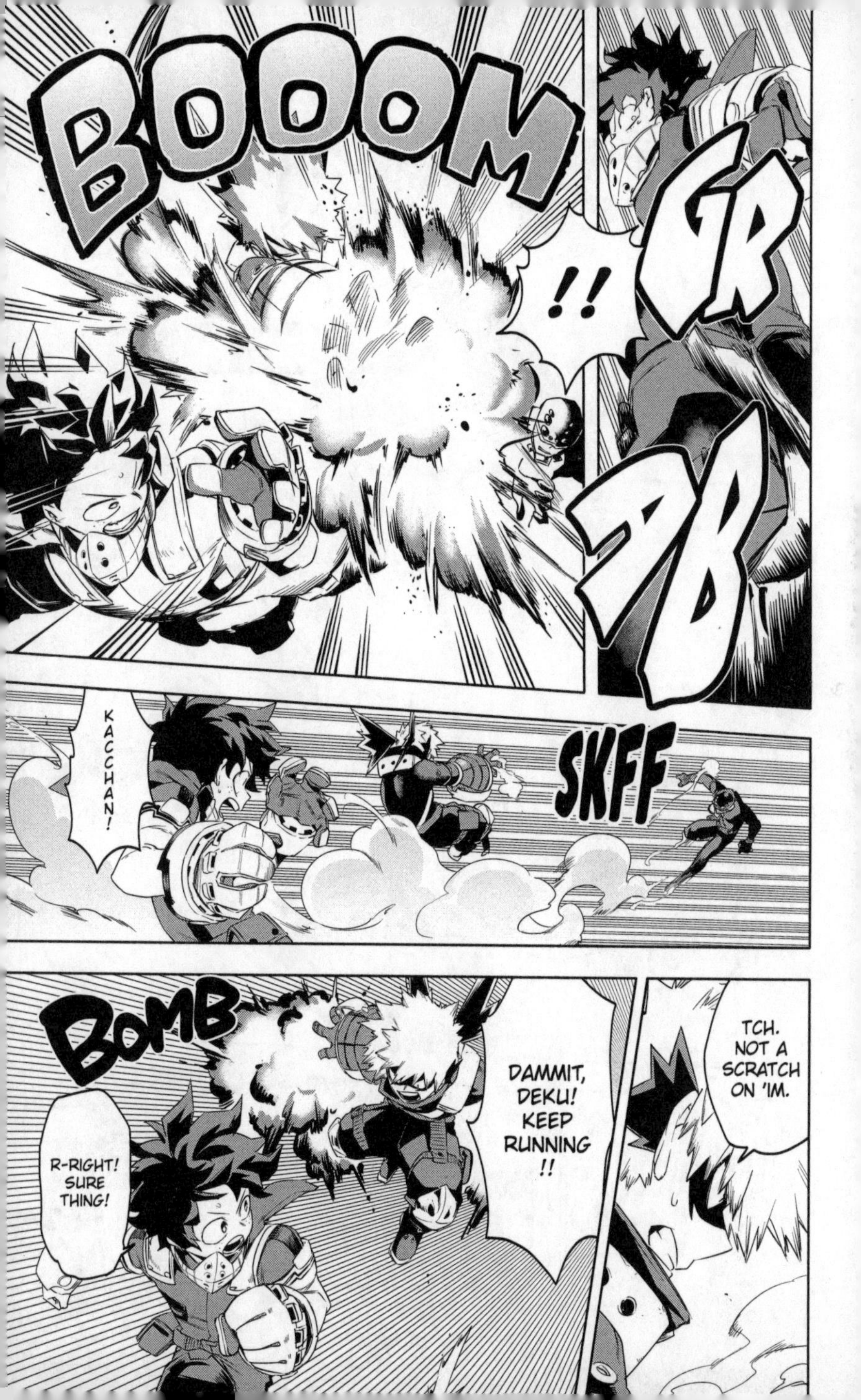
GR
BOOOM
!!
ZB
SKFF
KACCHAN!
TCH. NOT A SCRATCH ON 'IM.
BOMB
DAMMIT, DEKU! KEEP RUNNING!!
R-RIGHT! SURE THING!

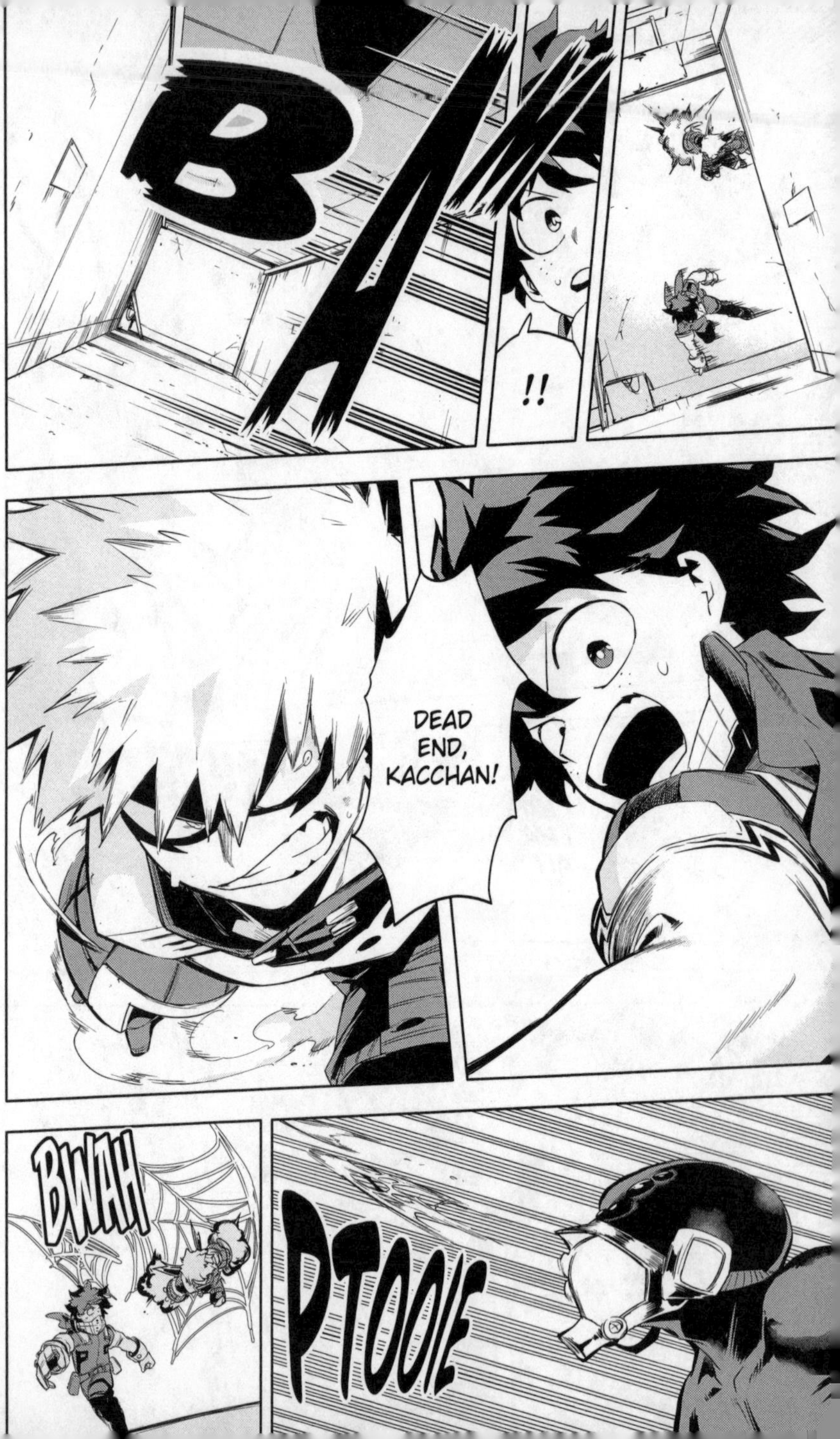
!!
BAM
DEAD END, KACCHAN!
PTOOIE
BWAH

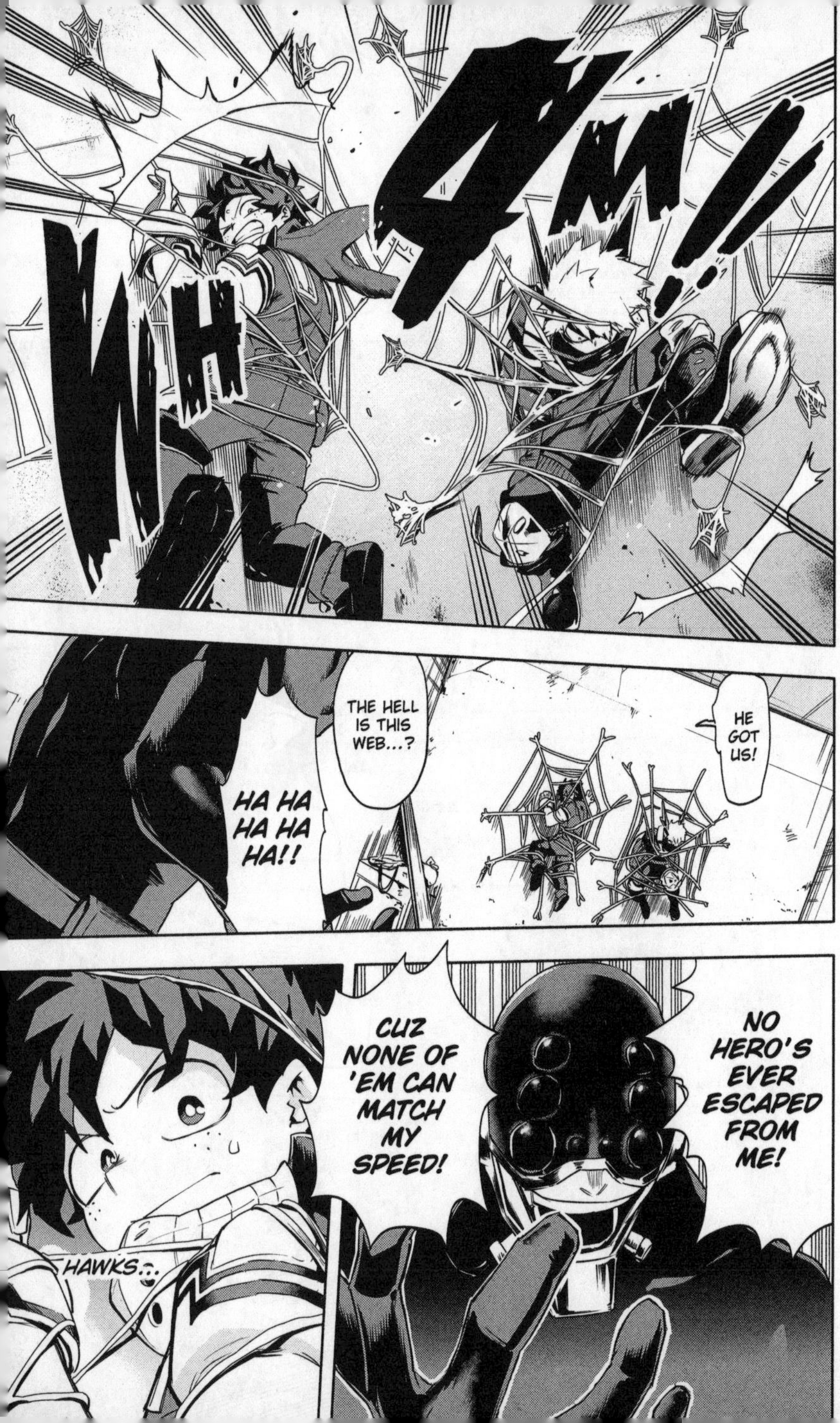
WHAM!!
HE GOT US!
THE HELL IS THIS WEB...?
HA HA HA HA HA!!
NO HERO'S EVER ESCAPED FROM ME!
CUZ NONE OF 'EM CAN MATCH MY SPEED!
HAWKS...

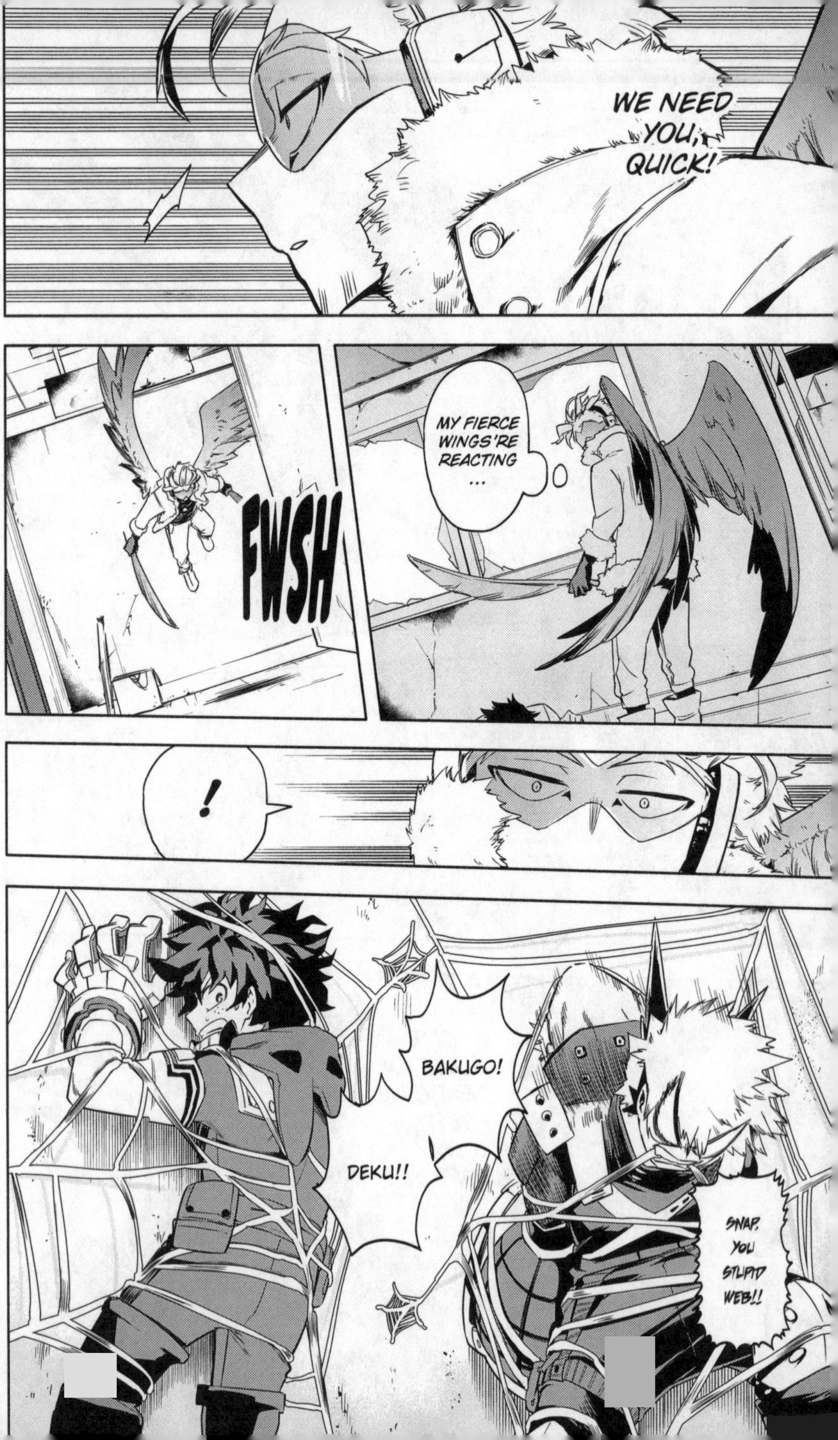
WE NEED YOU, QUICK!
MY FIERCE WINGS'RE REACTING ...
FWSH
!
BAKUGO!
DEKU!!
SNAP, YOU STUPID WEB!!

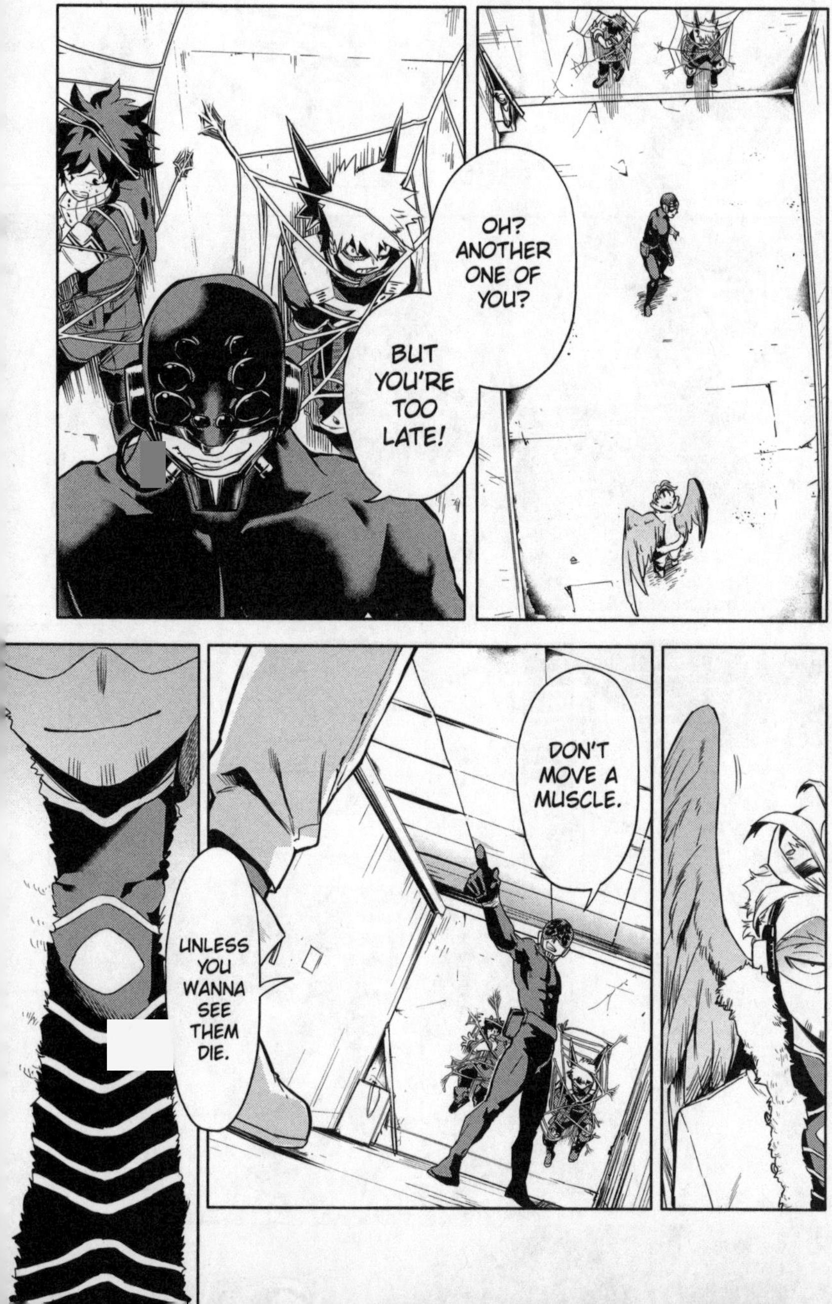
OH? ANOTHER ONE OF YOU?
BUT YOU'RE TOO LATE!
DON'T MOVE A MUSCLE.
UNLESS YOU WANNA SEE THEM DIE.

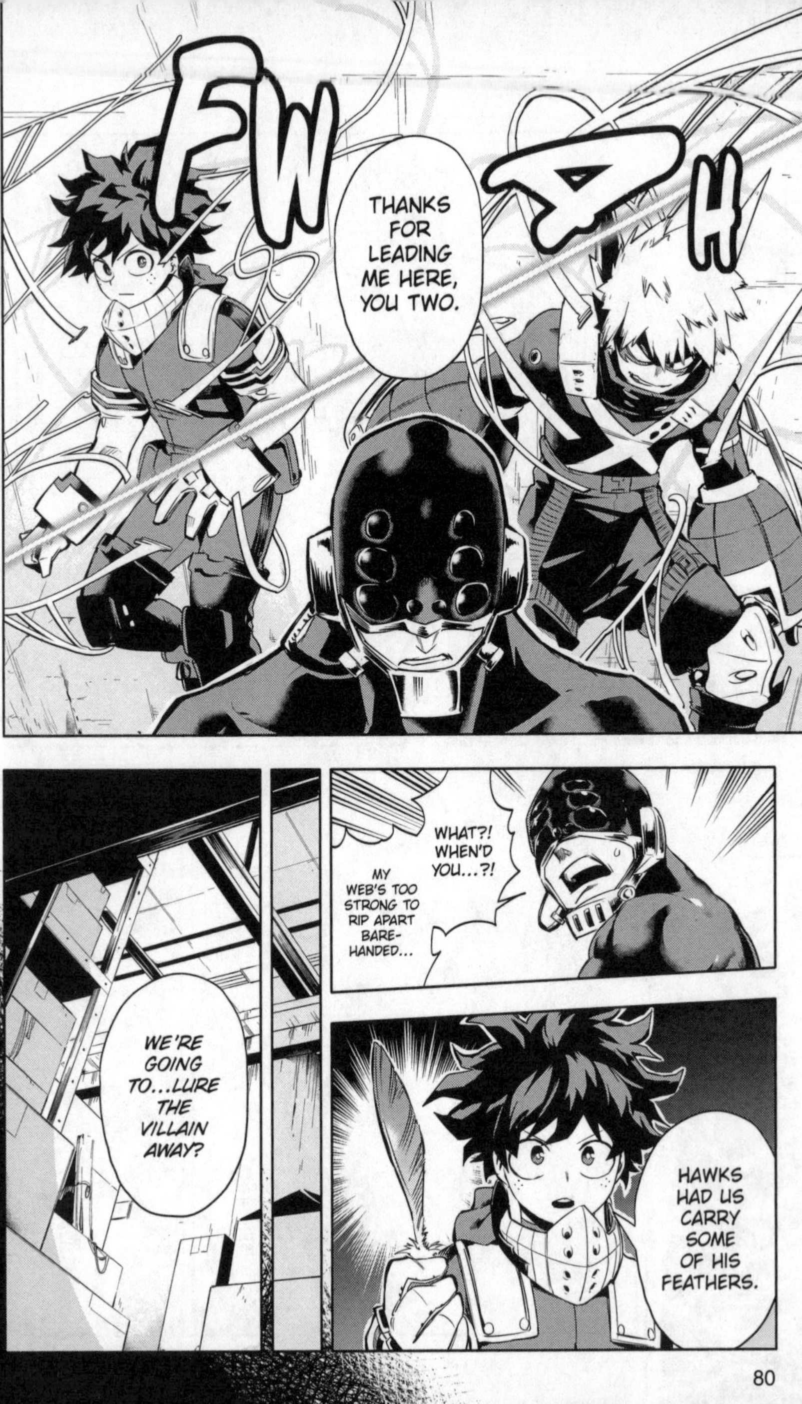
FWAH
THANKS FOR LEADING ME HERE, YOU TWO.
WHAT?! WHEN'D YOU...?!
MY WEB'S TOO STRONG TO RIP APART BARE-HANDED...
HAWKS HAD US CARRY SOME OF HIS FEATHERS.
WE'RE GOING TO...LURE THE VILLAIN AWAY?

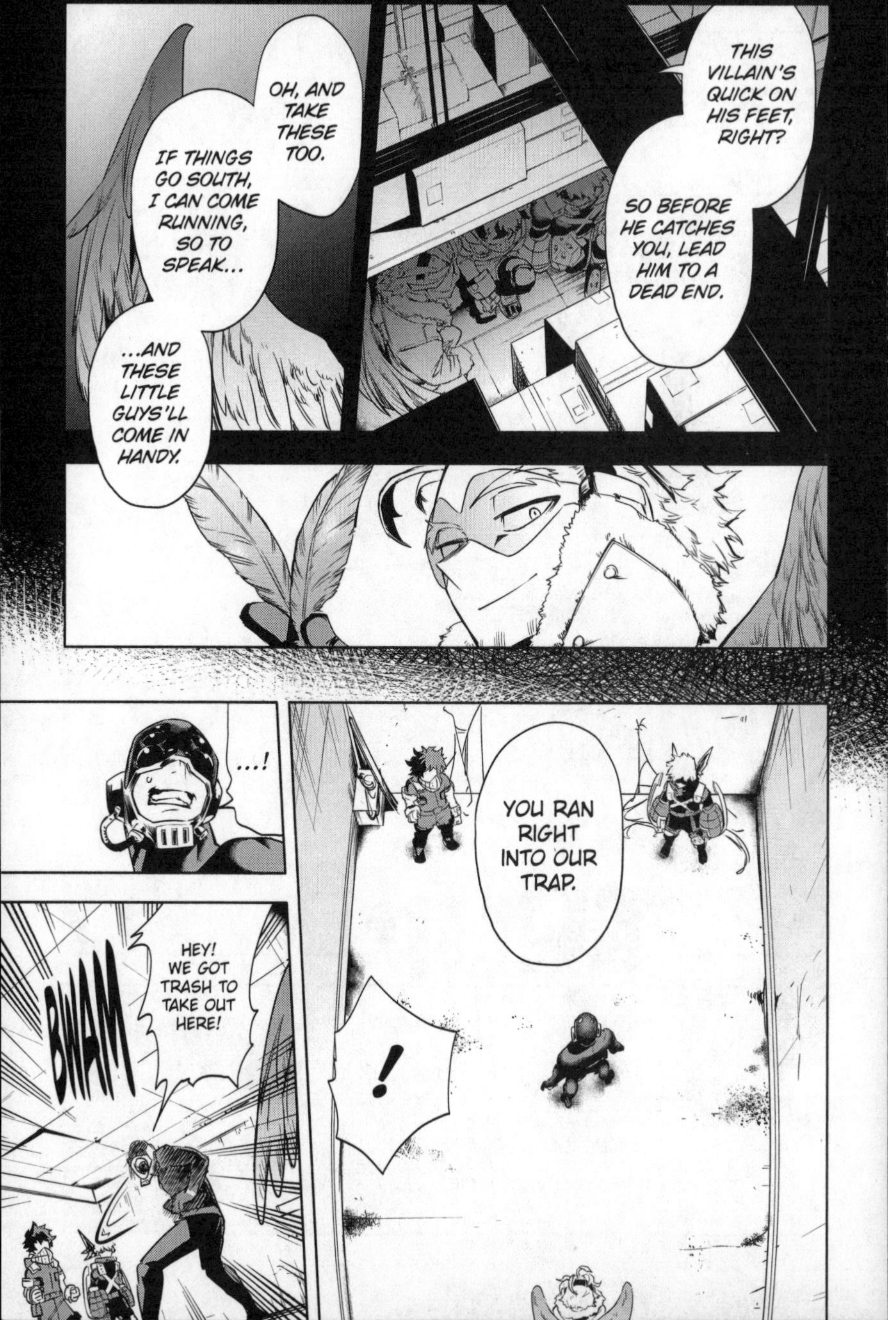
THIS VILLAIN'S QUICK ON HIS FEET, RIGHT?
SO BEFORE HE CATCHES YOU, LEAD HIM TO A DEAD END.
OH, AND TAKE THESE TOO.
IF THINGS GO SOUTH, I CAN COME RUNNING, SO TO SPEAK...
...AND THESE LITTLE GUYS'LL COME IN HANDY.
YOU RAN RIGHT INTO OUR TRAP.
!
...!
HEY! WE GOT TRASH TO TAKE OUT HERE!
BWAM

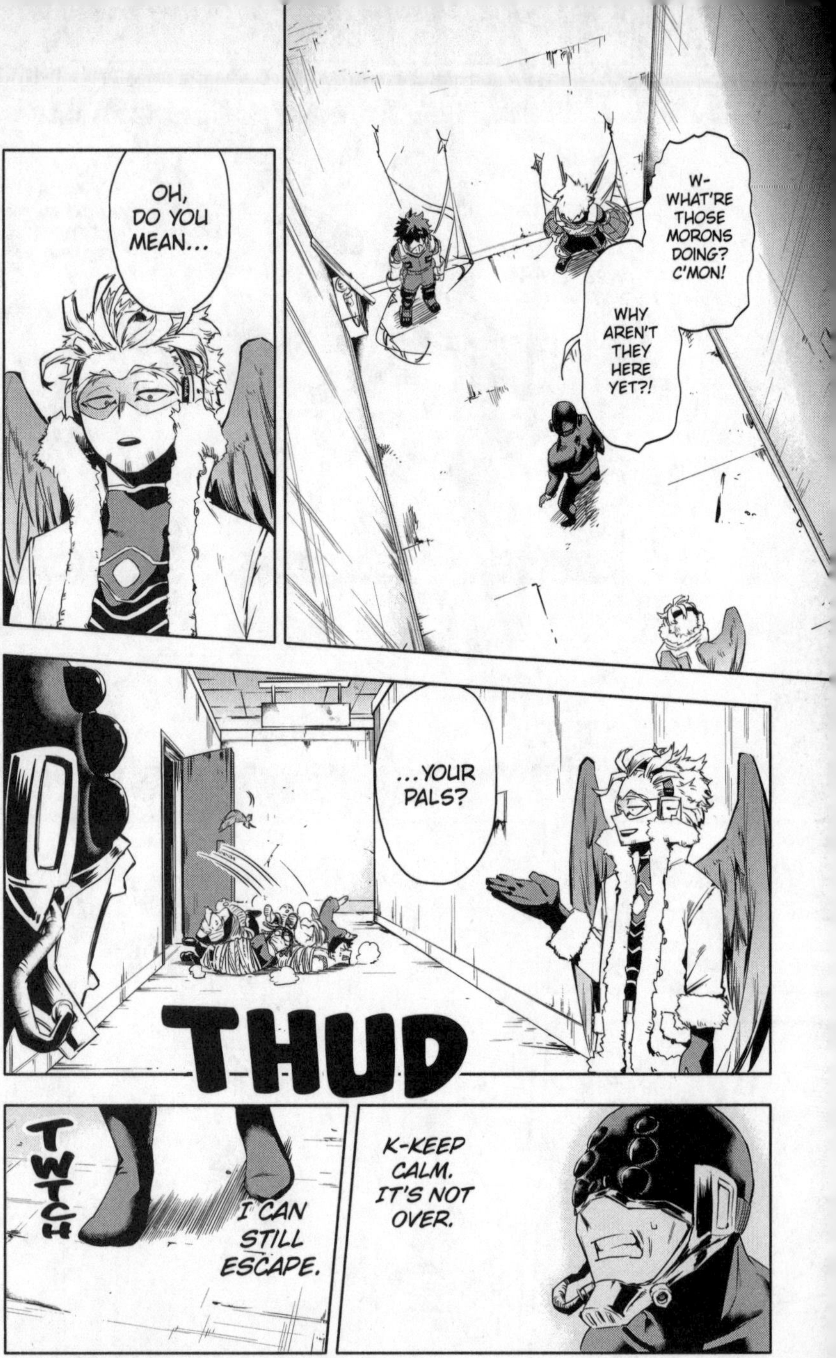
W-WHAT'RE THOSE MORONS DOING? C'MON!
WHY AREN'T THEY HERE YET?!
OH, DO YOU MEAN...
...YOUR PALS?
THUD
K-KEEP CALM. IT'S NOT OVER.
TWTCH
I CAN STILL ESCAPE.

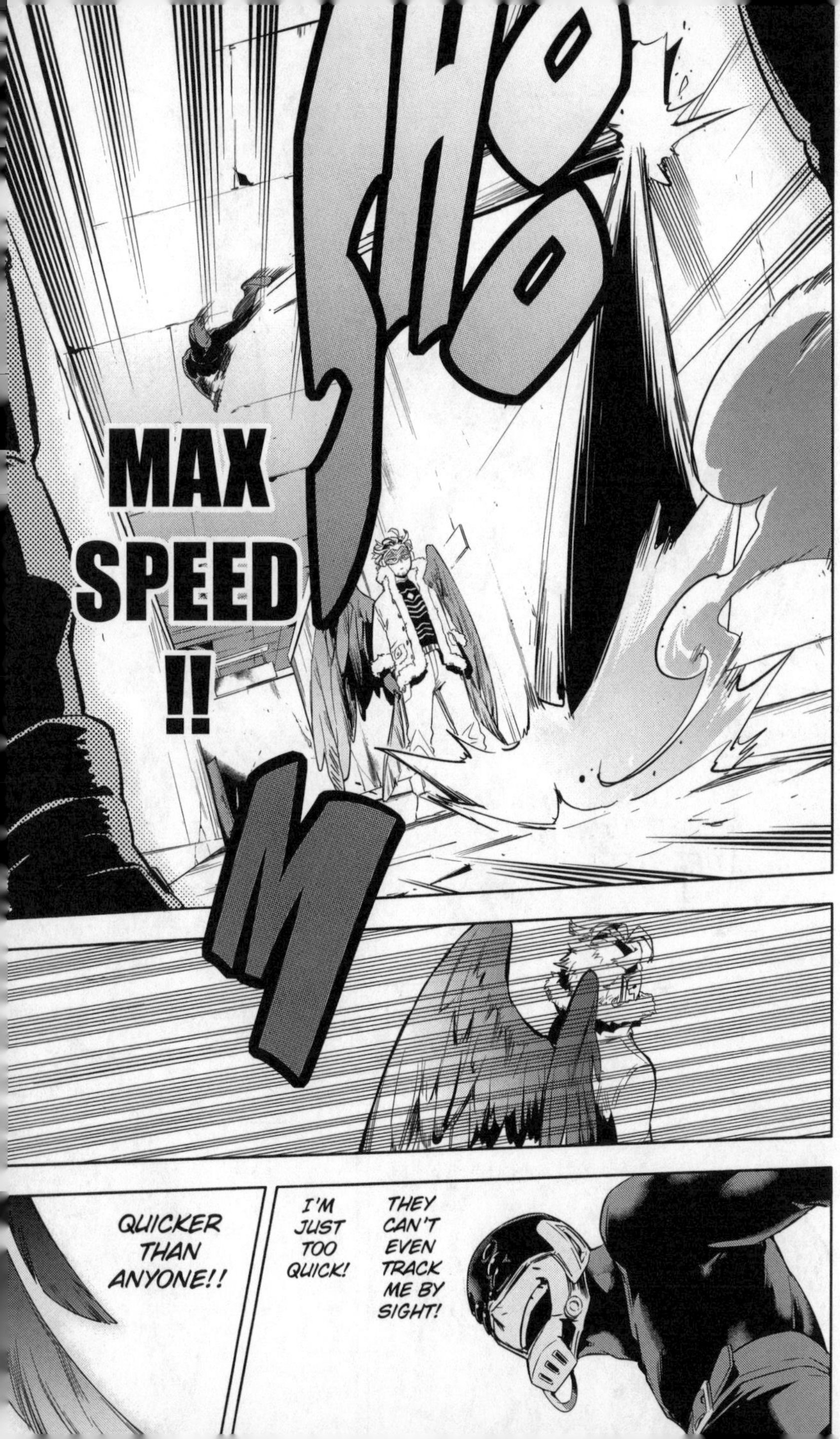
MAX SPEED!!
THEY CAN'T EVEN TRACK ME BY SIGHT!
I'M JUST TOO QUICK!
QUICKER THAN ANYONE!!

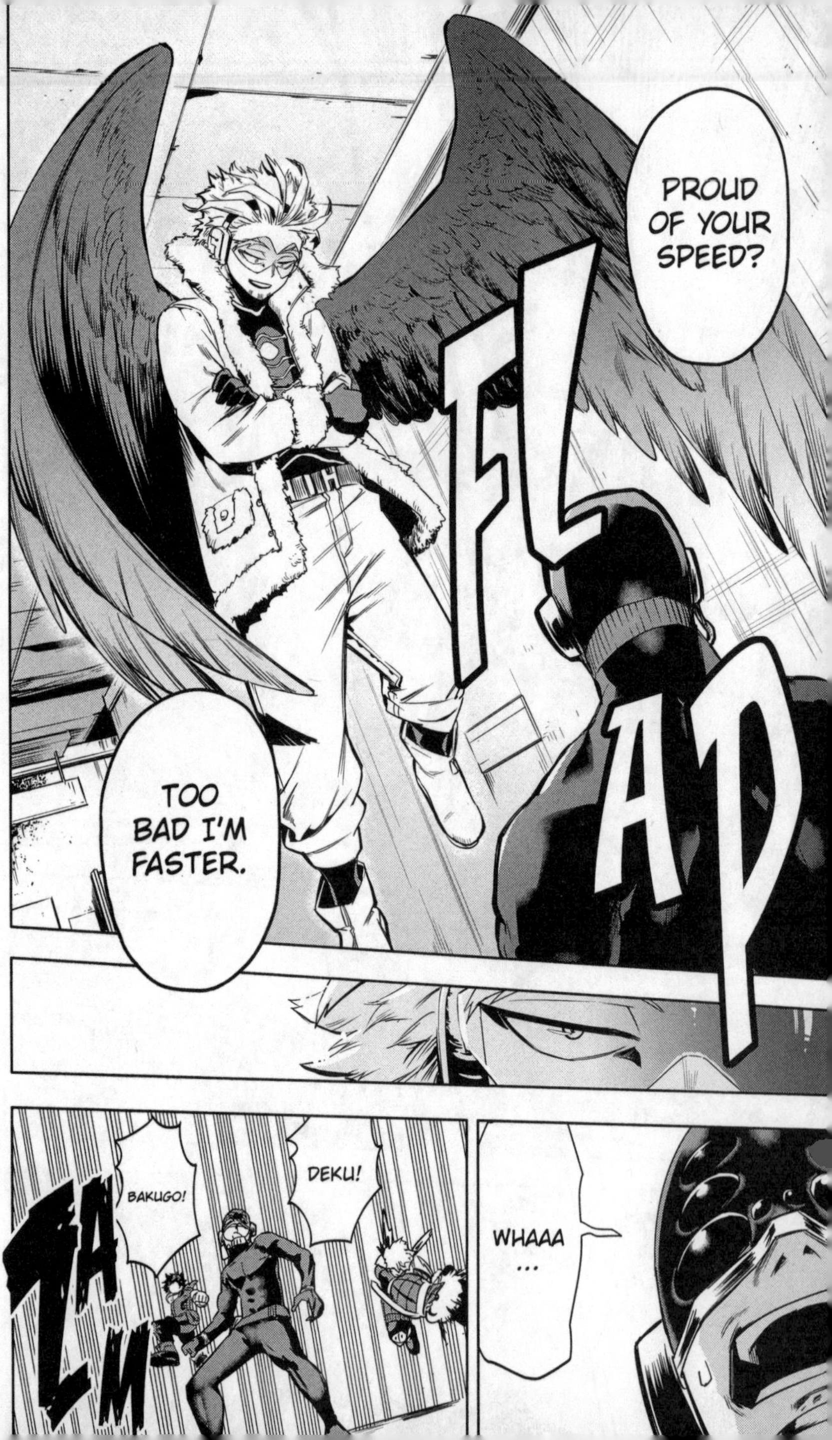
PROUD OF YOUR SPEED?
FLAP
TOO BAD I'M FASTER.
WHAAA ...
DEKU!
BAKUGO!

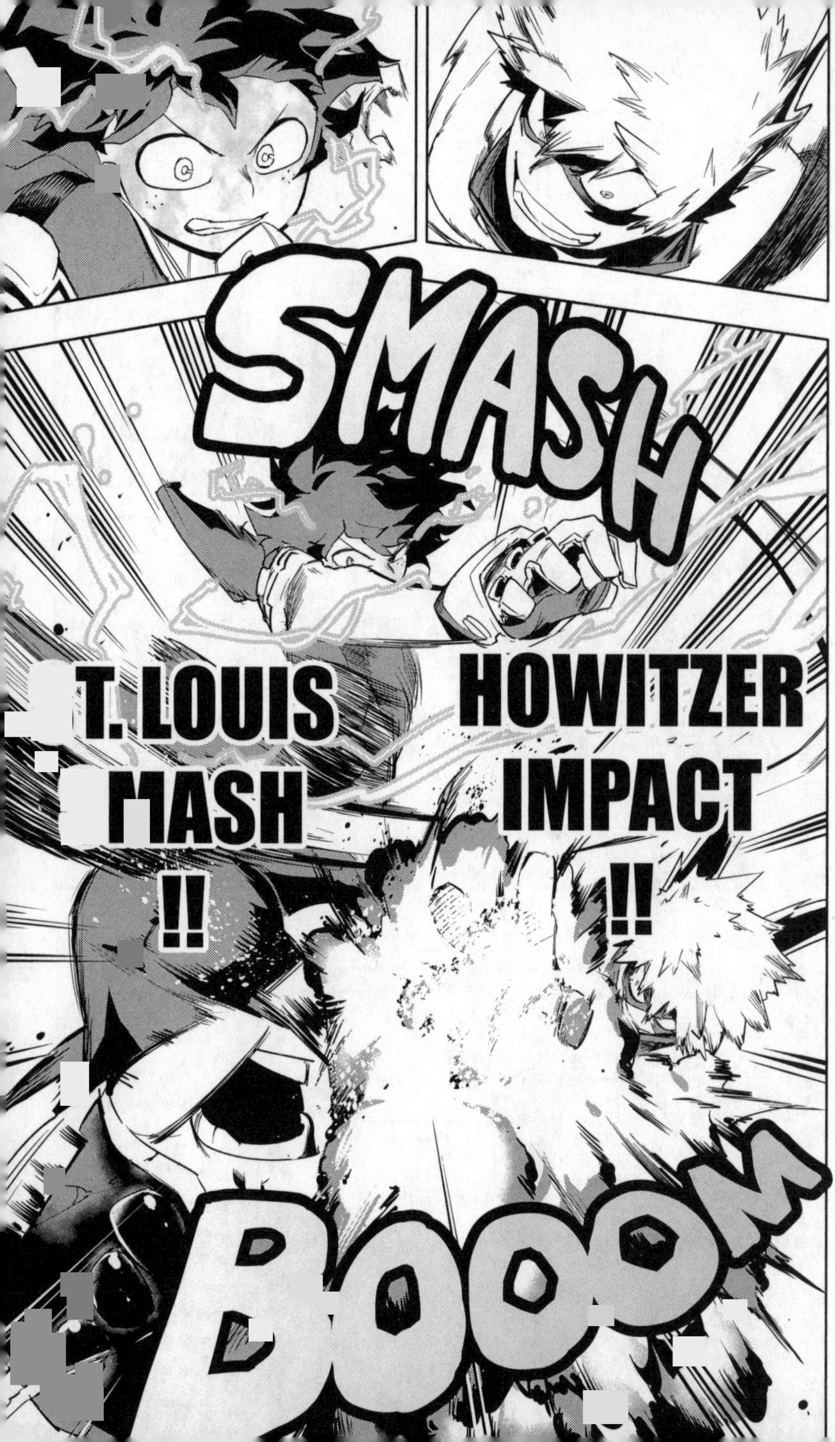
SMASH
HOWITZER IMPACT!!
T. LOUIS MASH!!
BOOOM

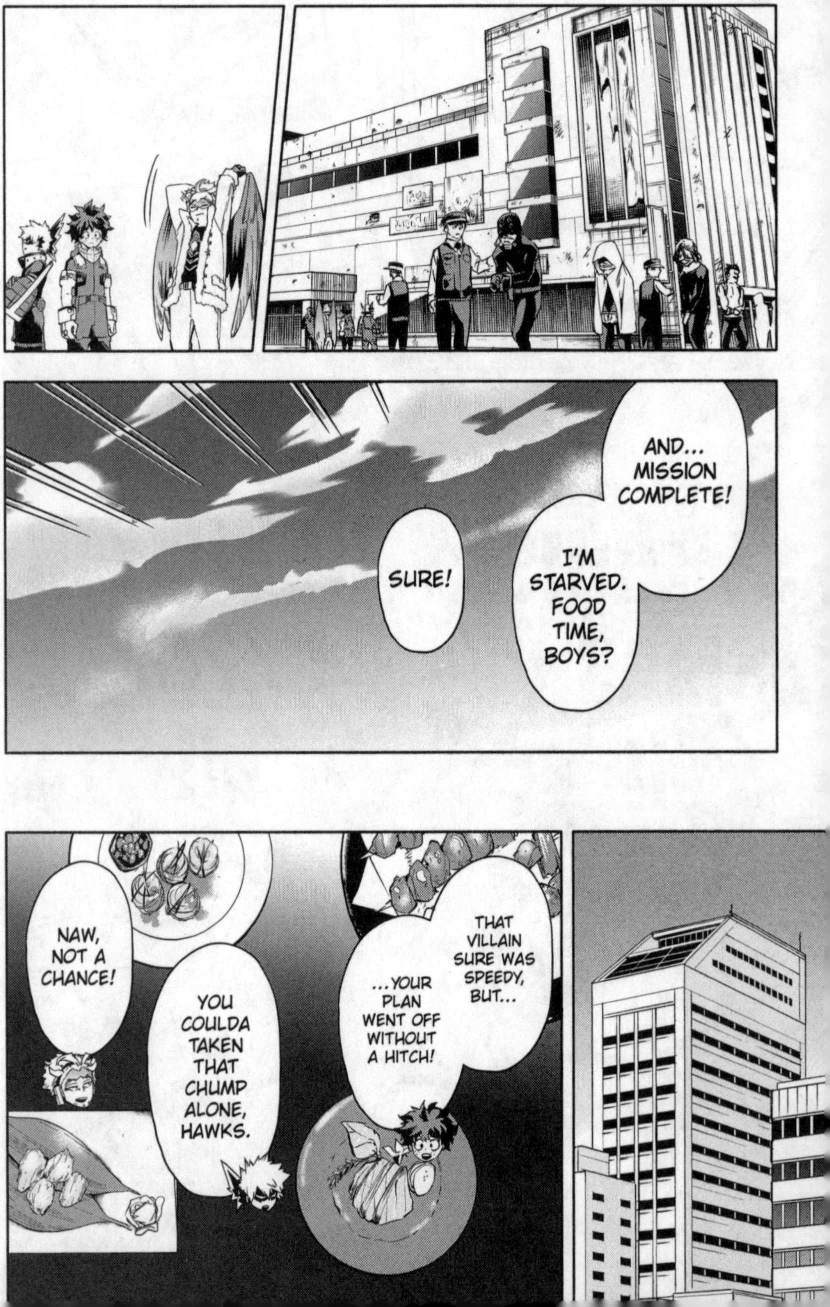
AND... MISSION COMPLETE!
I'M STARVED. FOOD TIME, BOYS?
SURE!
THAT VILLAIN SURE WAS SPEEDY, BUT...
...YOUR PLAN WENT OFF WITHOUT A HITCH!
YOU COULDA TAKEN THAT CHUMP ALONE, HAWKS.
NAW, NOT A CHANCE!

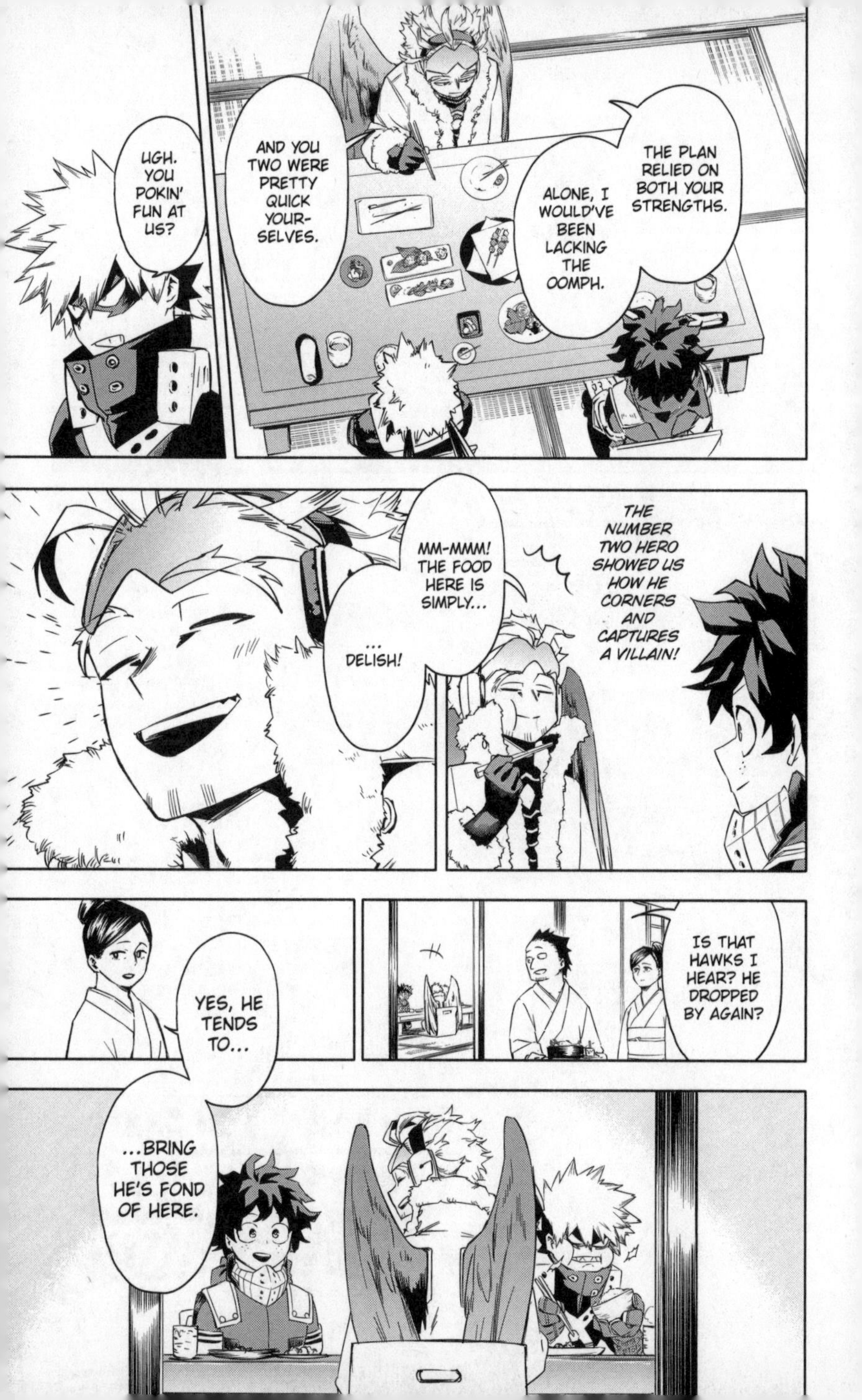
THE PLAN RELIED ON BOTH YOUR STRENGTHS.
ALONE, I WOULD'VE BEEN LACKING THE OOMPH.
AND YOU TWO WERE PRETTY QUICK YOUR-SELVES.
UGH. YOU POKIN' FUN AT US?
THE NUMBER TWO HERO SHOWED US HOW HE CORNERS AND CAPTURES A VILLAIN!
MM-MMM! THE FOOD HERE IS SIMPLY...
...DELISH!
IS THAT HAWKS I HEAR? HE DROPPED BY AGAIN?
YES, HE TENDS TO...
...BRING THOSE HE'S FOND OF HERE.

MY HERO ACADEMIA
Team-Up Missions

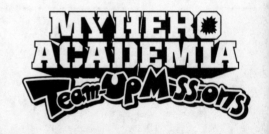

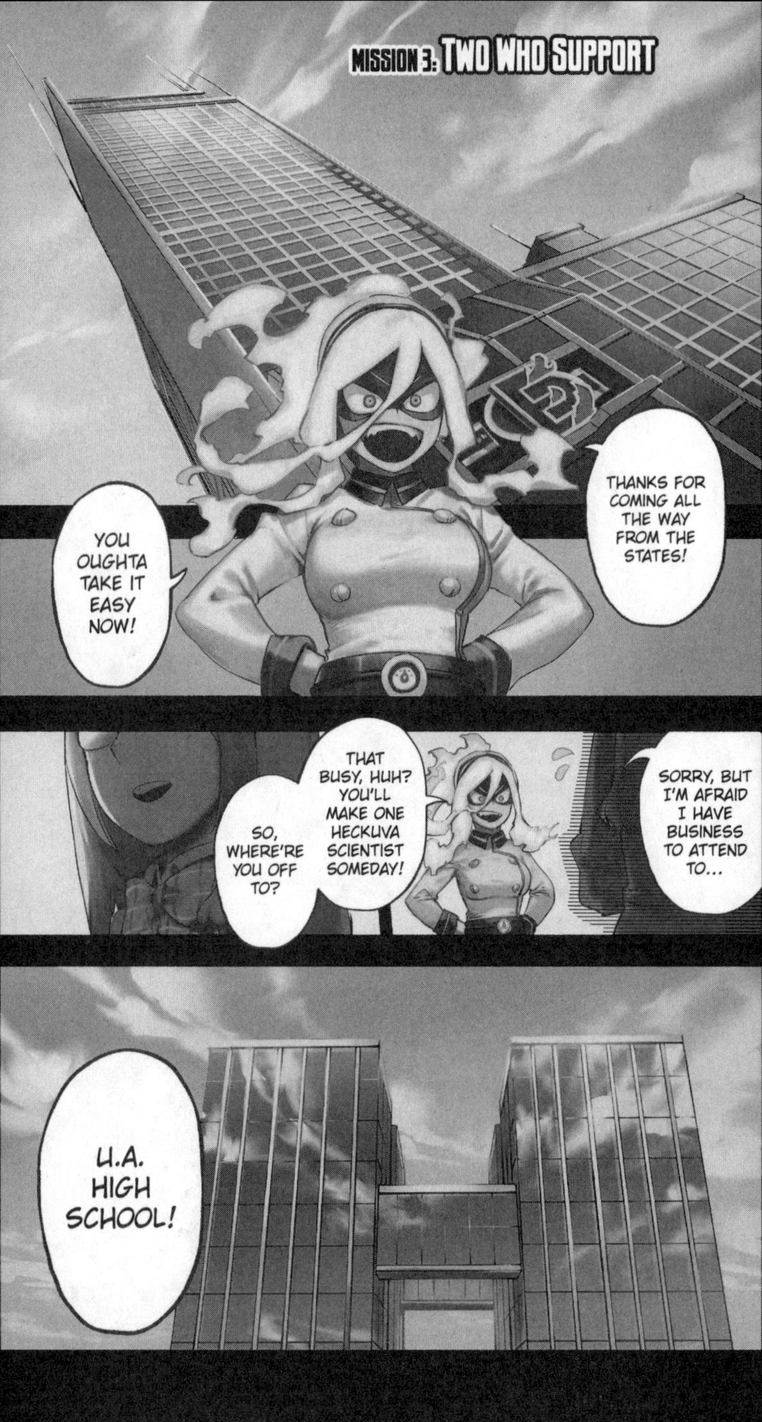
MISSION 3: TWO WHO SUPPORT
THANKS FOR COMING ALL THE WAY FROM THE STATES!
YOU OUGHTA TAKE IT EASY NOW!
SORRY, BUT I'M AFRAID I HAVE BUSINESS TO ATTEND TO...
THAT BUSY, HUH? YOU'LL MAKE ONE HECKUVA SCIENTIST SOMEDAY!
SO, WHERE'RE YOU OFF TO?
U.A. HIGH SCHOOL!

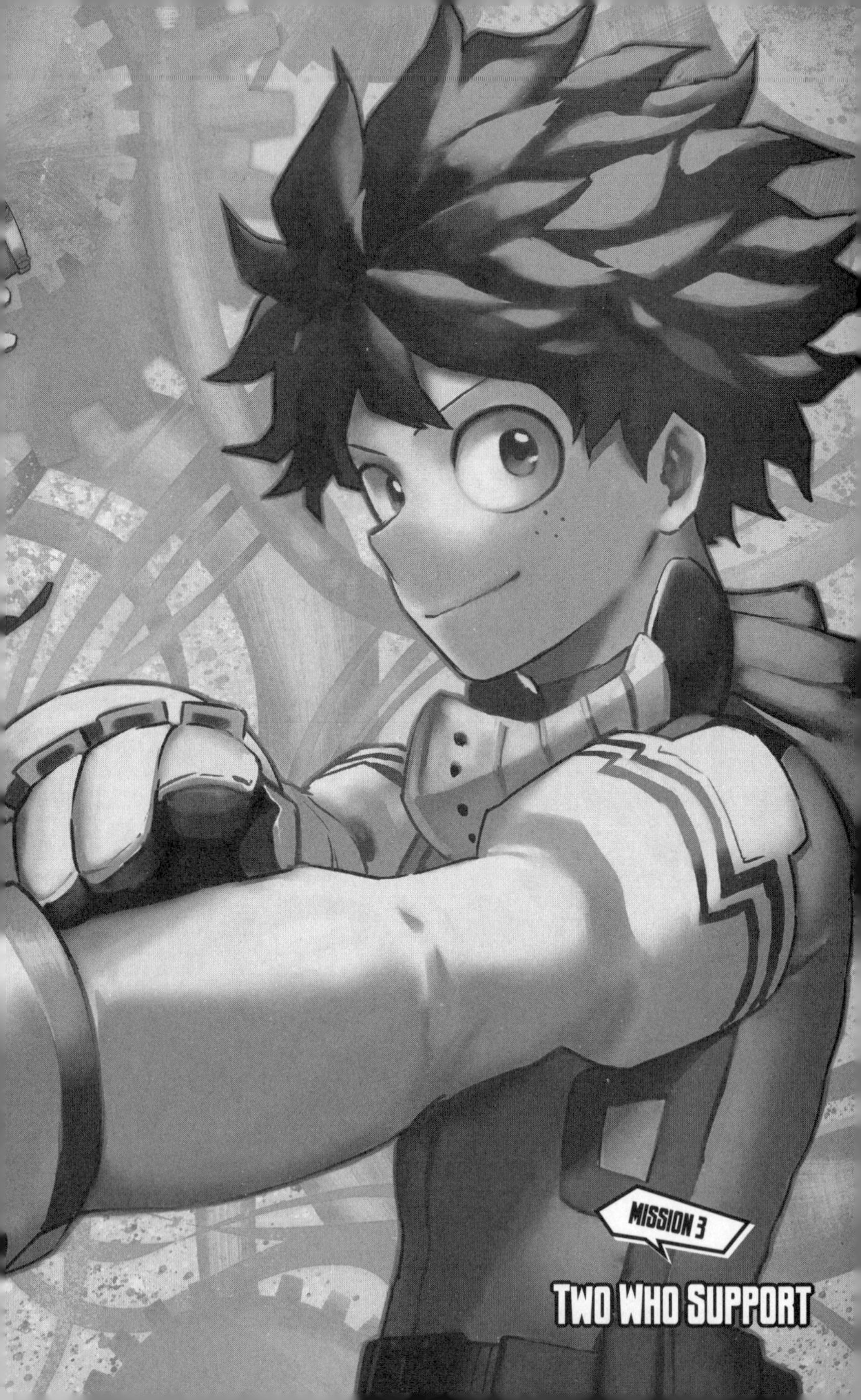
MISSION 3
TWO WHO SUPPORT

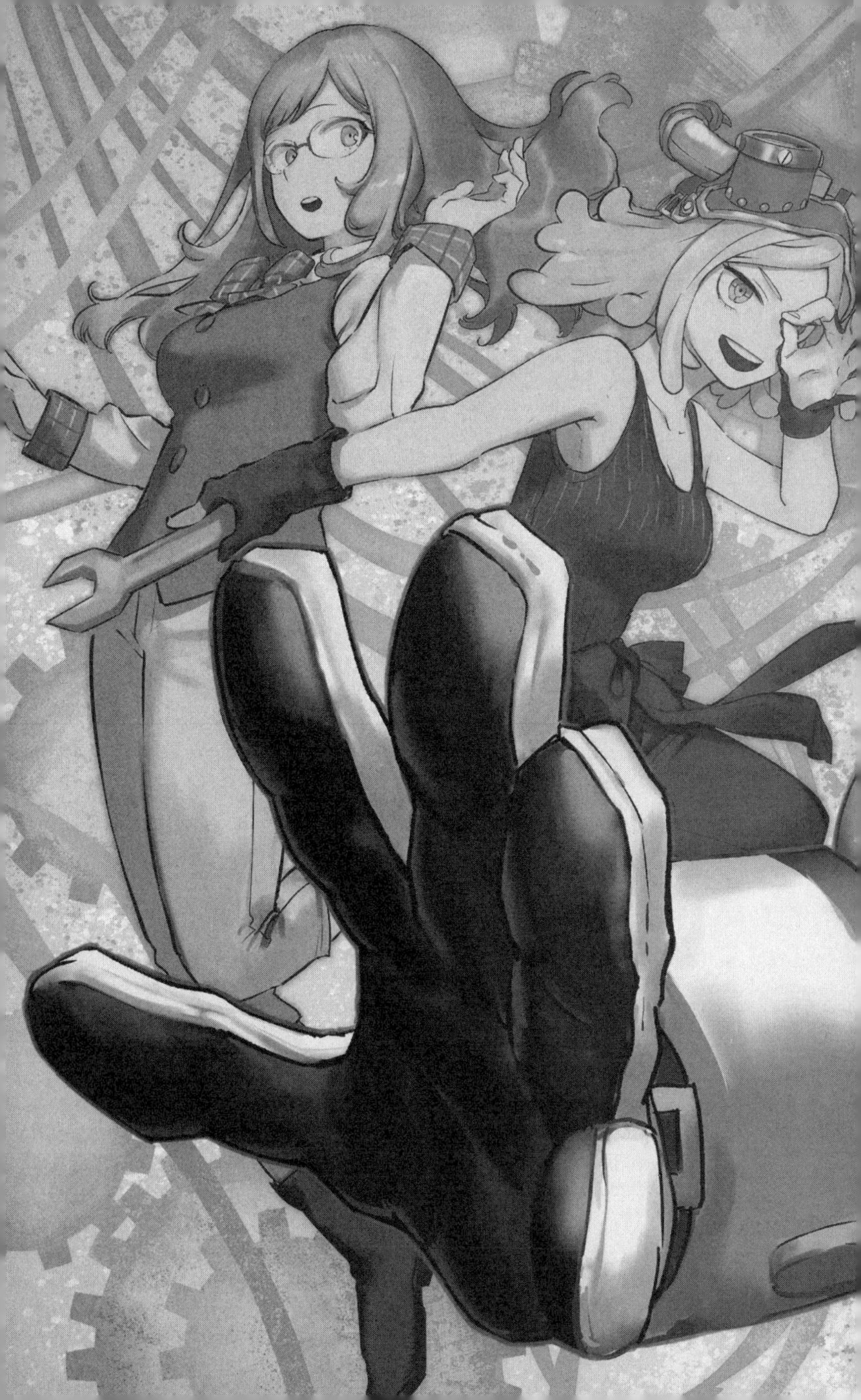

MY HERO ACADEMIA
Team-Up Missions

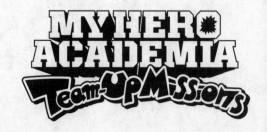

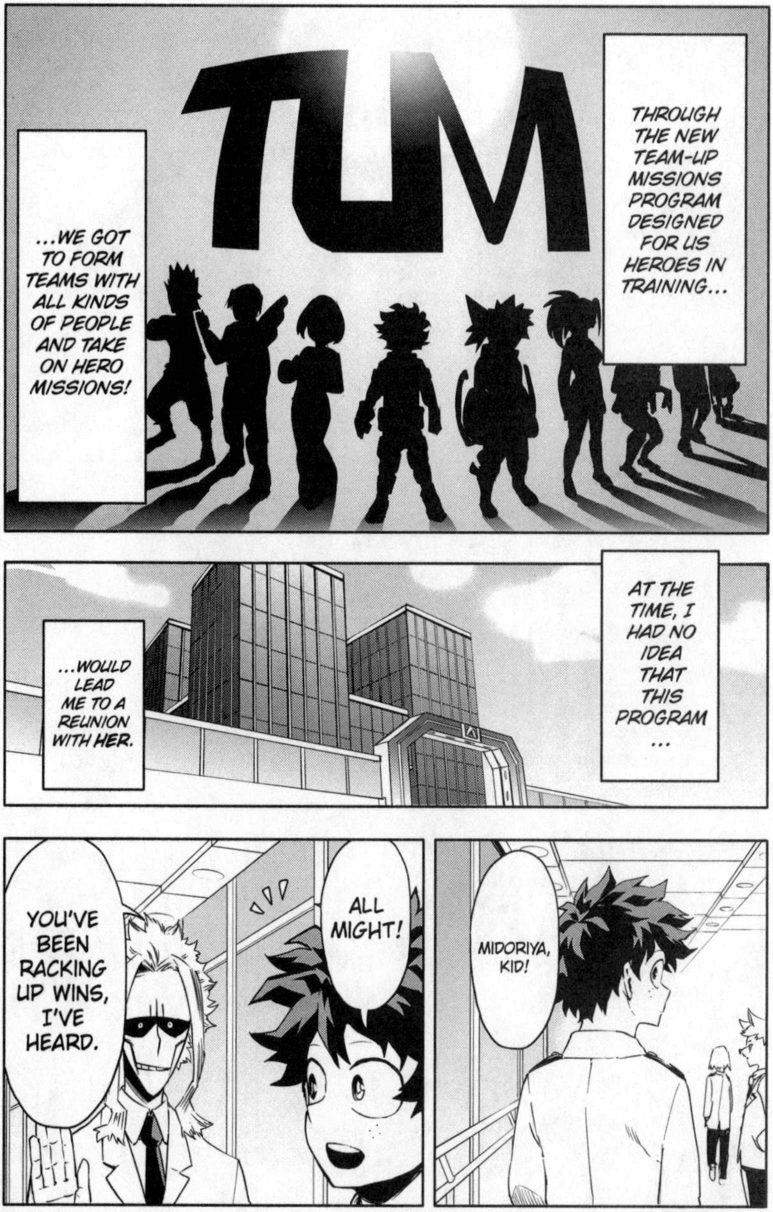
THROUGH THE NEW TEAM-UP MISSIONS PROGRAM DESIGNED FOR US HEROES IN TRAINING...
TUM
...WE GOT TO FORM TEAMS WITH ALL KINDS OF PEOPLE AND TAKE ON HERO MISSIONS!
AT THE TIME, I HAD NO IDEA THAT THIS PROGRAM ...
...WOULD LEAD ME TO A REUNION WITH HER.
MIDORIYA, KID!
ALL MIGHT!
YOU'VE BEEN RACKING UP WINS, I'VE HEARD.

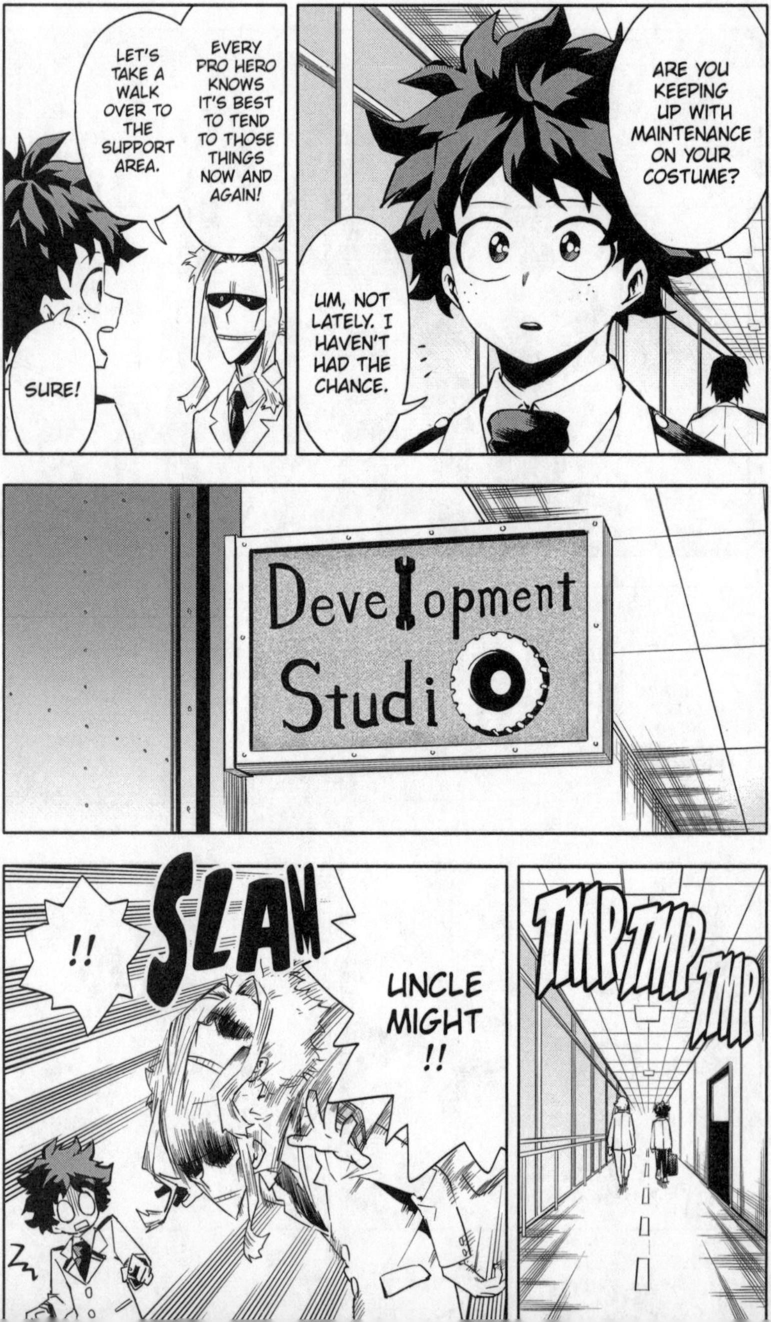
ARE YOU KEEPING UP WITH MAINTENANCE ON YOUR COSTUME?
UM, NOT LATELY. I HAVEN'T HAD THE CHANCE.
EVERY PRO HERO KNOWS IT'S BEST TO TEND TO THOSE THINGS NOW AND AGAIN!
LET'S TAKE A WALK OVER TO THE SUPPORT AREA.
SURE!
Development Studio
TMP TMP TMP
SLAM
UNCLE MIGHT!!
!!

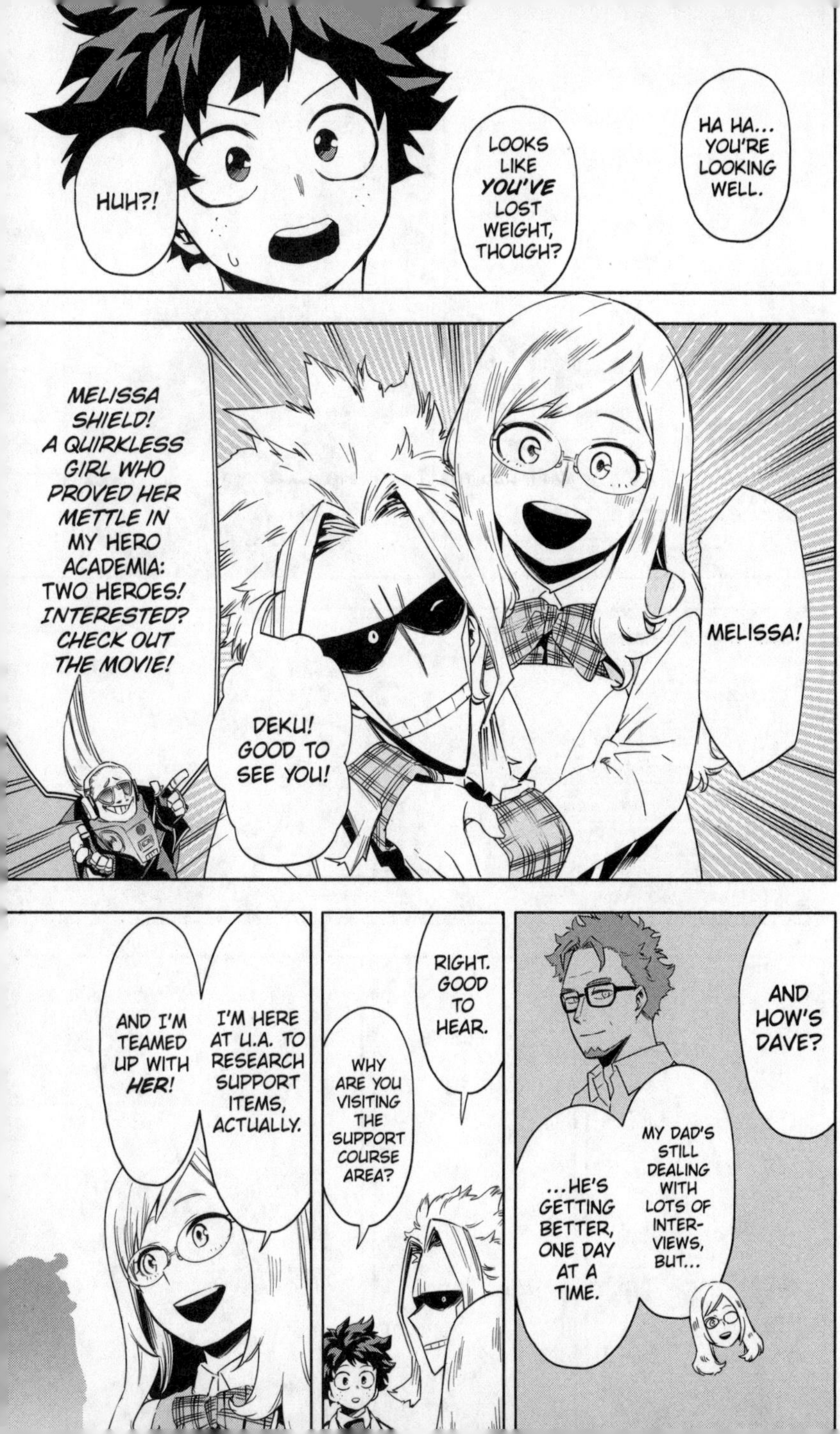
HA HA... YOU'RE LOOKING WELL.
LOOKS LIKE *YOU'VE* LOST WEIGHT, THOUGH?
HUH?!
MELISSA!
DEKU! GOOD TO SEE YOU!
MELISSA SHIELD! A QUIRKLESS GIRL WHO PROVED HER METTLE IN MY HERO ACADEMIA: TWO HEROES! INTERESTED? CHECK OUT THE MOVIE!
AND HOW'S DAVE?
MY DAD'S STILL DEALING WITH LOTS OF INTER-VIEWS, BUT...
...HE'S GETTING BETTER, ONE DAY AT A TIME.
RIGHT. GOOD TO HEAR.
WHY ARE YOU VISITING THE SUPPORT COURSE AREA?
I'M HERE AT U.A. TO RESEARCH SUPPORT ITEMS, ACTUALLY.
AND I'M TEAMED UP WITH *HER*!

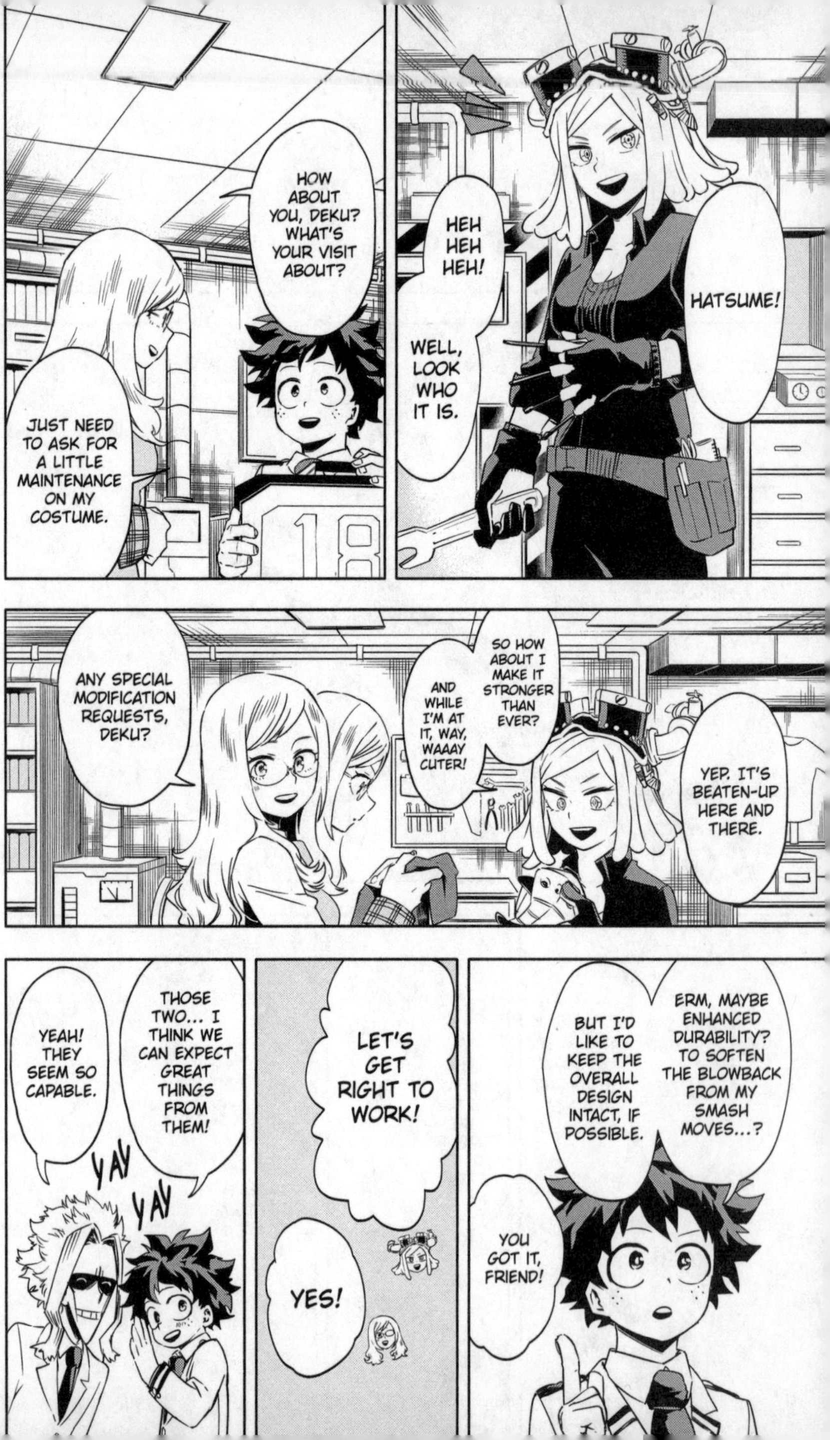
HATSUME!
HEH HEH HEH!
WELL, LOOK WHO IT IS.
HOW ABOUT YOU, DEKU? WHAT'S YOUR VISIT ABOUT?
JUST NEED TO ASK FOR A LITTLE MAINTENANCE ON MY COSTUME.
YEP. IT'S BEATEN-UP HERE AND THERE.
SO HOW ABOUT I MAKE IT STRONGER THAN EVER?
AND WHILE I'M AT IT, WAY, WAAAY CUTER!
ANY SPECIAL MODIFICATION REQUESTS, DEKU?
ERM, MAYBE ENHANCED DURABILITY? TO SOFTEN THE BLOWBACK FROM MY SMASH MOVES...?
BUT I'D LIKE TO KEEP THE OVERALL DESIGN INTACT, IF POSSIBLE.
YOU GOT IT, FRIEND!
LET'S GET RIGHT TO WORK!
YES!
THOSE TWO... I THINK WE CAN EXPECT GREAT THINGS FROM THEM!
YEAH! THEY SEEM SO CAPABLE.
YAY
YAY

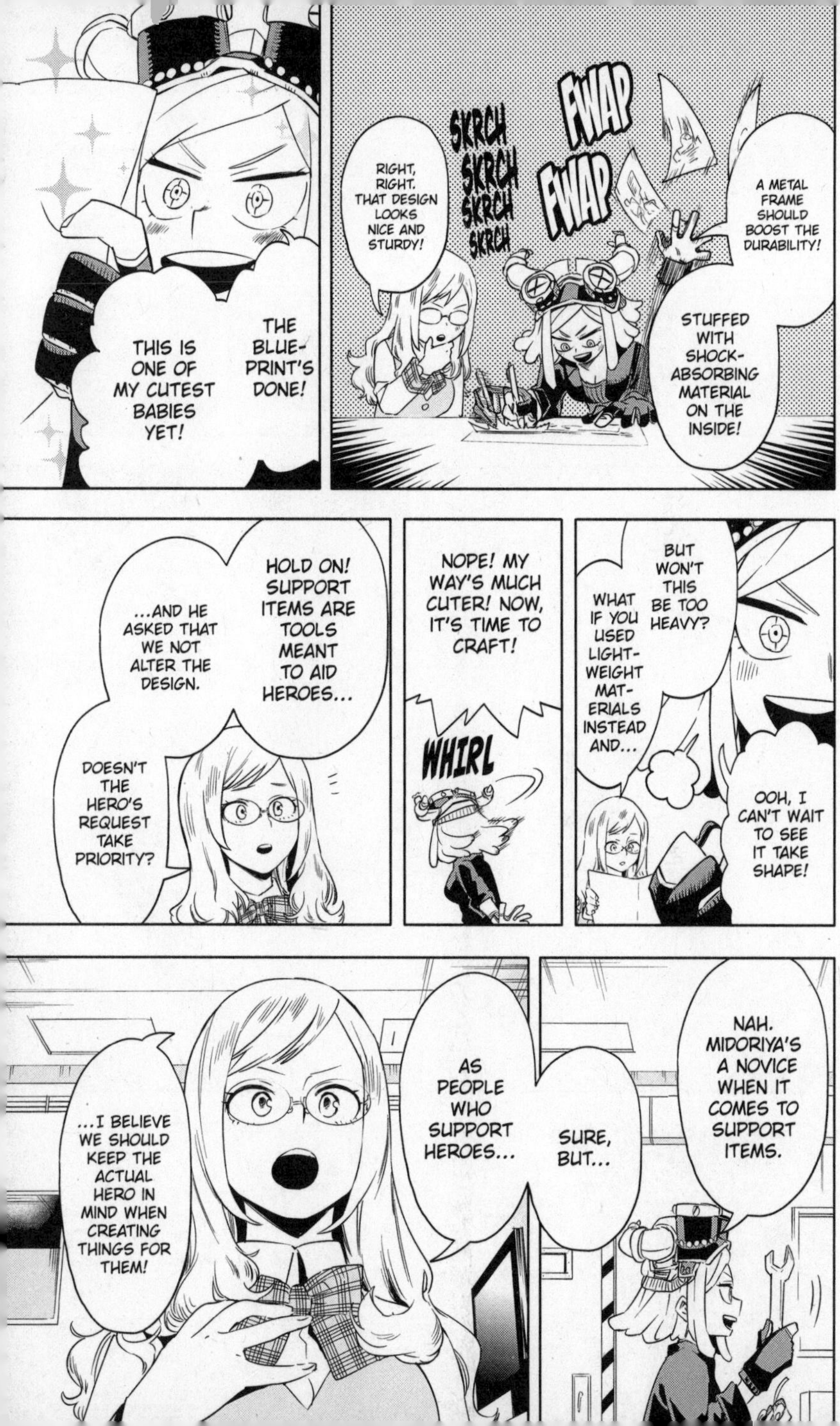
A METAL FRAME SHOULD BOOST THE DURABILITY!
FWAP FWAP
STUFFED WITH SHOCK-ABSORBING MATERIAL ON THE INSIDE!
SKRCH SKRCH SKRCH SKRCH
RIGHT, RIGHT. THAT DESIGN LOOKS NICE AND STURDY!
THE BLUE-PRINT'S DONE!
THIS IS ONE OF MY CUTEST BABIES YET!
BUT WON'T THIS BE TOO HEAVY?
WHAT IF YOU USED LIGHT-WEIGHT MAT-ERIALS INSTEAD AND...
OOH, I CAN'T WAIT TO SEE IT TAKE SHAPE!
NOPE! MY WAY'S MUCH CUTER! NOW, IT'S TIME TO CRAFT!
WHIRL
HOLD ON! SUPPORT ITEMS ARE TOOLS MEANT TO AID HEROES...
...AND HE ASKED THAT WE NOT ALTER THE DESIGN.
DOESN'T THE HERO'S REQUEST TAKE PRIORITY?
NAH. MIDORIYA'S A NOVICE WHEN IT COMES TO SUPPORT ITEMS.
SURE, BUT...
AS PEOPLE WHO SUPPORT HEROES...
...I BELIEVE WE SHOULD KEEP THE ACTUAL HERO IN MIND WHEN CREATING THINGS FOR THEM!

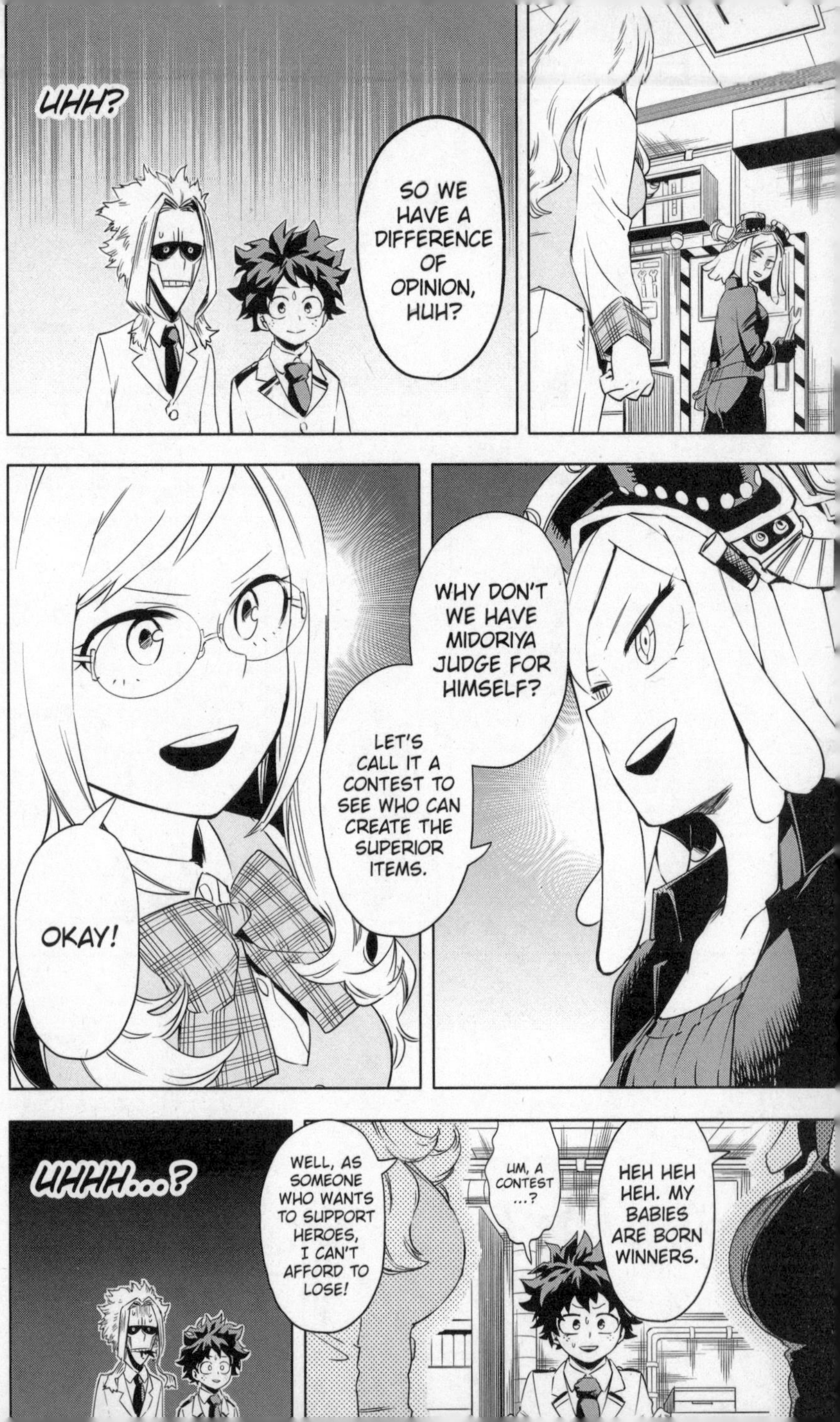
SO WE HAVE A DIFFERENCE OF OPINION, HUH?
UHH?
WHY DON'T WE HAVE MIDORIYA JUDGE FOR HIMSELF?
LET'S CALL IT A CONTEST TO SEE WHO CAN CREATE THE SUPERIOR ITEMS.
OKAY!
HEH HEH HEH. MY BABIES ARE BORN WINNERS.
UM, A CONTEST ...?
WELL, AS SOMEONE WHO WANTS TO SUPPORT HEROES, I CAN'T AFFORD TO LOSE!
UHHH...?

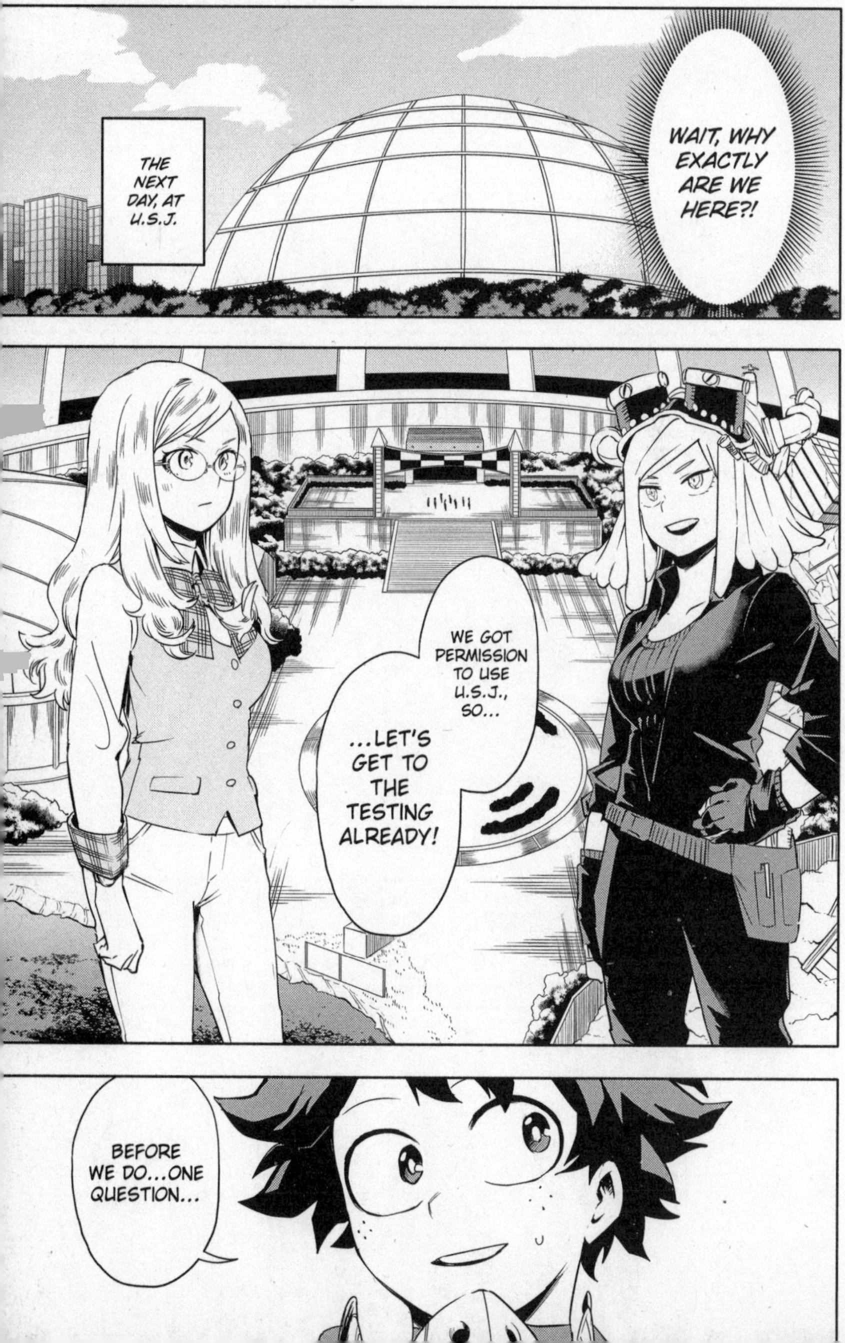
WAIT, WHY EXACTLY ARE WE HERE?!
THE NEXT DAY, AT U.S.J.
WE GOT PERMISSION TO USE U.S.J., SO...
...LET'S GET TO THE TESTING ALREADY!
BEFORE WE DO...ONE QUESTION...

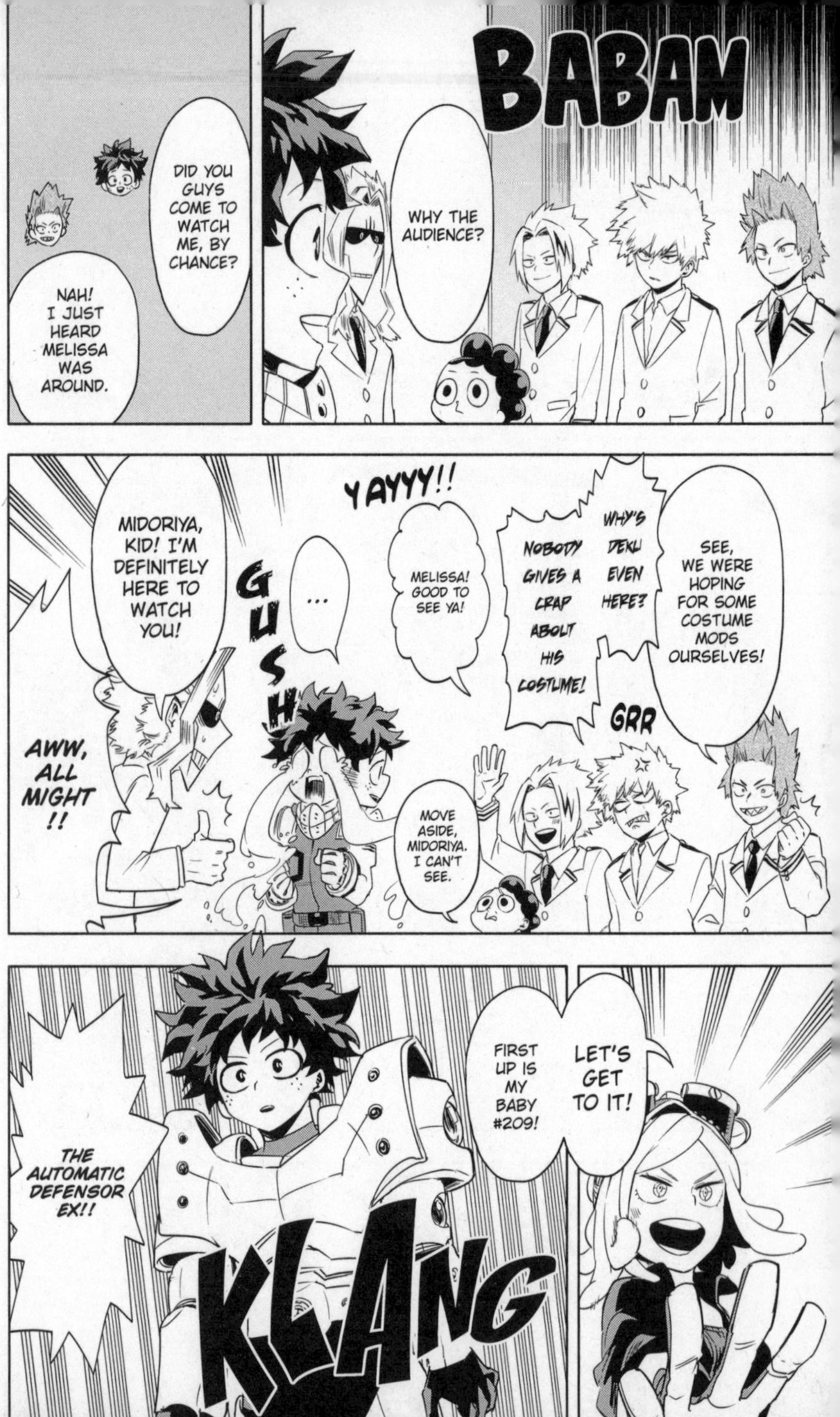
BABAM
WHY THE AUDIENCE?
DID YOU GUYS COME TO WATCH ME, BY CHANCE?
NAH! I JUST HEARD MELISSA WAS AROUND.
SEE, WE WERE HOPING FOR SOME COSTUME MODS OURSELVES!
WHY'S DEKU EVEN HERE?
NOBODY GIVES A CRAP ABOUT HIS COSTUME!
GRR
YAYYY!!
MELISSA! GOOD TO SEE YA!
...
GUSH
MIDORIYA, KID! I'M DEFINITELY HERE TO WATCH YOU!
MOVE ASIDE, MIDORIYA. I CAN'T SEE.
AWW, ALL MIGHT!!
LET'S GET TO IT!
FIRST UP IS MY BABY #209!
THE AUTOMATIC DEFENSOR EX!!
KLANG

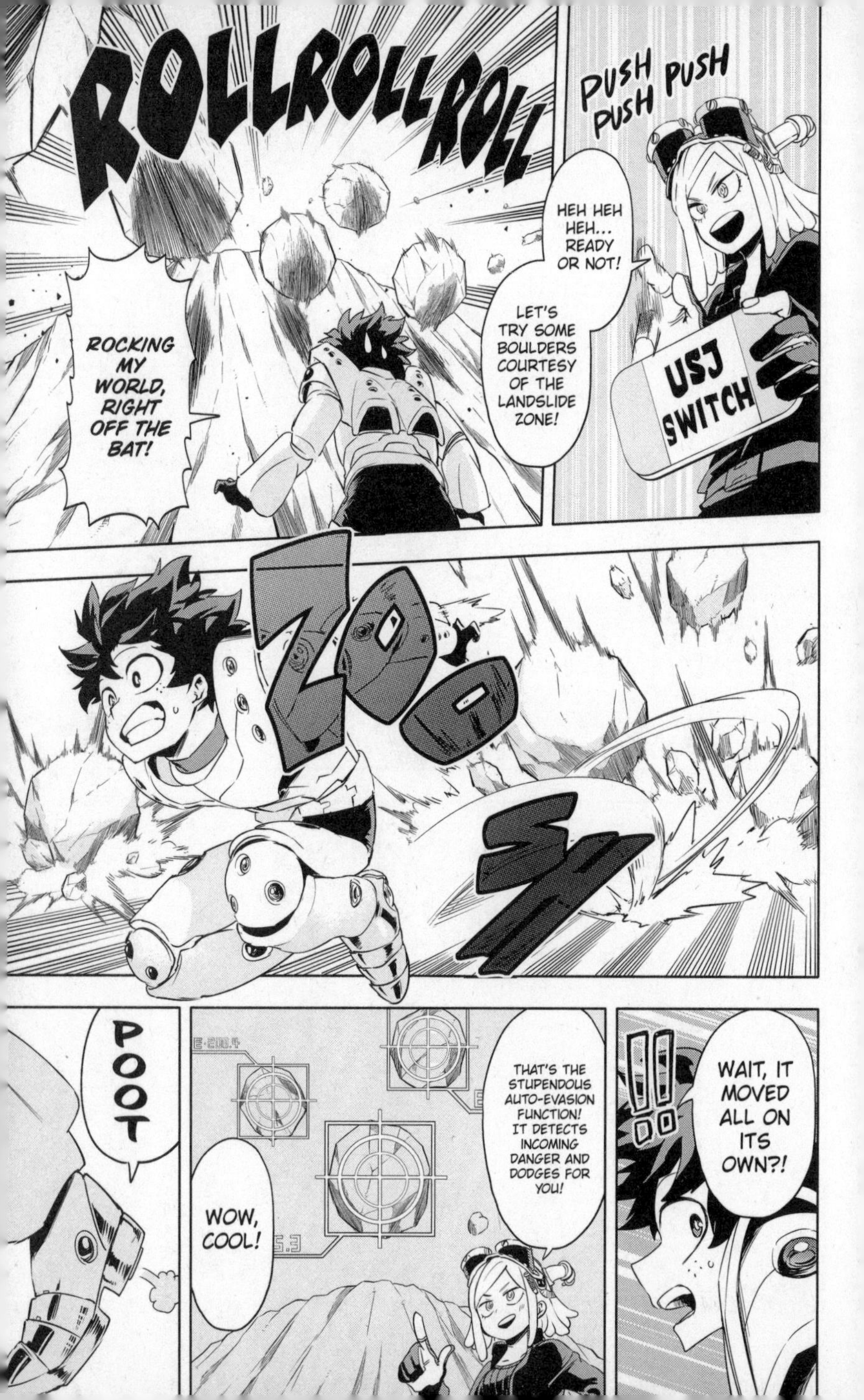
PUSH PUSH PUSH
USJ SWITCH
HEH HEH HEH... READY OR NOT!
LET'S TRY SOME BOULDERS COURTESY OF THE LANDSLIDE ZONE!
ROLLROLLROLL
ROCKING MY WORLD, RIGHT OFF THE BAT!
ZOOSH
!!
WAIT, IT MOVED ALL ON ITS OWN?!
THAT'S THE STUPENDOUS AUTO-EVASION FUNCTION! IT DETECTS INCOMING DANGER AND DODGES FOR YOU!
WOW, COOL!
POOT

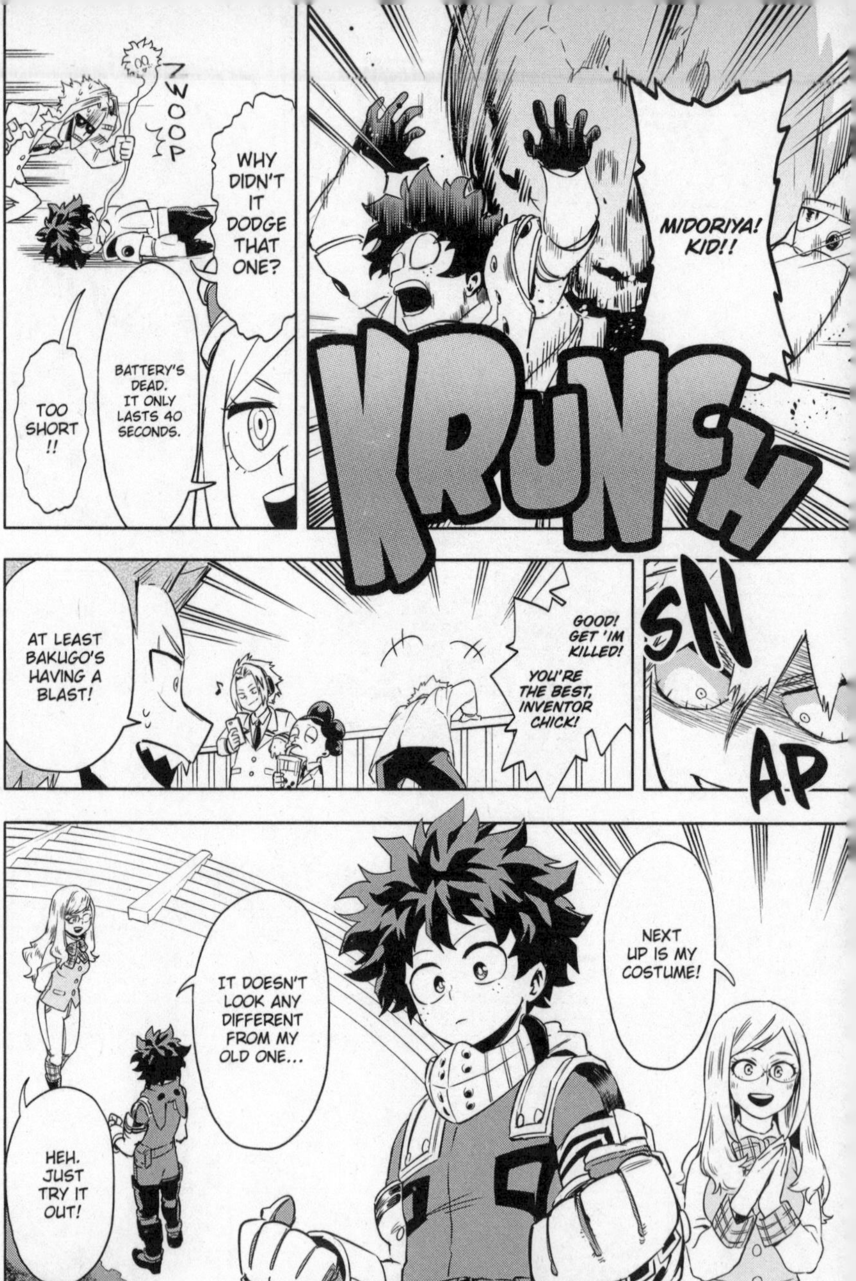
MIDORIYA! KID!!
KRUNCH
WOOP
WHY DIDN'T IT DODGE THAT ONE?
BATTERY'S DEAD. IT ONLY LASTS 40 SECONDS.
TOO SHORT!!
SNAP
GOOD! GET 'IM KILLED!
YOU'RE THE BEST, INVENTOR CHICK!
AT LEAST BAKUGO'S HAVING A BLAST!
NEXT UP IS MY COSTUME!
IT DOESN'T LOOK ANY DIFFERENT FROM MY OLD ONE...
HEH. JUST TRY IT OUT!

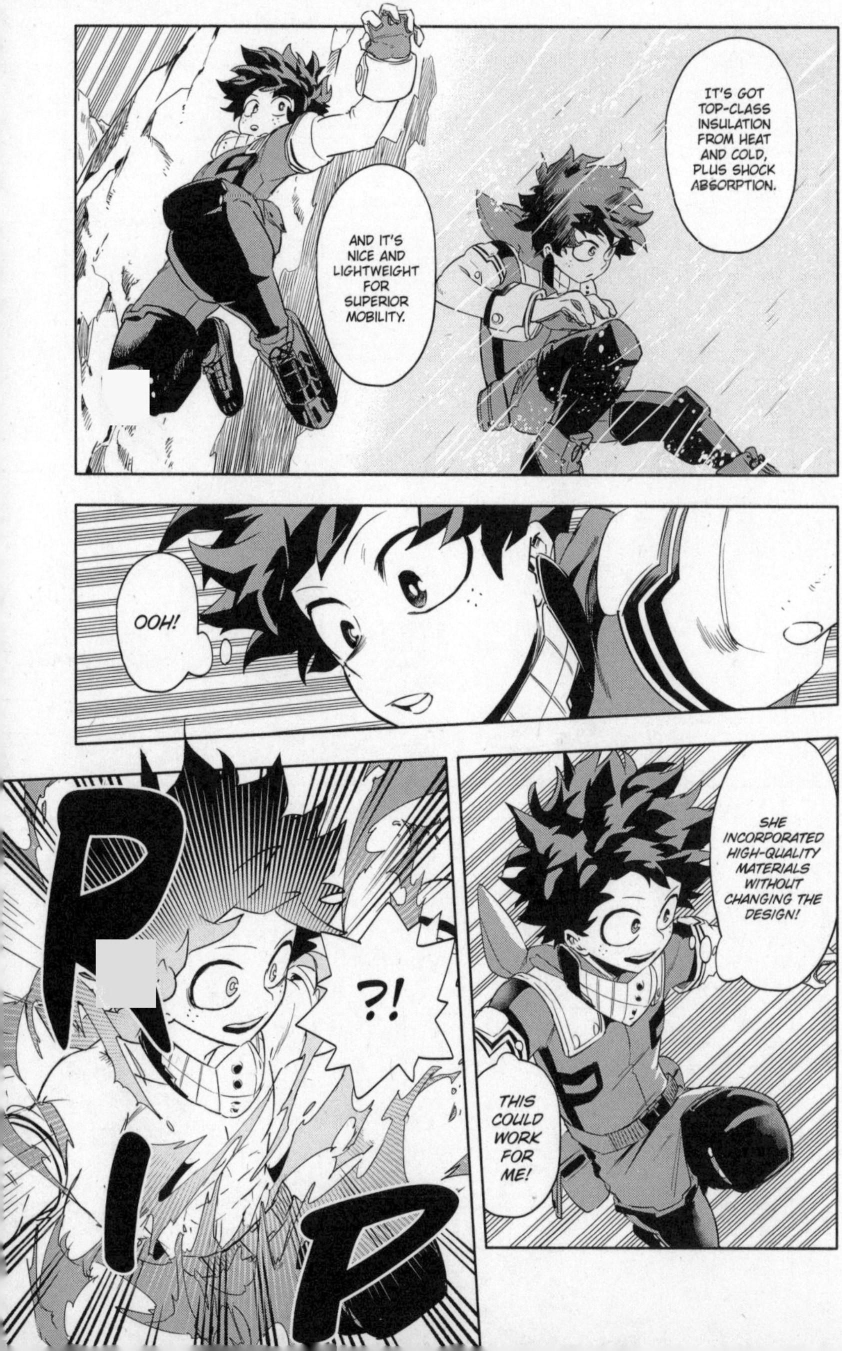
IT'S GOT TOP-CLASS INSULATION FROM HEAT AND COLD, PLUS SHOCK ABSORPTION.
AND IT'S NICE AND LIGHTWEIGHT FOR SUPERIOR MOBILITY.
OOH!
SHE INCORPORATED HIGH-QUALITY MATERIALS WITHOUT CHANGING THE DESIGN!
THIS COULD WORK FOR ME!
?!

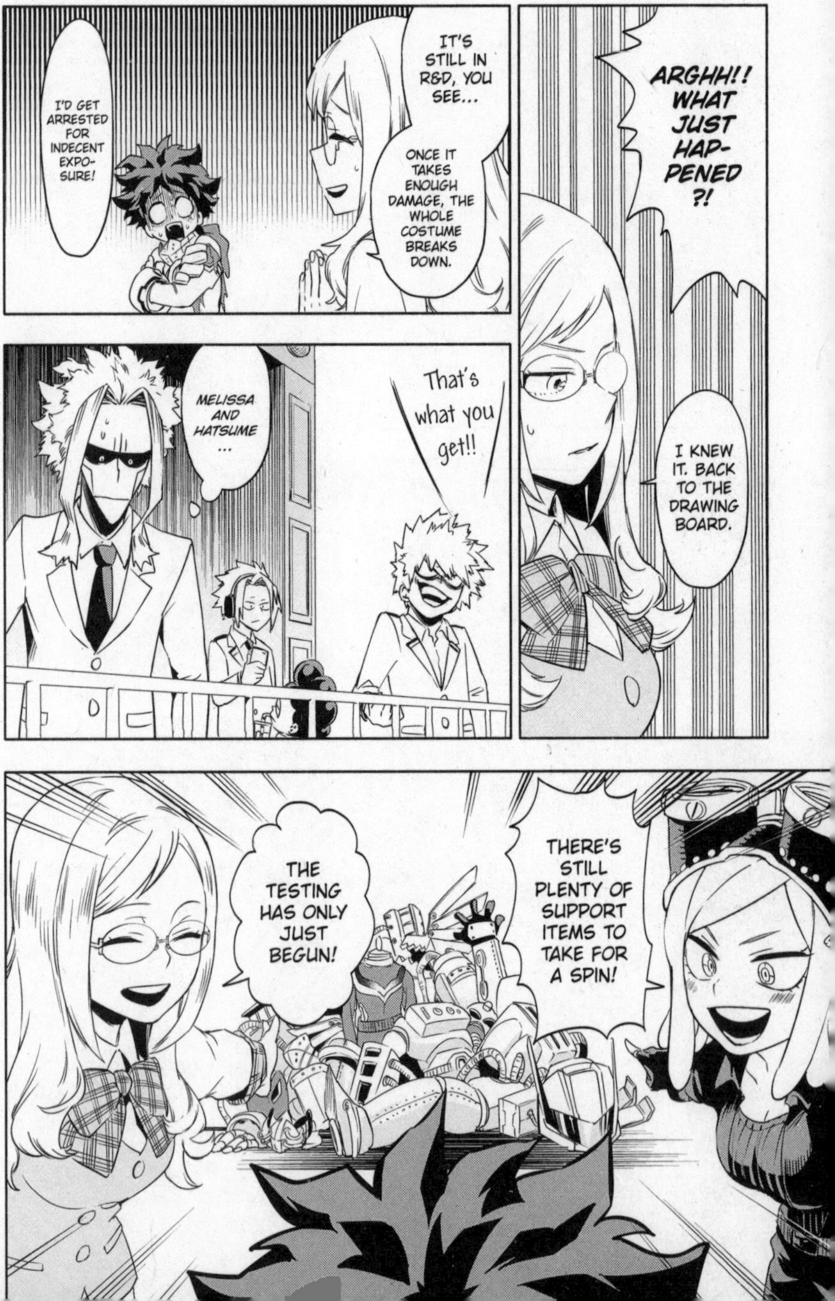
ARGHH!! WHAT JUST HAP-PENED?!
I KNEW IT. BACK TO THE DRAWING BOARD.
IT'S STILL IN R&D, YOU SEE...
ONCE IT TAKES ENOUGH DAMAGE, THE WHOLE COSTUME BREAKS DOWN.
I'D GET ARRESTED FOR INDECENT EXPO-SURE!
That's what you get!!
MELISSA AND HATSUME ...
THERE'S STILL PLENTY OF SUPPORT ITEMS TO TAKE FOR A SPIN!
THE TESTING HAS ONLY JUST BEGUN!

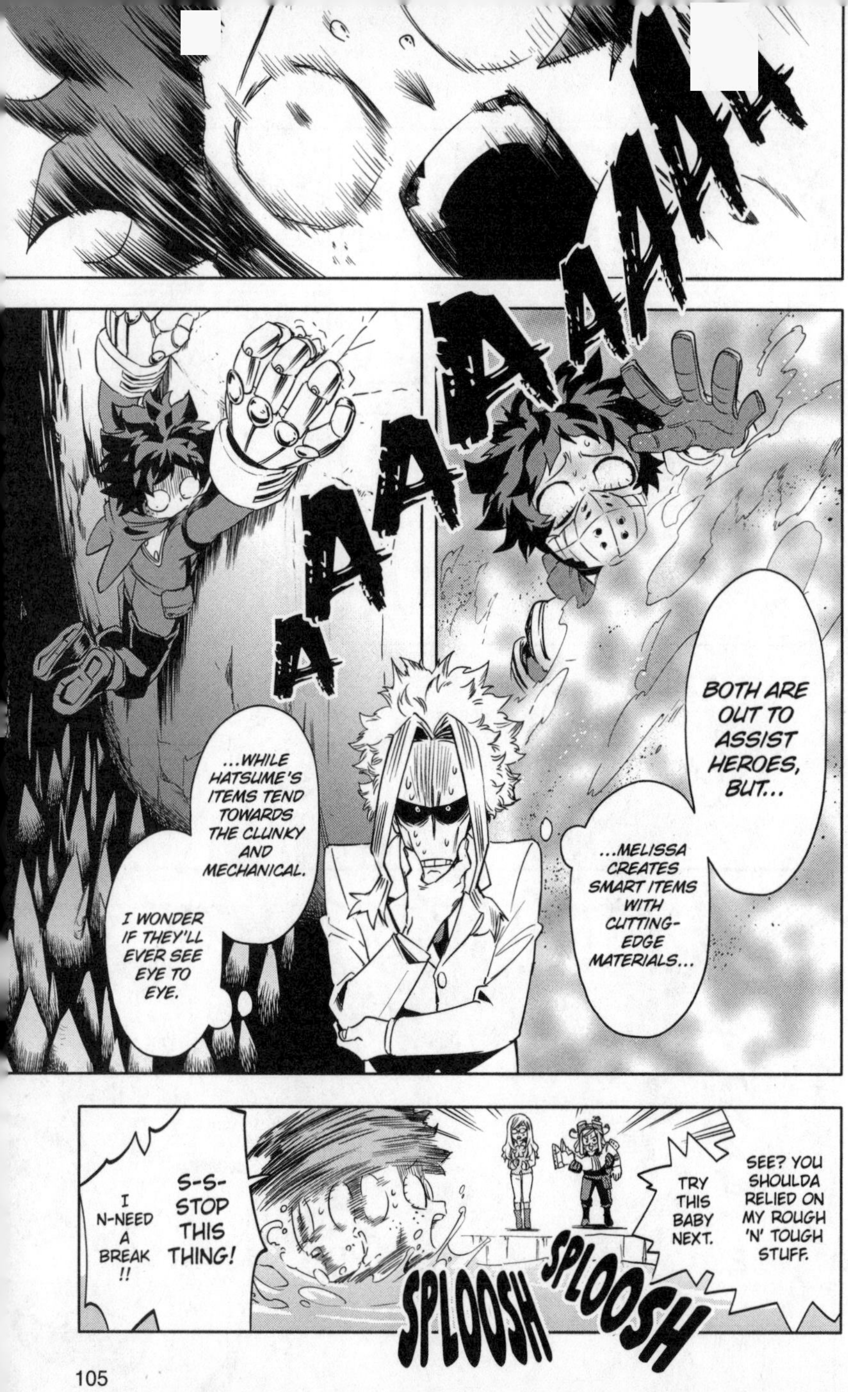
AAAAAAAAAAH
BOTH ARE OUT TO ASSIST HEROES, BUT...
...MELISSA CREATES SMART ITEMS WITH CUTTING-EDGE MATERIALS...
...WHILE HATSUME'S ITEMS TEND TOWARDS THE CLUNKY AND MECHANICAL.
I WONDER IF THEY'LL EVER SEE EYE TO EYE.
SEE? YOU SHOULDA RELIED ON MY ROUGH 'N' TOUGH STUFF.
TRY THIS BABY NEXT.
SPLOOSH
SPLOOSH
S-S-STOP THIS THING!
I N-NEED A BREAK !!

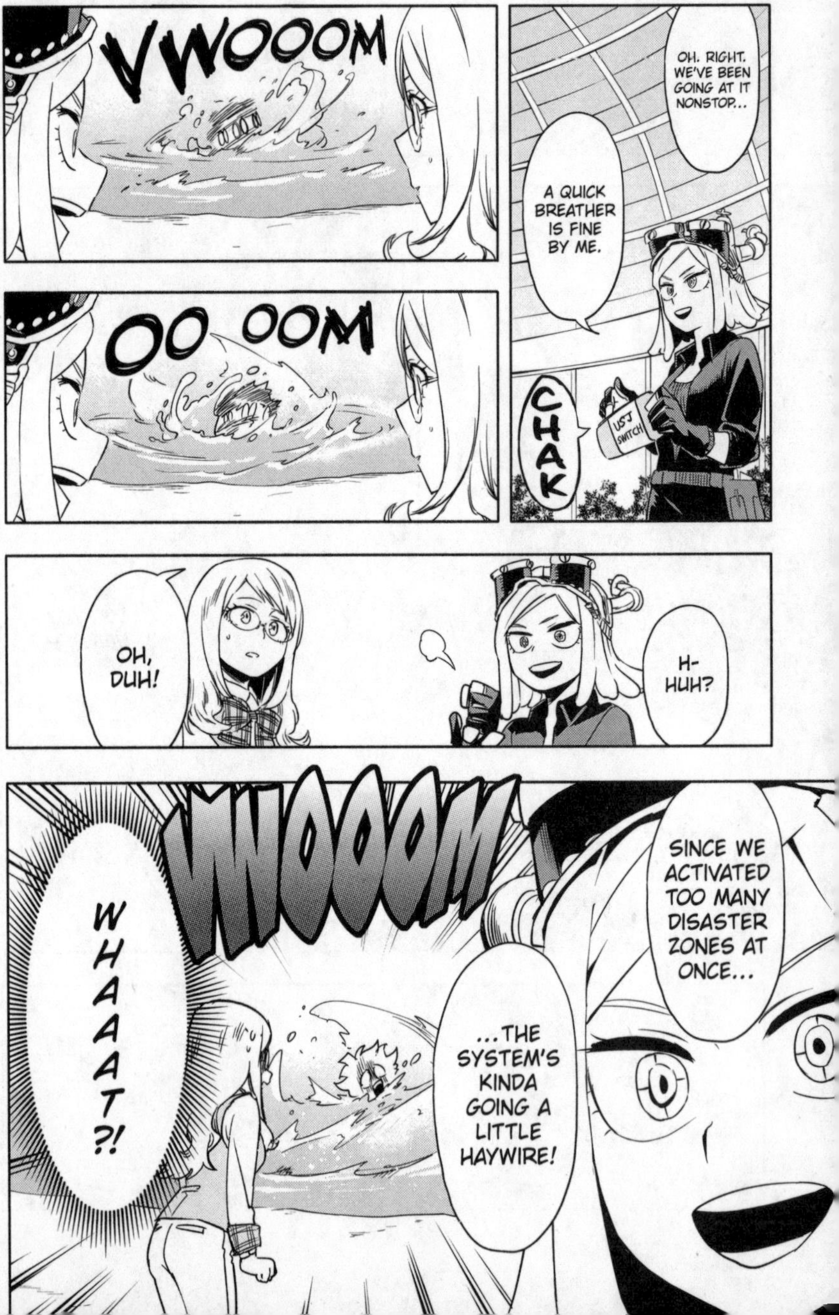
OH. RIGHT. WE'VE BEEN GOING AT IT NONSTOP...
A QUICK BREATHER IS FINE BY ME.
CHAK
USJ SWITCH
VWOOOM
OO OOM
H-HUH?
OH, DUH!
SINCE WE ACTIVATED TOO MANY DISASTER ZONES AT ONCE...
...THE SYSTEM'S KINDA GOING A LITTLE HAYWIRE!
VWOOOM
WHAAAAT?!

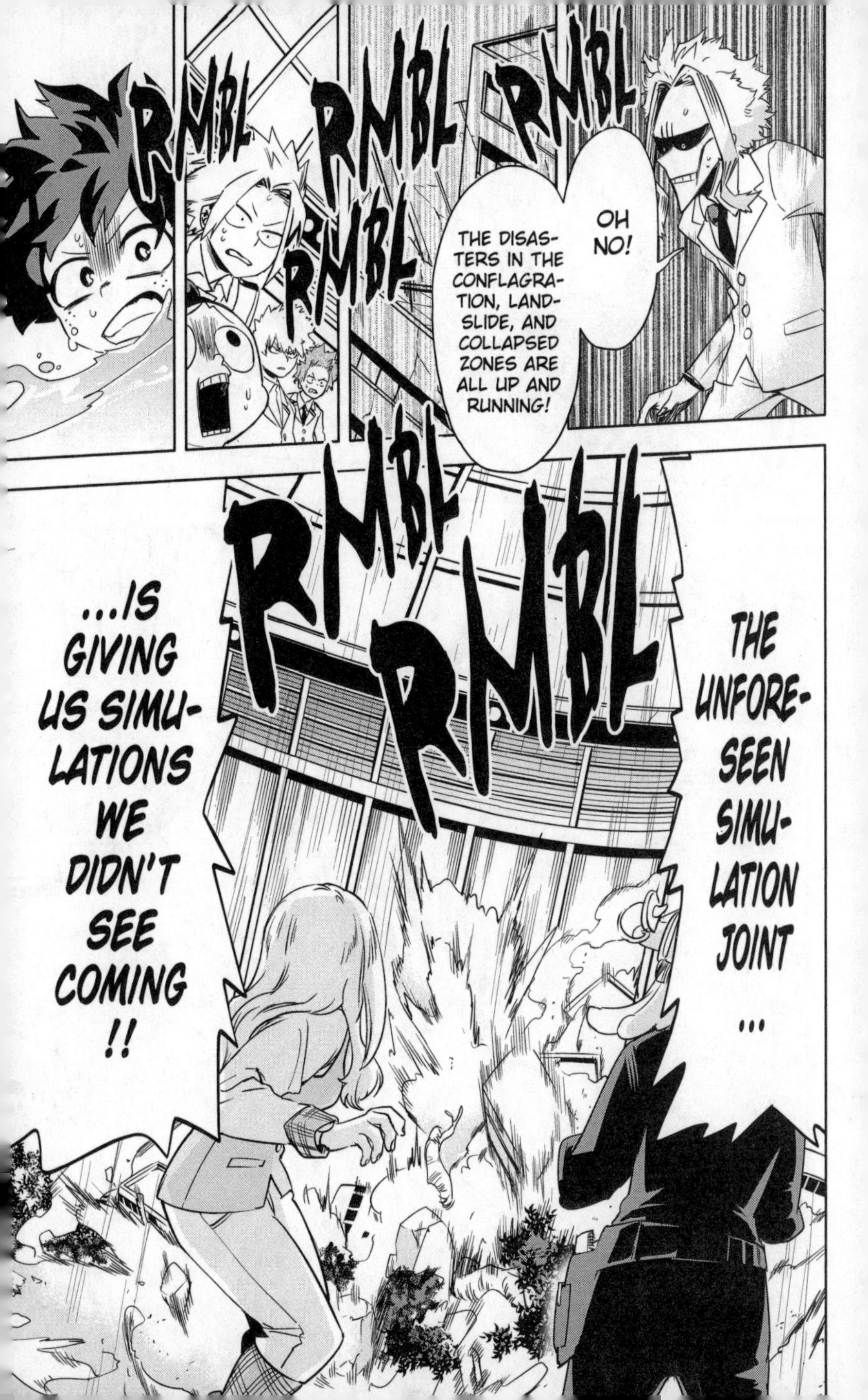
RMBL RMBL RMBL RMBL
OH NO!
THE DISASTERS IN THE CONFLAGRATION, LANDSLIDE, AND COLLAPSED ZONES ARE ALL UP AND RUNNING!
RMBL
RMBL RMBL RMBL
THE UNFORESEEN SIMULATION JOINT...
...IS GIVING US SIMULATIONS WE DIDN'T SEE COMING!!

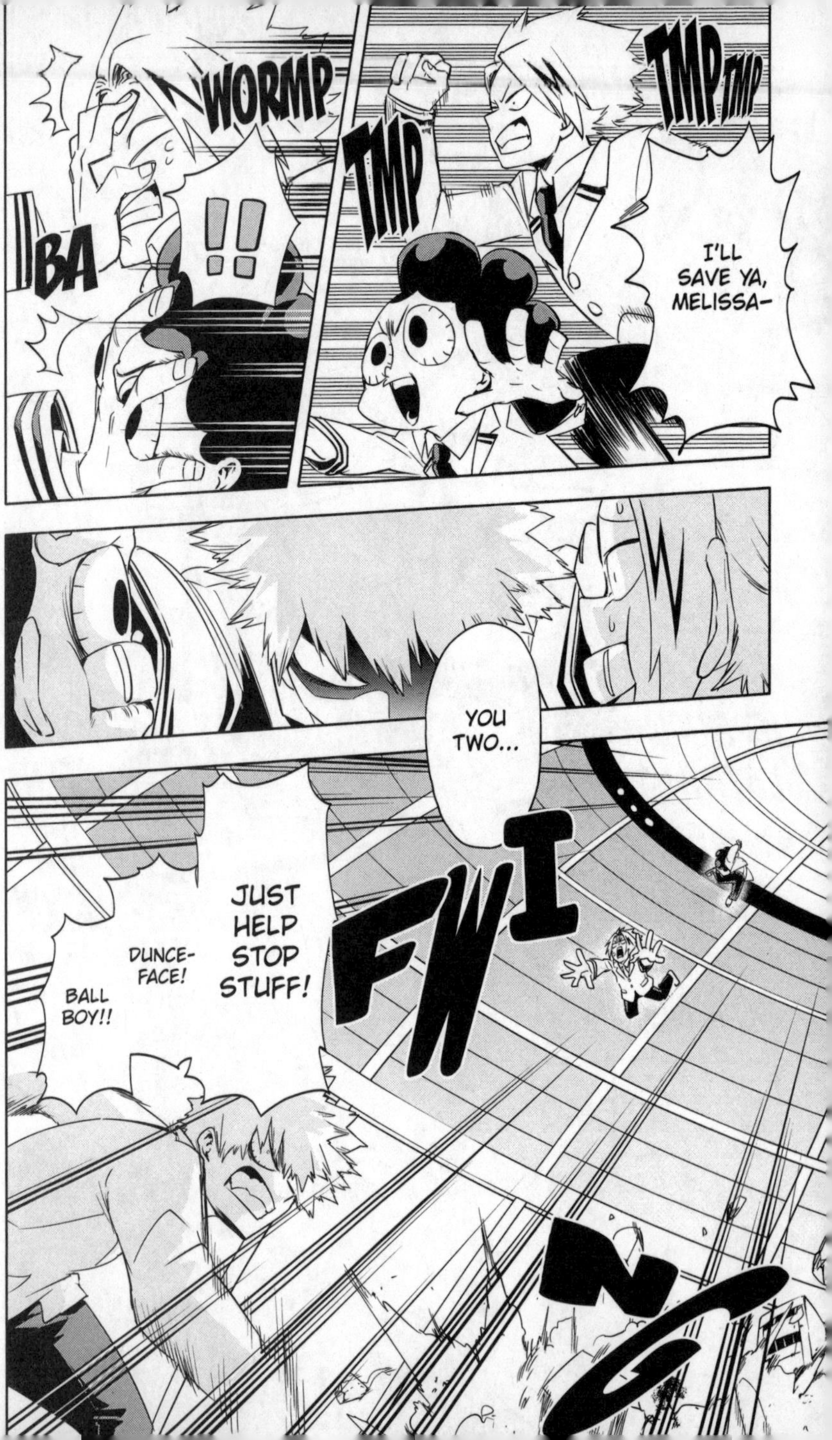
TMP TMP
TMP
I'LL SAVE YA, MELISSA-
WORMP
!!
BA
YOU TWO...
JUST HELP STOP STUFF!
DUNCE-FACE!
BALL BOY!!
FWI
NG

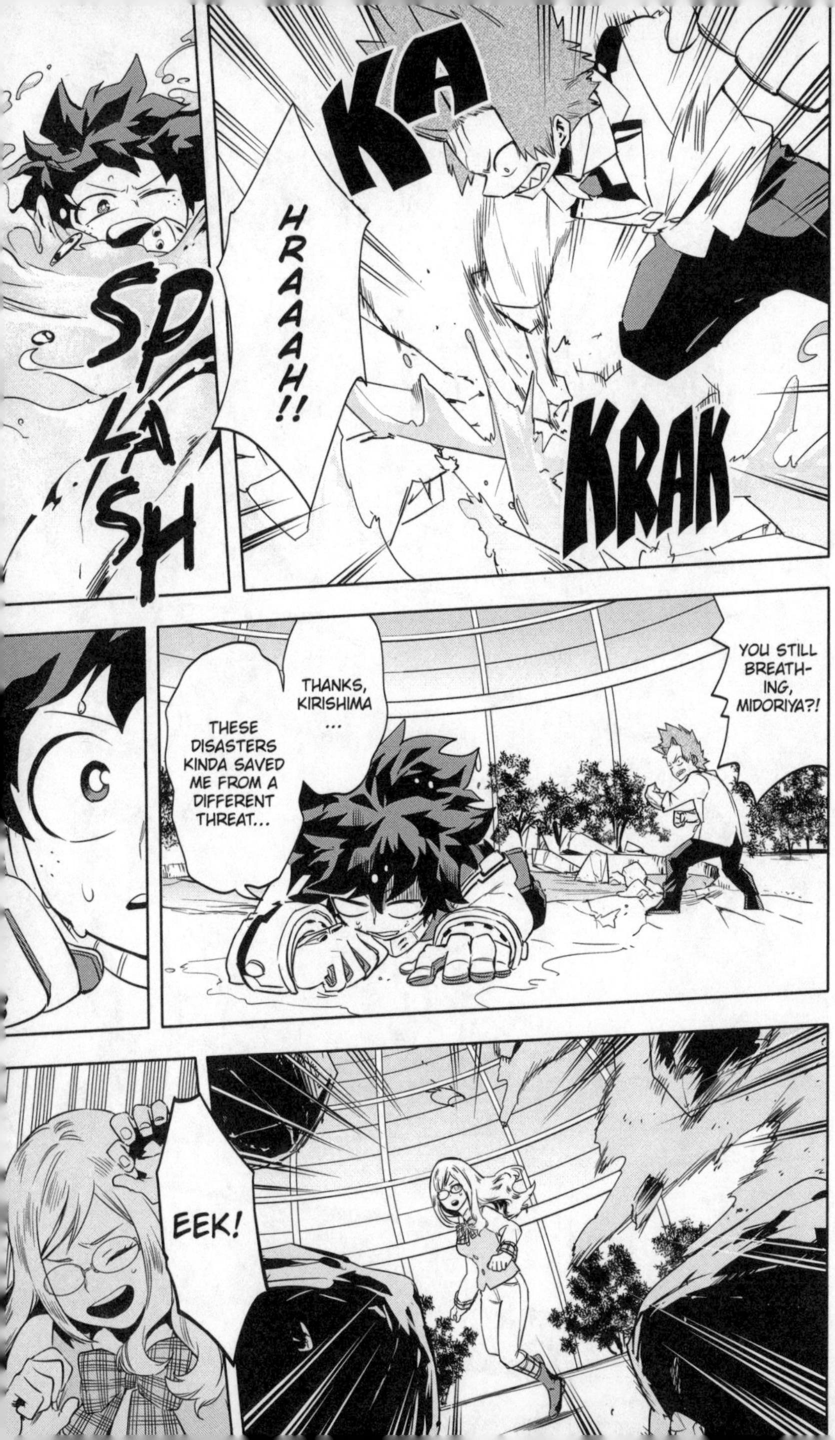
KA
HRAAAAH!!
KRAK
SPLASH
YOU STILL BREATHING, MIDORIYA?!
THANKS, KIRISHIMA...
THESE DISASTERS KINDA SAVED ME FROM A DIFFERENT THREAT...
EEK!

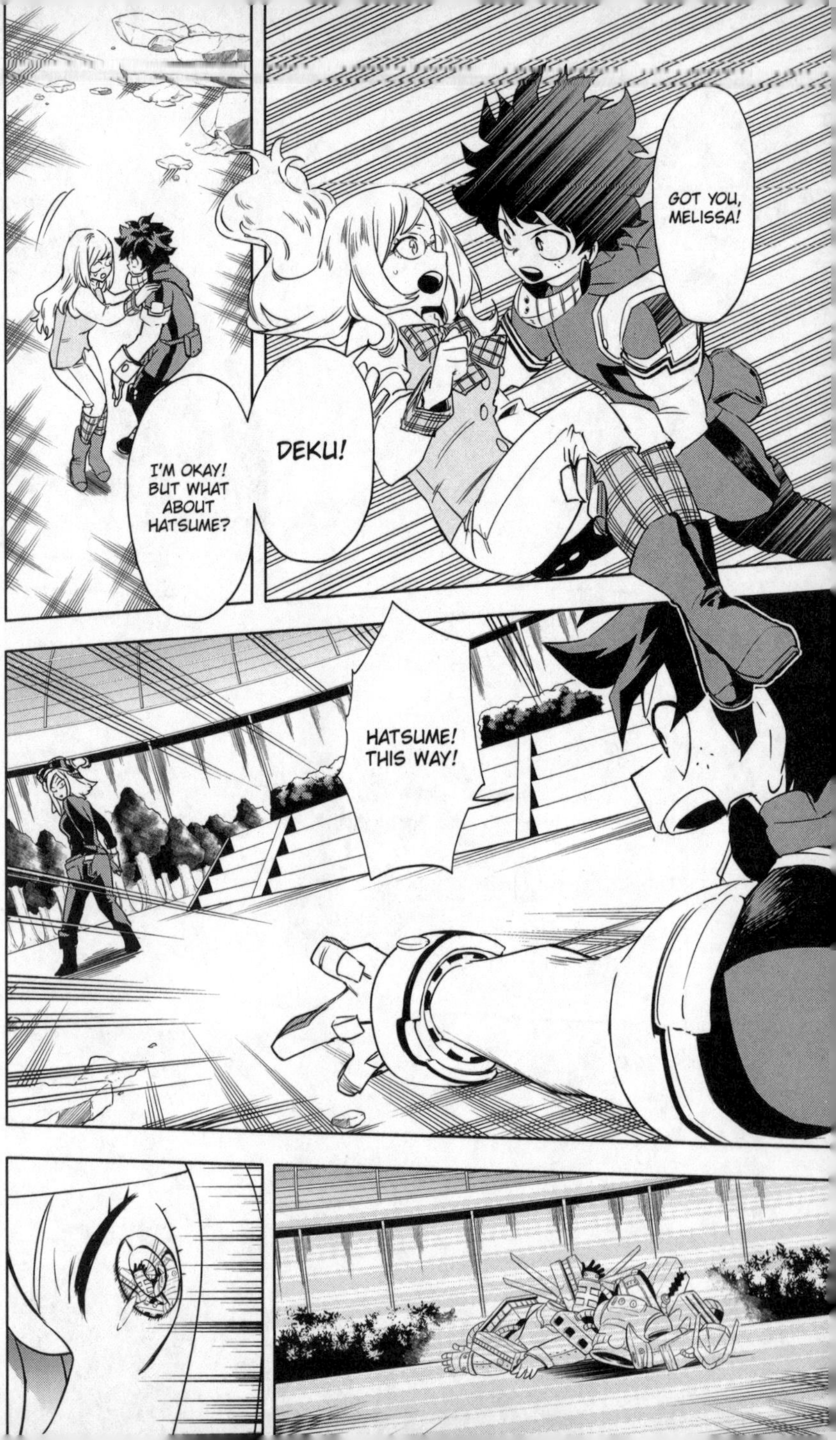
GOT YOU, MELISSA!
DEKU!
I'M OKAY! BUT WHAT ABOUT HATSUME?
HATSUME! THIS WAY!

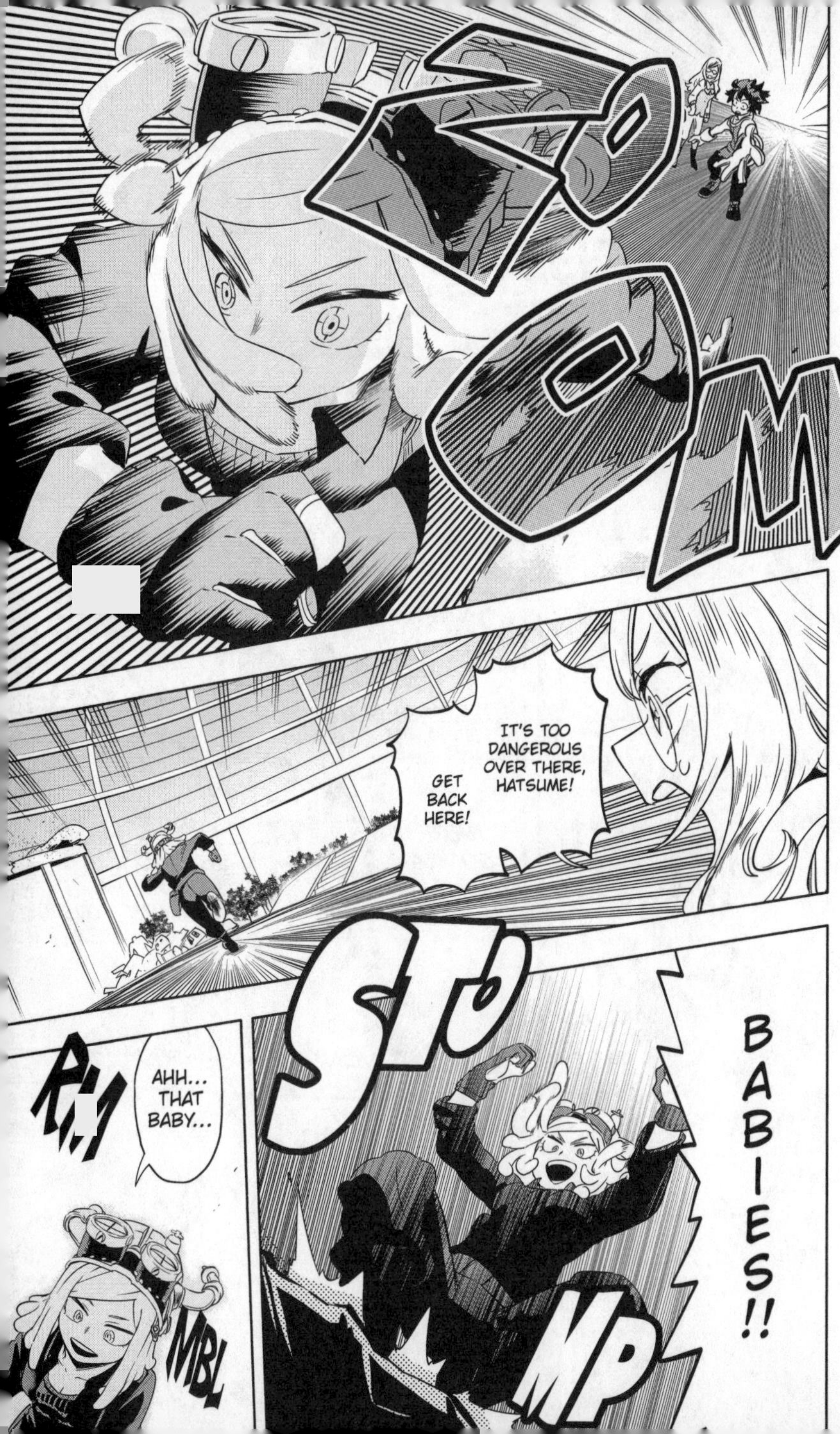
ZOOM
IT'S TOO DANGEROUS OVER THERE, HATSUME!
GET BACK HERE!
STOMP
BABIES!!
AHH... THAT BABY...

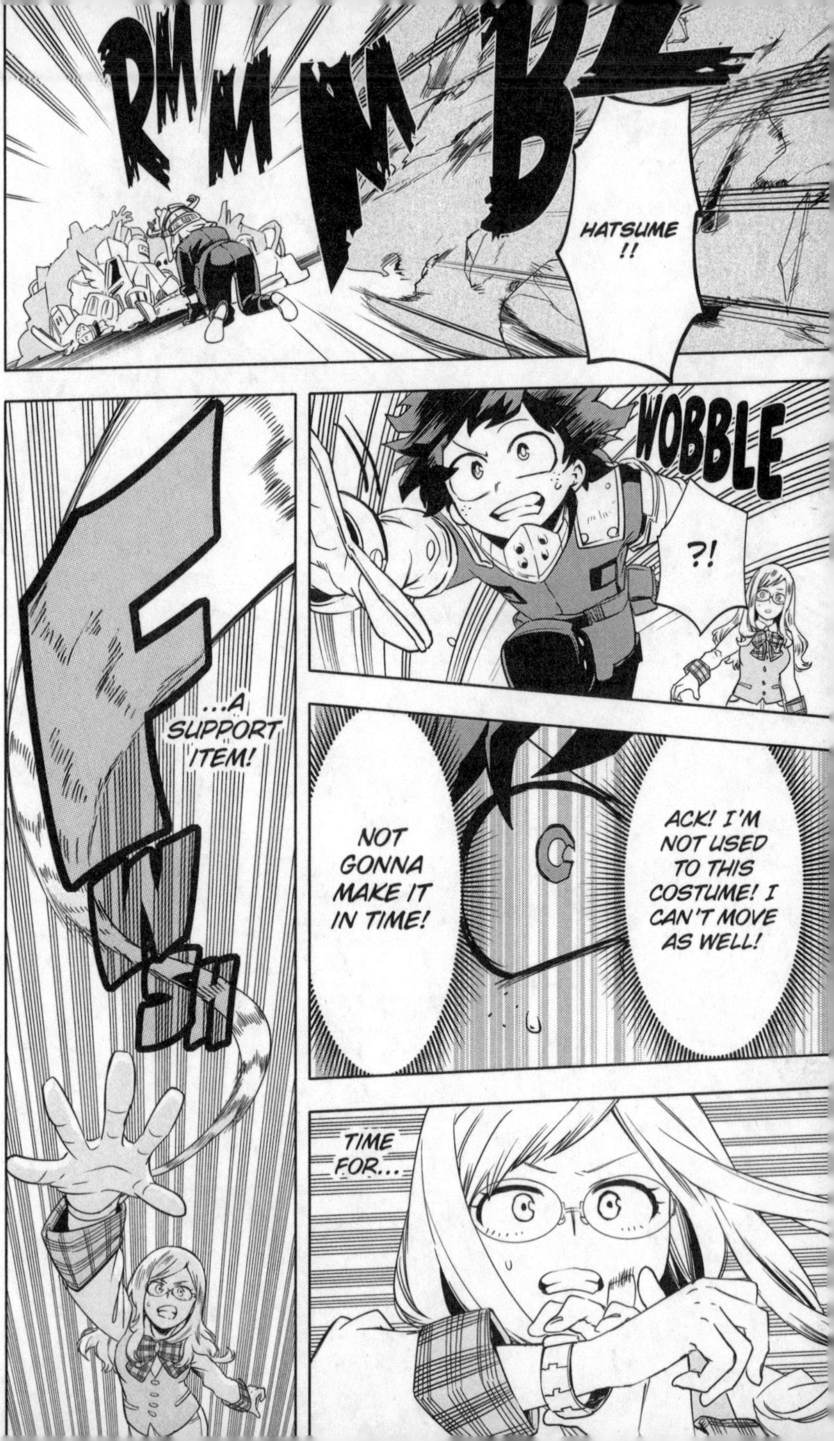
RMMMB
HATSUME !!
WOBBLE
?!
ACK! I'M NOT USED TO THIS COSTUME! I CAN'T MOVE AS WELL!
NOT GONNA MAKE IT IN TIME!
TIME FOR...
...A SUPPORT ITEM!
WSH

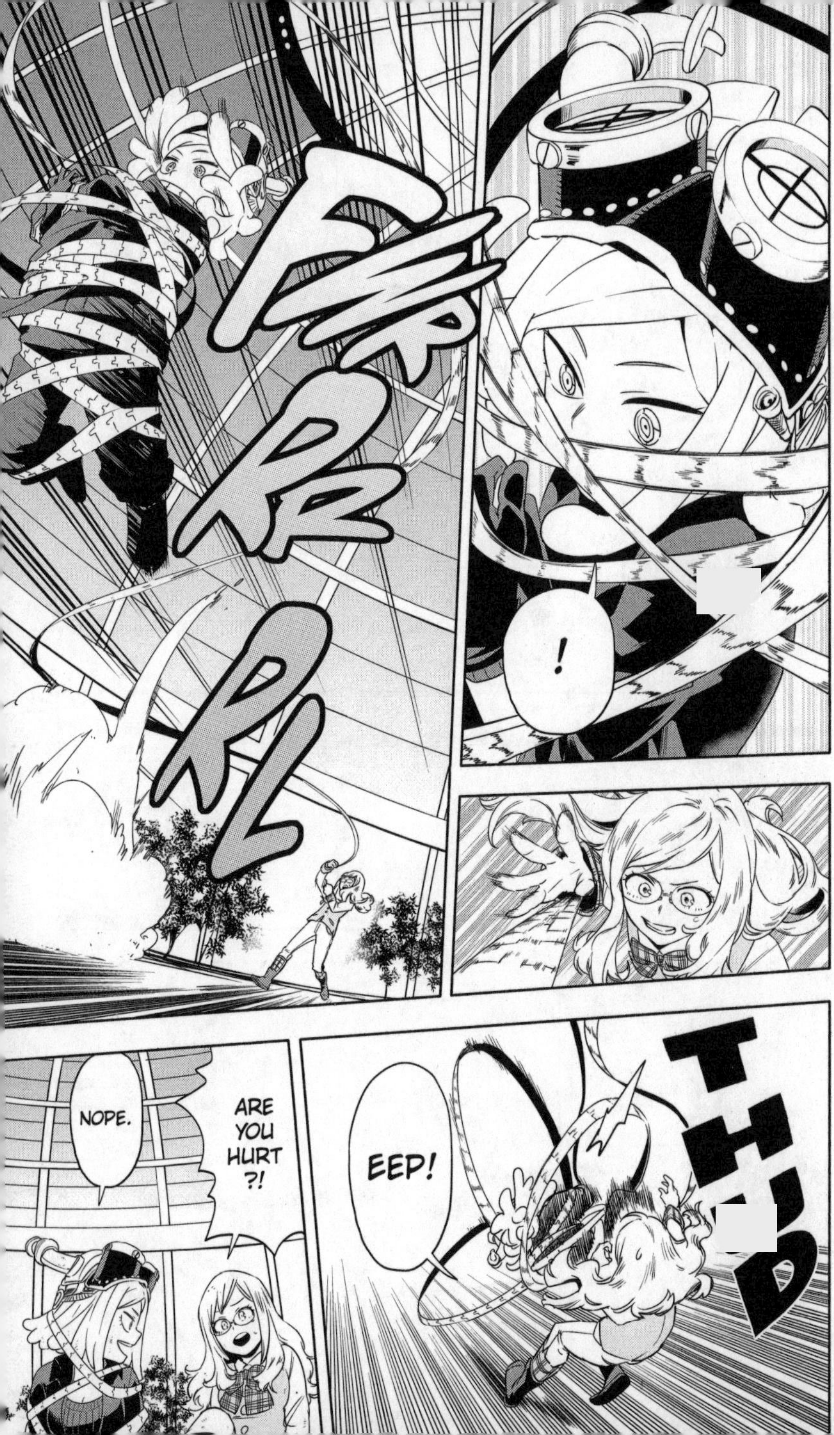
!
THUD
EEP!
ARE YOU HURT ?!
NOPE.

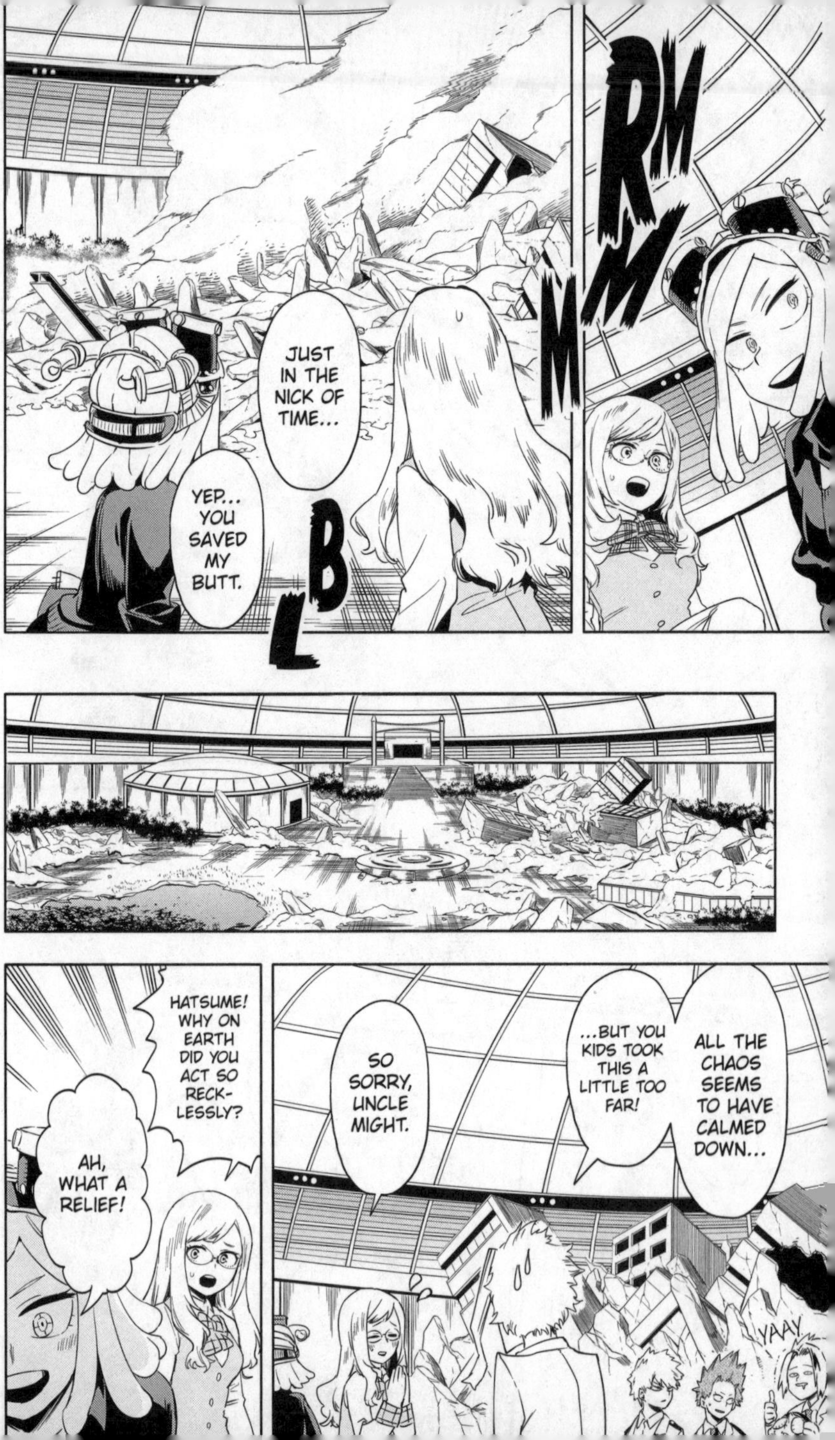
RMMM
JUST IN THE NICK OF TIME...
YEP... YOU SAVED MY BUTT.
BL
ALL THE CHAOS SEEMS TO HAVE CALMED DOWN...
...BUT YOU KIDS TOOK THIS A LITTLE TOO FAR!
SO SORRY, UNCLE MIGHT.
YAAY
HATSUME! WHY ON EARTH DID YOU ACT SO RECK-LESSLY?
AH, WHAT A RELIEF!

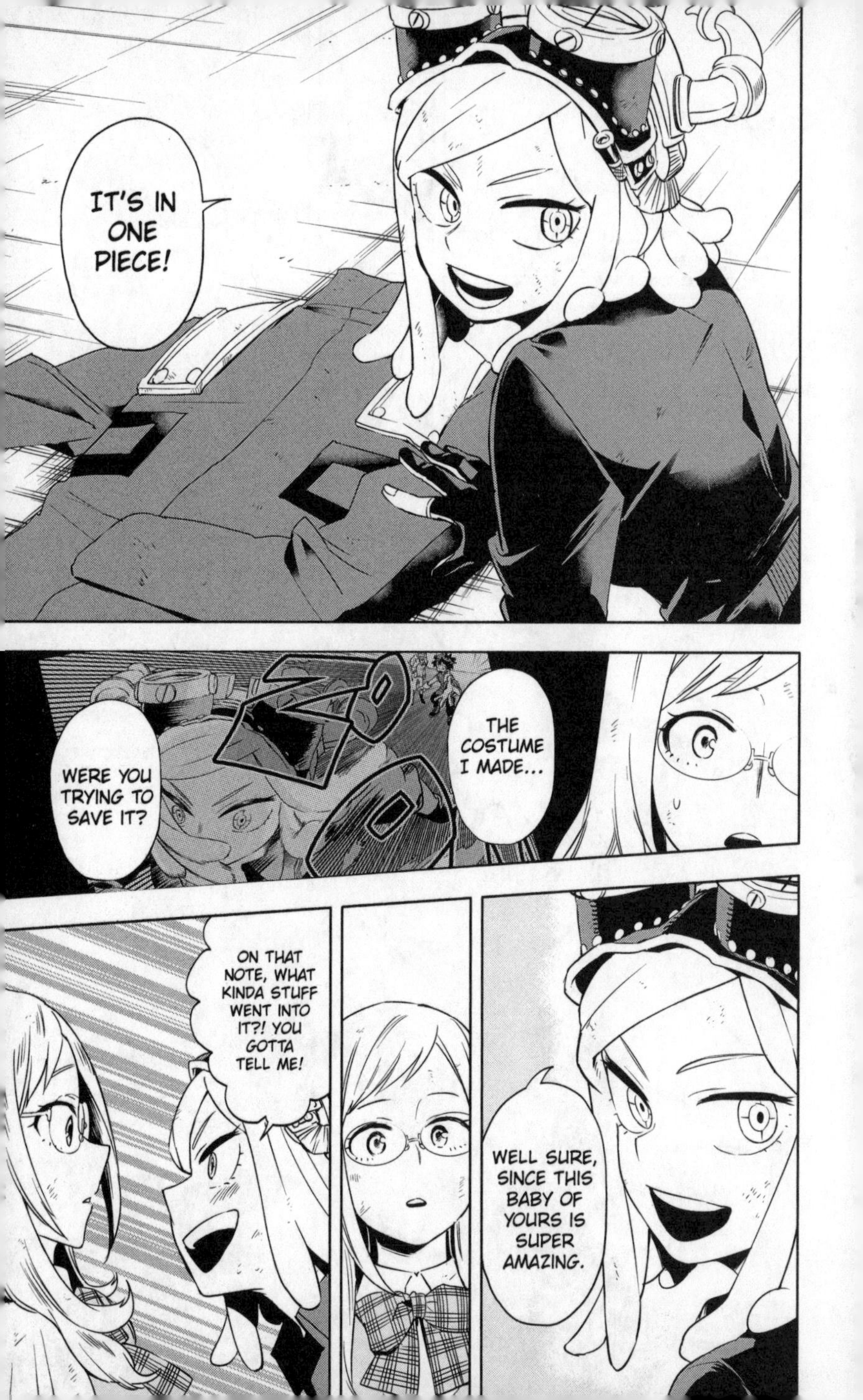
IT'S IN ONE PIECE!
THE COSTUME I MADE...
WERE YOU TRYING TO SAVE IT?
WELL SURE, SINCE THIS BABY OF YOURS IS SUPER AMAZING.
ON THAT NOTE, WHAT KINDA STUFF WENT INTO IT?! YOU GOTTA TELL ME!

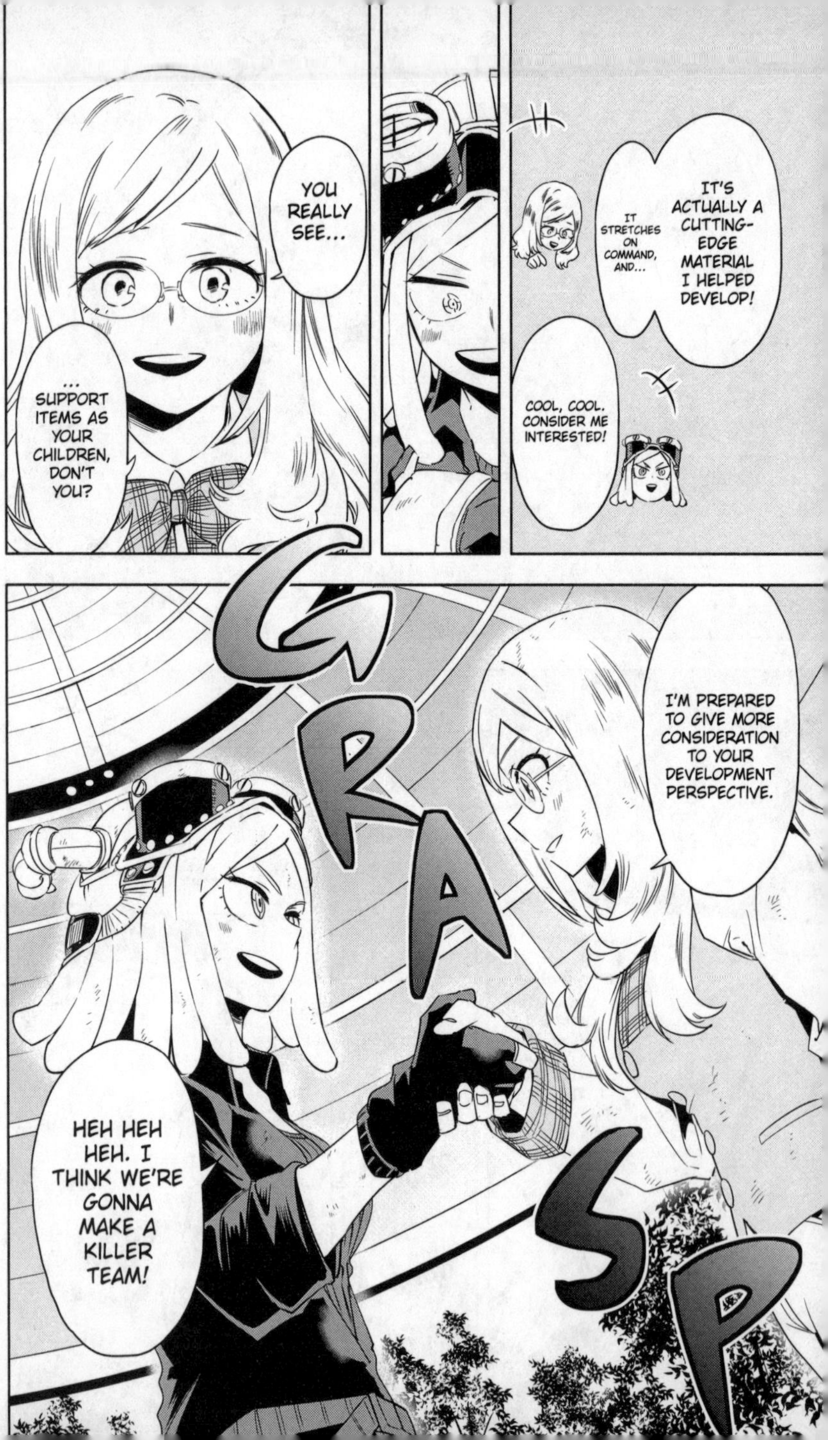
IT'S ACTUALLY A CUTTING-EDGE MATERIAL I HELPED DEVELOP!
IT STRETCHES ON COMMAND, AND...
COOL, COOL. CONSIDER ME INTERESTED!
YOU REALLY SEE...
...SUPPORT ITEMS AS YOUR CHILDREN, DON'T YOU?
I'M PREPARED TO GIVE MORE CONSIDERATION TO YOUR DEVELOPMENT PERSPECTIVE.
GRASP
HEH HEH HEH. I THINK WE'RE GONNA MAKE A KILLER TEAM!

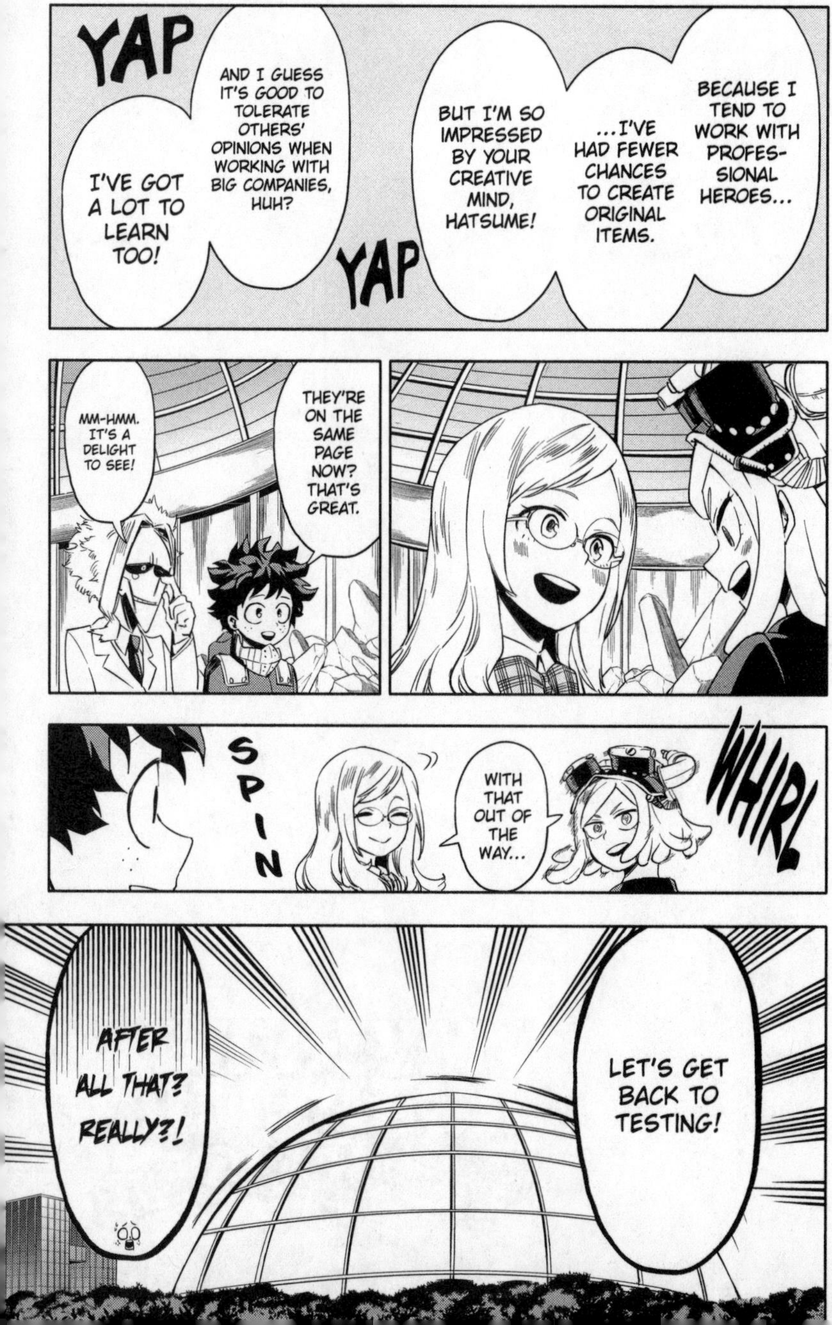
BECAUSE I TEND TO WORK WITH PROFES-SIONAL HEROES...
...I'VE HAD FEWER CHANCES TO CREATE ORIGINAL ITEMS.
BUT I'M SO IMPRESSED BY YOUR CREATIVE MIND, HATSUME!
YAP
AND I GUESS IT'S GOOD TO TOLERATE OTHERS' OPINIONS WHEN WORKING WITH BIG COMPANIES, HUH?
YAP
I'VE GOT A LOT TO LEARN TOO!
THEY'RE ON THE SAME PAGE NOW? THAT'S GREAT.
MM-HMM. IT'S A DELIGHT TO SEE!
WHIR!
WITH THAT OUT OF THE WAY...
SPIN
LET'S GET BACK TO TESTING!
AFTER ALL THAT? REALLY?!

MY HERO ACADEMIA

Team-Up Missions

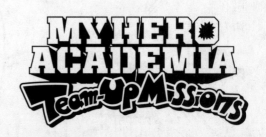

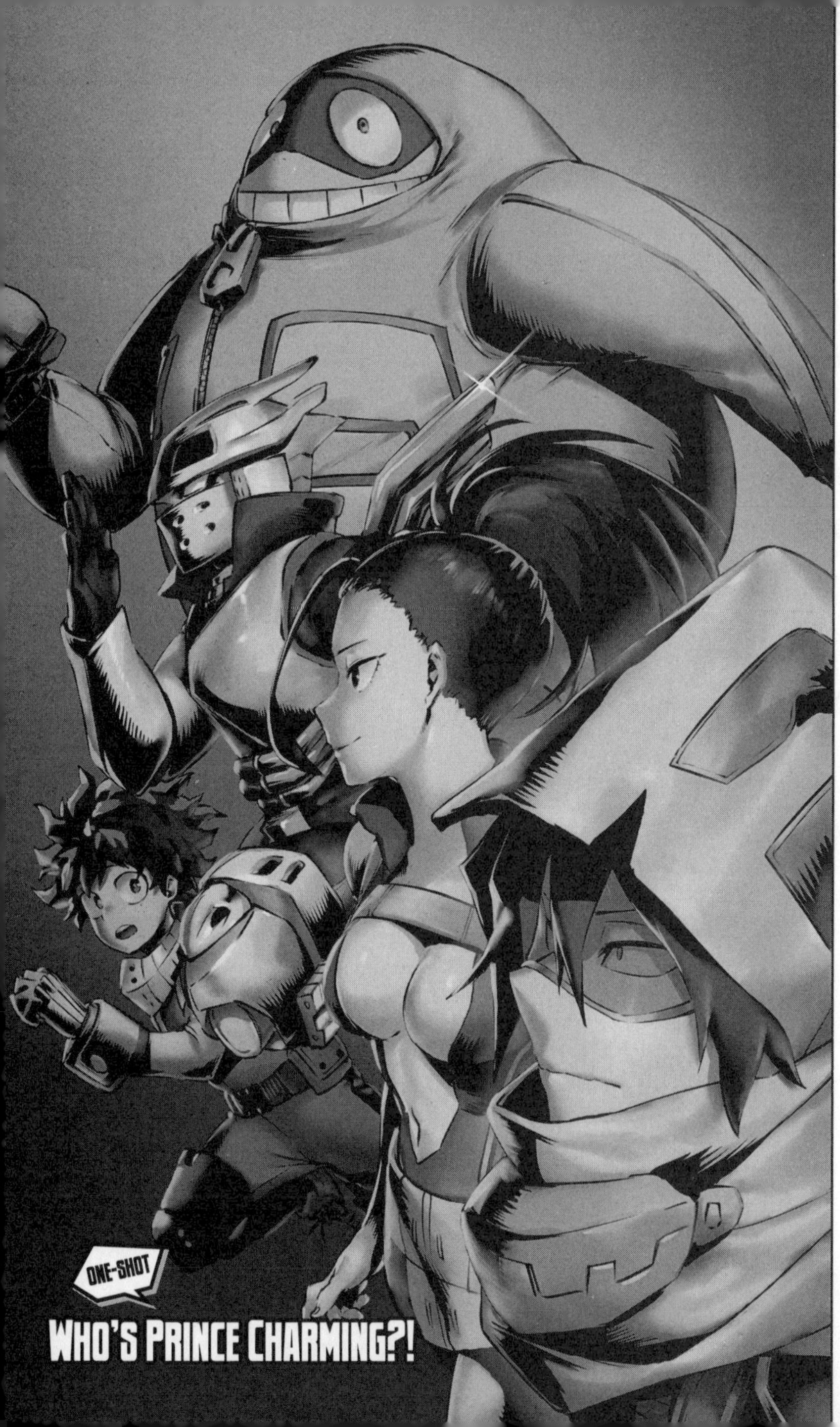
ONE-SHOT
WHO'S PRINCE CHARMING?!

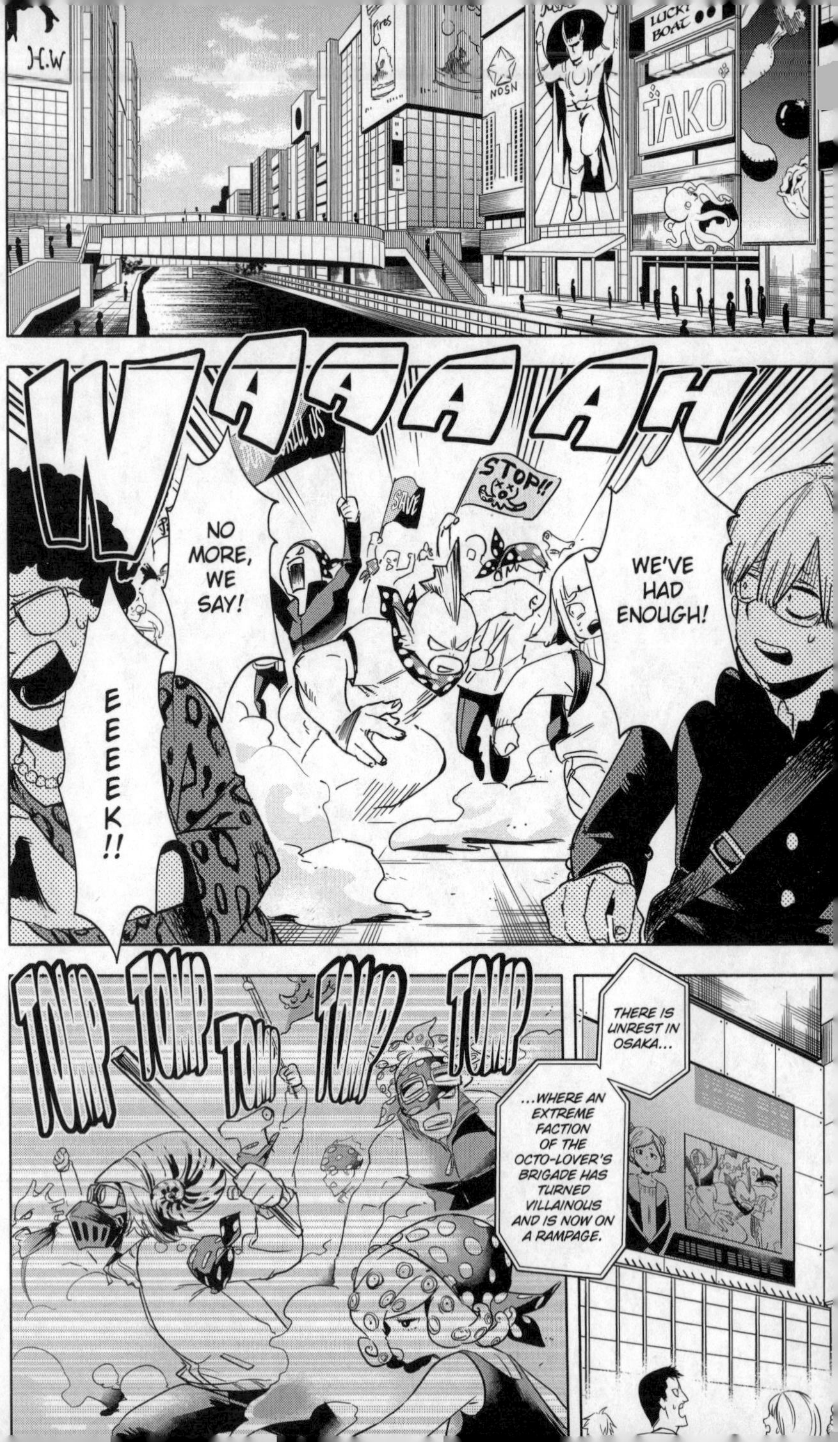
TAKO
NOSN
H.W
WAAAAH
WE'VE HAD ENOUGH!
STOP!!
SAVE
NO MORE, WE SAY!
EEEEEK!!
THERE IS UNREST IN OSAKA...
...WHERE AN EXTREME FACTION OF THE OCTO-LOVER'S BRIGADE HAS TURNED VILLAINOUS AND IS NOW ON A RAMPAGE.
TOMP TOMP TOMP TOMP TOMP

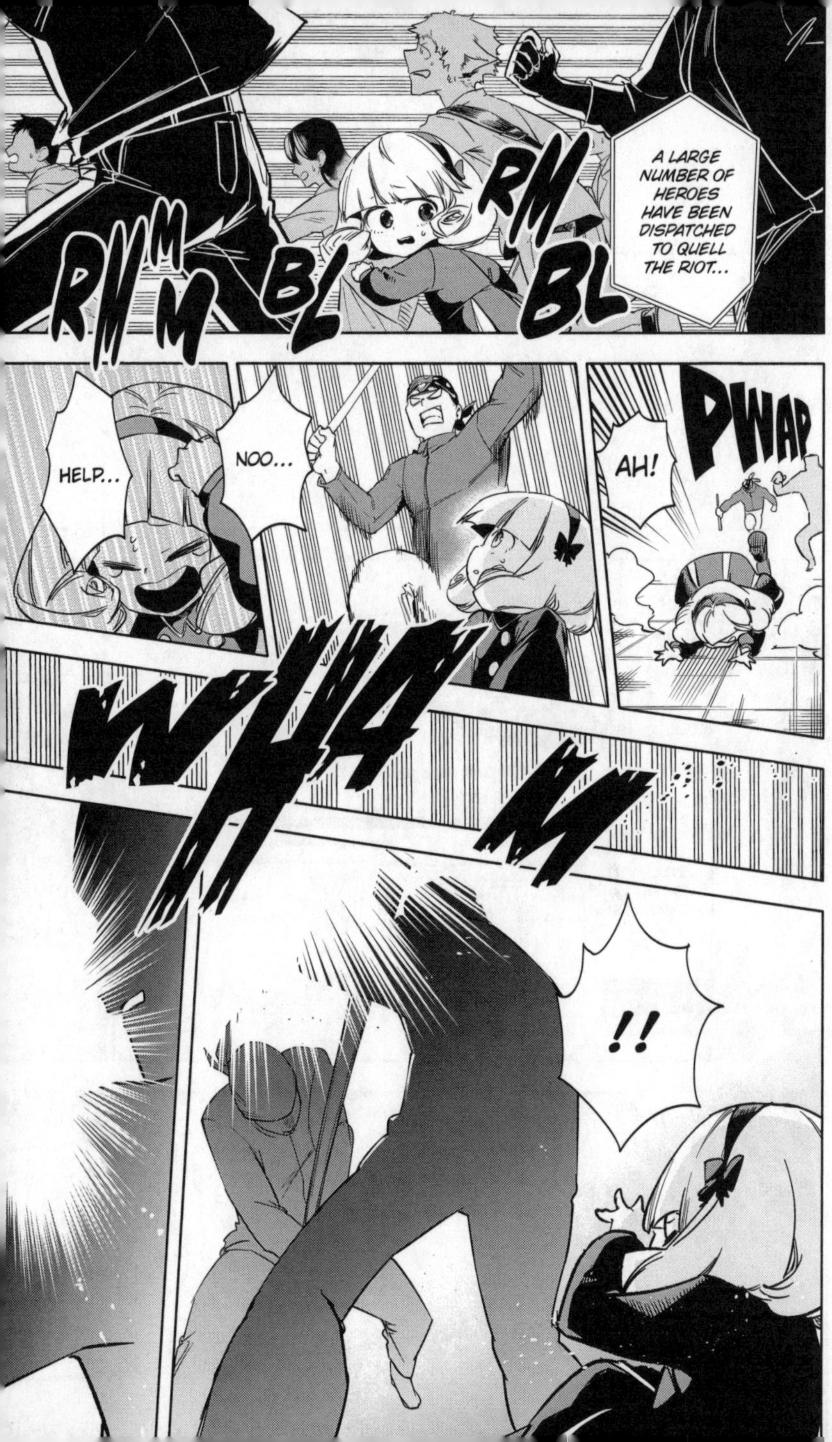
A LARGE NUMBER OF HEROES HAVE BEEN DISPATCHED TO QUELL THE RIOT...
RMBL
RMMBL
PWAP
AH!
NOO...
HELP...
WHAM
!!

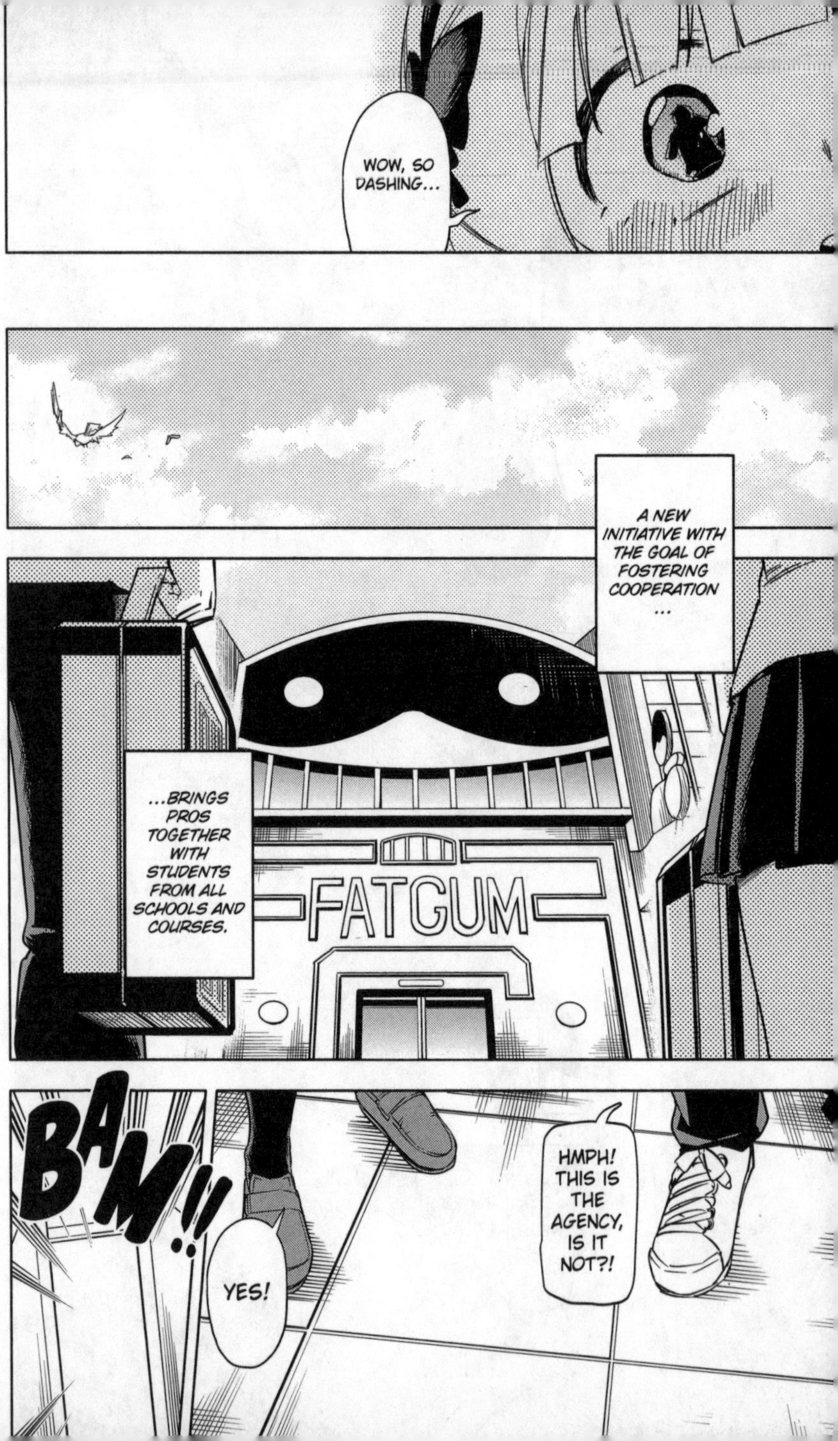
WOW, SO DASHING...
A NEW INITIATIVE WITH THE GOAL OF FOSTERING COOPERATION ...
FATGUM
...BRINGS PROS TOGETHER WITH STUDENTS FROM ALL SCHOOLS AND COURSES.
HMPH! THIS IS THE AGENCY, IS IT NOT?!
YES!
BAM!!

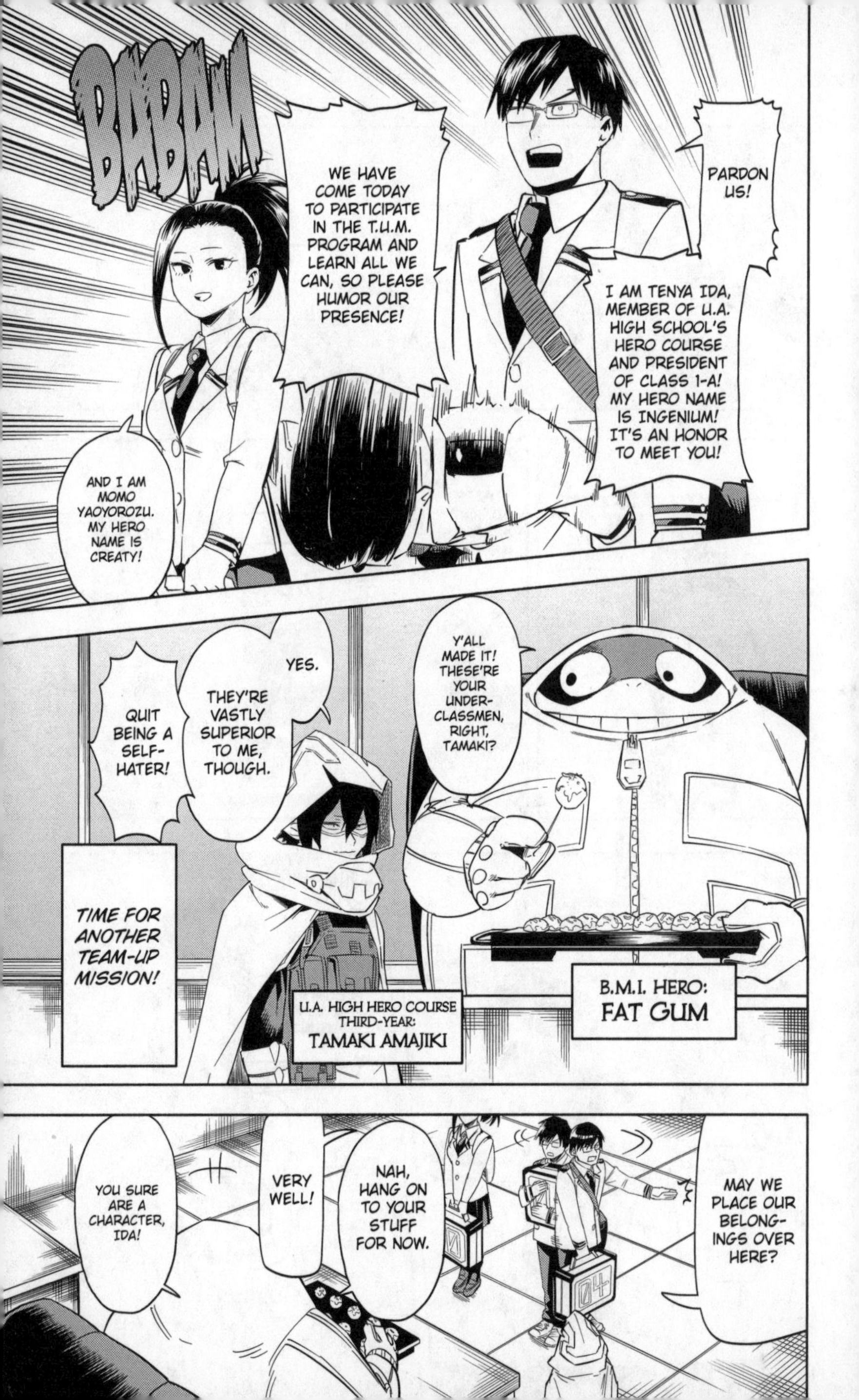
PARDON US!
I AM TENYA IDA, MEMBER OF U.A. HIGH SCHOOL'S HERO COURSE AND PRESIDENT OF CLASS 1-A! MY HERO NAME IS INGENIUM! IT'S AN HONOR TO MEET YOU!
WE HAVE COME TODAY TO PARTICIPATE IN THE T.U.M. PROGRAM AND LEARN ALL WE CAN, SO PLEASE HUMOR OUR PRESENCE!
BABAM
AND I AM MOMO YAOYOROZU. MY HERO NAME IS CREATY!
Y'ALL MADE IT! THESE'RE YOUR UNDER-CLASSMEN, RIGHT, TAMAKI?
B.M.I. HERO: FAT GUM
YES.
THEY'RE VASTLY SUPERIOR TO ME, THOUGH.
QUIT BEING A SELF-HATER!
U.A. HIGH HERO COURSE THIRD-YEAR: TAMAKI AMAJIKI
TIME FOR ANOTHER TEAM-UP MISSION!
MAY WE PLACE OUR BELONG-INGS OVER HERE?
NAH, HANG ON TO YOUR STUFF FOR NOW.
VERY WELL!
YOU SURE ARE A CHARACTER, IDA!

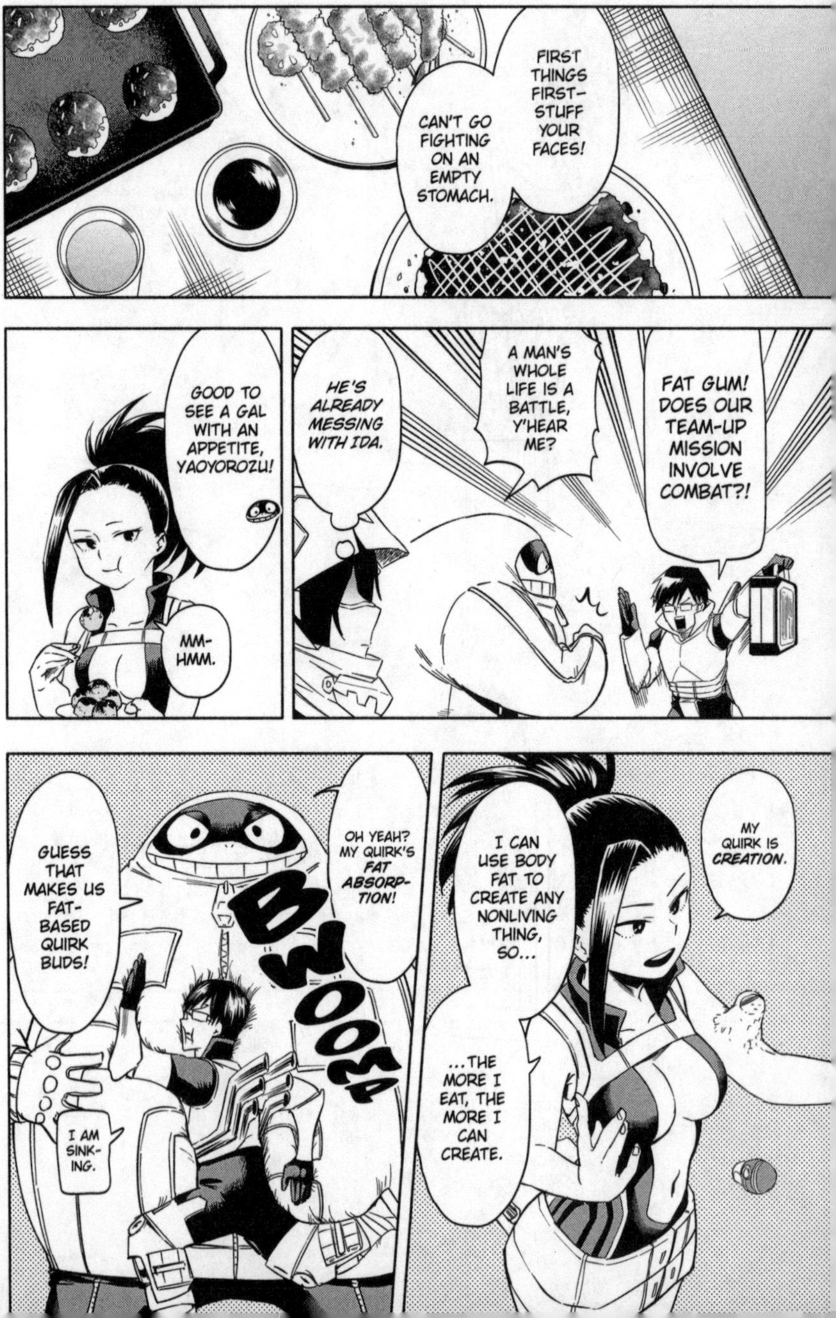
FIRST THINGS FIRST—STUFF YOUR FACES!
CAN'T GO FIGHTING ON AN EMPTY STOMACH.
FAT GUM! DOES OUR TEAM-UP MISSION INVOLVE COMBAT?!
A MAN'S WHOLE LIFE IS A BATTLE, Y'HEAR ME?
HE'S ALREADY MESSING WITH IDA.
GOOD TO SEE A GAL WITH AN APPETITE, YAOYOROZU!
MM-HMM.
MY QUIRK IS *CREATION*.
I CAN USE BODY FAT TO CREATE ANY NONLIVING THING, SO...
...THE MORE I EAT, THE MORE I CAN CREATE.
OH YEAH? MY QUIRK'S *FAT ABSORPTION!*
BWOOMP
GUESS THAT MAKES US FAT-BASED QUIRK BUDS!
I AM SINKING.

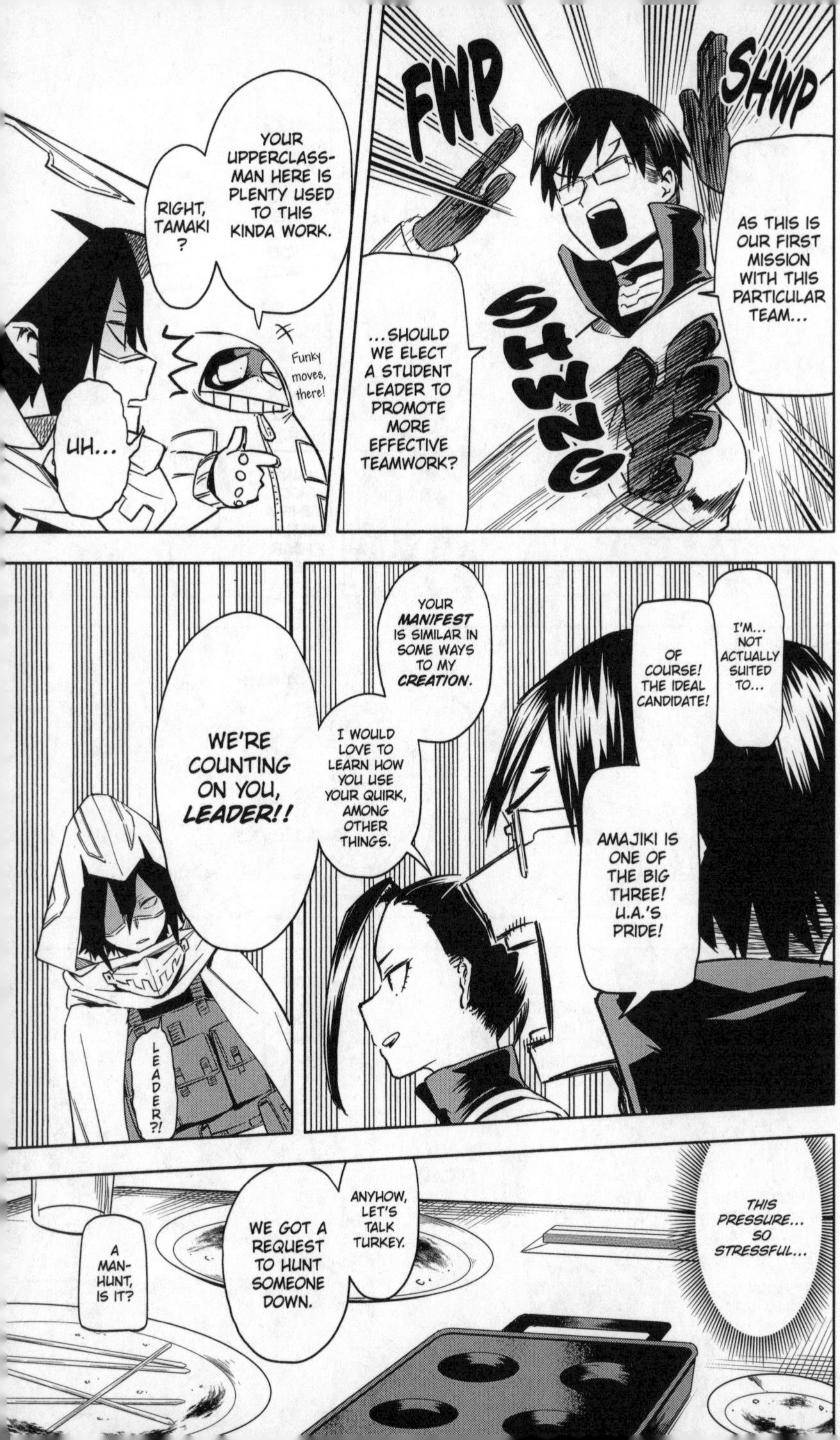
FWP
SHWP
AS THIS IS OUR FIRST MISSION WITH THIS PARTICULAR TEAM...
SHWNG
...SHOULD WE ELECT A STUDENT LEADER TO PROMOTE MORE EFFECTIVE TEAMWORK?
YOUR UPPERCLASSMAN HERE IS PLENTY USED TO THIS KINDA WORK.
RIGHT, TAMAKI?
Funky moves, there!
UH...
I'M... NOT ACTUALLY SUITED TO...
OF COURSE! THE IDEAL CANDIDATE!
YOUR *MANIFEST* IS SIMILAR IN SOME WAYS TO MY *CREATION*.
AMAJIKI IS ONE OF THE BIG THREE! U.A.'S PRIDE!
I WOULD LOVE TO LEARN HOW YOU USE YOUR QUIRK, AMONG OTHER THINGS.
WE'RE COUNTING ON YOU, *LEADER!!*
LEADER?!
THIS PRESSURE... SO STRESSFUL...
ANYHOW, LET'S TALK TURKEY.
WE GOT A REQUEST TO HUNT SOMEONE DOWN.
A MAN-HUNT, IS IT?

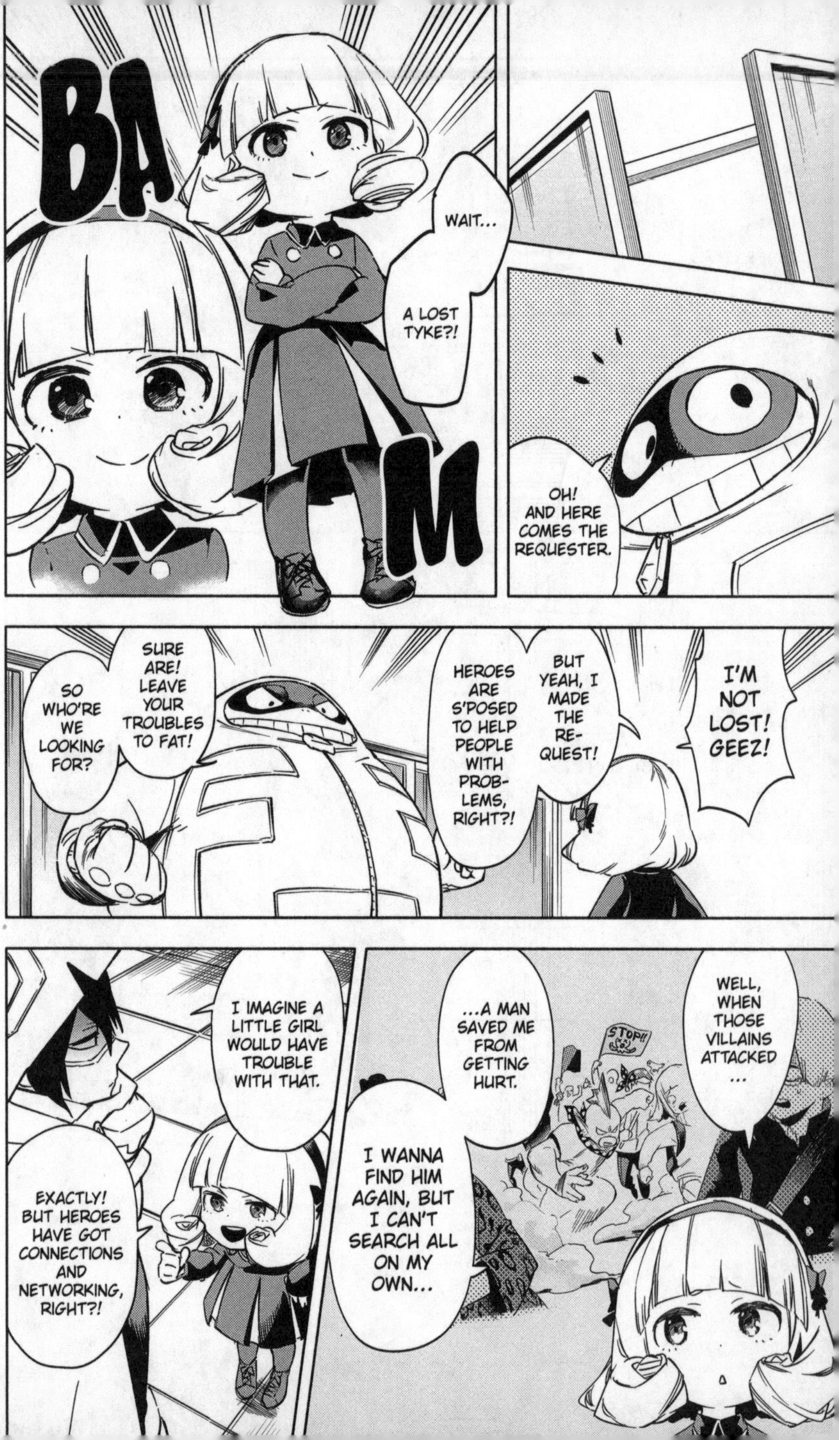
OH! AND HERE COMES THE REQUESTER.
WAIT...
A LOST TYKE?!
BAM
I'M NOT LOST! GEEZ!
BUT YEAH, I MADE THE RE-QUEST!
HEROES ARE S'POSED TO HELP PEOPLE WITH PROB-LEMS, RIGHT?!
SURE ARE! LEAVE YOUR TROUBLES TO FAT!
SO WHO'RE WE LOOKING FOR?
WELL, WHEN THOSE VILLAINS ATTACKED...
...A MAN SAVED ME FROM GETTING HURT.
STOP!!
I WANNA FIND HIM AGAIN, BUT I CAN'T SEARCH ALL ON MY OWN...
I IMAGINE A LITTLE GIRL WOULD HAVE TROUBLE WITH THAT.
EXACTLY! BUT HEROES HAVE GOT CONNECTIONS AND NETWORKING, RIGHT?!

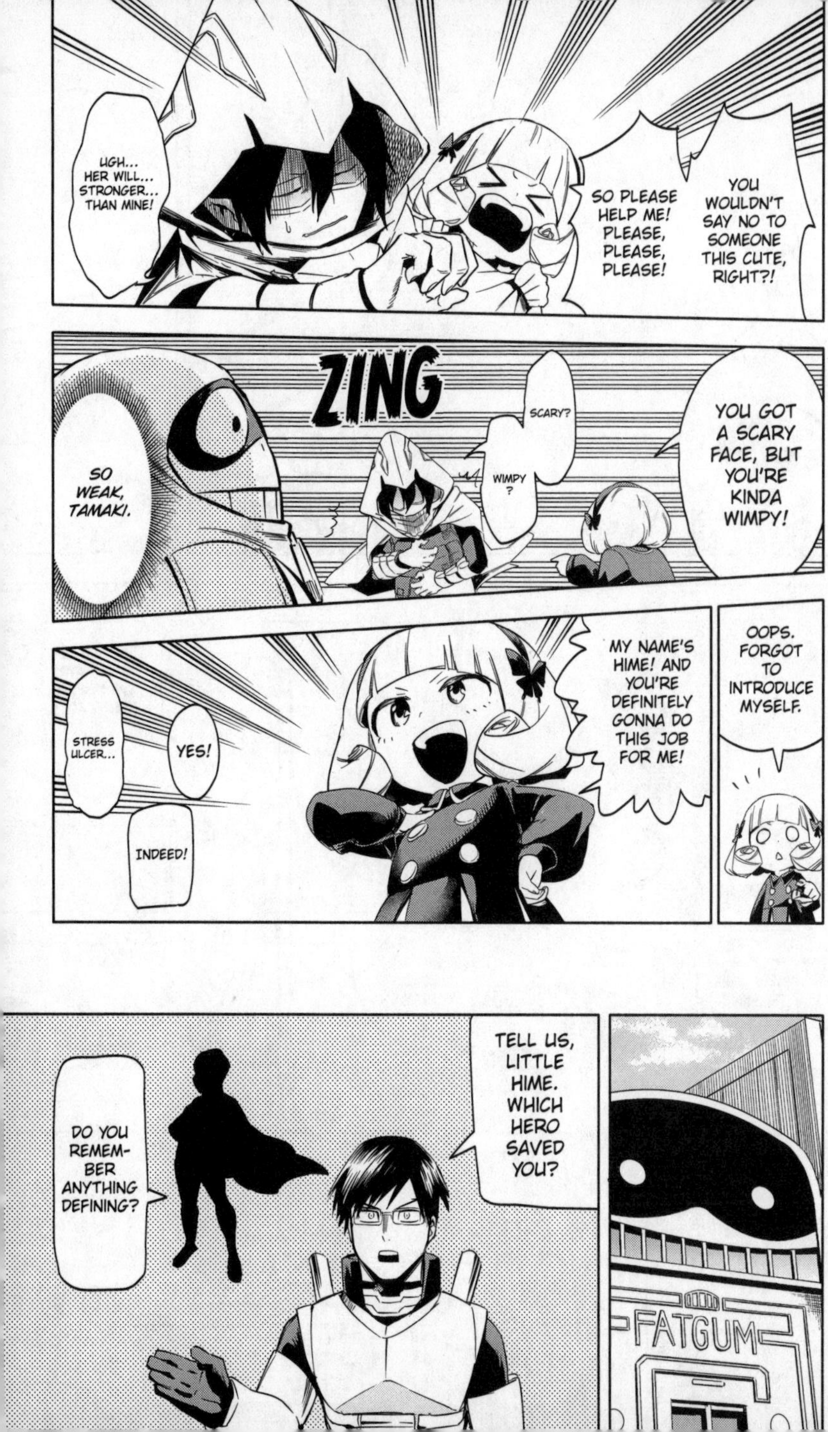

YOU WOULDN'T SAY NO TO SOMEONE THIS CUTE, RIGHT?!
SO PLEASE HELP ME! PLEASE, PLEASE, PLEASE!
UGH... HER WILL... STRONGER... THAN MINE!
YOU GOT A SCARY FACE, BUT YOU'RE KINDA WIMPY!
ZING
SCARY?
WIMPY?
SO WEAK, TAMAKI.
OOPS. FORGOT TO INTRODUCE MYSELF.
MY NAME'S HIME! AND YOU'RE DEFINITELY GONNA DO THIS JOB FOR ME!
YES!
STRESS ULCER...
INDEED!
FATGUM
TELL US, LITTLE HIME. WHICH HERO SAVED YOU?
DO YOU REMEM-BER ANYTHING DEFINING?

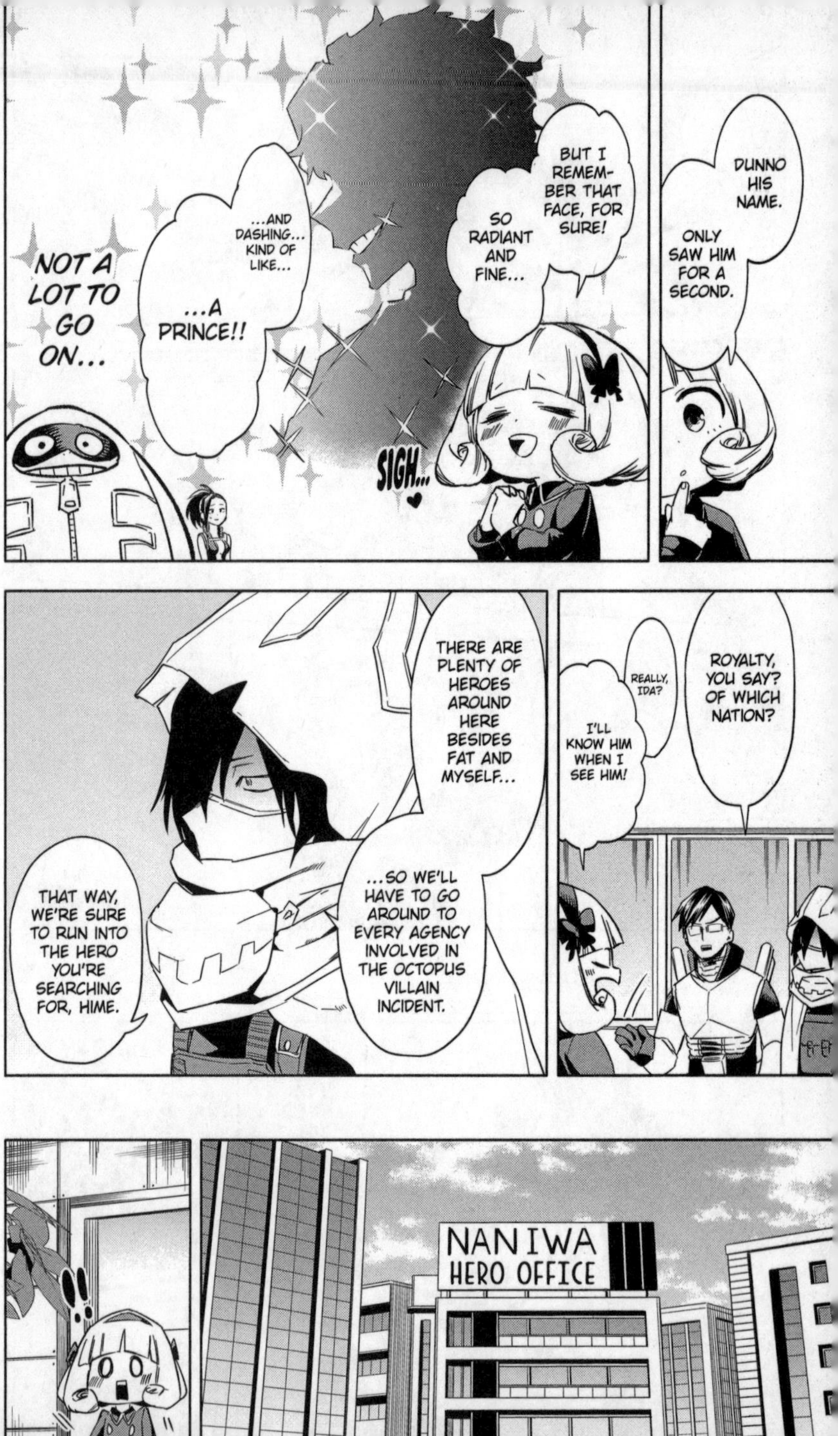
DUNNO HIS NAME.
ONLY SAW HIM FOR A SECOND.
BUT I REMEMBER THAT FACE, FOR SURE!
SO RADIANT AND FINE...
...AND DASHING... KIND OF LIKE...
...A PRINCE!!
SIGH...
NOT A LOT TO GO ON...
ROYALTY, YOU SAY? OF WHICH NATION?
REALLY, IDA?
I'LL KNOW HIM WHEN I SEE HIM!
THERE ARE PLENTY OF HEROES AROUND HERE BESIDES FAT AND MYSELF...
...SO WE'LL HAVE TO GO AROUND TO EVERY AGENCY INVOLVED IN THE OCTOPUS VILLAIN INCIDENT.
THAT WAY, WE'RE SURE TO RUN INTO THE HERO YOU'RE SEARCHING FOR, HIME.
NANIWA HERO OFFICE

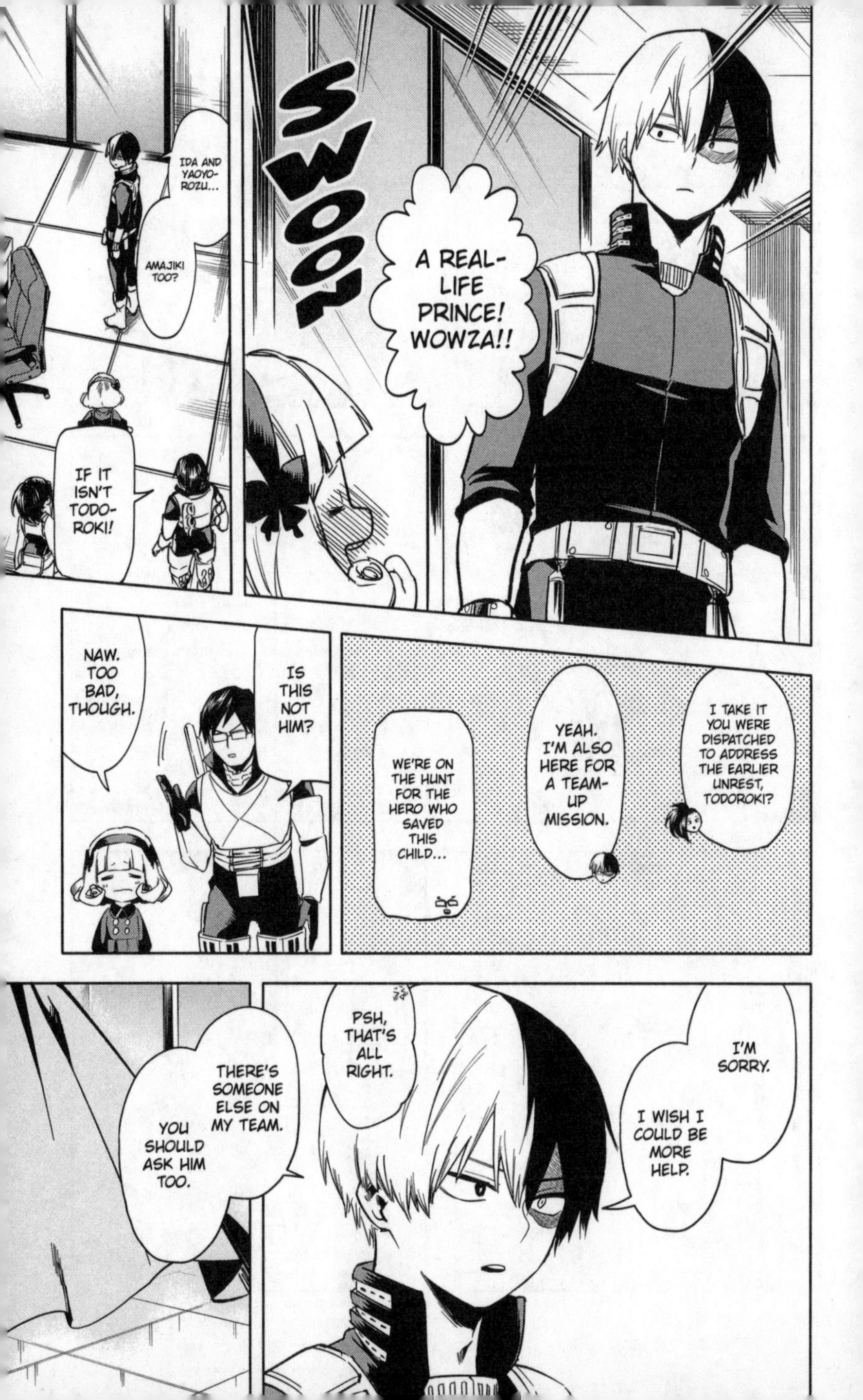
SWOON
A REAL-LIFE PRINCE! WOWZA!!
IDA AND YAOYOROZU...
AMAJIKI TOO?
IF IT ISN'T TODOROKI!
I TAKE IT YOU WERE DISPATCHED TO ADDRESS THE EARLIER UNREST, TODOROKI?
YEAH. I'M ALSO HERE FOR A TEAM-UP MISSION.
WE'RE ON THE HUNT FOR THE HERO WHO SAVED THIS CHILD...
IS THIS NOT HIM?
NAW. TOO BAD, THOUGH.
I'M SORRY.
I WISH I COULD BE MORE HELP.
PSH, THAT'S ALL RIGHT.
THERE'S SOMEONE ELSE ON MY TEAM.
YOU SHOULD ASK HIM TOO.

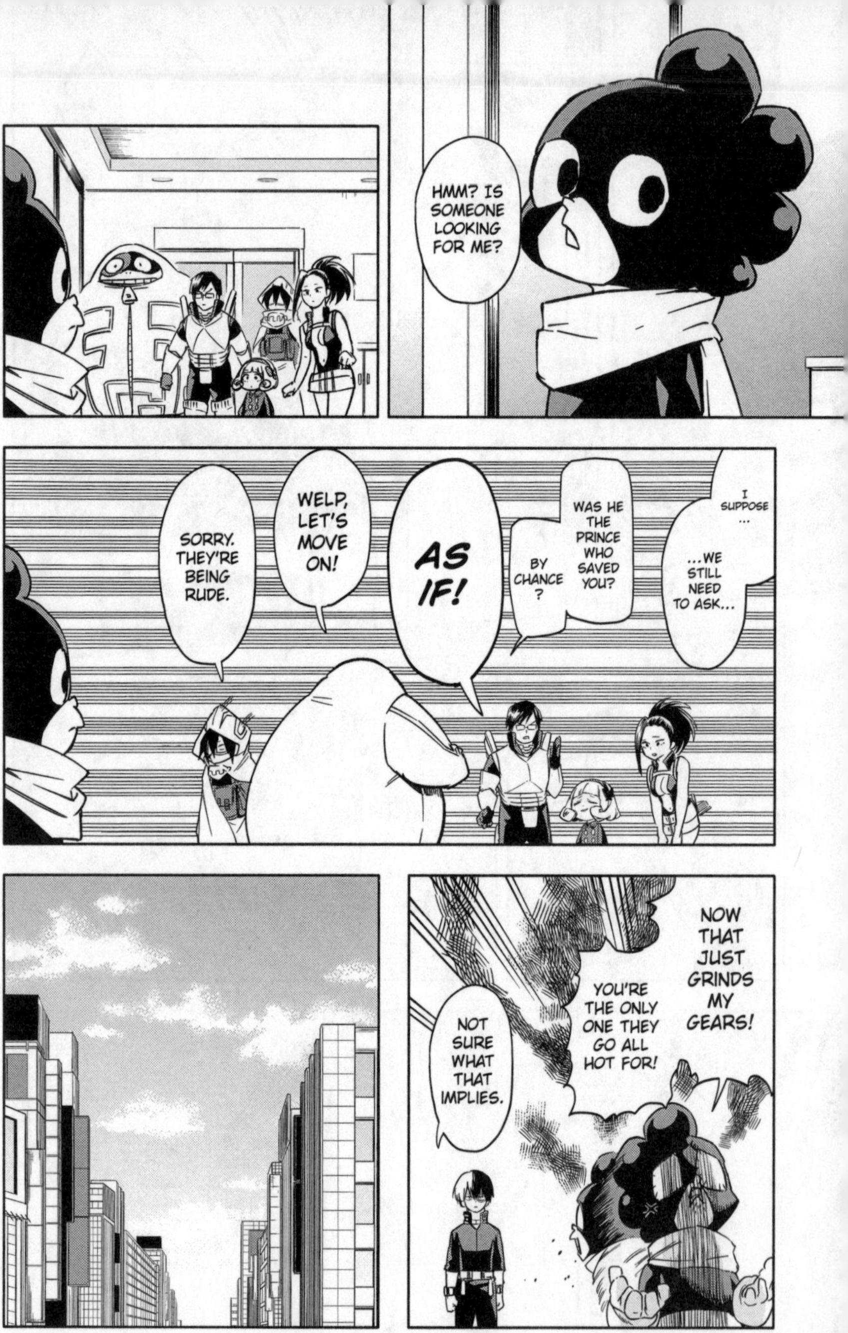
HMM? IS SOMEONE LOOKING FOR ME?
I SUPPOSE... ...WE STILL NEED TO ASK...
WAS HE THE PRINCE WHO SAVED YOU?
BY CHANCE?
AS IF!
WELP, LET'S MOVE ON!
SORRY. THEY'RE BEING RUDE.
NOW THAT JUST GRINDS MY GEARS!
YOU'RE THE ONLY ONE THEY GO ALL HOT FOR!
NOT SURE WHAT THAT IMPLIES.

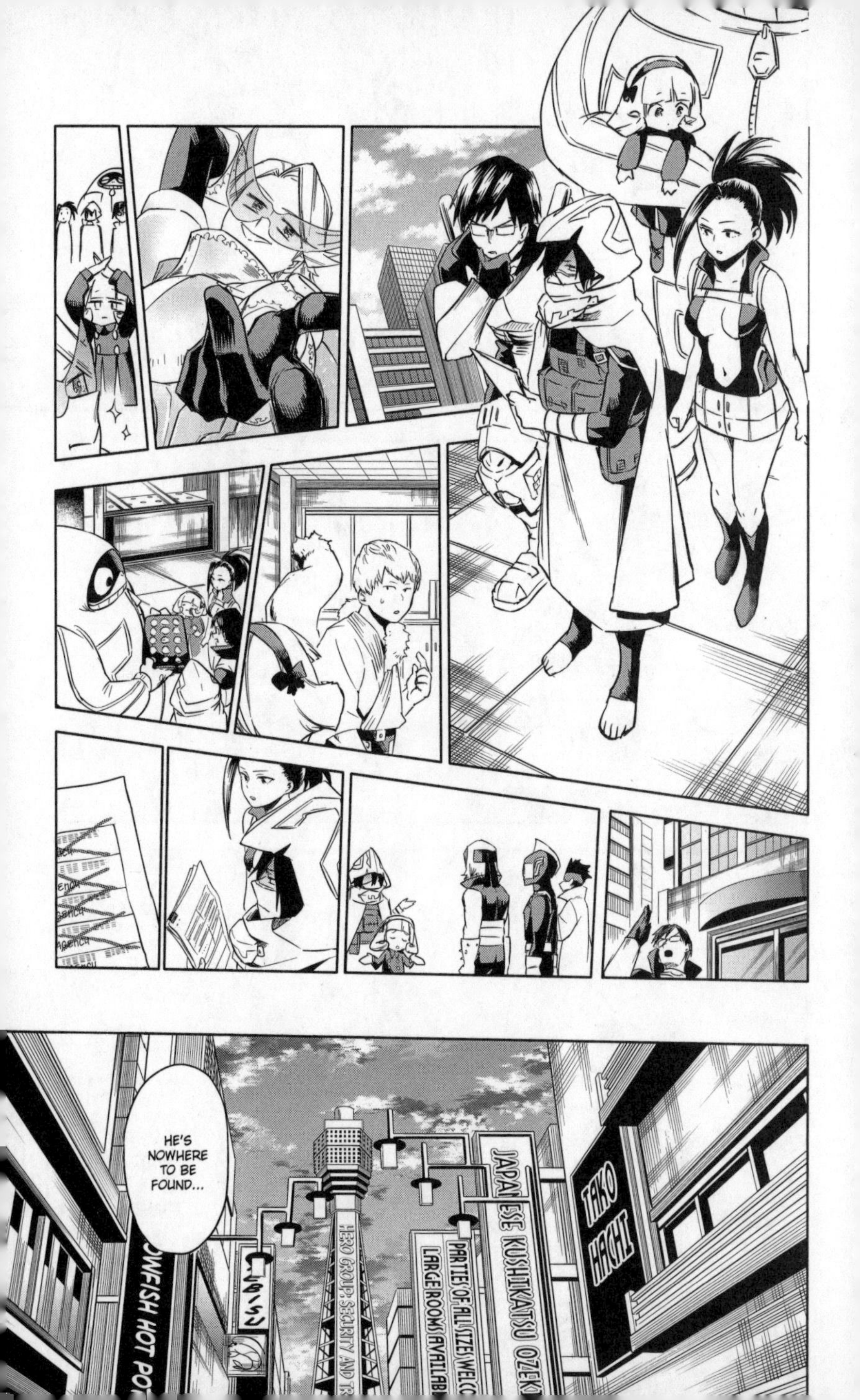
TAKO HACHI
JAPANESE KUSHIKATSU OZEK
PARTIES OF ALL SIZES WELCO
LARGE ROOMS AVAILAB
HERO GROUP: SECURITY AND T
HE'S NOWHERE TO BE FOUND...
OWFISH HOT PO

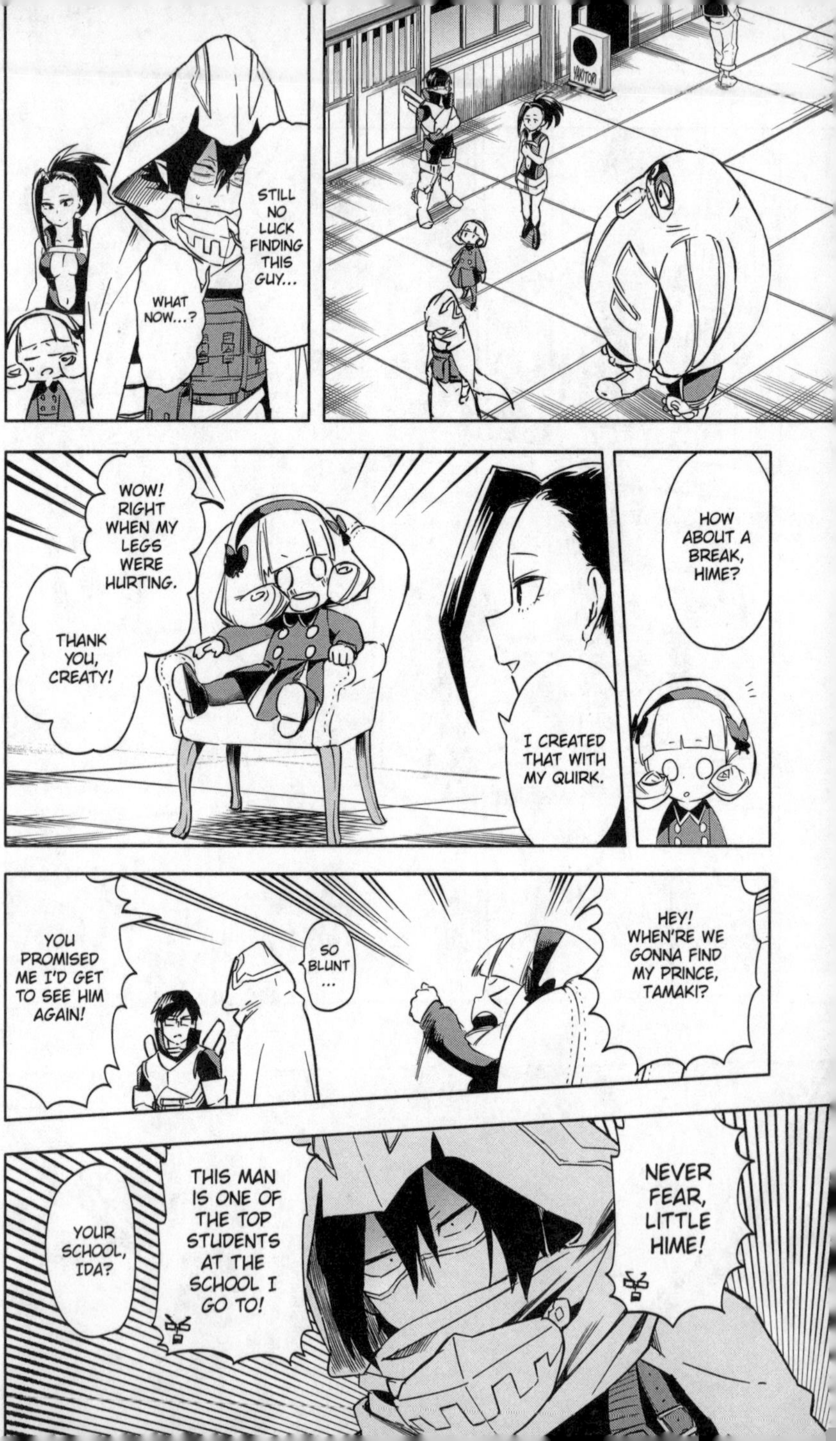
YAKITORI
STILL NO LUCK FINDING THIS GUY...
WHAT NOW...?
HOW ABOUT A BREAK, HIME?
I CREATED THAT WITH MY QUIRK.
WOW! RIGHT WHEN MY LEGS WERE HURTING.
THANK YOU, CREATY!
HEY! WHEN'RE WE GONNA FIND MY PRINCE, TAMAKI?
SO BLUNT...
YOU PROMISED ME I'D GET TO SEE HIM AGAIN!
NEVER FEAR, LITTLE HIME!
THIS MAN IS ONE OF THE TOP STUDENTS AT THE SCHOOL I GO TO!
YOUR SCHOOL, IDA?

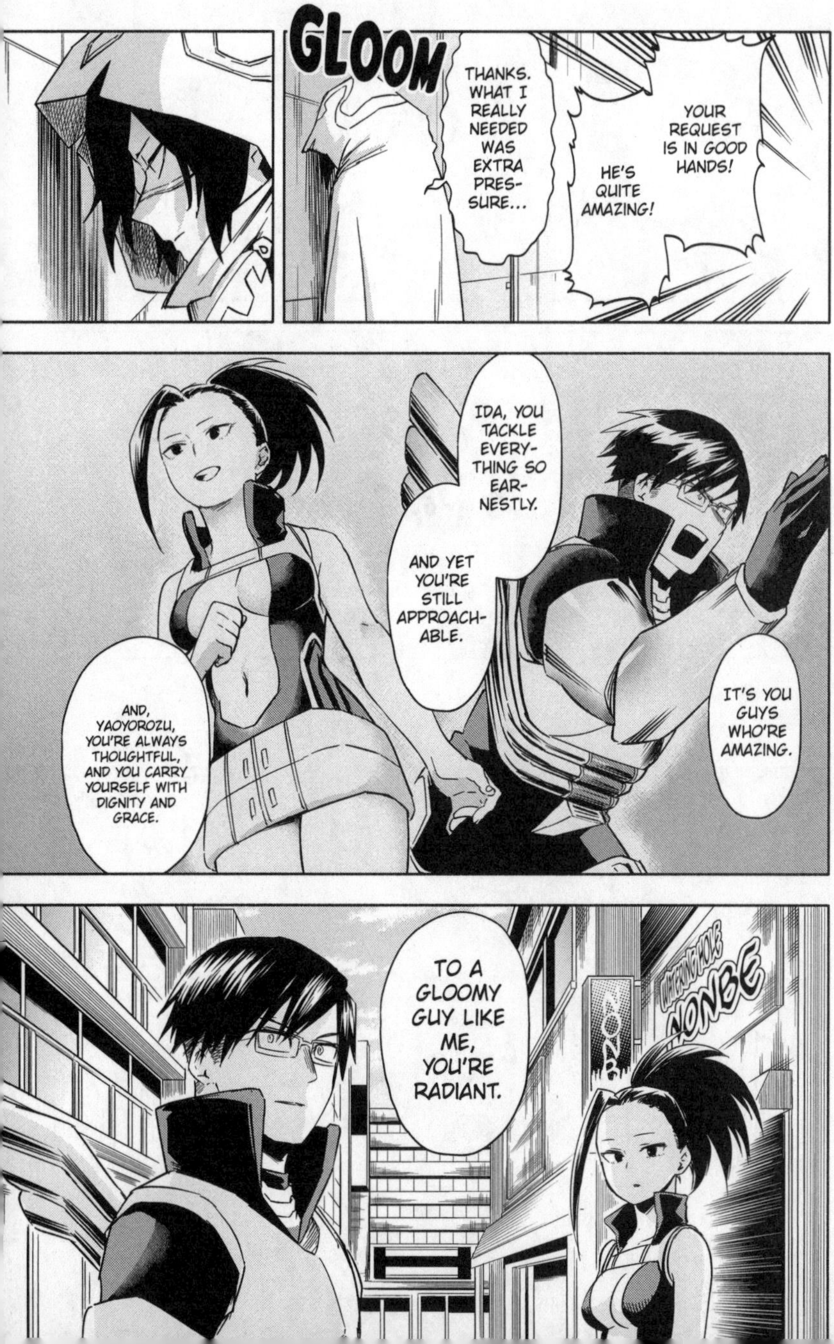
YOUR REQUEST IS IN GOOD HANDS!
HE'S QUITE AMAZING!
THANKS. WHAT I REALLY NEEDED WAS EXTRA PRES-SURE...
GLOOM
IT'S YOU GUYS WHO'RE AMAZING.
IDA, YOU TACKLE EVERY-THING SO EAR-NESTLY.
AND YET YOU'RE STILL APPROACH-ABLE.
AND, YAOYOROZU, YOU'RE ALWAYS THOUGHTFUL, AND YOU CARRY YOURSELF WITH DIGNITY AND GRACE.
TO A GLOOMY GUY LIKE ME, YOU'RE RADIANT.
NONBE

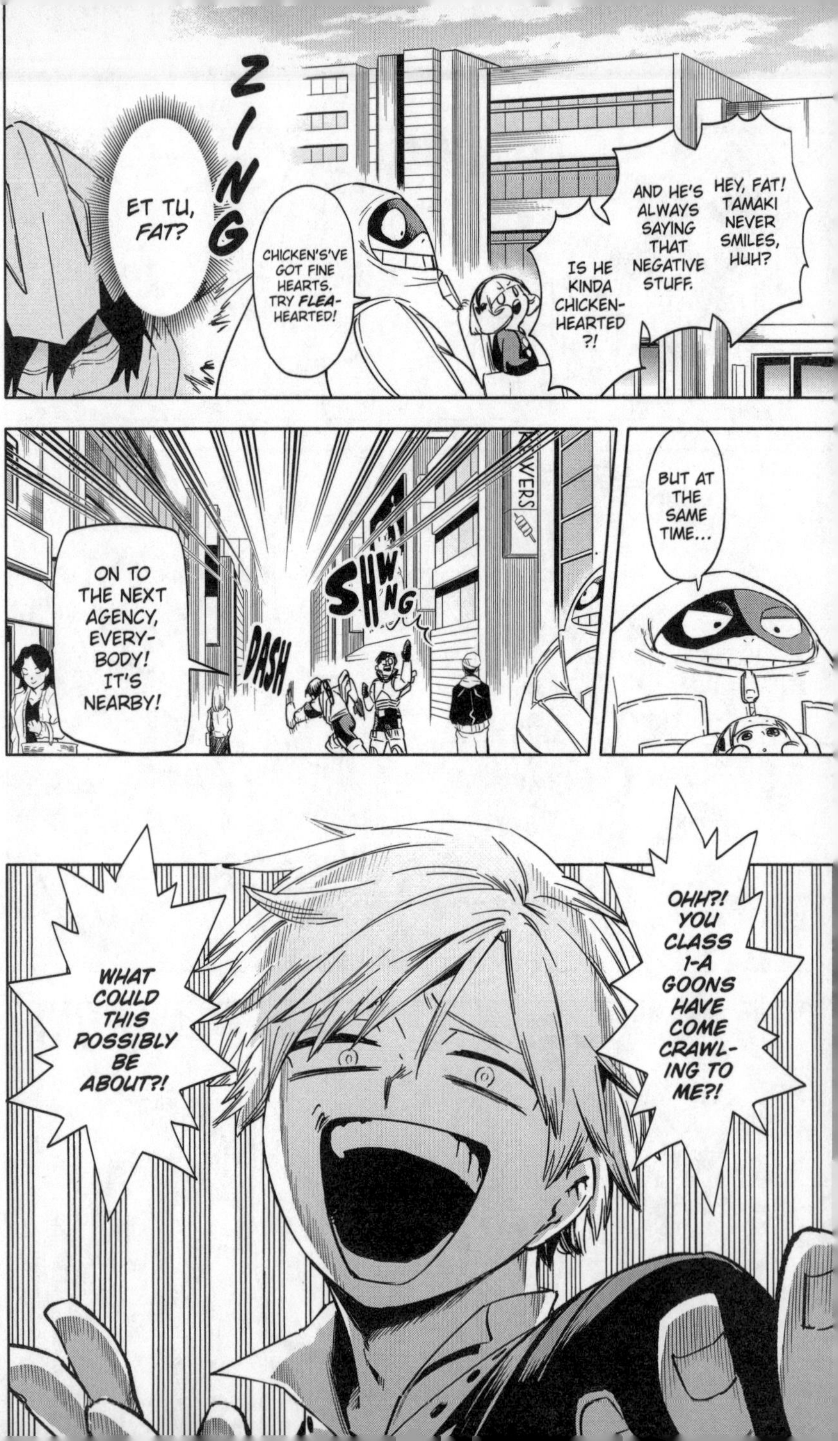
HEY, FAT! TAMAKI NEVER SMILES, HUH?
AND HE'S ALWAYS SAYING THAT NEGATIVE STUFF.
IS HE KINDA CHICKEN-HEARTED?!
CHICKEN'S'VE GOT FINE HEARTS. TRY FLEA-HEARTED!
ZING
ET TU, FAT?
BUT AT THE SAME TIME...
SHWNG
DASH
ON TO THE NEXT AGENCY, EVERYBODY! IT'S NEARBY!
OHH?! YOU CLASS 1-A GOONS HAVE COME CRAWLING TO ME?!
WHAT COULD THIS POSSIBLY BE ABOUT?!

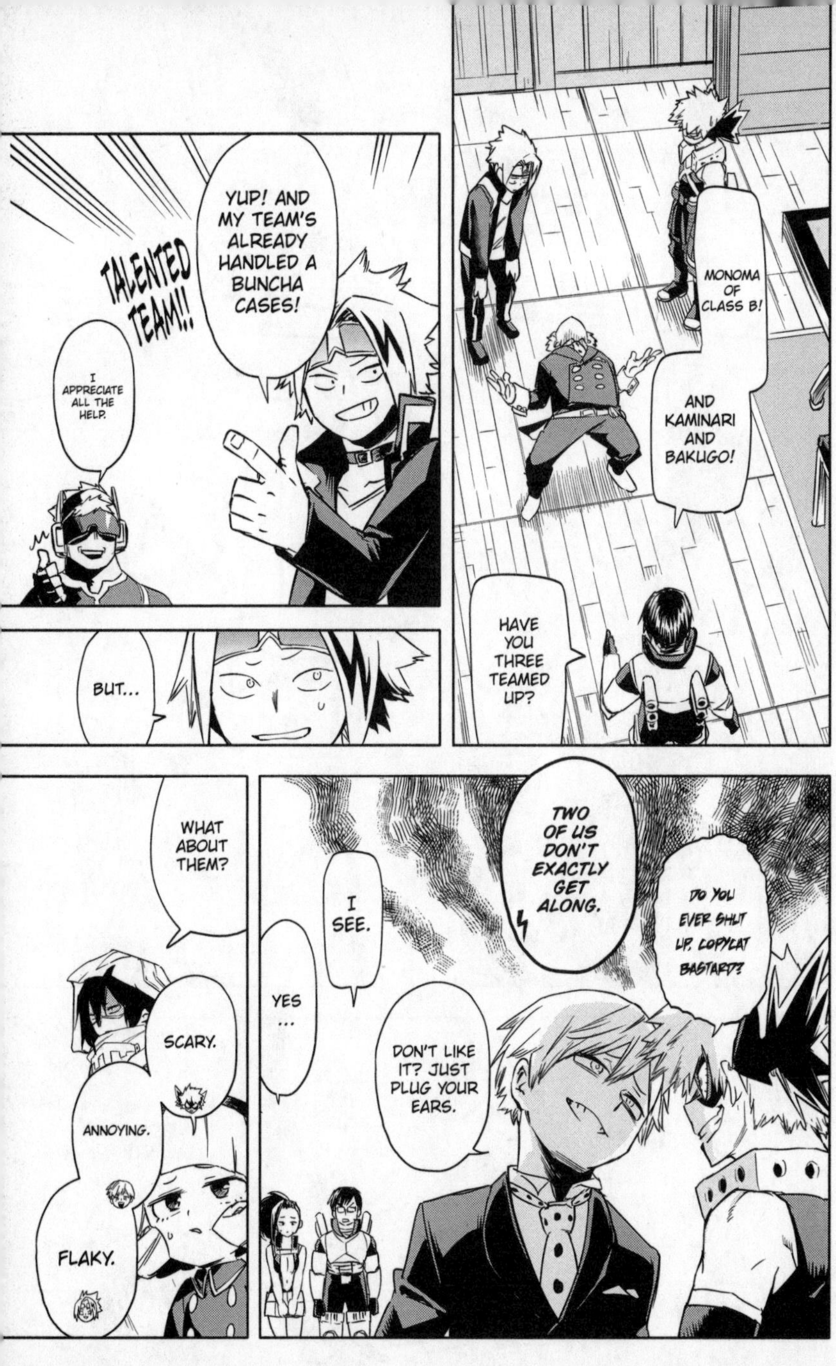
MONOMA OF CLASS B!
AND KAMINARI AND BAKUGO!
HAVE YOU THREE TEAMED UP?
TALENTED TEAM!!
YUP! AND MY TEAM'S ALREADY HANDLED A BUNCHA CASES!
I APPRECIATE ALL THE HELP.
BUT...
TWO OF US DON'T EXACTLY GET ALONG.
DO YOU EVER SHUT UP, COPYCAT BASTARD?
I SEE.
DON'T LIKE IT? JUST PLUG YOUR EARS.
YES...
WHAT ABOUT THEM?
SCARY.
ANNOYING.
FLAKY.

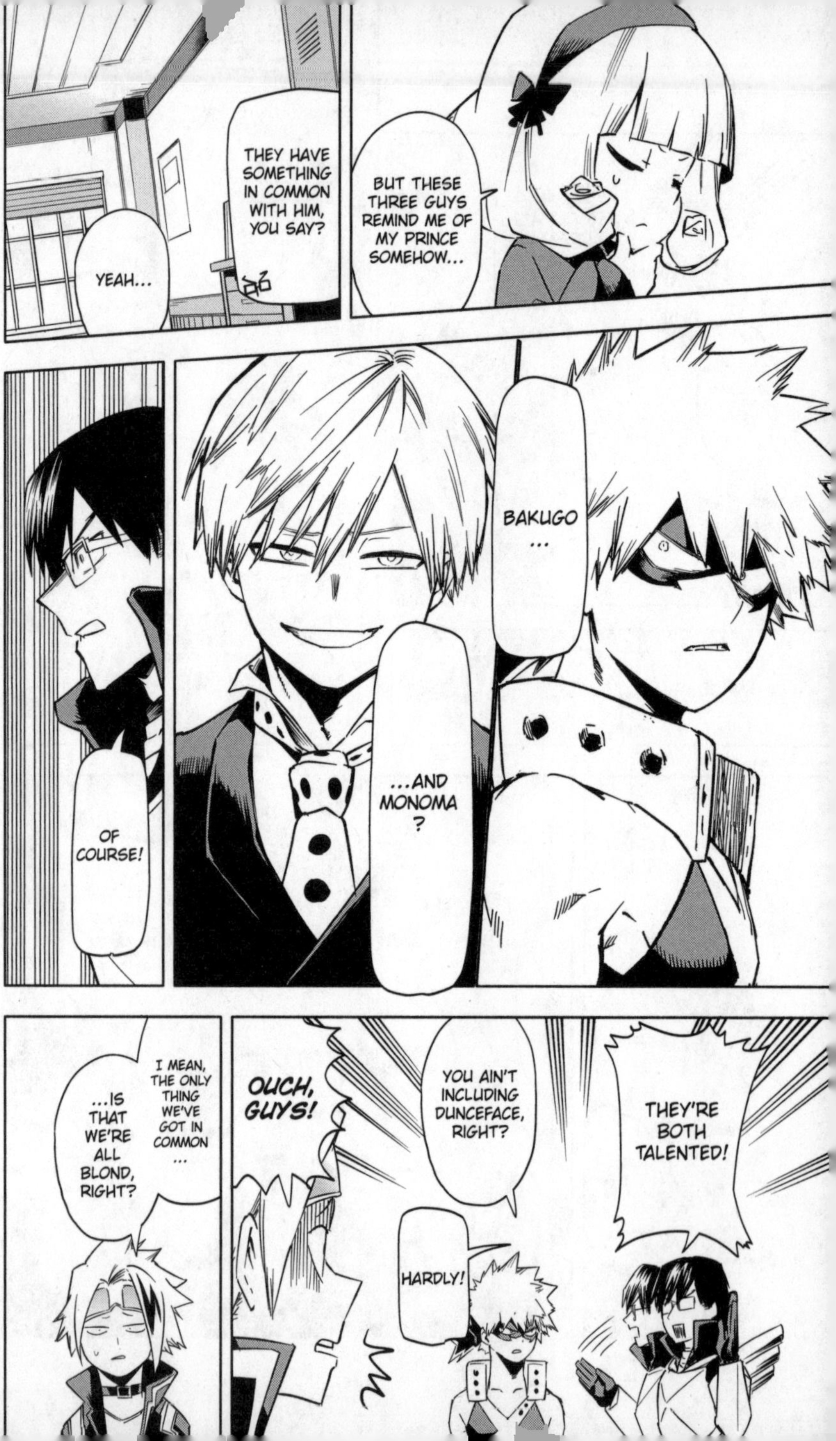
BUT THESE THREE GUYS REMIND ME OF MY PRINCE SOMEHOW...
THEY HAVE SOMETHING IN COMMON WITH HIM, YOU SAY?
YEAH...
BAKUGO ...
...AND MONOMA ?
OF COURSE!
THEY'RE BOTH TALENTED!
YOU AIN'T INCLUDING DUNCEFACE, RIGHT?
HARDLY!
OUCH, GUYS!
I MEAN, THE ONLY THING WE'VE GOT IN COMMON ...
...IS THAT WE'RE ALL BLOND, RIGHT?

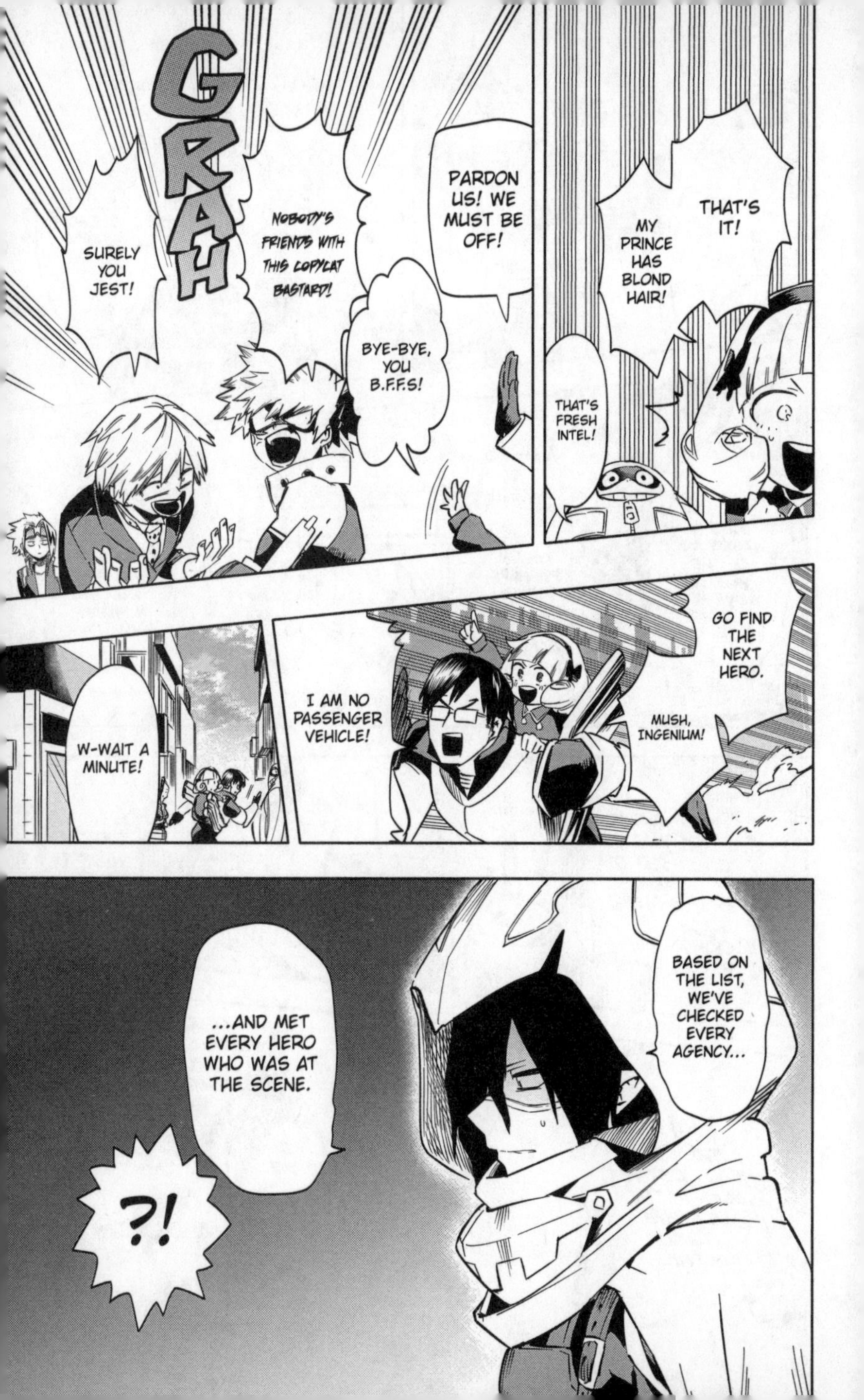
THAT'S IT!
MY PRINCE HAS BLOND HAIR!
THAT'S FRESH INTEL!
PARDON US! WE MUST BE OFF!
BYE-BYE, YOU B.F.F.S!
NOBODY'S FRIENDS WITH THIS COPYCAT BASTARD!
GRAH
SURELY YOU JEST!
GO FIND THE NEXT HERO.
MUSH, INGENIUM!
I AM NO PASSENGER VEHICLE!
W-WAIT A MINUTE!
BASED ON THE LIST, WE'VE CHECKED EVERY AGENCY...
...AND MET EVERY HERO WHO WAS AT THE SCENE.
?!

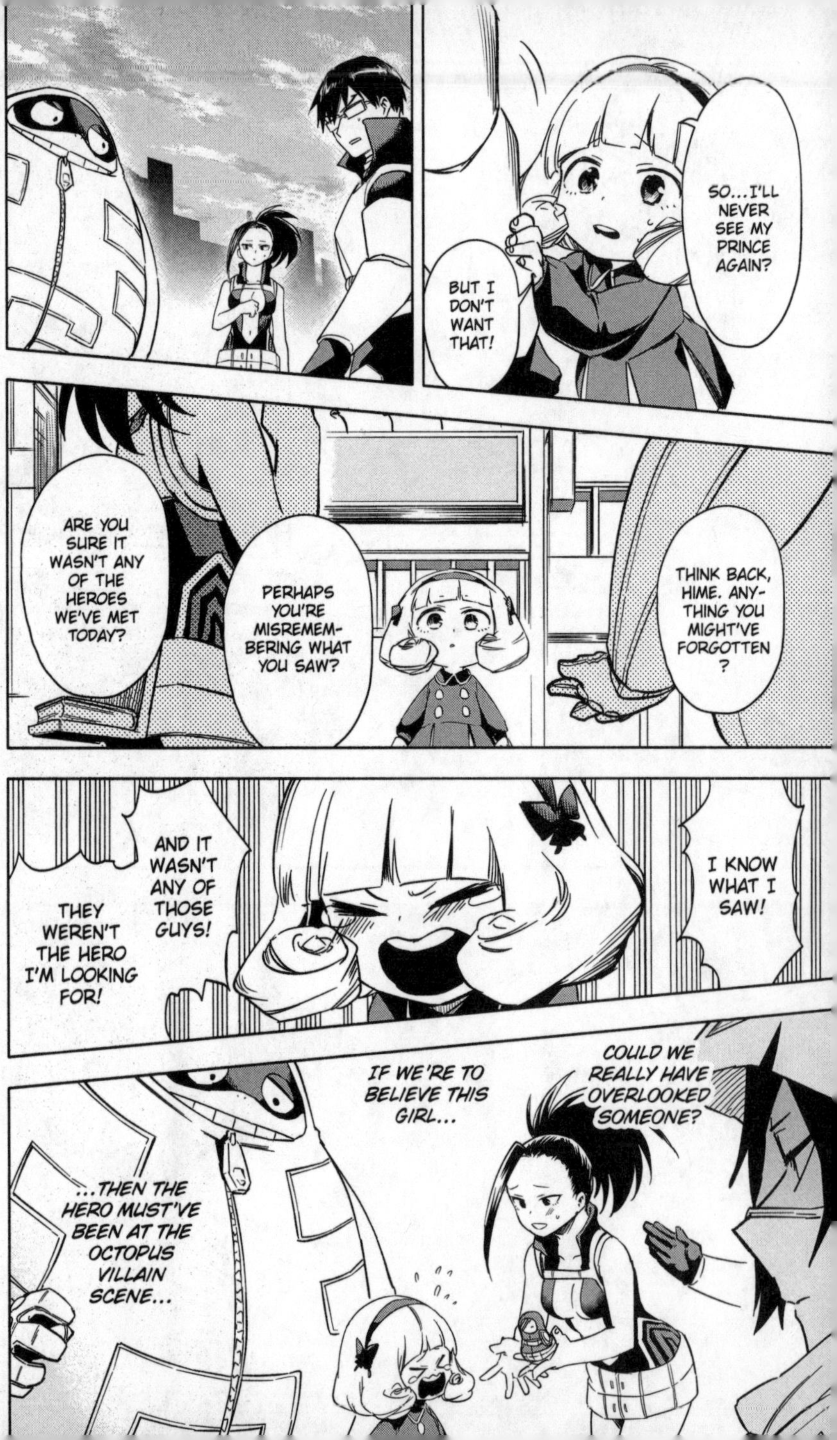
SO...I'LL NEVER SEE MY PRINCE AGAIN?
BUT I DON'T WANT THAT!
THINK BACK, HIME. ANYTHING YOU MIGHT'VE FORGOTTEN?
PERHAPS YOU'RE MISREMEMBERING WHAT YOU SAW?
ARE YOU SURE IT WASN'T ANY OF THE HEROES WE'VE MET TODAY?
I KNOW WHAT I SAW!
AND IT WASN'T ANY OF THOSE GUYS!
THEY WEREN'T THE HERO I'M LOOKING FOR!
COULD WE REALLY HAVE OVERLOOKED SOMEONE?
IF WE'RE TO BELIEVE THIS GIRL...
...THEN THE HERO MUST'VE BEEN AT THE OCTOPUS VILLAIN SCENE...

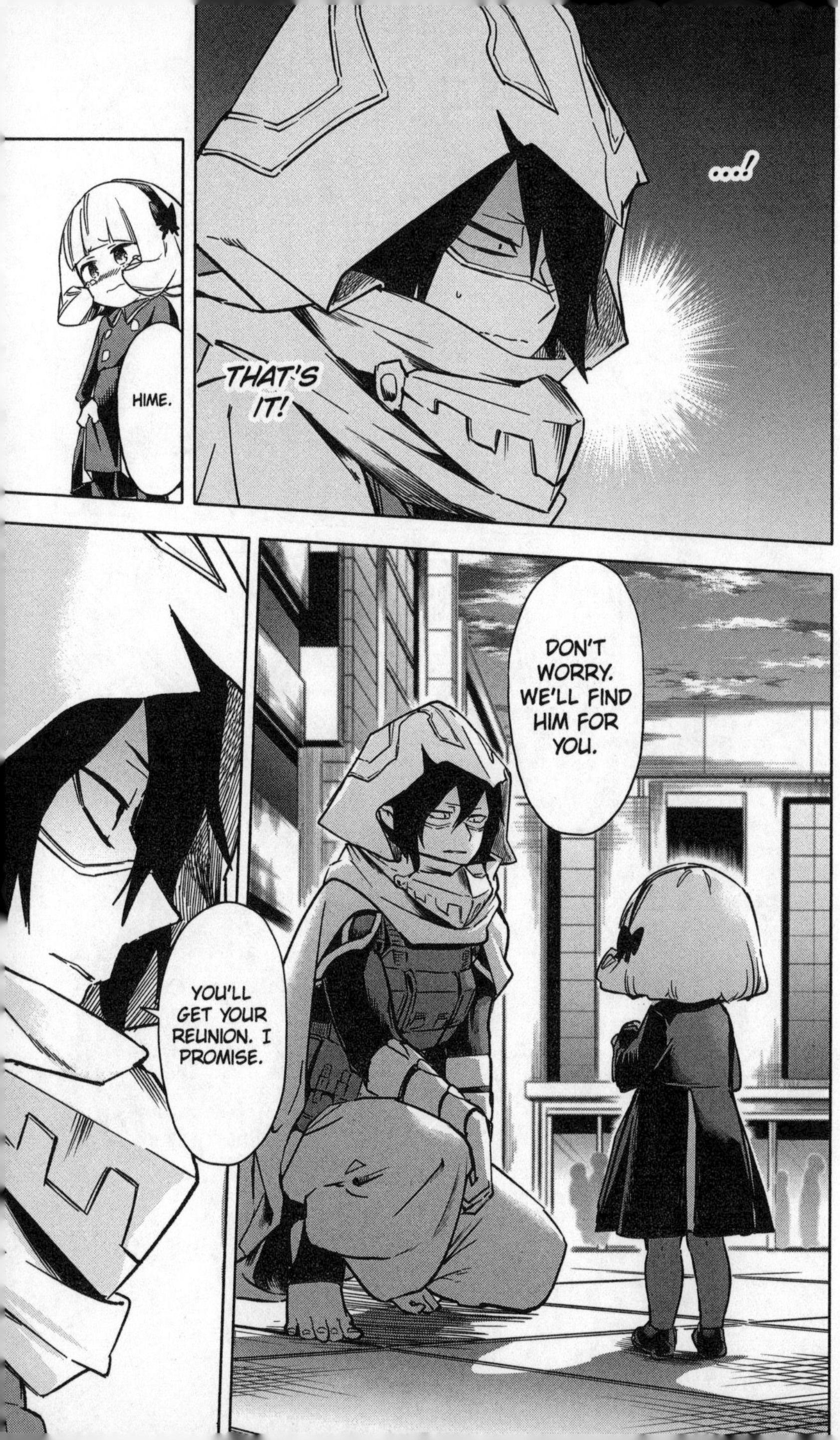
...!
THAT'S IT!
HIME.
DON'T WORRY. WE'LL FIND HIM FOR YOU.
YOU'LL GET YOUR REUNION. I PROMISE.

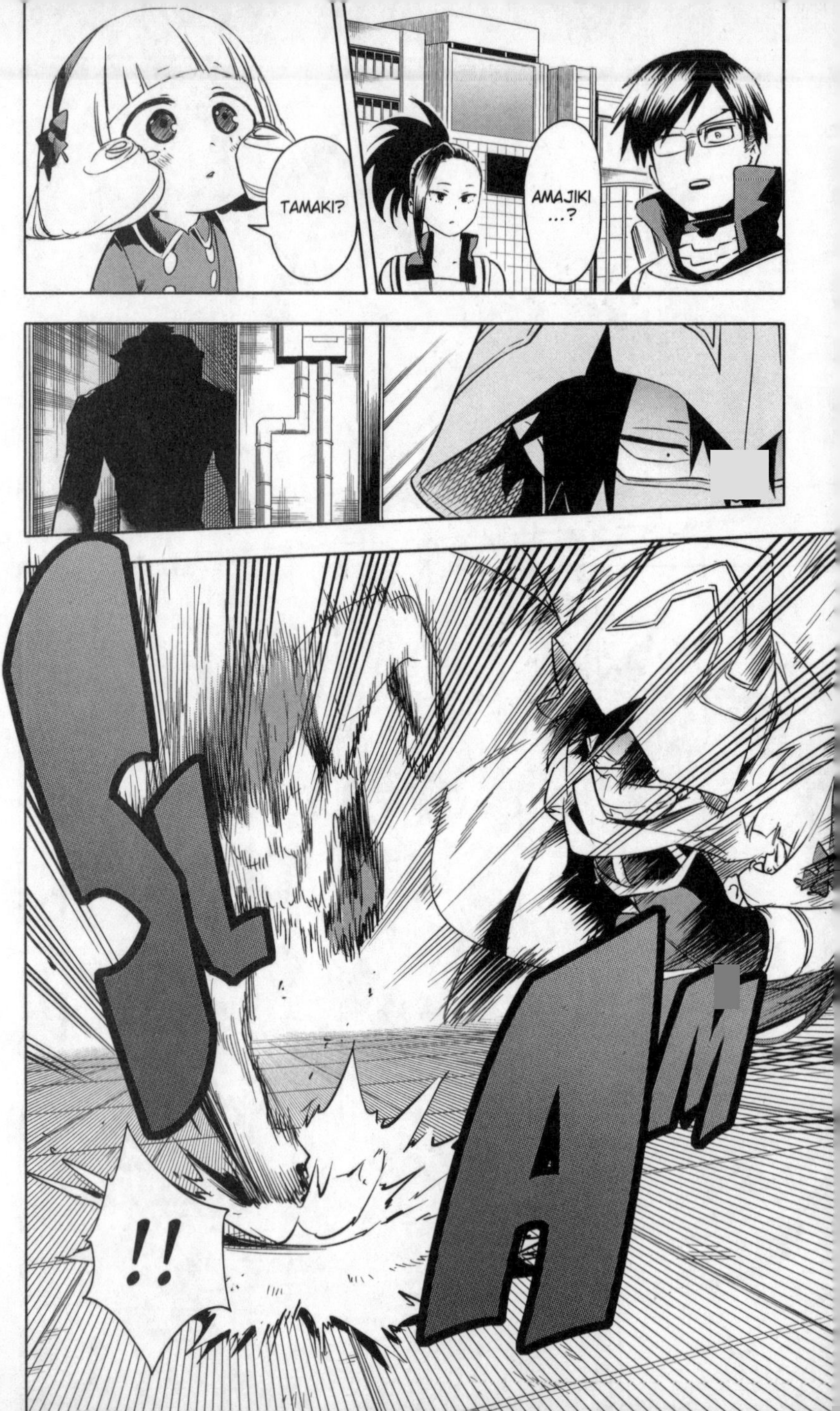
AMAJIKI ...?
TAMAKI?
SLAM
!!

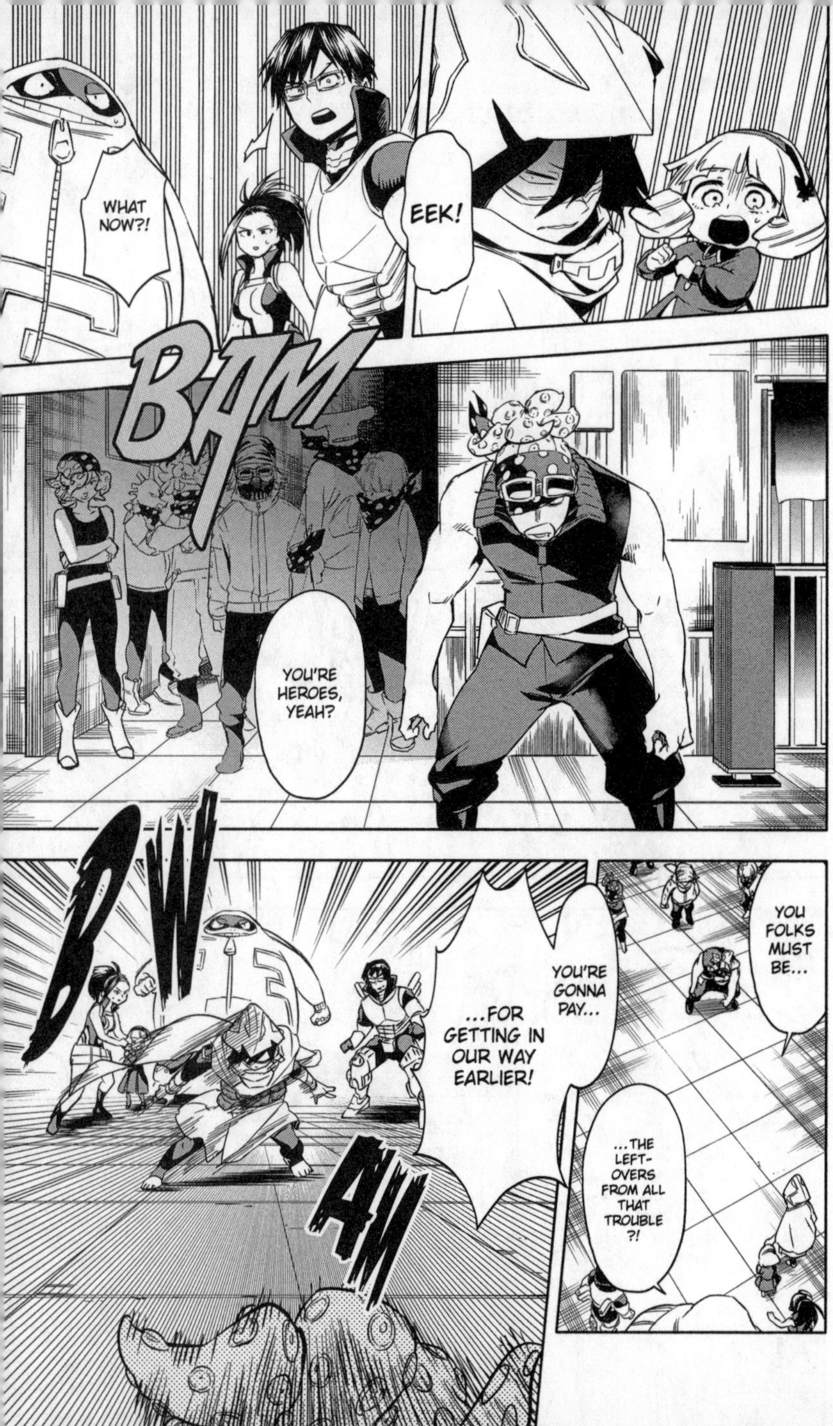
EEK!
WHAT NOW?!
BAM
YOU'RE HEROES, YEAH?
YOU FOLKS MUST BE...
...THE LEFT-OVERS FROM ALL THAT TROUBLE?!
YOU'RE GONNA PAY...
...FOR GETTING IN OUR WAY EARLIER!

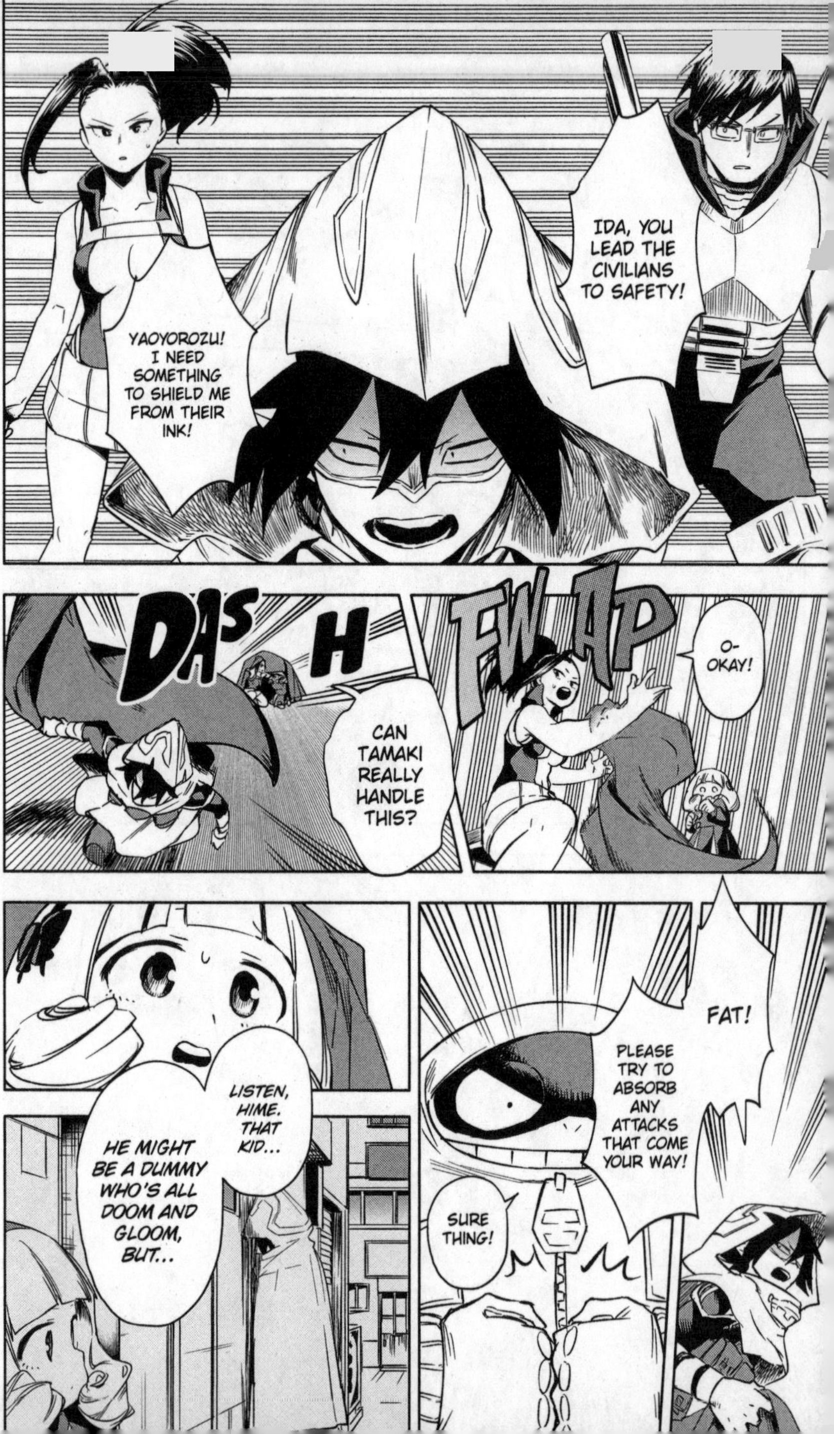
IDA, YOU LEAD THE CIVILIANS TO SAFETY!
YAOYOROZU! I NEED SOMETHING TO SHIELD ME FROM THEIR INK!
FWAP
O-OKAY!
DASH
CAN TAMAKI REALLY HANDLE THIS?
FAT!
PLEASE TRY TO ABSORB ANY ATTACKS THAT COME YOUR WAY!
SURE THING!
LISTEN, HIME. THAT KID...
HE MIGHT BE A DUMMY WHO'S ALL DOOM AND GLOOM, BUT...

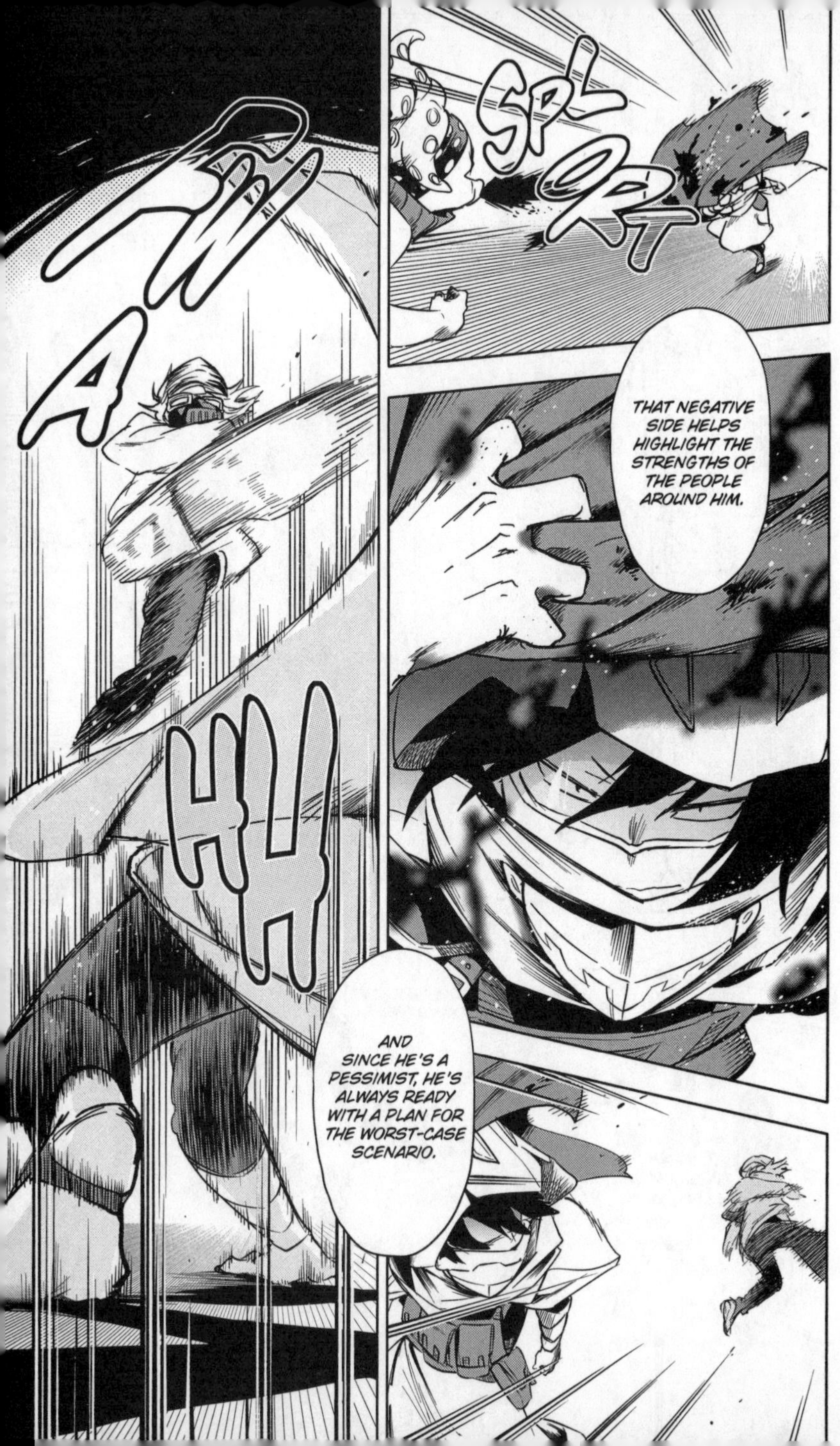
SPLORT
THAT NEGATIVE SIDE HELPS HIGHLIGHT THE STRENGTHS OF THE PEOPLE AROUND HIM.
AND SINCE HE'S A PESSIMIST, HE'S ALWAYS READY WITH A PLAN FOR THE WORST-CASE SCENARIO.

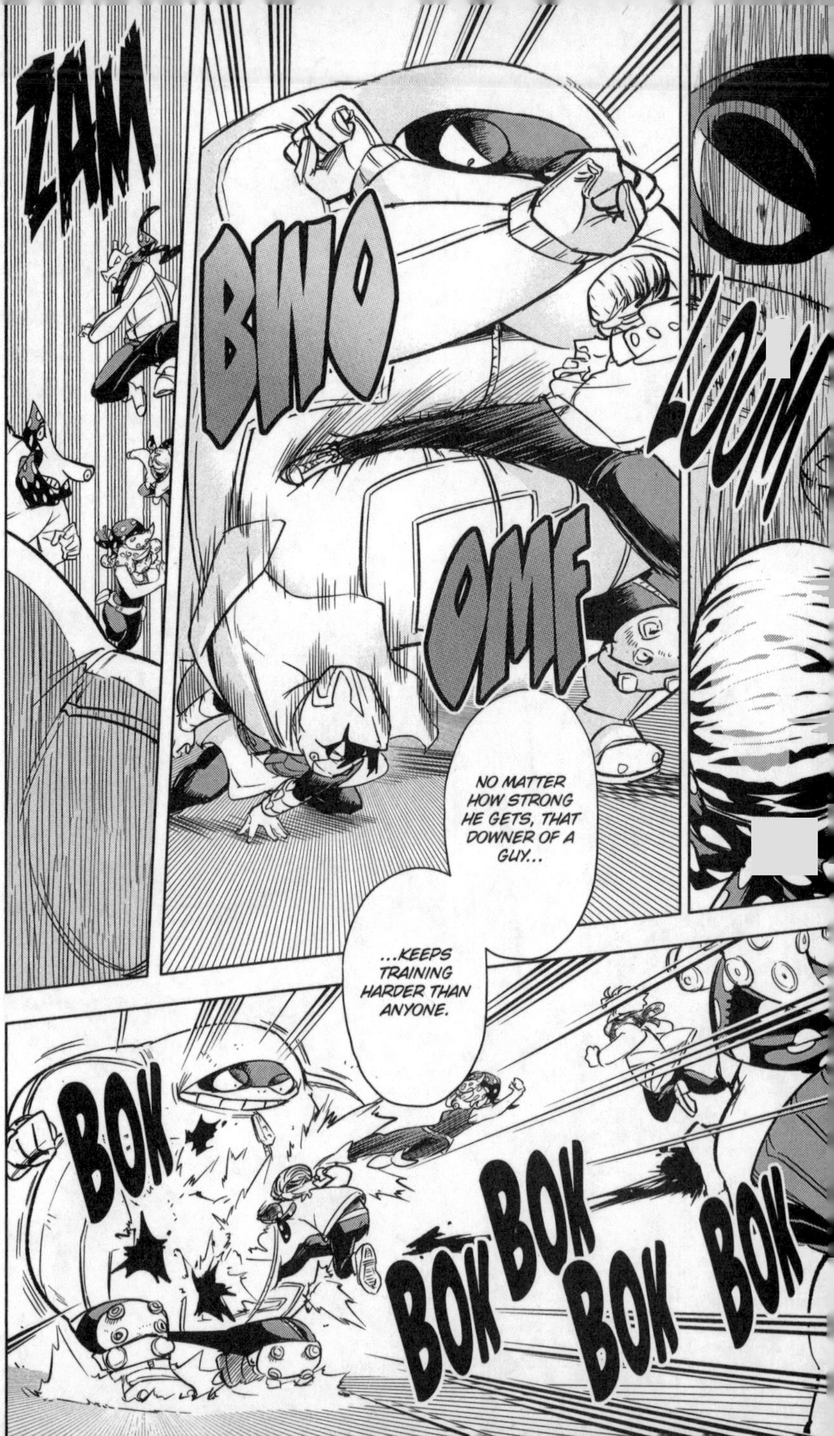
ZAM
BWO
OMF
NO MATTER HOW STRONG HE GETS, THAT DOWNER OF A GUY...
...KEEPS TRAINING HARDER THAN ANYONE.
BOK
BOK BOK
BOK BOK
BOK

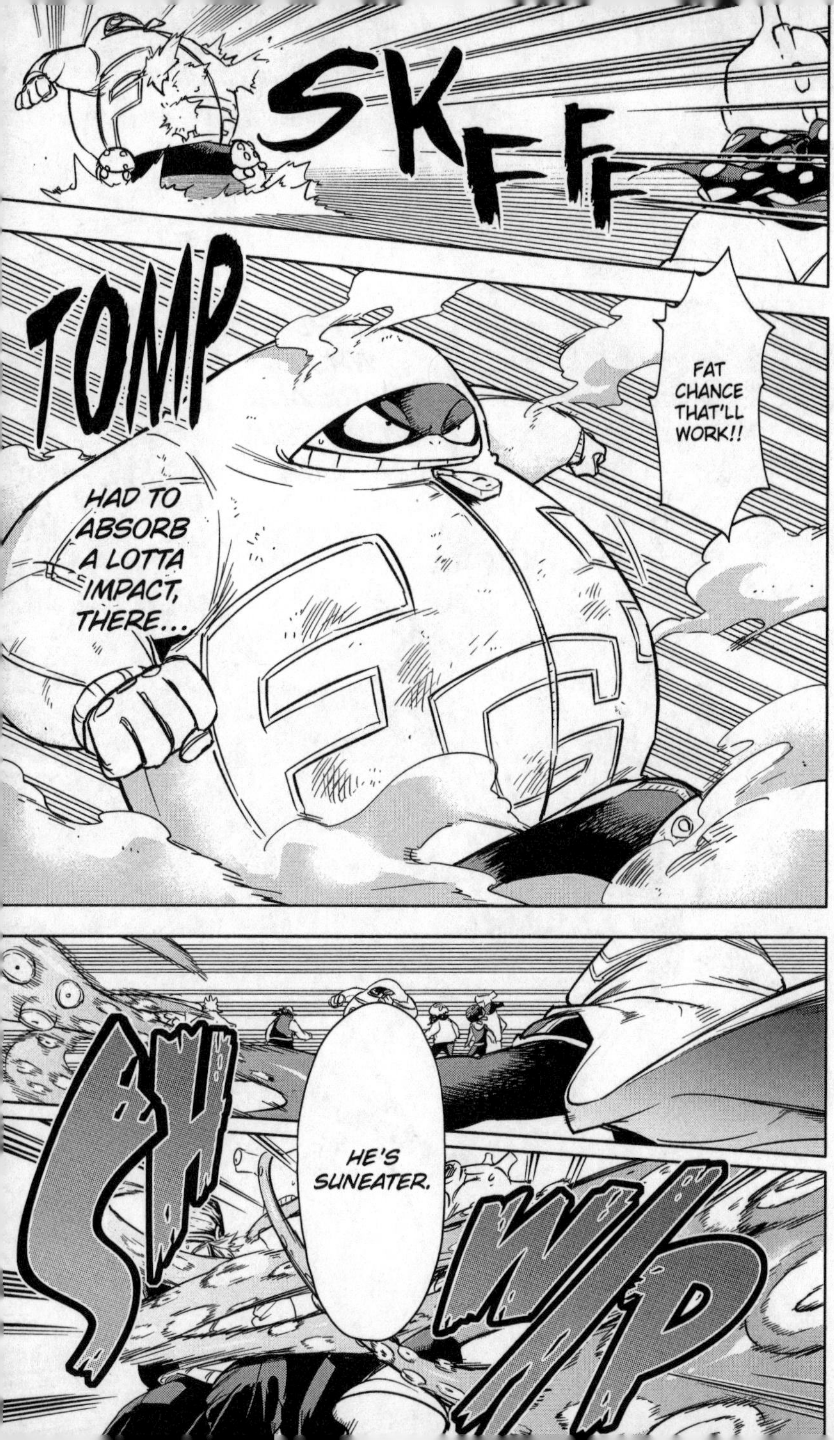
SKFFF
TOMP
FAT CHANCE THAT'LL WORK!!
HAD TO ABSORB A LOTTA IMPACT, THERE...
HE'S SUNEATER.
SHWIP

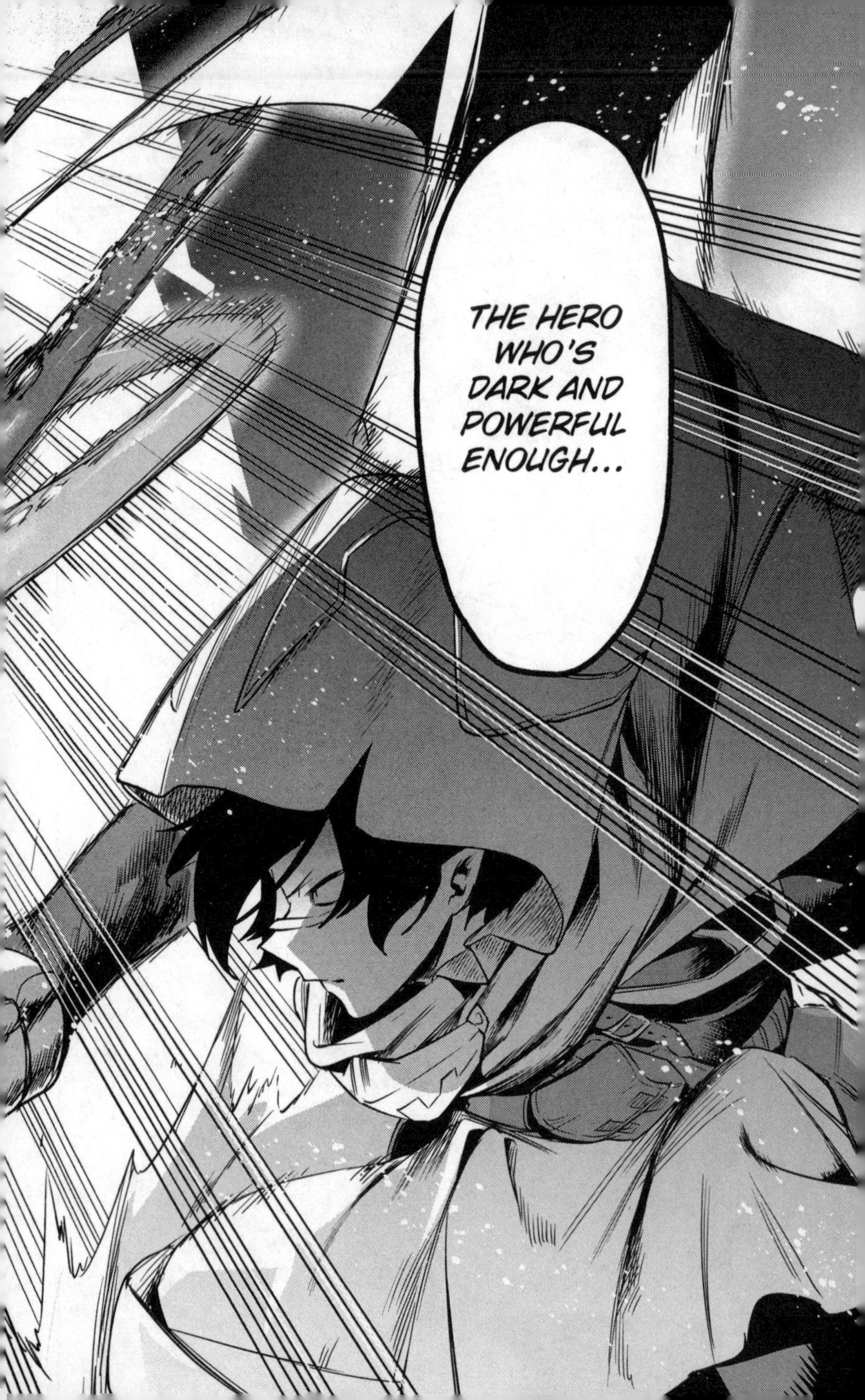
THE HERO WHO'S DARK AND POWERFUL ENOUGH...

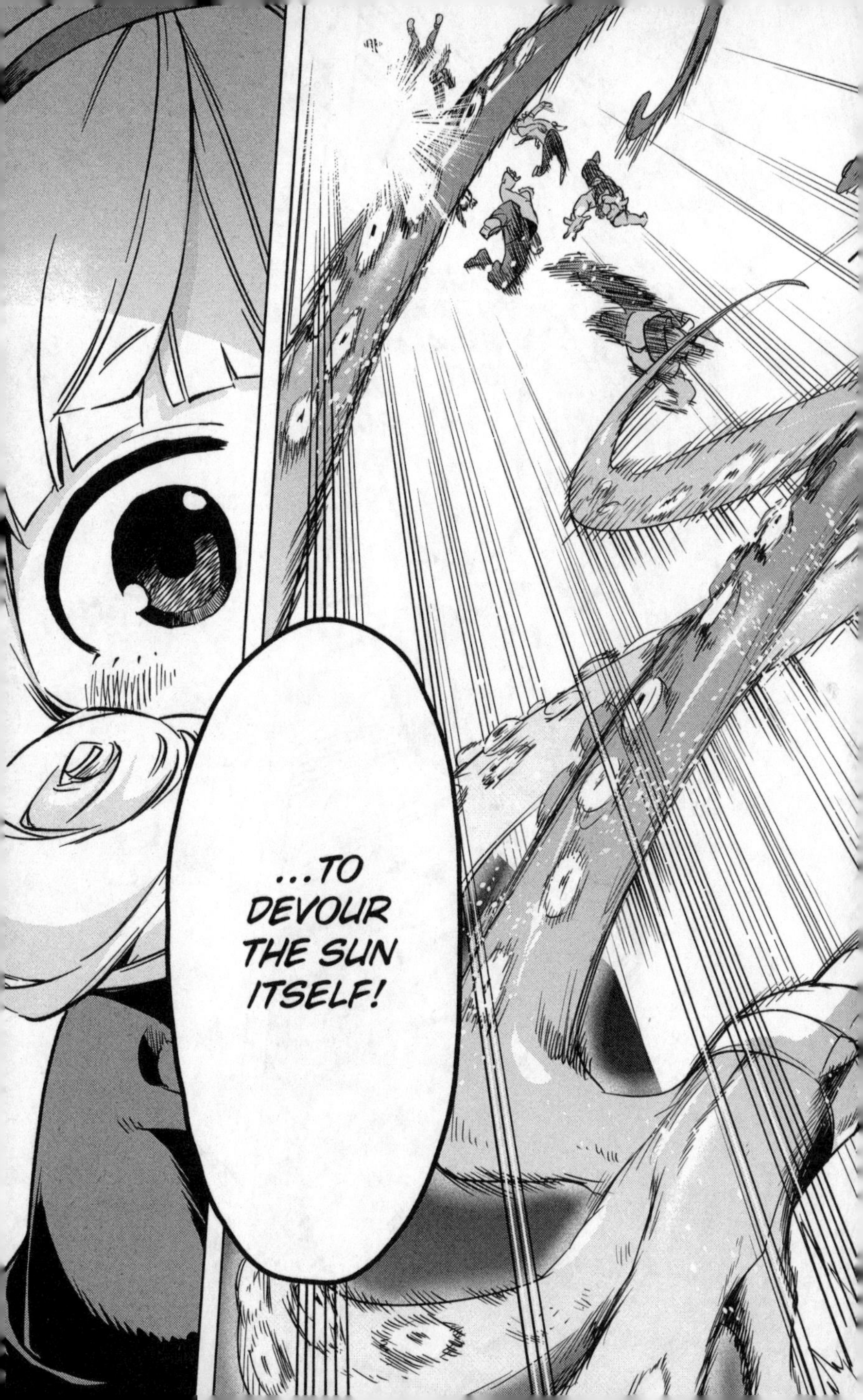
...TO DEVOUR THE SUN ITSELF!

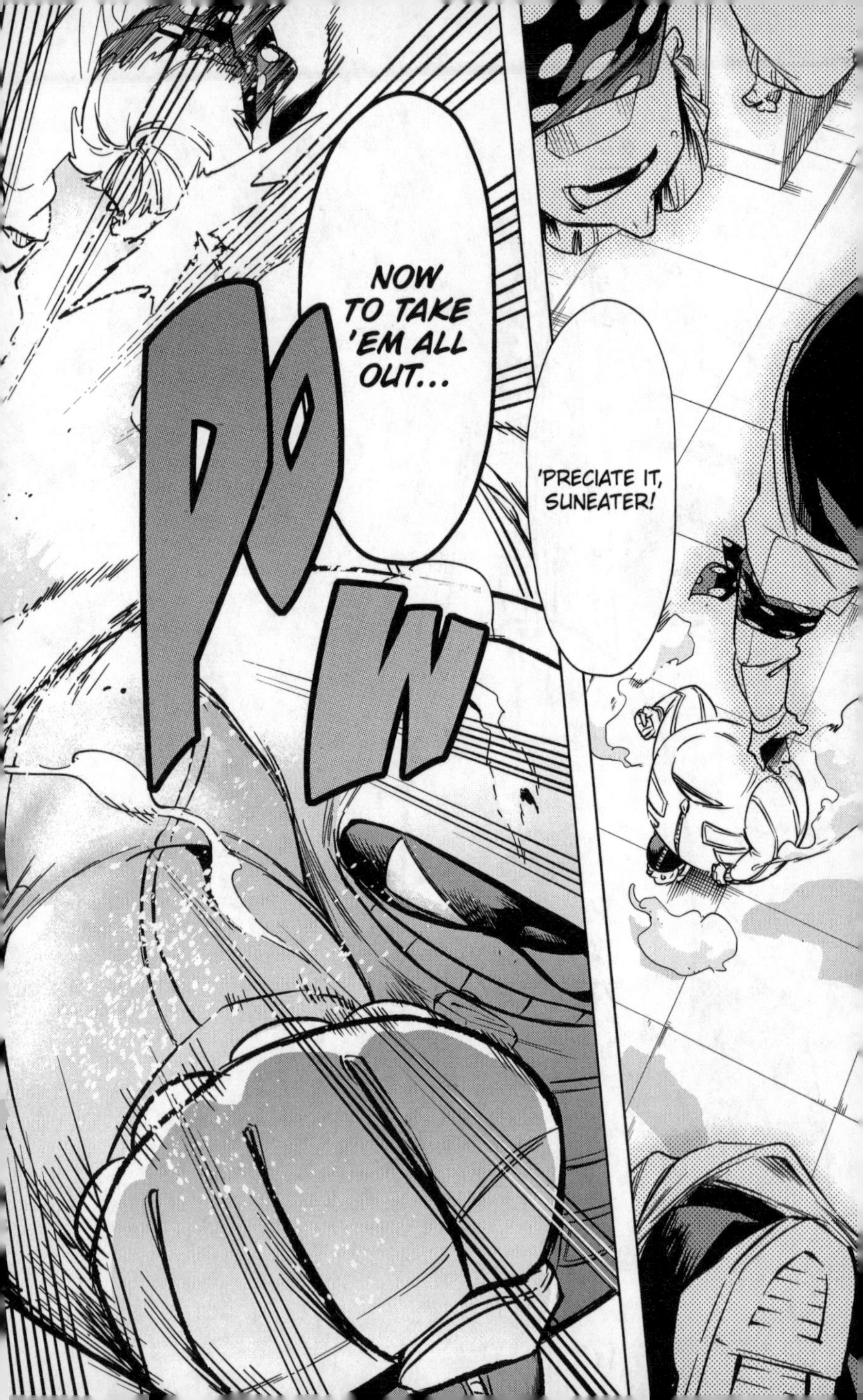
'PRECIATE IT, SUNEATER!
NOW TO TAKE 'EM ALL OUT...
POW

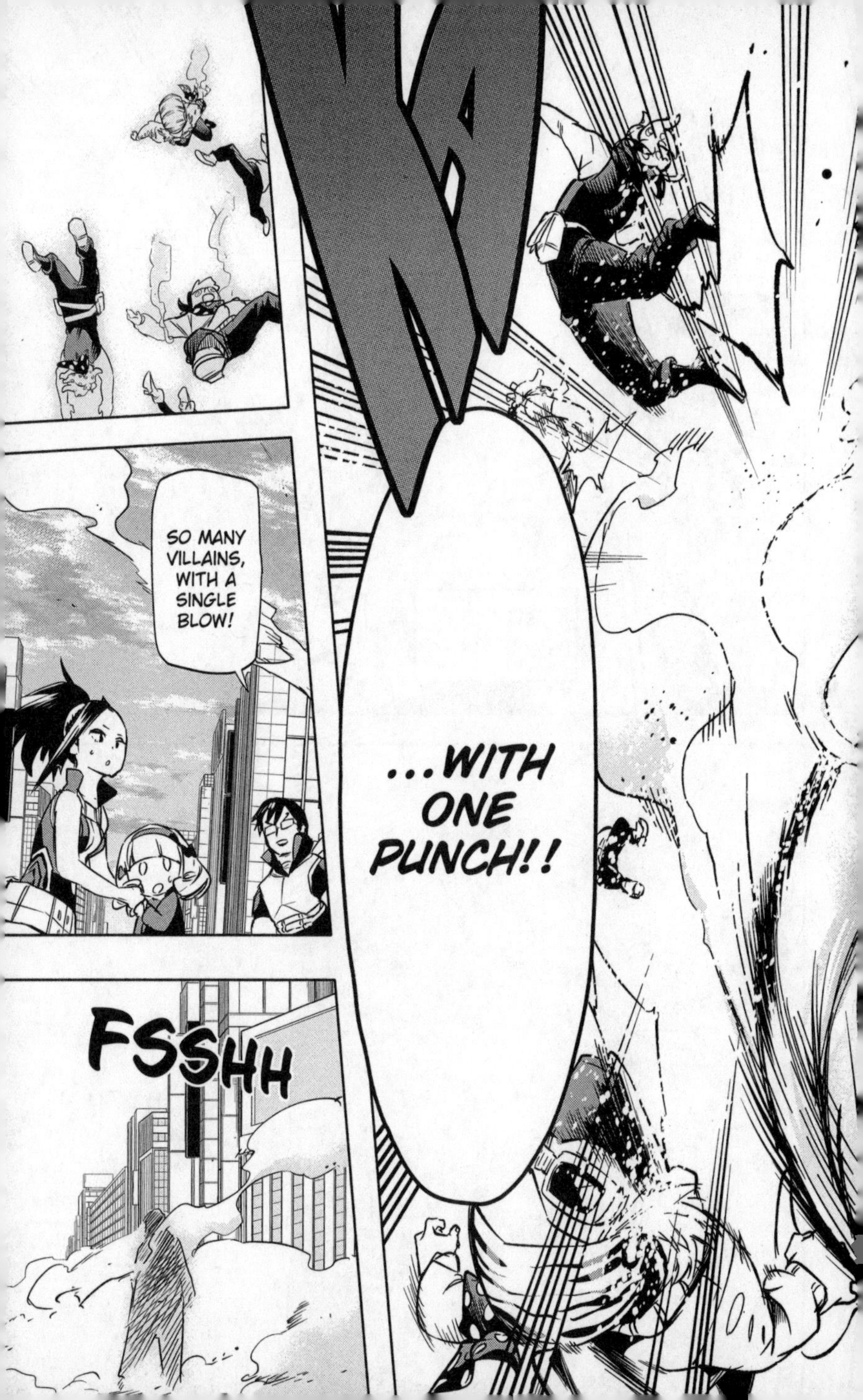
...WITH ONE PUNCH!!
SO MANY VILLAINS, WITH A SINGLE BLOW!
FSSHH

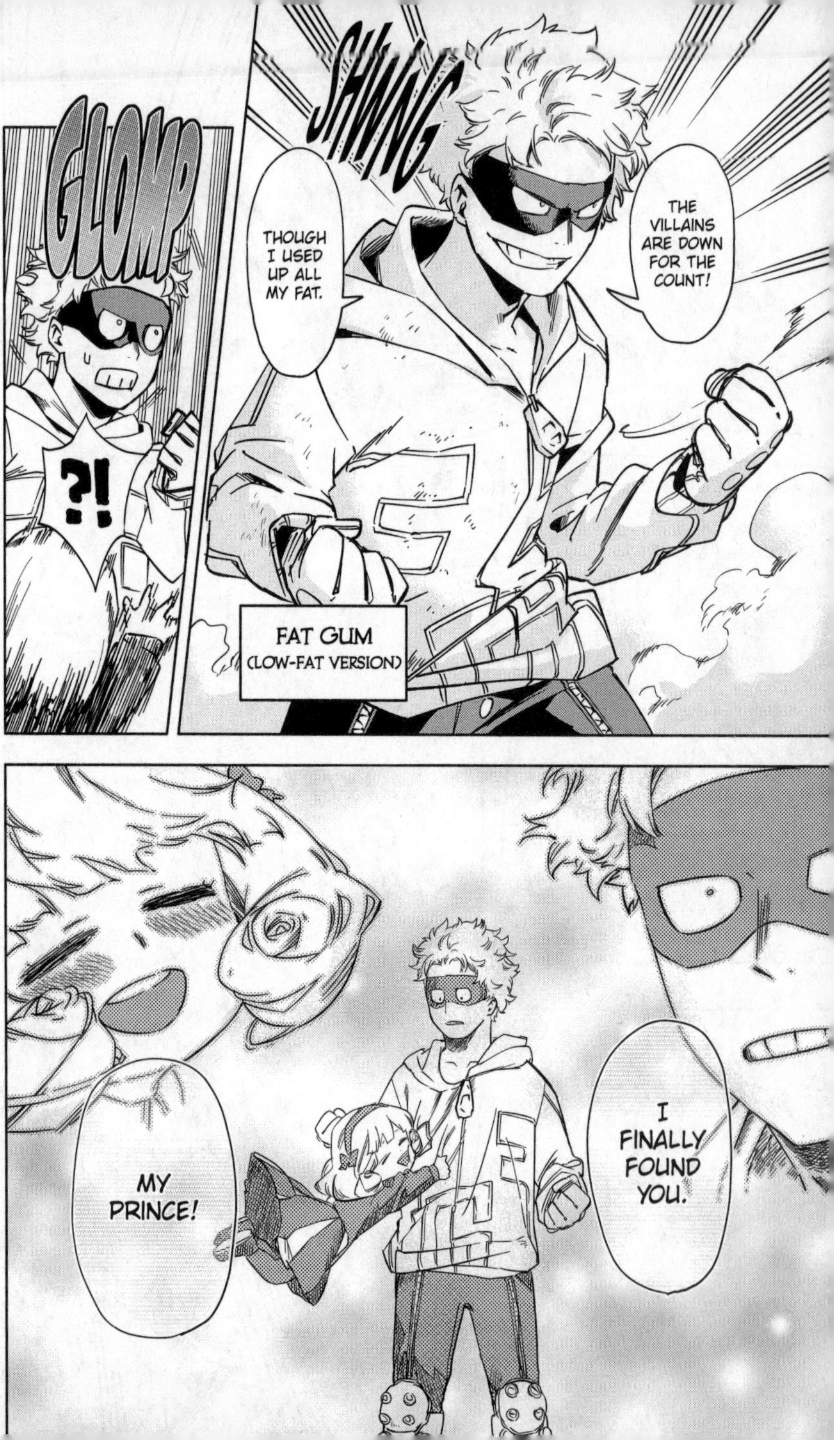
SHWING
THE VILLAINS ARE DOWN FOR THE COUNT!
THOUGH I USED UP ALL MY FAT.
FAT GUM (LOW-FAT VERSION)
GLOMP
?!
I FINALLY FOUND YOU.
MY PRINCE!

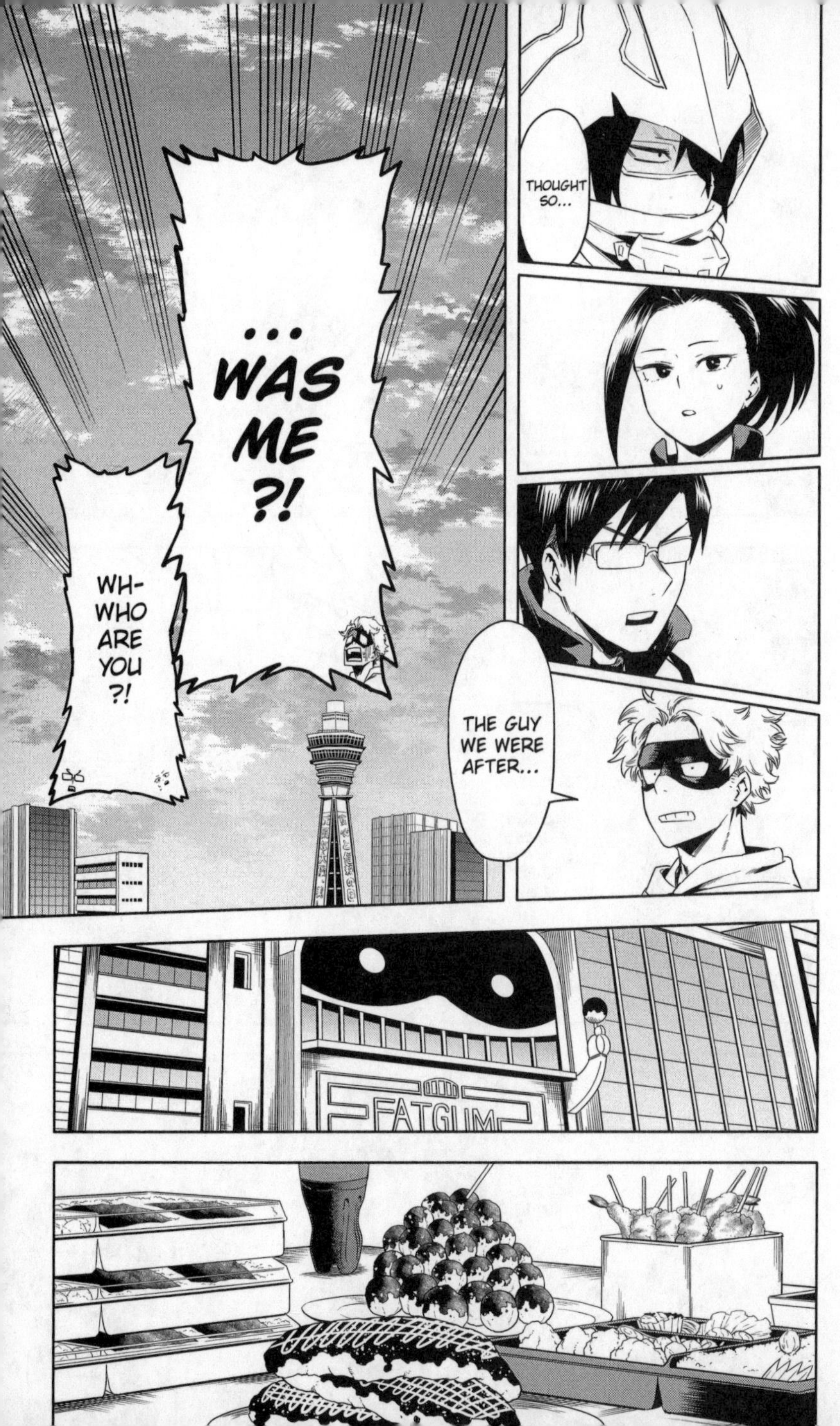
THOUGHT SO...
THE GUY WE WERE AFTER...
...WAS ME?!
WH-WHO ARE YOU?!
FATGUM

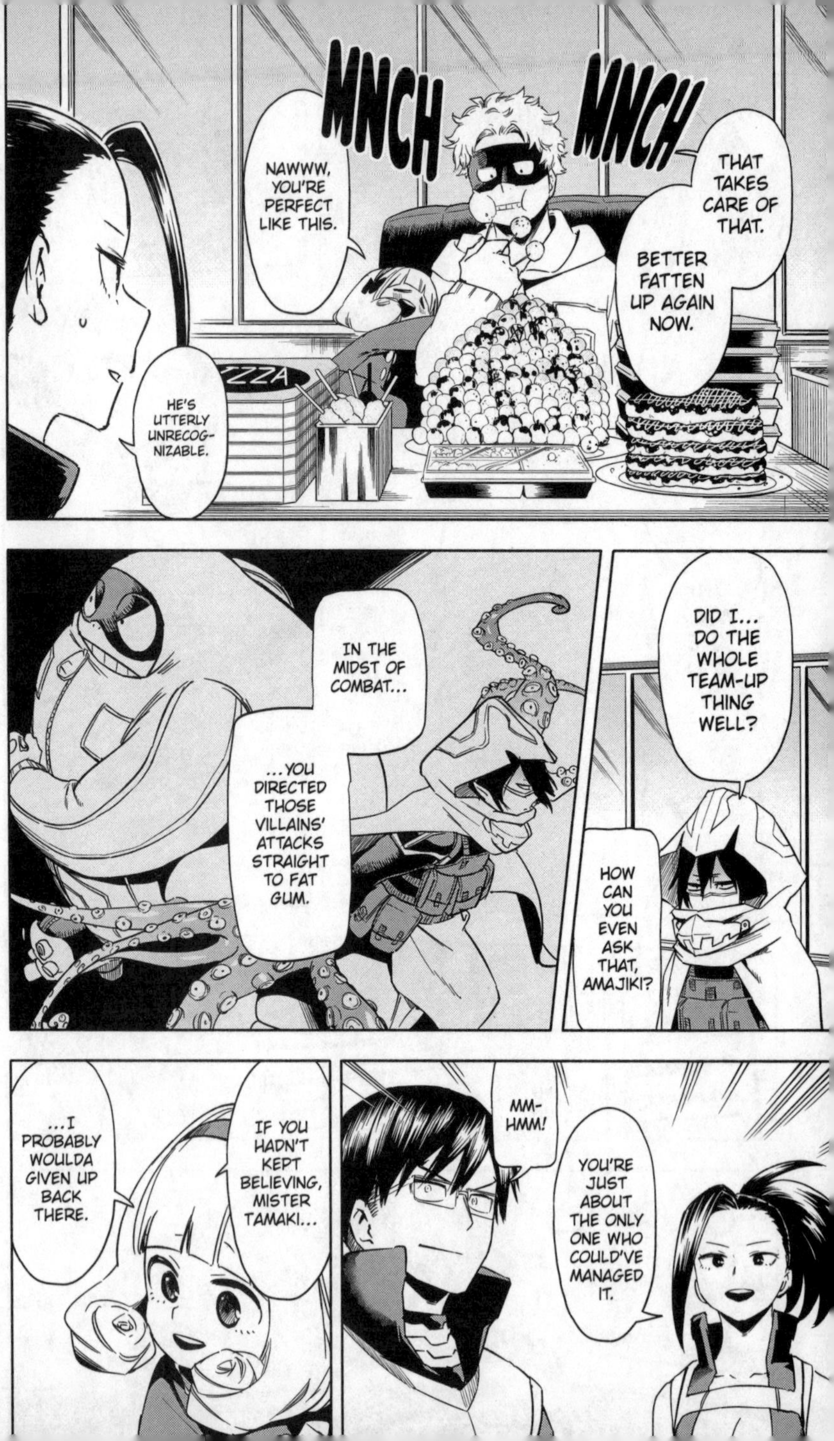
MNCH
MNCH
THAT TAKES CARE OF THAT.
BETTER FATTEN UP AGAIN NOW.
NAWWW, YOU'RE PERFECT LIKE THIS.
HE'S UTTERLY UNRECOG-NIZABLE.
DID I... DO THE WHOLE TEAM-UP THING WELL?
HOW CAN YOU EVEN ASK THAT, AMAJIKI?
IN THE MIDST OF COMBAT...
...YOU DIRECTED THOSE VILLAINS' ATTACKS STRAIGHT TO FAT GUM.
YOU'RE JUST ABOUT THE ONLY ONE WHO COULD'VE MANAGED IT.
MM-HMM!
IF YOU HADN'T KEPT BELIEVING, MISTER TAMAKI...
...I PROBABLY WOULDA GIVEN UP BACK THERE.

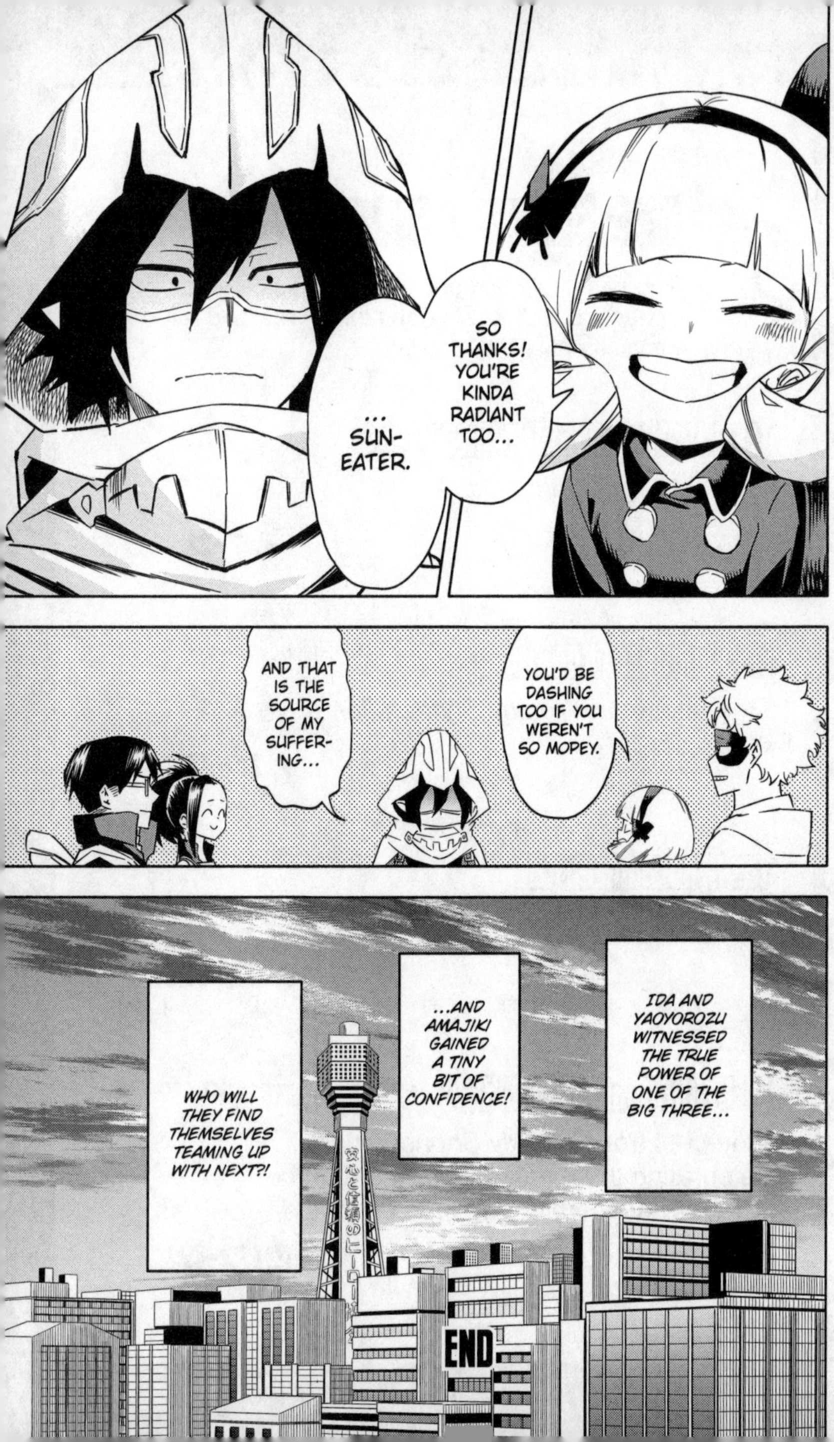
SO THANKS! YOU'RE KINDA RADIANT TOO...
... SUN-EATER.
YOU'D BE DASHING TOO IF YOU WEREN'T SO MOPEY.
AND THAT IS THE SOURCE OF MY SUFFERING...
IDA AND YAOYOROZU WITNESSED THE TRUE POWER OF ONE OF THE BIG THREE...
...AND AMAJIKI GAINED A TINY BIT OF CONFIDENCE!
WHO WILL THEY FIND THEMSELVES TEAMING UP WITH NEXT?!
END

ONE-SHOTS / SIDE STORIES

A good half of this book consists of side stories, doesn't it…? I don't think I realized it myself until it was too late.

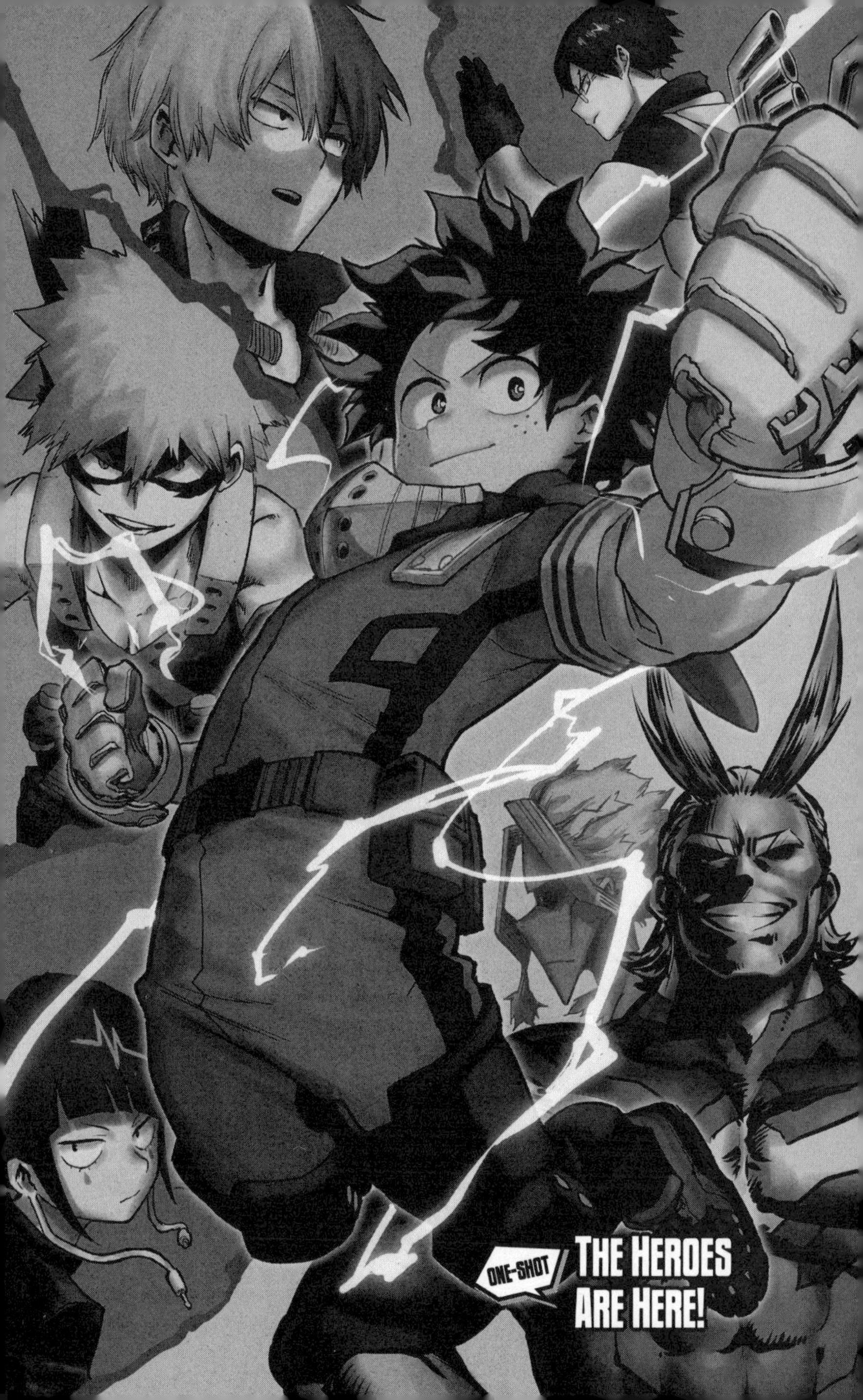
ONE-SHOT
THE HEROES ARE HERE!

MY HERO ACADEMIA
Team-Up Missions

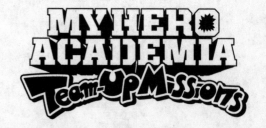

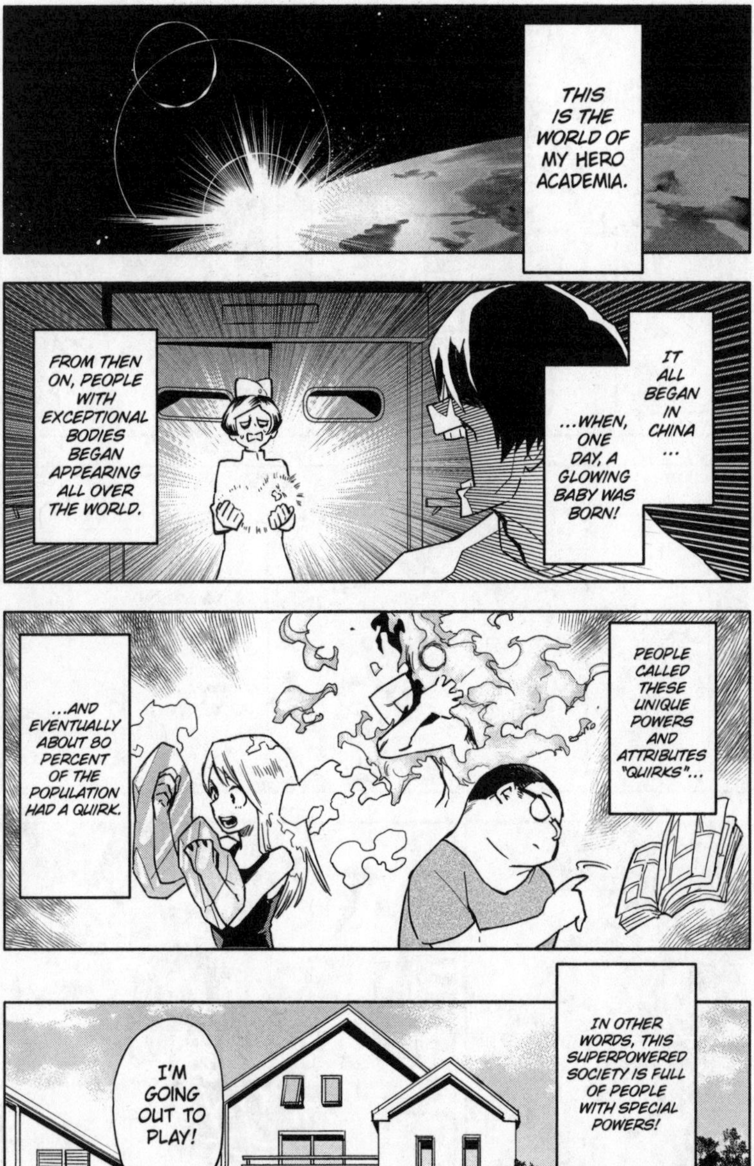
THIS IS THE WORLD OF MY HERO ACADEMIA.
IT ALL BEGAN IN CHINA...
...WHEN, ONE DAY, A GLOWING BABY WAS BORN!
FROM THEN ON, PEOPLE WITH EXCEPTIONAL BODIES BEGAN APPEARING ALL OVER THE WORLD.
PEOPLE CALLED THESE UNIQUE POWERS AND ATTRIBUTES "QUIRKS"...
...AND EVENTUALLY ABOUT 80 PERCENT OF THE POPULATION HAD A QUIRK.
IN OTHER WORDS, THIS SUPERPOWERED SOCIETY IS FULL OF PEOPLE WITH SPECIAL POWERS!
I'M GOING OUT TO PLAY!

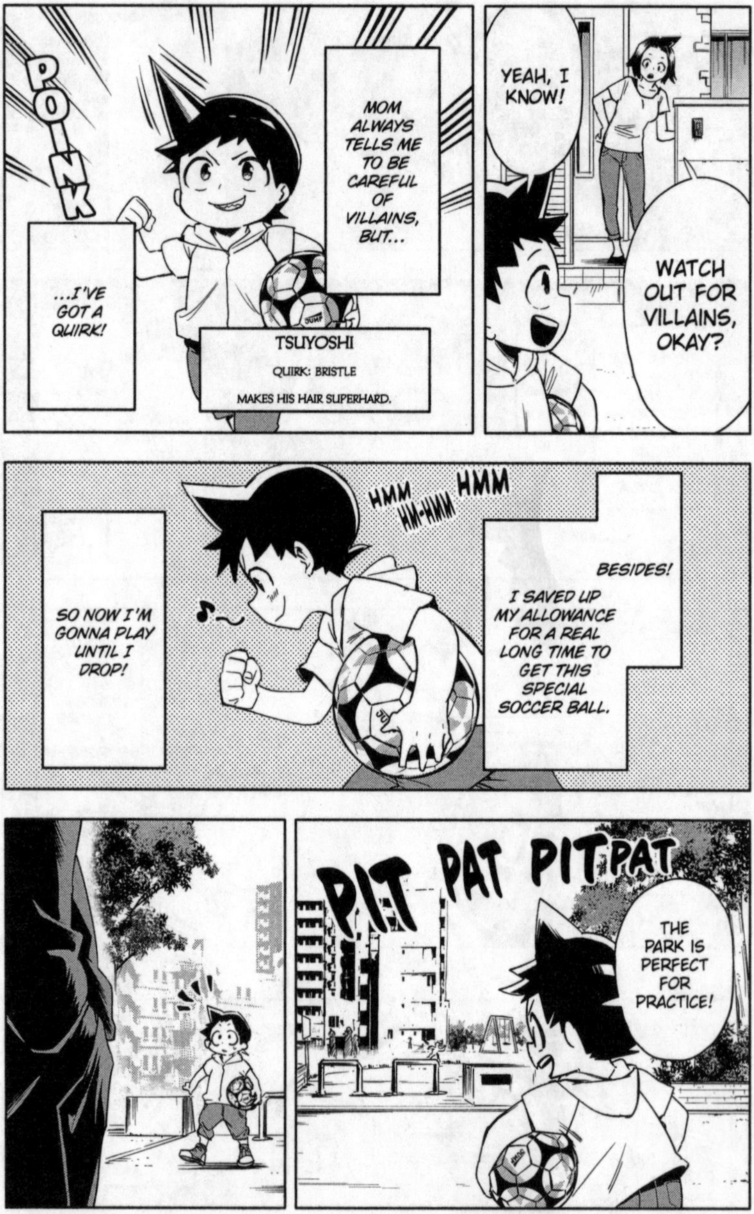
WATCH OUT FOR VILLAINS, OKAY?
YEAH, I KNOW!
POINK
MOM ALWAYS TELLS ME TO BE CAREFUL OF VILLAINS, BUT...
...I'VE GOT A QUIRK!
TSUYOSHI
QUIRK: BRISTLE
MAKES HIS HAIR SUPERHARD.
BESIDES!
I SAVED UP MY ALLOWANCE FOR A REAL LONG TIME TO GET THIS SPECIAL SOCCER BALL.
HMM HM-HMM HMM
SO NOW I'M GONNA PLAY UNTIL I DROP!
PIT PAT PIT PAT
THE PARK IS PERFECT FOR PRACTICE!

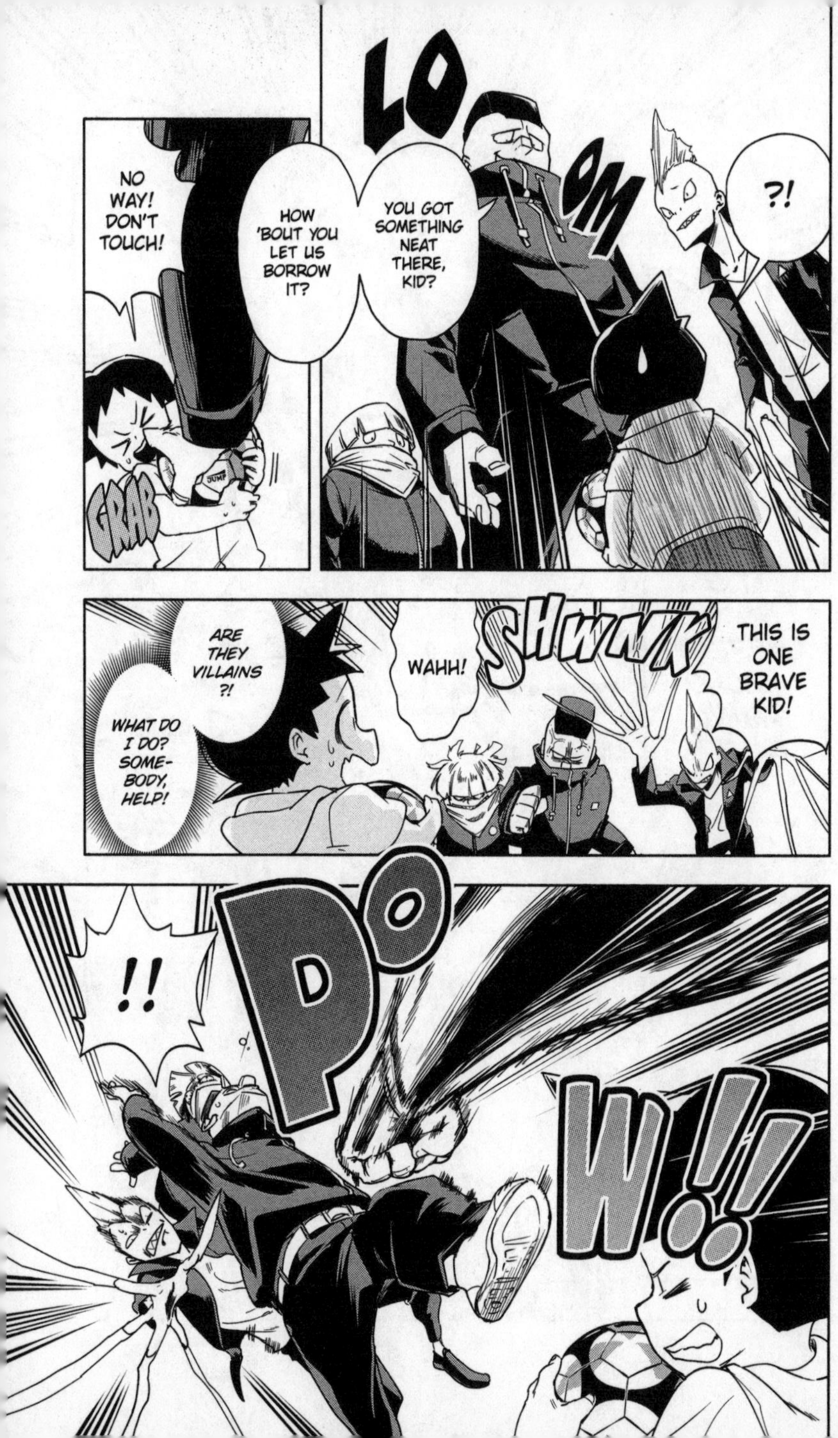
LOOM
?!
YOU GOT SOMETHING NEAT THERE, KID?
HOW 'BOUT YOU LET US BORROW IT?
NO WAY! DON'T TOUCH!
GRAB
THIS IS ONE BRAVE KID!
SHWNK
WAHH!
ARE THEY VILLAINS?!
WHAT DO I DO? SOMEBODY, HELP!
DOW!!
!!

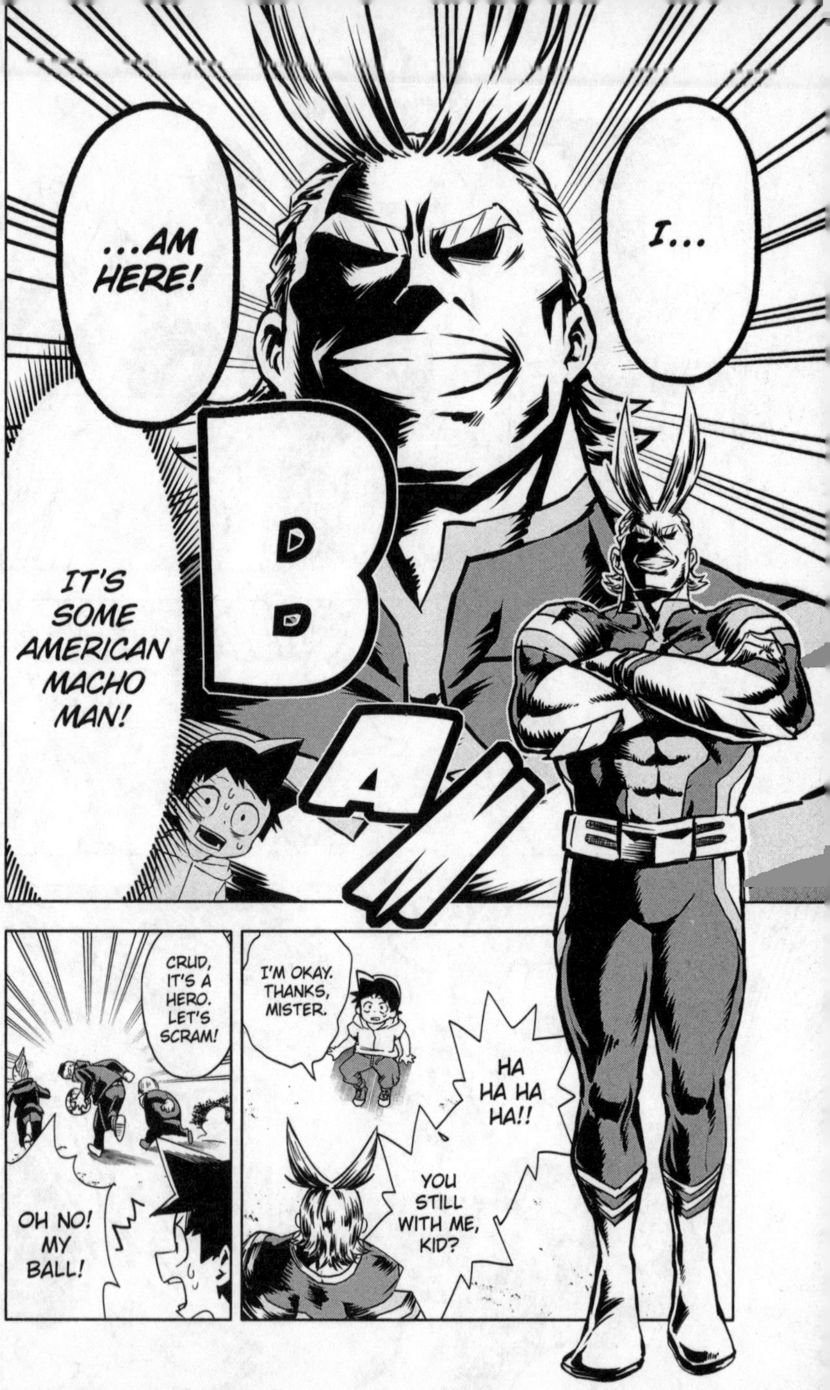
I...
...AM HERE!
BA
IT'S SOME AMERICAN MACHO MAN!
HA HA HA HA!!
I'M OKAY. THANKS, MISTER.
YOU STILL WITH ME, KID?
CRUD, IT'S A HERO. LET'S SCRAM!
OH NO! MY BALL!

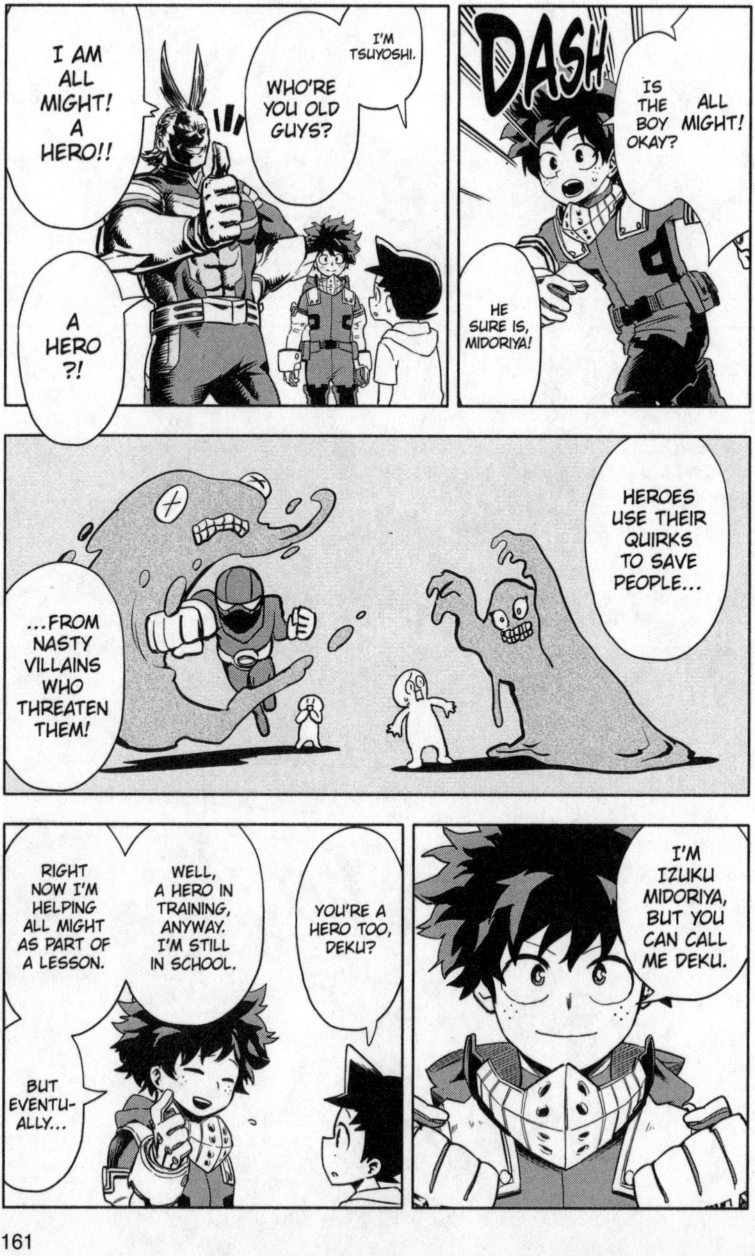
DASH
ALL MIGHT!
IS THE BOY OKAY?
HE SURE IS, MIDORIYA!
I'M TSUYOSHI.
WHO'RE YOU OLD GUYS?
I AM ALL MIGHT! A HERO!!
A HERO ?!
HEROES USE THEIR QUIRKS TO SAVE PEOPLE...
...FROM NASTY VILLAINS WHO THREATEN THEM!
I'M IZUKU MIDORIYA, BUT YOU CAN CALL ME DEKU.
YOU'RE A HERO TOO, DEKU?
WELL, A HERO IN TRAINING, ANYWAY. I'M STILL IN SCHOOL.
RIGHT NOW I'M HELPING ALL MIGHT AS PART OF A LESSON.
BUT EVENTU-ALLY...

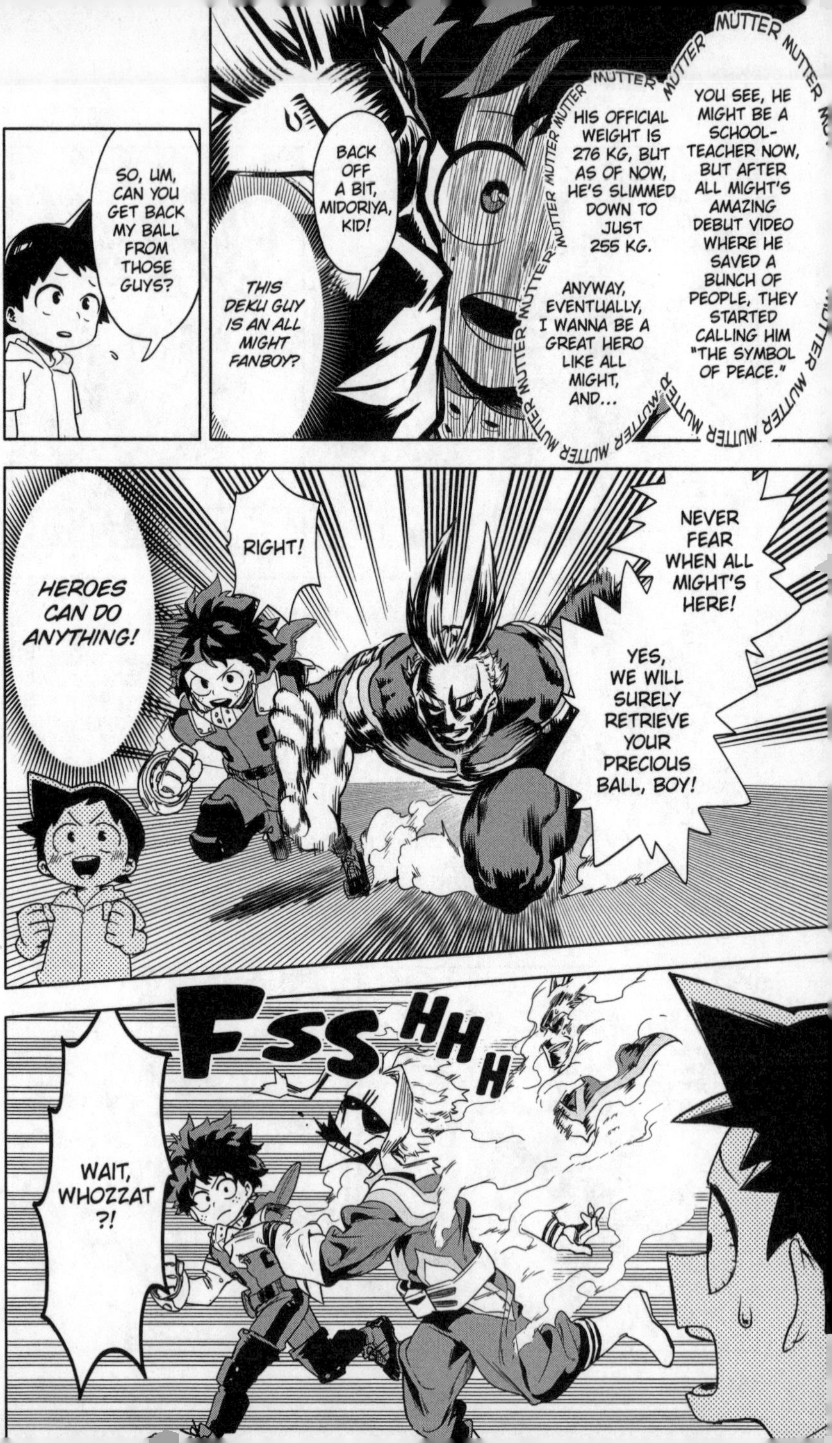
MUTTER MUTTER MUTTER MUTTER
YOU SEE, HE MIGHT BE A SCHOOL-TEACHER NOW, BUT AFTER ALL MIGHT'S AMAZING DEBUT VIDEO WHERE HE SAVED A BUNCH OF PEOPLE, THEY STARTED CALLING HIM "THE SYMBOL OF PEACE."
HIS OFFICIAL WEIGHT IS 276 KG, BUT AS OF NOW, HE'S SLIMMED DOWN TO JUST 255 KG.
ANYWAY, EVENTUALLY, I WANNA BE A GREAT HERO LIKE ALL MIGHT, AND...
BACK OFF A BIT, MIDORIYA, KID!
THIS DEKU GUY IS AN ALL MIGHT FANBOY?
SO, UM, CAN YOU GET BACK MY BALL FROM THOSE GUYS?
NEVER FEAR WHEN ALL MIGHT'S HERE!
YES, WE WILL SURELY RETRIEVE YOUR PRECIOUS BALL, BOY!
RIGHT!
HEROES CAN DO ANYTHING!
FSSHHHH
WAIT, WHOZZAT ?!

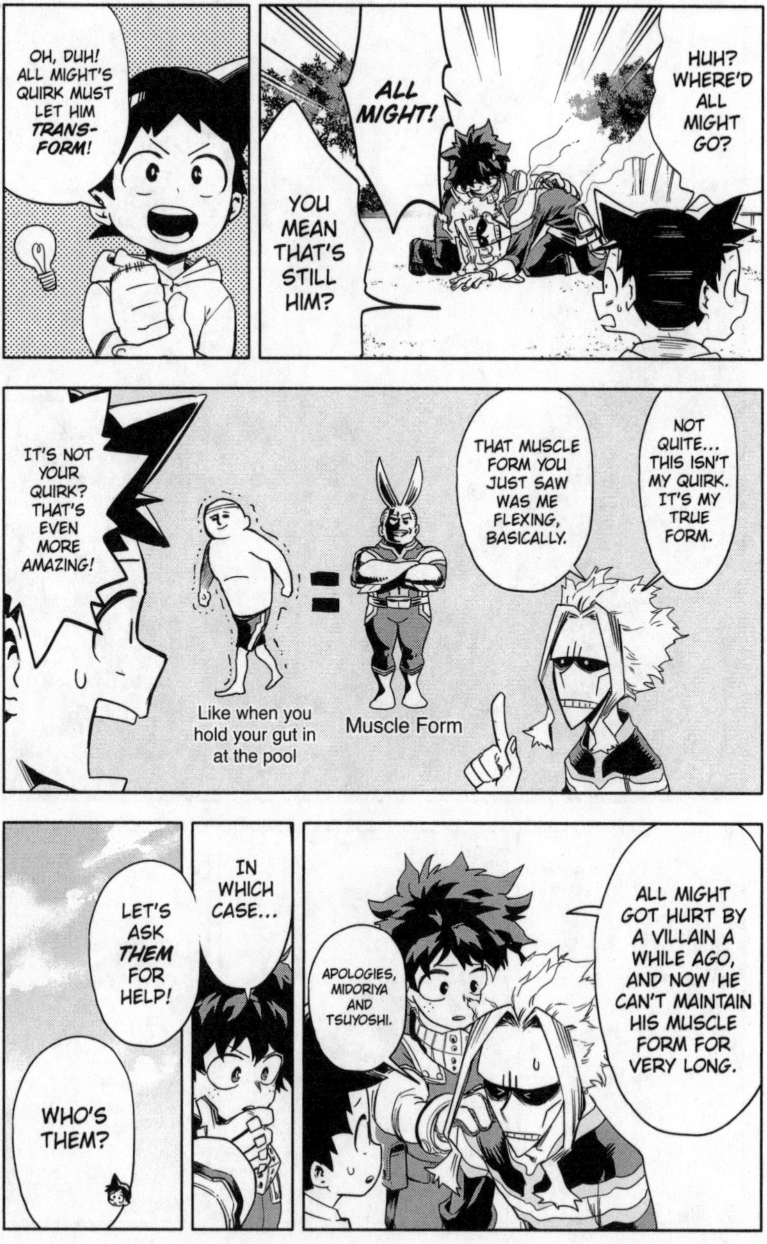
HUH? WHERE'D ALL MIGHT GO?
ALL MIGHT!
YOU MEAN THAT'S STILL HIM?
OH, DUH! ALL MIGHT'S QUIRK MUST LET HIM TRANSFORM!
NOT QUITE... THIS ISN'T MY QUIRK. IT'S MY TRUE FORM.
THAT MUSCLE FORM YOU JUST SAW WAS ME FLEXING, BASICALLY.
Muscle Form
Like when you hold your gut in at the pool
IT'S NOT YOUR QUIRK? THAT'S EVEN MORE AMAZING!
ALL MIGHT GOT HURT BY A VILLAIN A WHILE AGO, AND NOW HE CAN'T MAINTAIN HIS MUSCLE FORM FOR VERY LONG.
APOLOGIES, MIDORIYA AND TSUYOSHI.
IN WHICH CASE...
LET'S ASK THEM FOR HELP!
WHO'S THEM?

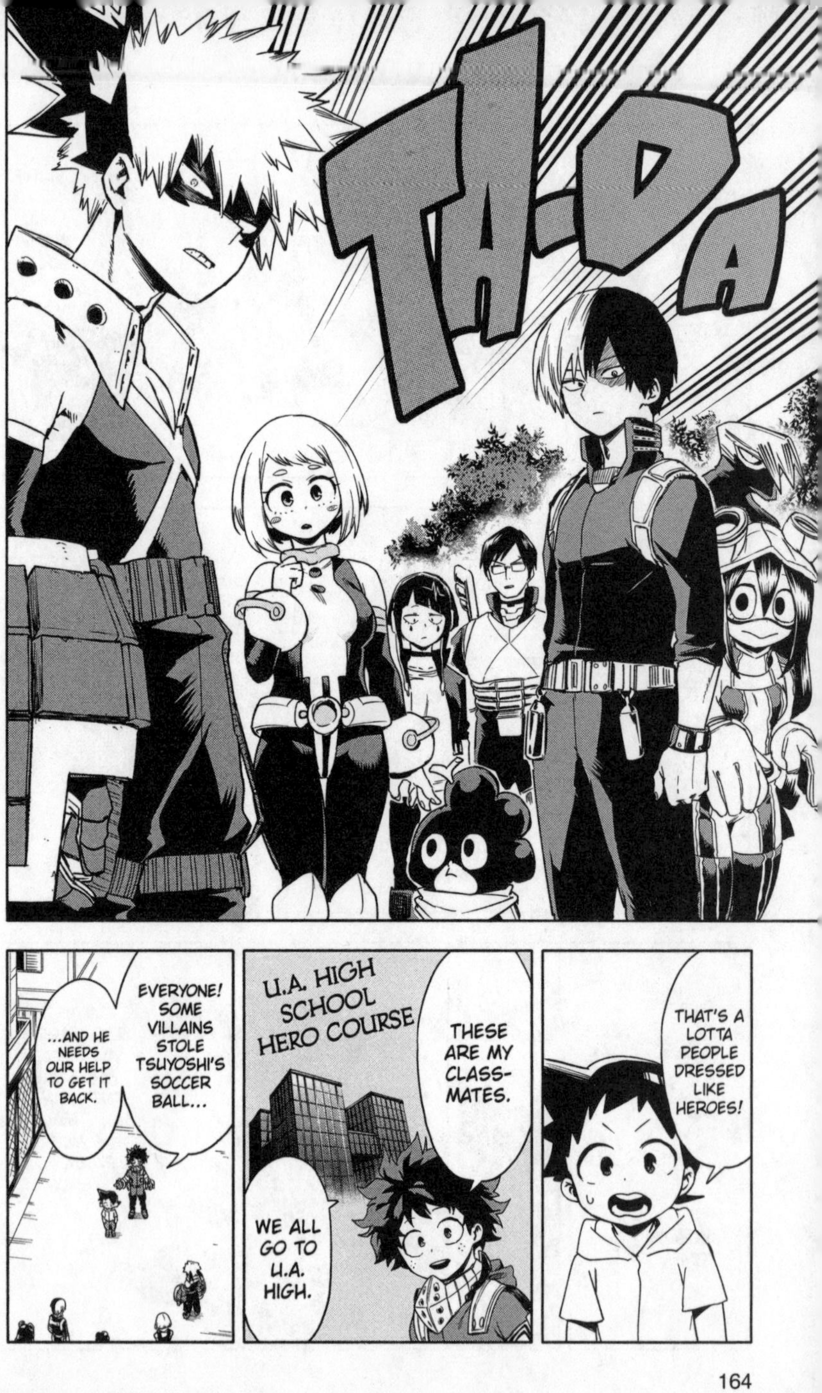
TA-DA
THAT'S A LOTTA PEOPLE DRESSED LIKE HEROES!
U.A. HIGH SCHOOL HERO COURSE
THESE ARE MY CLASS-MATES.
WE ALL GO TO U.A. HIGH.
EVERYONE! SOME VILLAINS STOLE TSUYOSHI'S SOCCER BALL...
...AND HE NEEDS OUR HELP TO GET IT BACK.

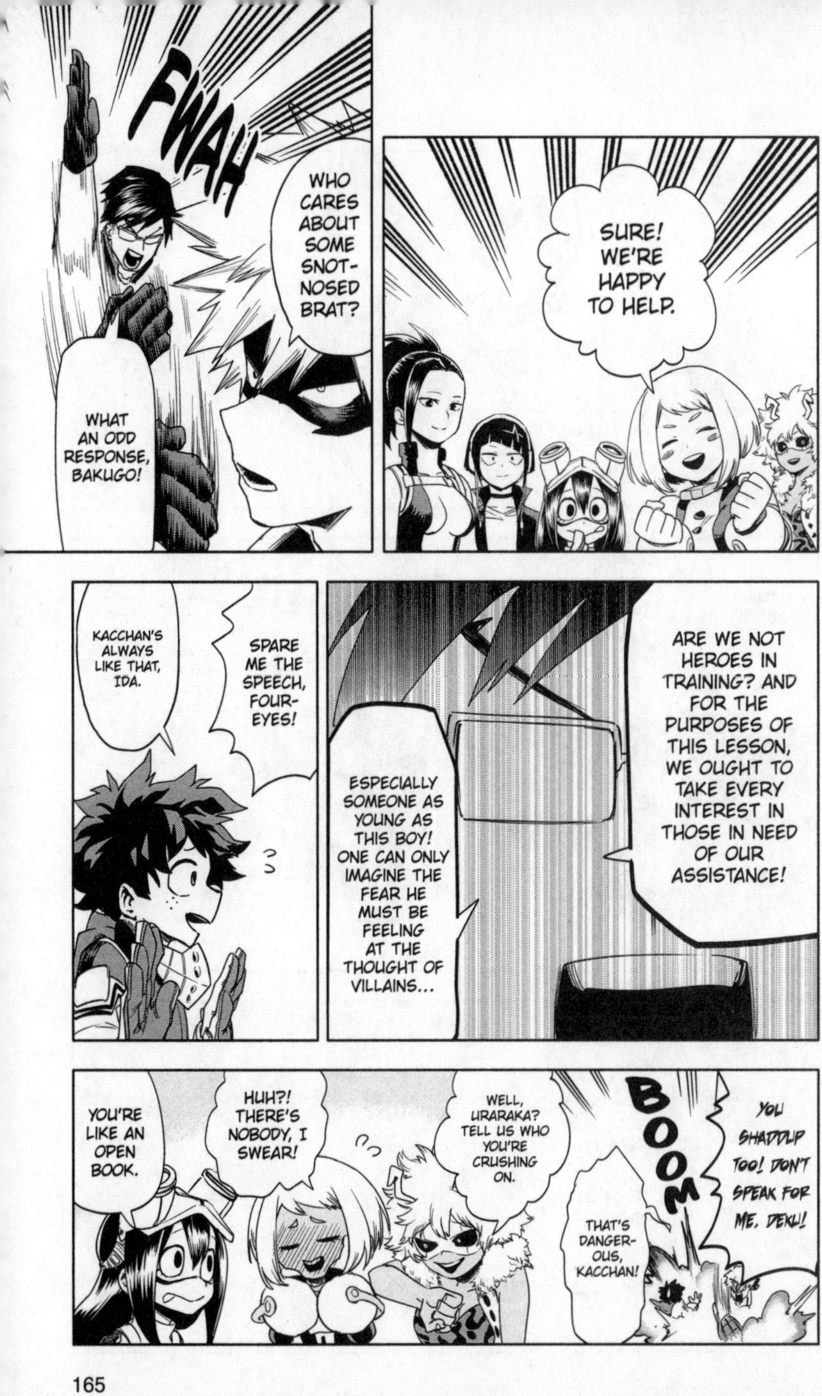
SURE! WE'RE HAPPY TO HELP.
WHO CARES ABOUT SOME SNOT-NOSED BRAT?
FWAH
WHAT AN ODD RESPONSE, BAKUGO!
ARE WE NOT HEROES IN TRAINING? AND FOR THE PURPOSES OF THIS LESSON, WE OUGHT TO TAKE EVERY INTEREST IN THOSE IN NEED OF OUR ASSISTANCE!
ESPECIALLY SOMEONE AS YOUNG AS THIS BOY! ONE CAN ONLY IMAGINE THE FEAR HE MUST BE FEELING AT THE THOUGHT OF VILLAINS...
SPARE ME THE SPEECH, FOUR-EYES!
KACCHAN'S ALWAYS LIKE THAT, IDA.
YOU SHADDUP TOO! DON'T SPEAK FOR ME, DEKU!
BOOM
THAT'S DANGER-OUS, KACCHAN!
WELL, URARAKA? TELL US WHO YOU'RE CRUSHING ON.
HUH?! THERE'S NOBODY, I SWEAR!
YOU'RE LIKE AN OPEN BOOK.

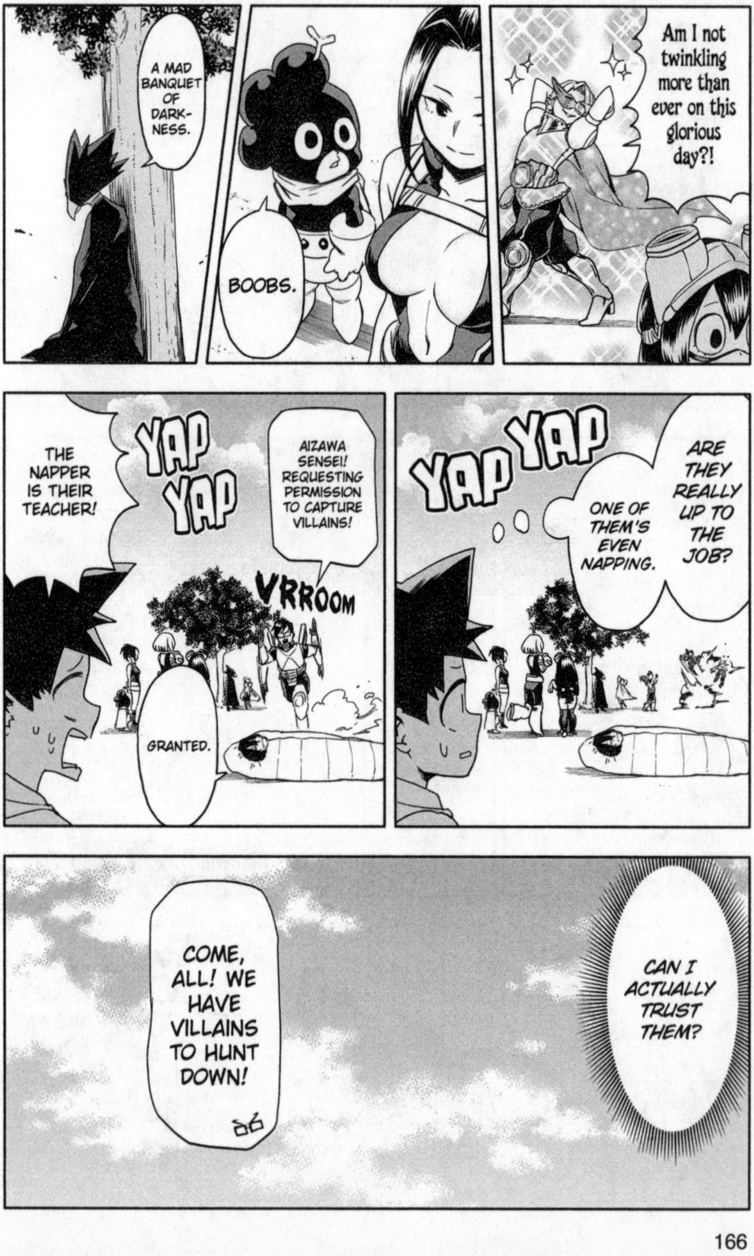
Am I not twinkling more than ever on this glorious day?!
BOOBS.
A MAD BANQUET OF DARKNESS.
ARE THEY REALLY UP TO THE JOB?
YAP YAP
ONE OF THEM'S EVEN NAPPING.
AIZAWA SENSEI! REQUESTING PERMISSION TO CAPTURE VILLAINS!
YAP YAP
THE NAPPER IS THEIR TEACHER!
VRROOM
GRANTED.
CAN I ACTUALLY TRUST THEM?
COME, ALL! WE HAVE VILLAINS TO HUNT DOWN!

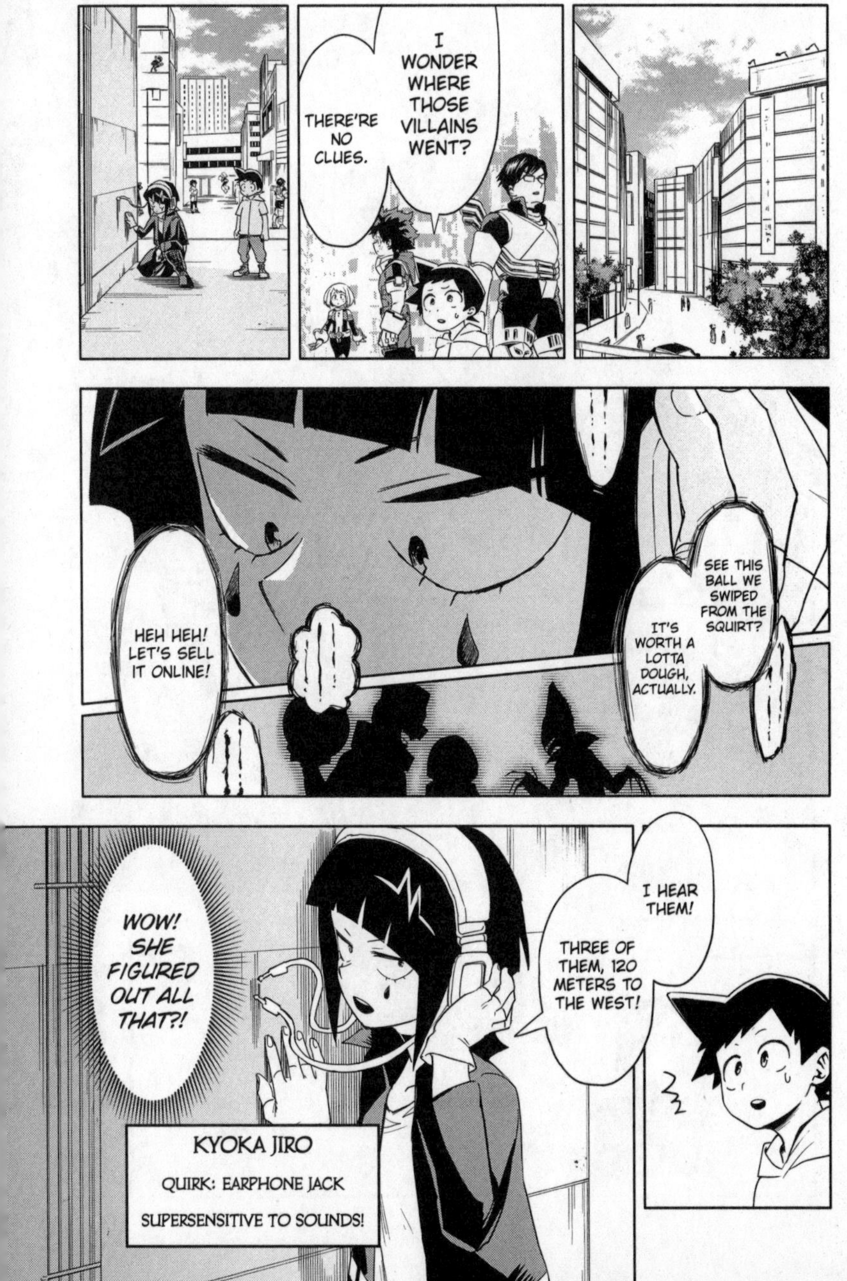
I WONDER WHERE THOSE VILLAINS WENT?
THERE'RE NO CLUES.
SEE THIS BALL WE SWIPED FROM THE SQUIRT?
IT'S WORTH A LOTTA DOUGH, ACTUALLY.
HEH HEH! LET'S SELL IT ONLINE!
I HEAR THEM!
THREE OF THEM, 120 METERS TO THE WEST!
WOW! SHE FIGURED OUT ALL THAT?!
KYOKA JIRO
QUIRK: EARPHONE JACK
SUPERSENSITIVE TO SOUNDS!

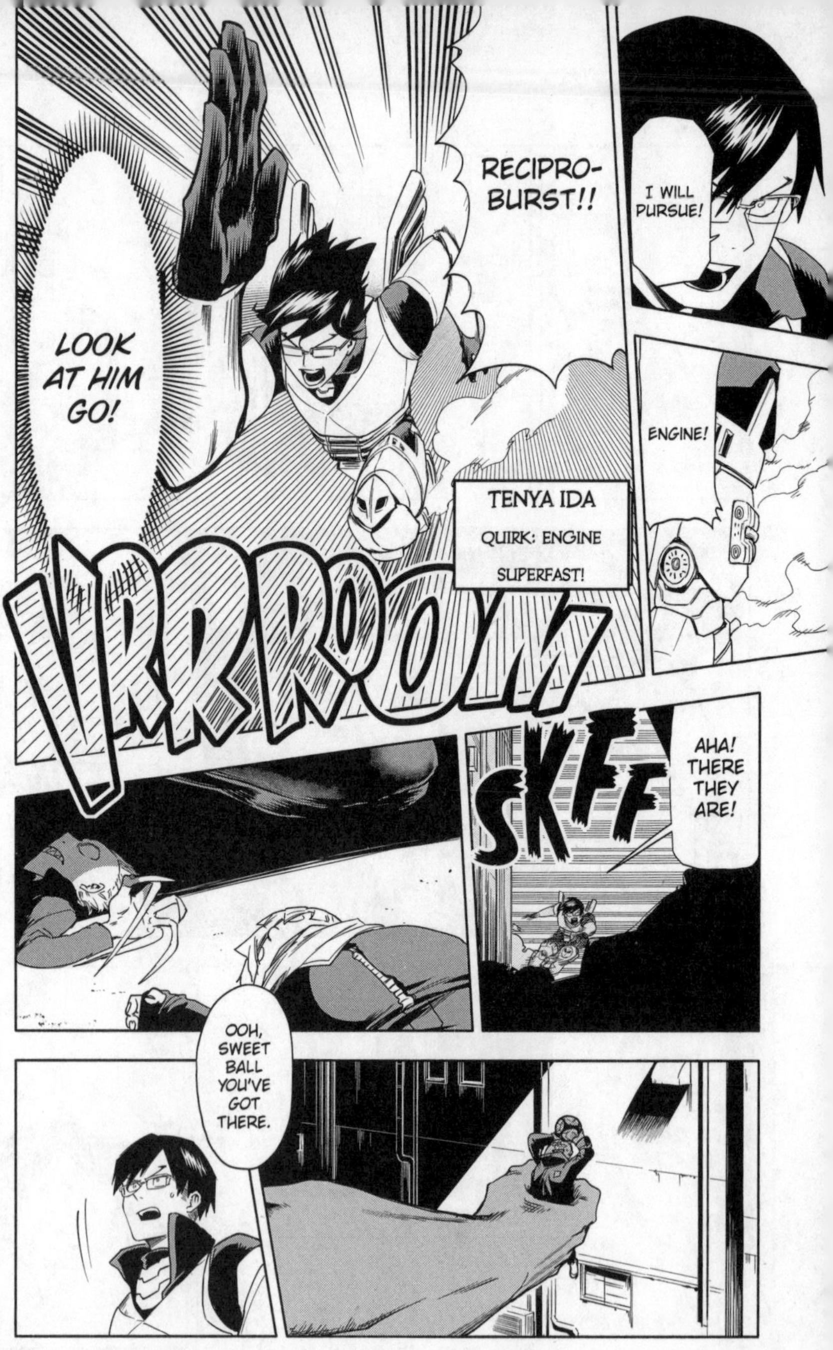
I WILL PURSUE!
ENGINE!
RECIPRO-BURST!!
LOOK AT HIM GO!
TENYA IDA
QUIRK: ENGINE
SUPERFAST!
VRRROOM
SKFF
AHA! THERE THEY ARE!
OOH, SWEET BALL YOU'VE GOT THERE.

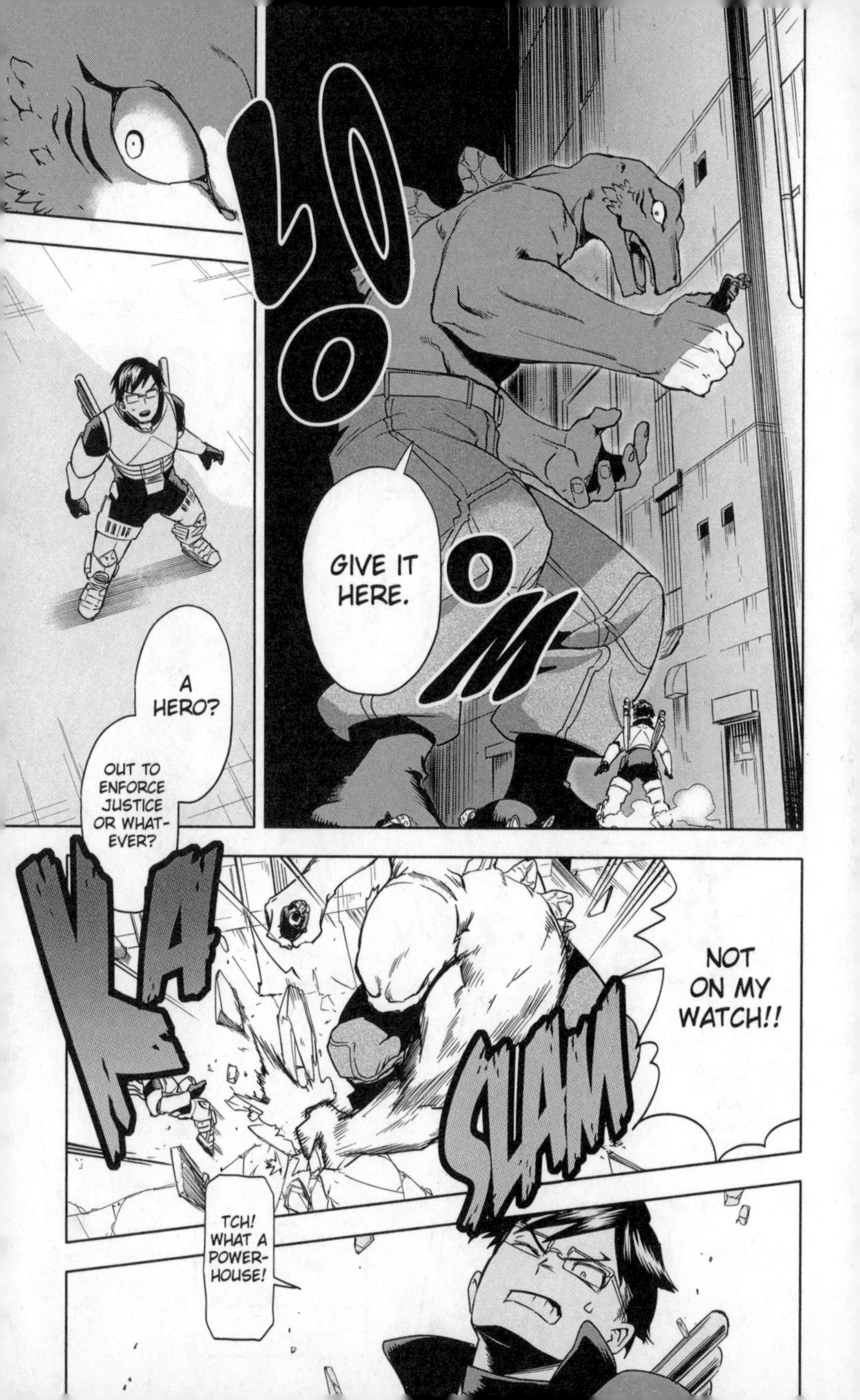
DOOOM
GIVE IT HERE.
A HERO?
OUT TO ENFORCE JUSTICE OR WHAT-EVER?
NOT ON MY WATCH!!
SLAM
KA
TCH! WHAT A POWER-HOUSE!

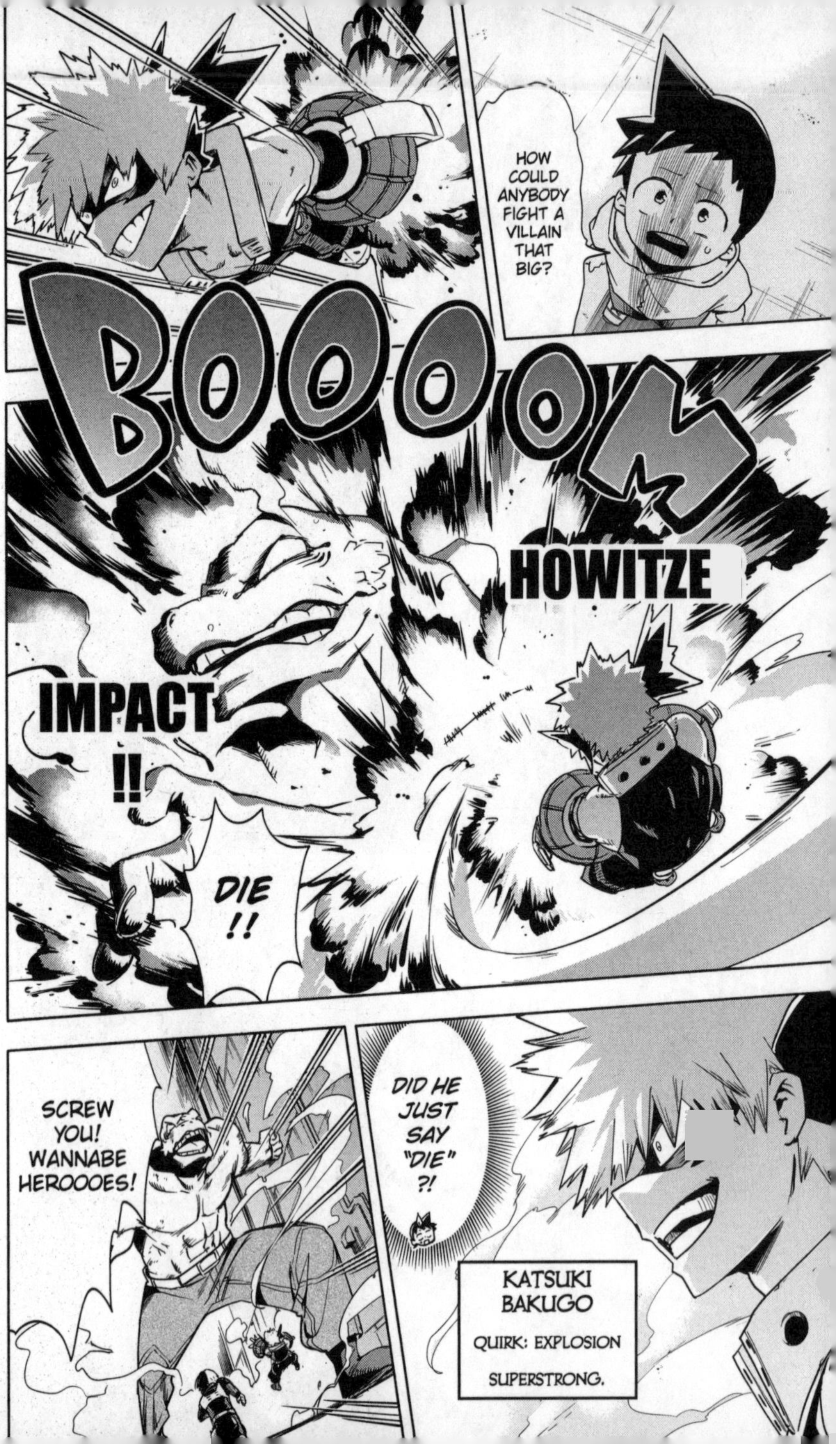
HOW COULD ANYBODY FIGHT A VILLAIN THAT BIG?
BOOOOM
HOWITZE
IMPACT !!
DIE !!
DID HE JUST SAY "DIE" ?!
KATSUKI BAKUGO
QUIRK: EXPLOSION
SUPERSTRONG.
SCREW YOU! WANNABE HEROOOES!

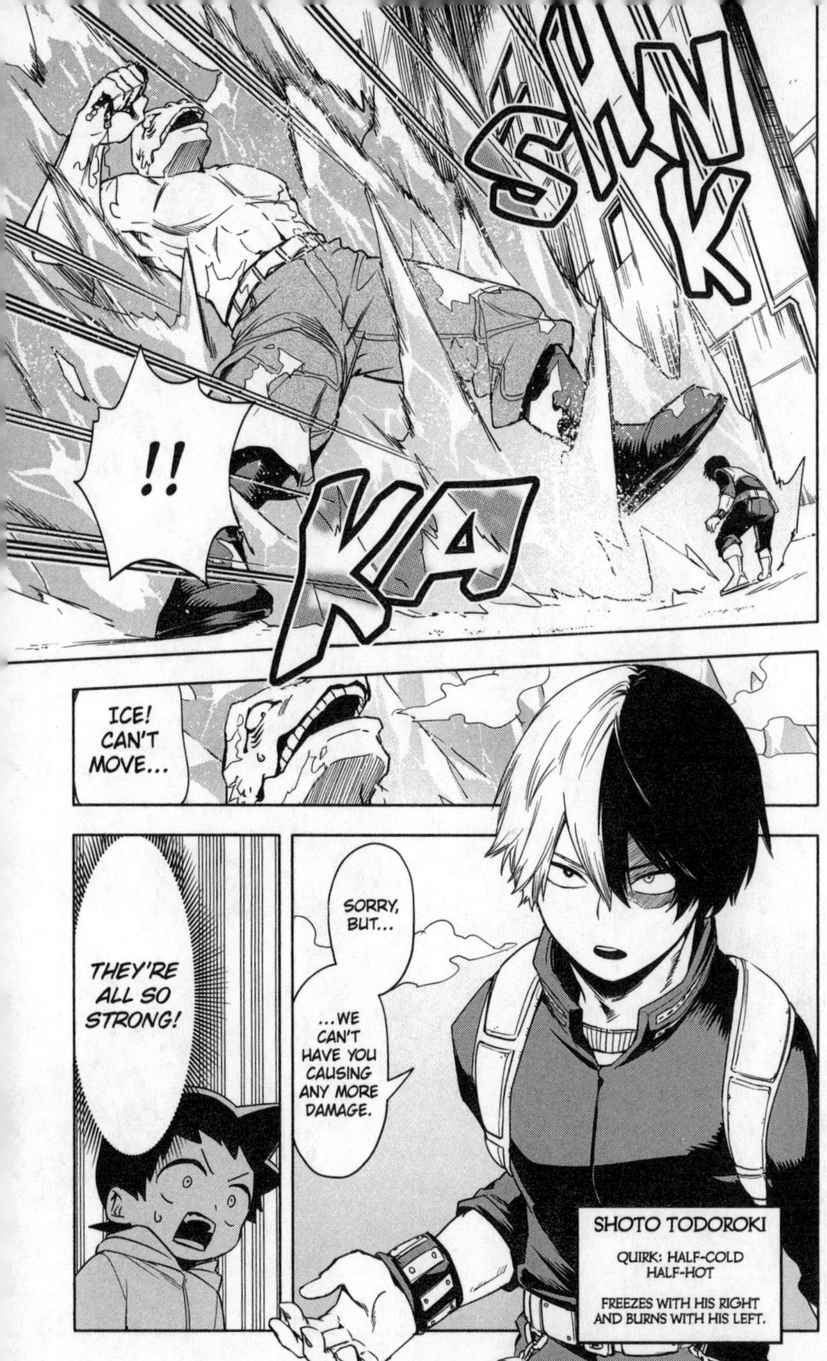
SHNK
!!
KA
ICE! CAN'T MOVE...
SORRY, BUT...
...WE CAN'T HAVE YOU CAUSING ANY MORE DAMAGE.
SHOTO TODOROKI
QUIRK: HALF-COLD HALF-HOT
FREEZES WITH HIS RIGHT AND BURNS WITH HIS LEFT.
THEY'RE ALL SO STRONG!

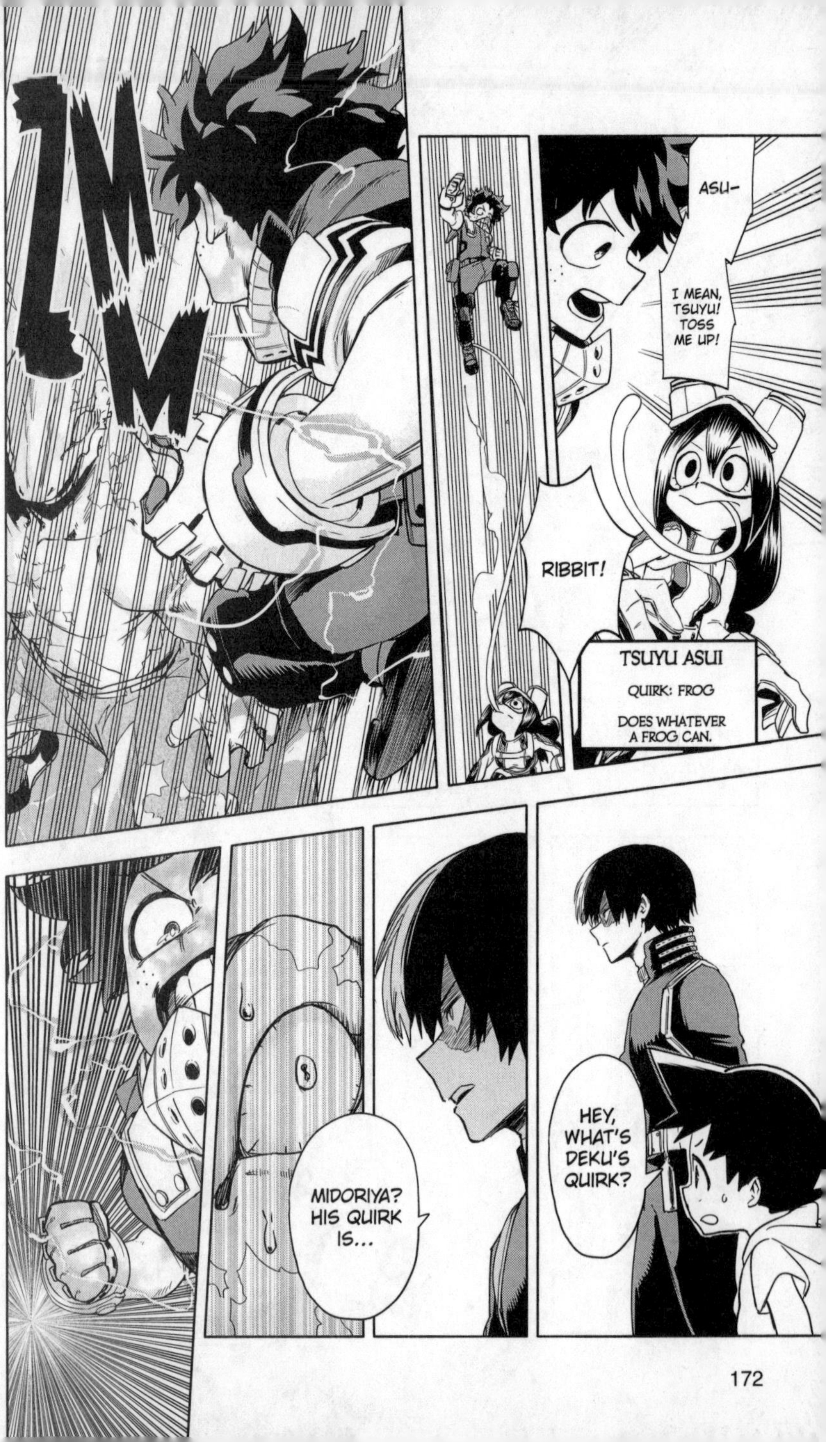
ASU-
I MEAN, TSUYU! TOSS ME UP!
RIBBIT!
TSUYU ASUI
QUIRK: FROG
DOES WHATEVER A FROG CAN.
ZMM
HEY, WHAT'S DEKU'S QUIRK?
MIDORIYA? HIS QUIRK IS...

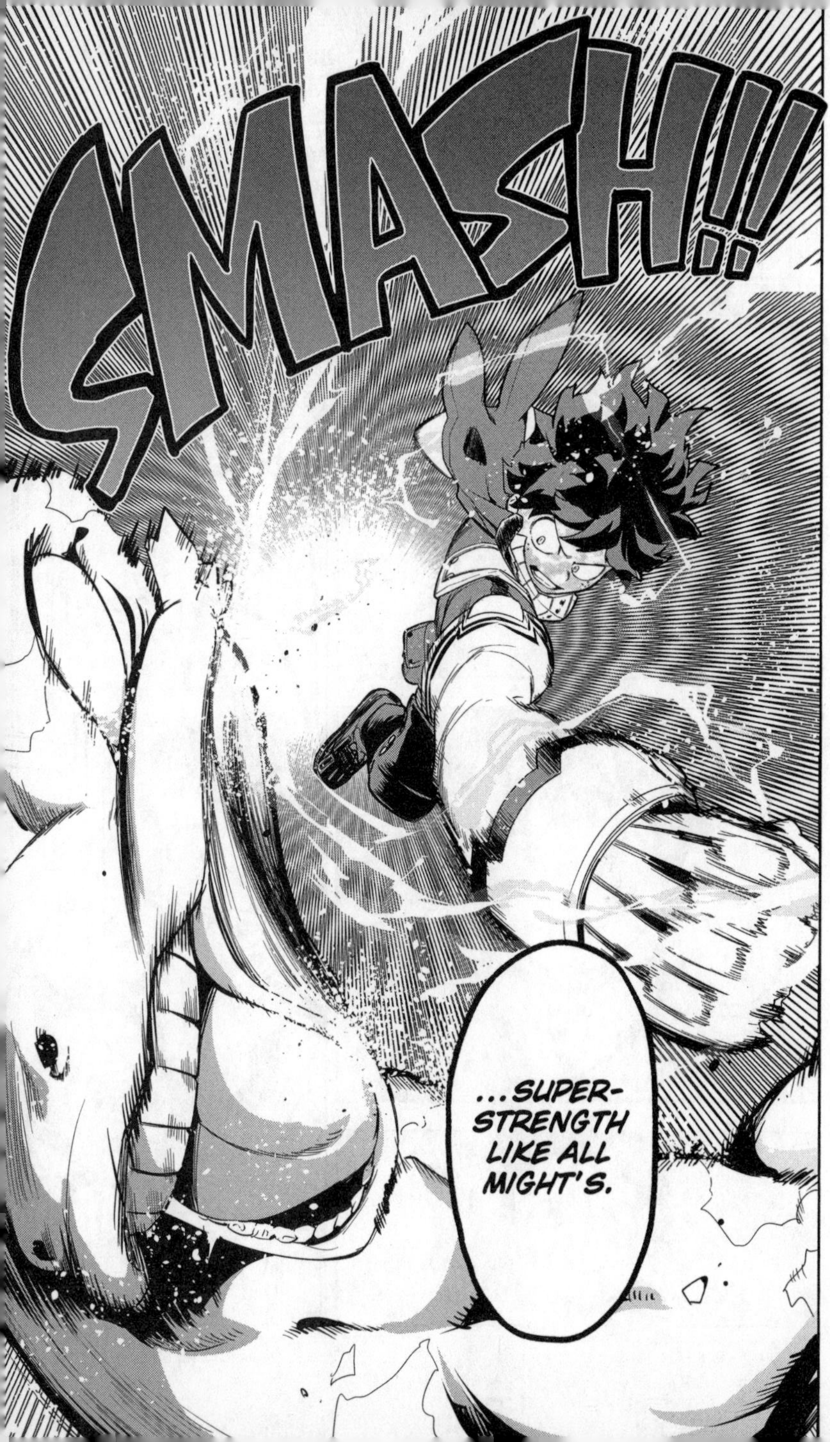
SMASH!!
...SUPER-STRENGTH LIKE ALL MIGHT'S.

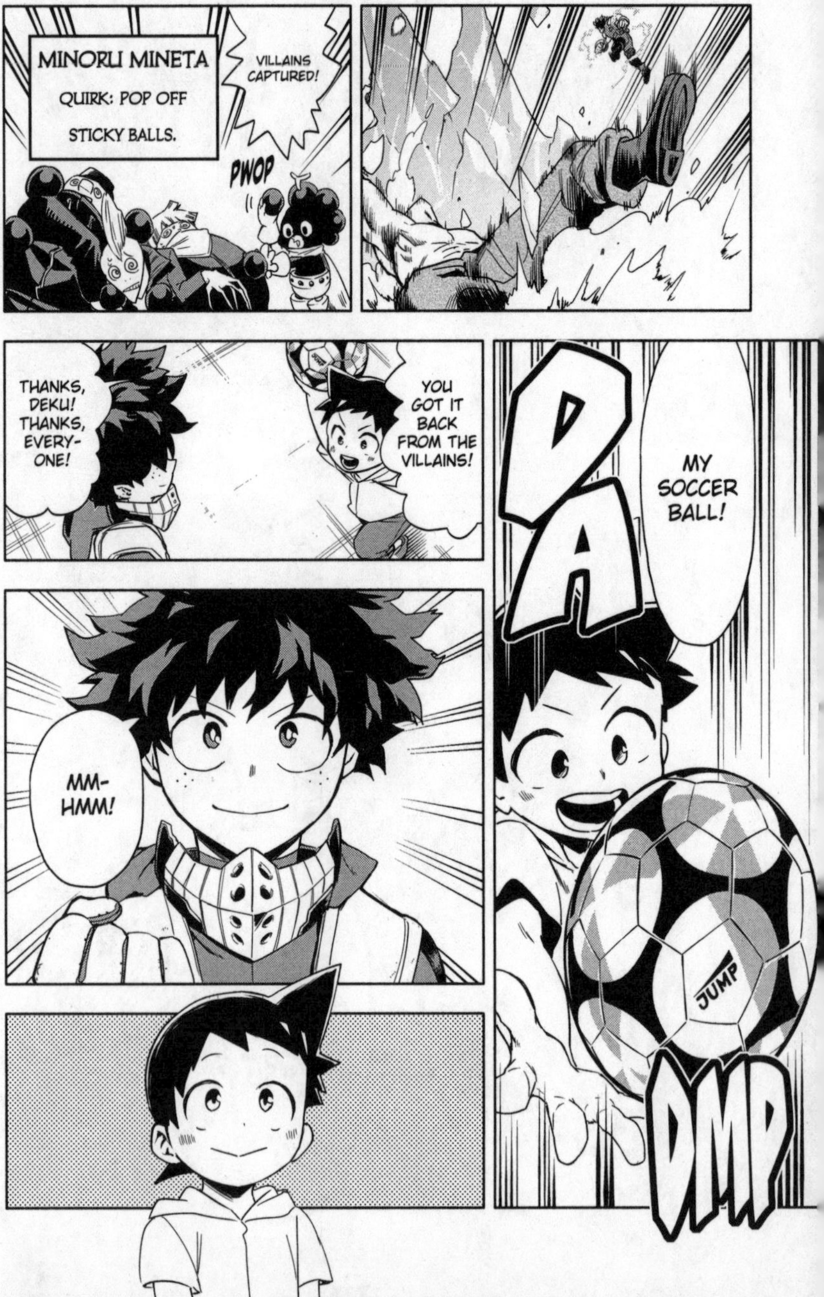
MINORU MINETA
QUIRK: POP OFF STICKY BALLS.
VILLAINS CAPTURED!
PWOP
DA
MY SOCCER BALL!
DMP
YOU GOT IT BACK FROM THE VILLAINS!
THANKS, DEKU! THANKS, EVERY-ONE!
MM-HMM!

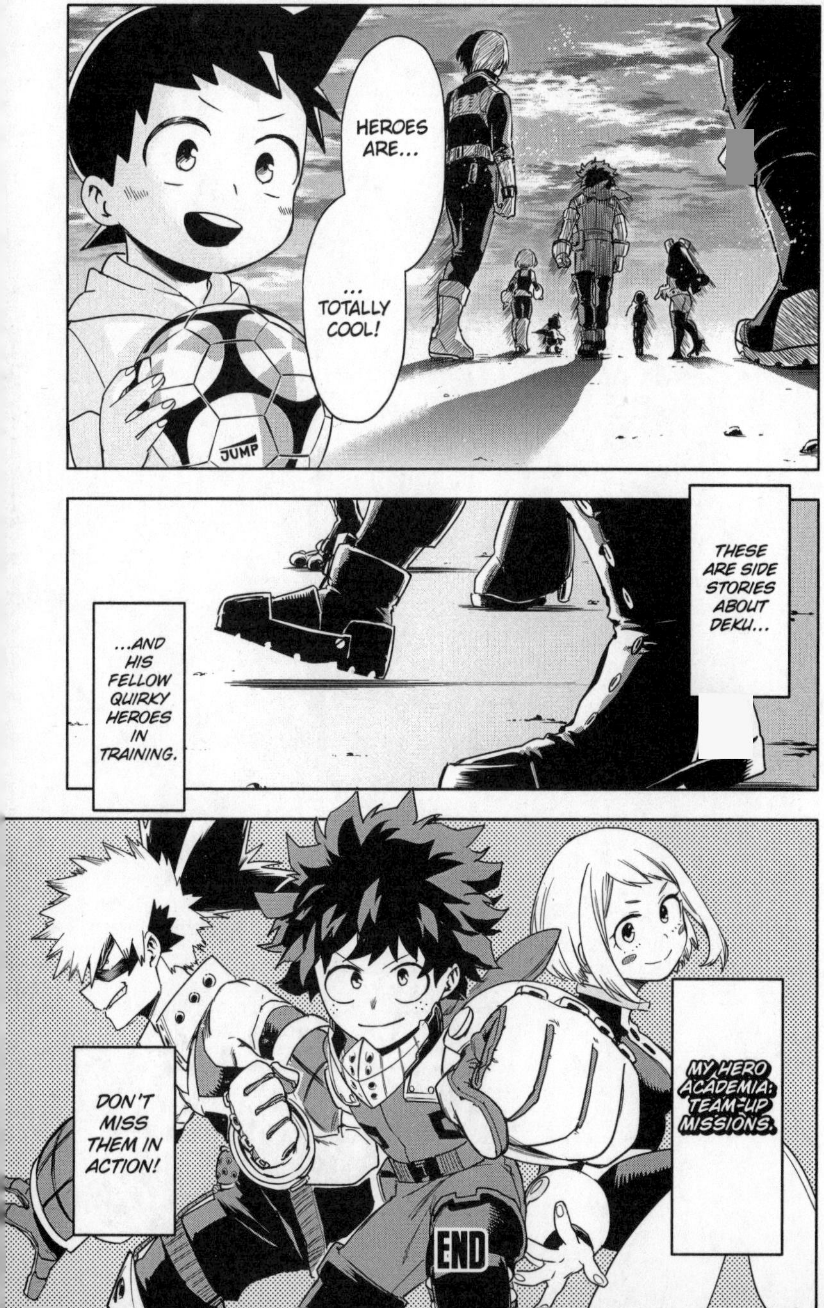
HEROES ARE...
... TOTALLY COOL!
JUMP
THESE ARE SIDE STORIES ABOUT DEKU...
...AND HIS FELLOW QUIRKY HEROES IN TRAINING.
MY HERO ACADEMIA: TEAM-UP MISSIONS.
DON'T MISS THEM IN ACTION!
END

MY HERO ACADEMIA
Team-Up Missions

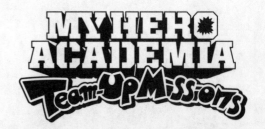

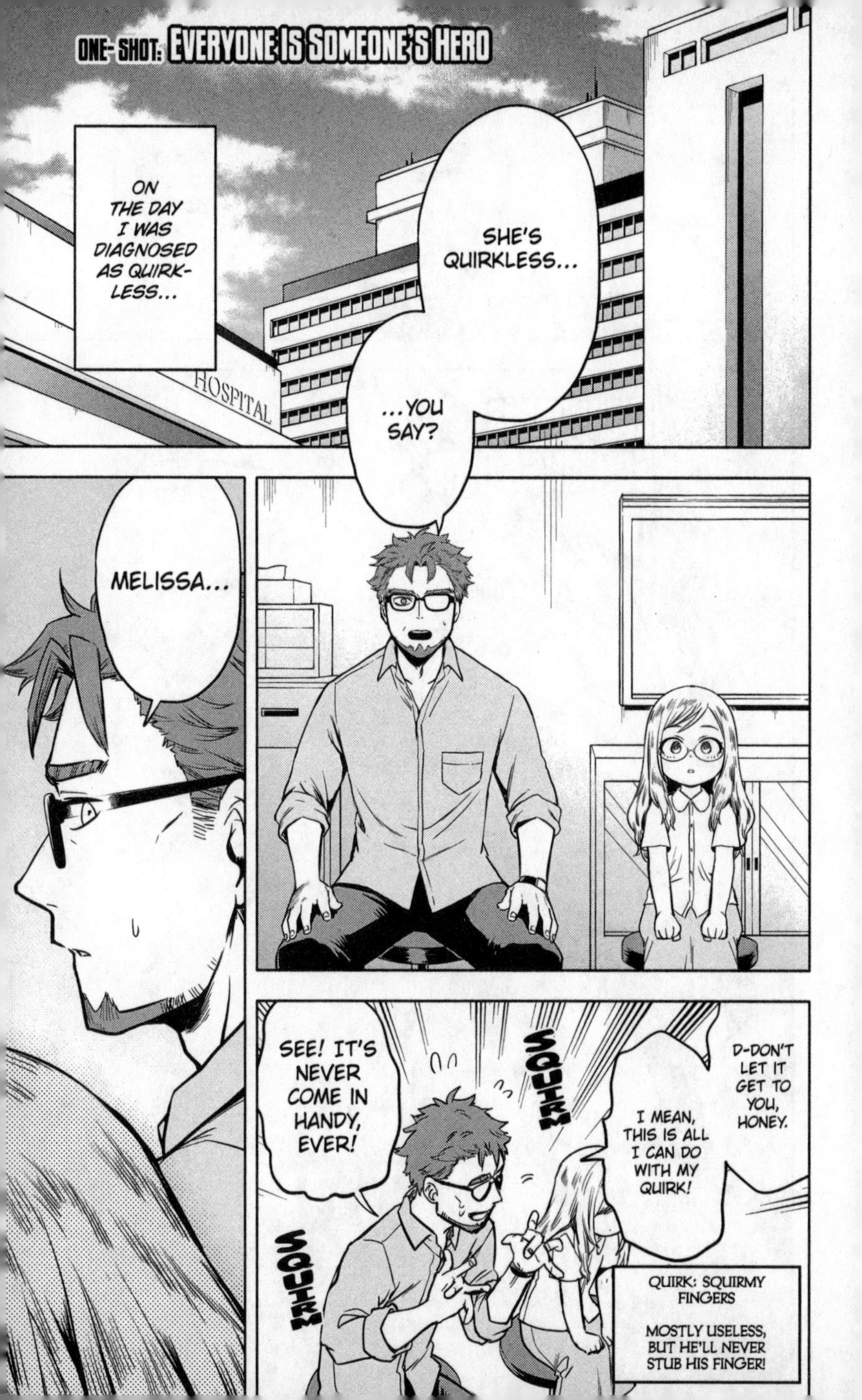
ONE-SHOT: EVERYONE IS SOMEONE'S HERO
SHE'S QUIRKLESS...
...YOU SAY?
ON THE DAY I WAS DIAGNOSED AS QUIRK-LESS...
HOSPITAL
D-DON'T LET IT GET TO YOU, HONEY.
I MEAN, THIS IS ALL I CAN DO WITH MY QUIRK!
SQUIRM
SEE! IT'S NEVER COME IN HANDY, EVER!
SQUIRM
QUIRK: SQUIRMY FINGERS
MOSTLY USELESS, BUT HE'LL NEVER STUB HIS FINGER!
MELISSA...

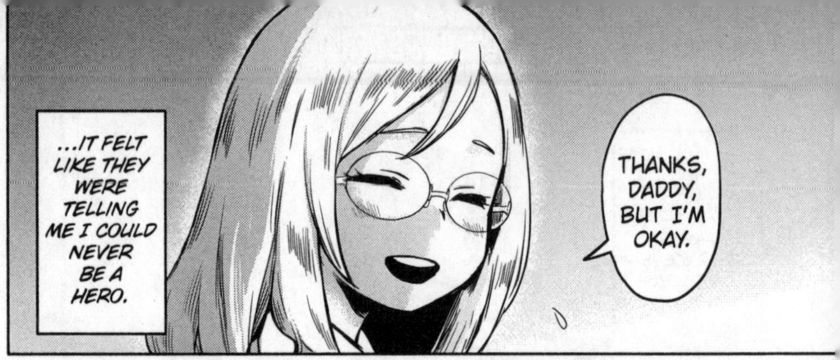
THANKS, DADDY, BUT I'M OKAY.
...IT FELT LIKE THEY WERE TELLING ME I COULD NEVER BE A HERO.

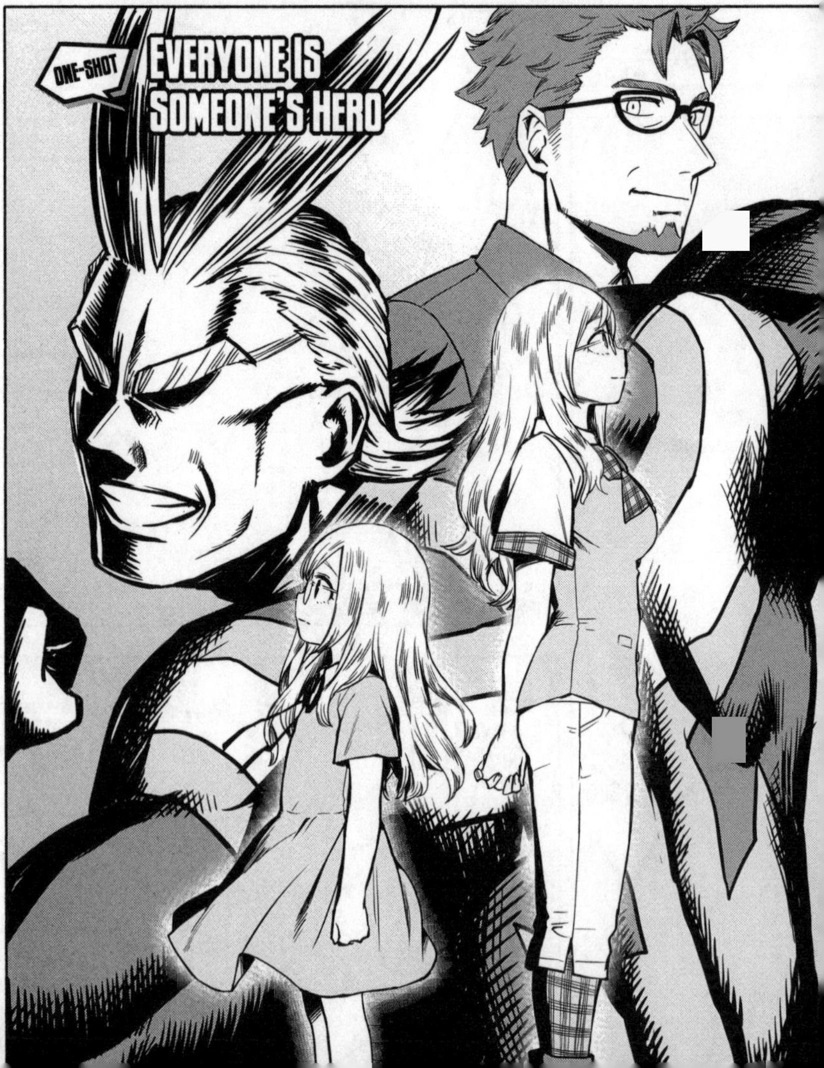
ONE-SHOT
EVERYONE IS SOMEONE'S HERO

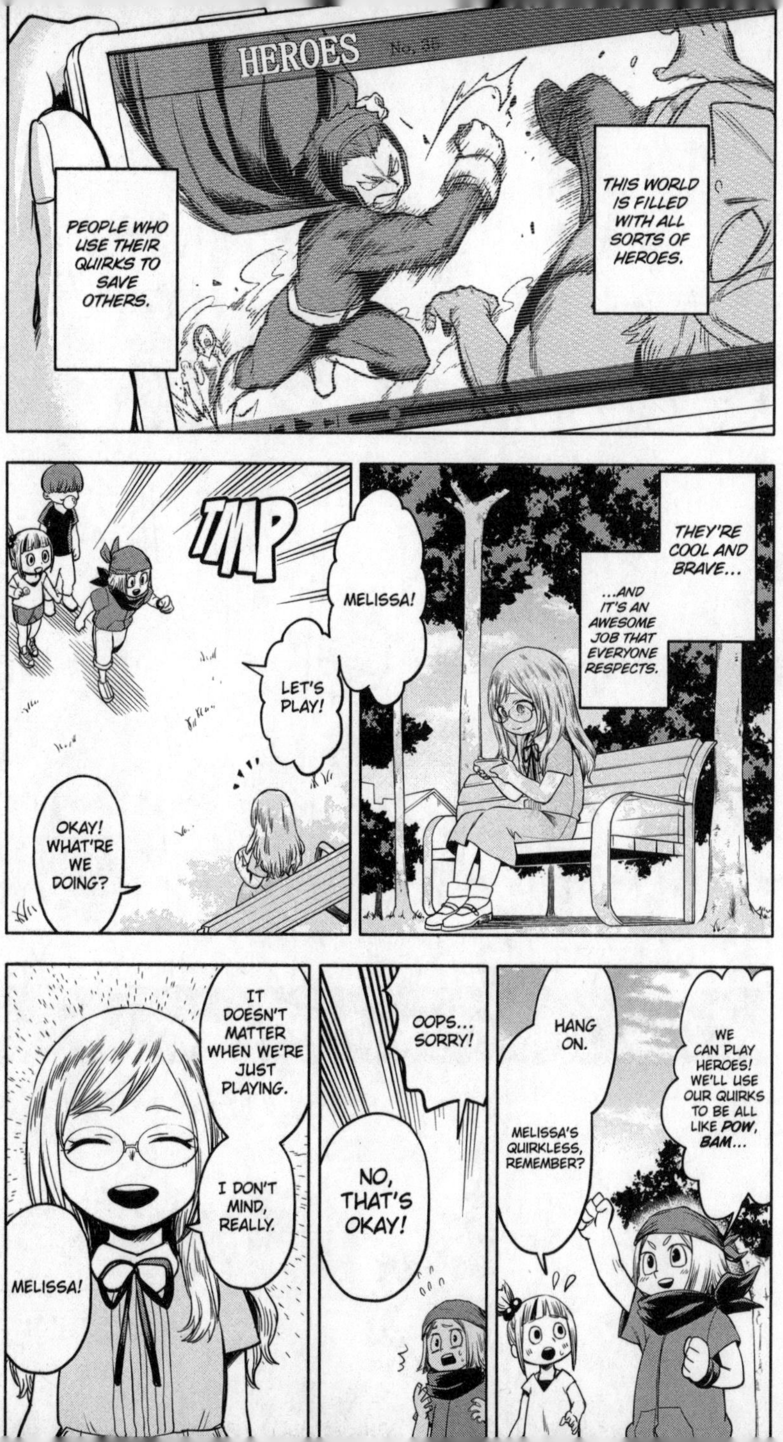
HEROES
THIS WORLD IS FILLED WITH ALL SORTS OF HEROES.
PEOPLE WHO USE THEIR QUIRKS TO SAVE OTHERS.
THEY'RE COOL AND BRAVE...
...AND IT'S AN AWESOME JOB THAT EVERYONE RESPECTS.
TMP
MELISSA!
LET'S PLAY!
OKAY! WHAT'RE WE DOING?
WE CAN PLAY HEROES! WE'LL USE OUR QUIRKS TO BE ALL LIKE *POW, BAM*...
HANG ON.
MELISSA'S QUIRKLESS, REMEMBER?
OOPS... SORRY!
NO, THAT'S OKAY!
IT DOESN'T MATTER WHEN WE'RE JUST PLAYING.
I DON'T MIND, REALLY.
MELISSA!

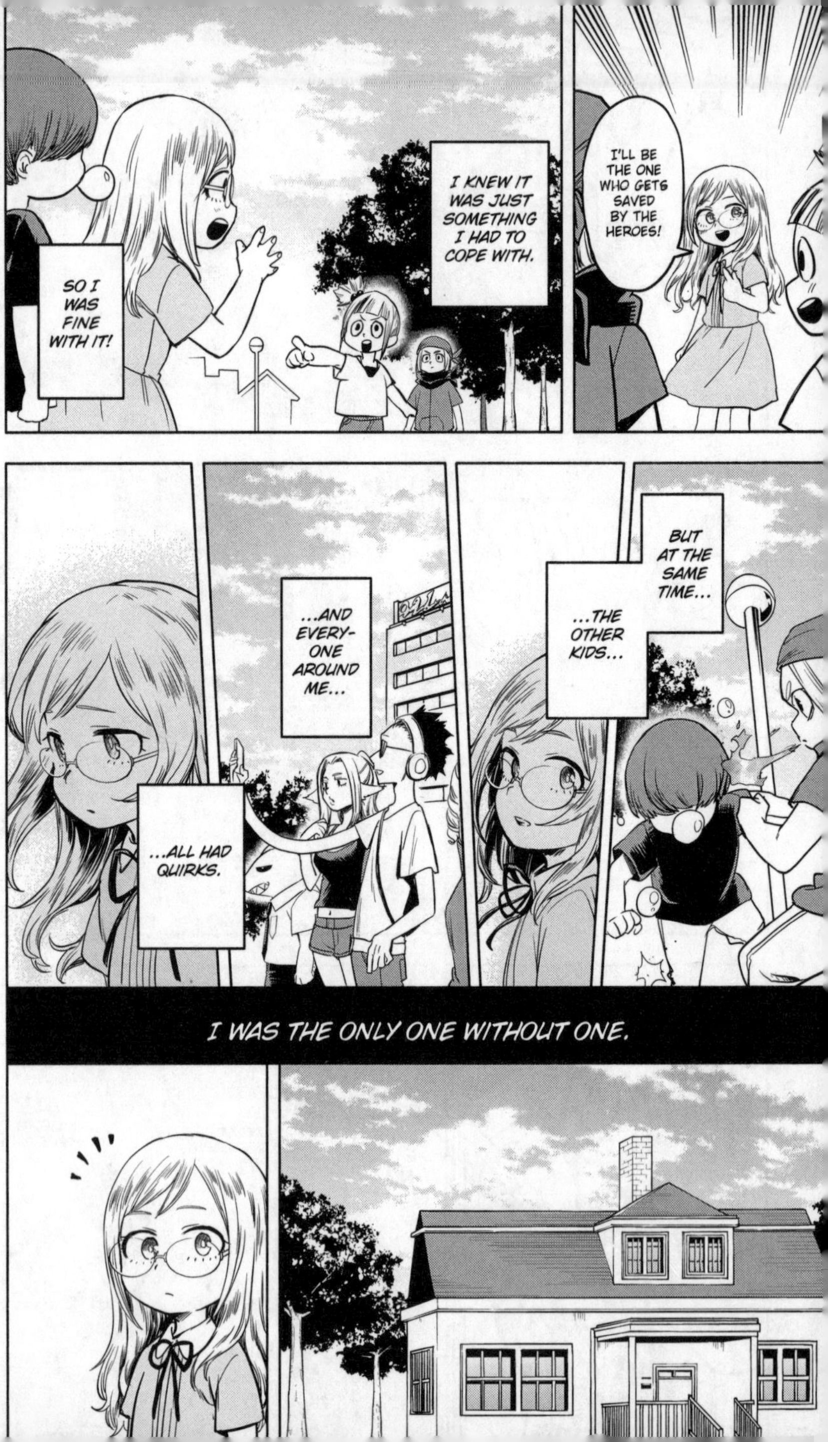
I'LL BE THE ONE WHO GETS SAVED BY THE HEROES!
I KNEW IT WAS JUST SOMETHING I HAD TO COPE WITH.
SO I WAS FINE WITH IT!
BUT AT THE SAME TIME...
...THE OTHER KIDS...
...AND EVERY-ONE AROUND ME...
...ALL HAD QUIRKS.
I WAS THE ONLY ONE WITHOUT ONE.

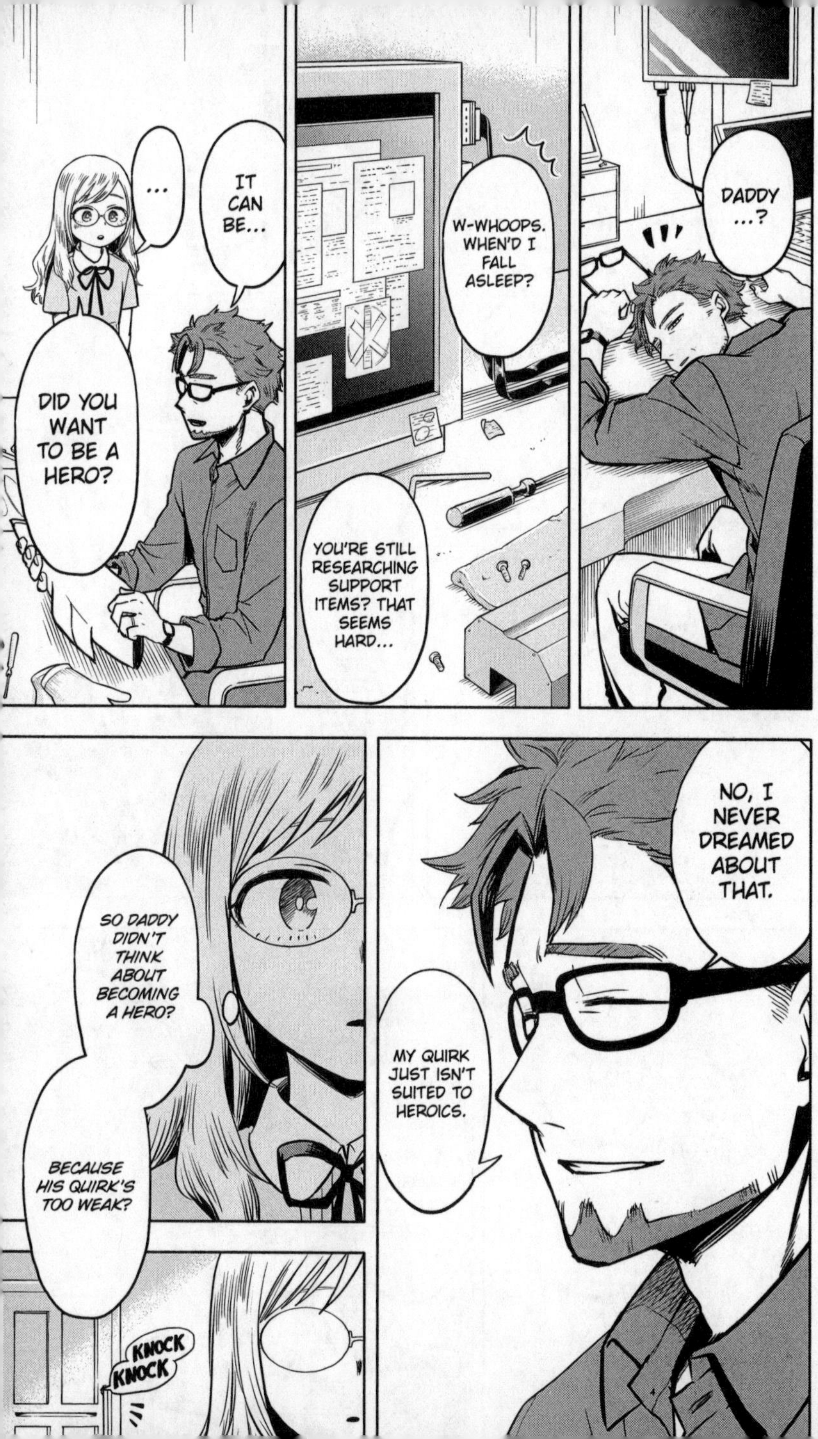

DADDY ...?
W-WHOOPS. WHEN'D I FALL ASLEEP?
YOU'RE STILL RESEARCHING SUPPORT ITEMS? THAT SEEMS HARD...
IT CAN BE...
...
DID YOU WANT TO BE A HERO?
NO, I NEVER DREAMED ABOUT THAT.
MY QUIRK JUST ISN'T SUITED TO HEROICS.
SO DADDY DIDN'T THINK ABOUT BECOMING A HERO?
BECAUSE HIS QUIRK'S TOO WEAK?
KNOCK KNOCK

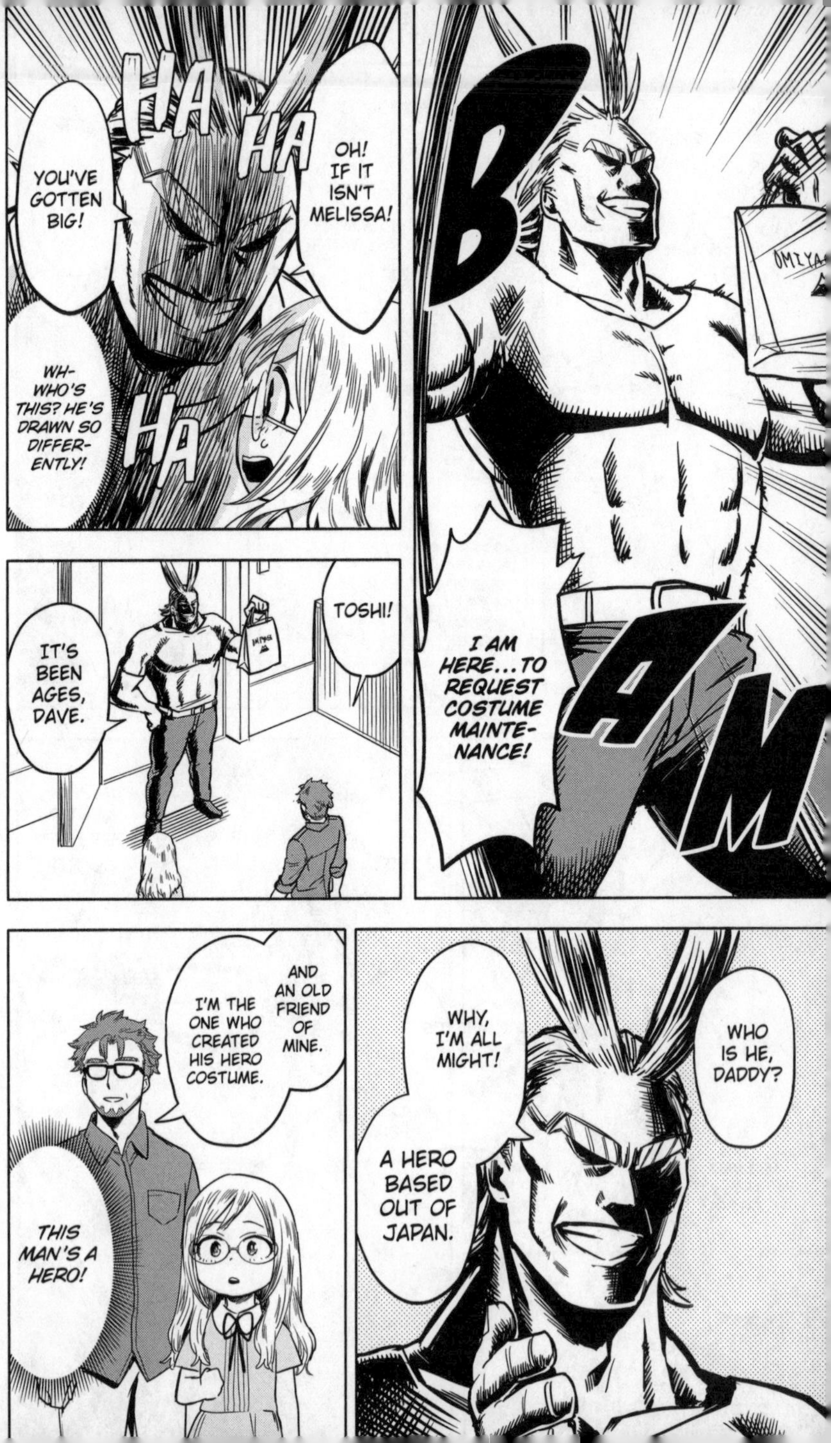
BAM
I AM HERE...TO REQUEST COSTUME MAINTENANCE!
OMIYA
HA HA HA
OH! IF IT ISN'T MELISSA!
YOU'VE GOTTEN BIG!
WH-WHO'S THIS? HE'S DRAWN SO DIFFERENTLY!
TOSHI!
IT'S BEEN AGES, DAVE.
WHO IS HE, DADDY?
WHY, I'M ALL MIGHT!
A HERO BASED OUT OF JAPAN.
AND AN OLD FRIEND OF MINE.
I'M THE ONE WHO CREATED HIS HERO COSTUME.
THIS MAN'S A HERO!

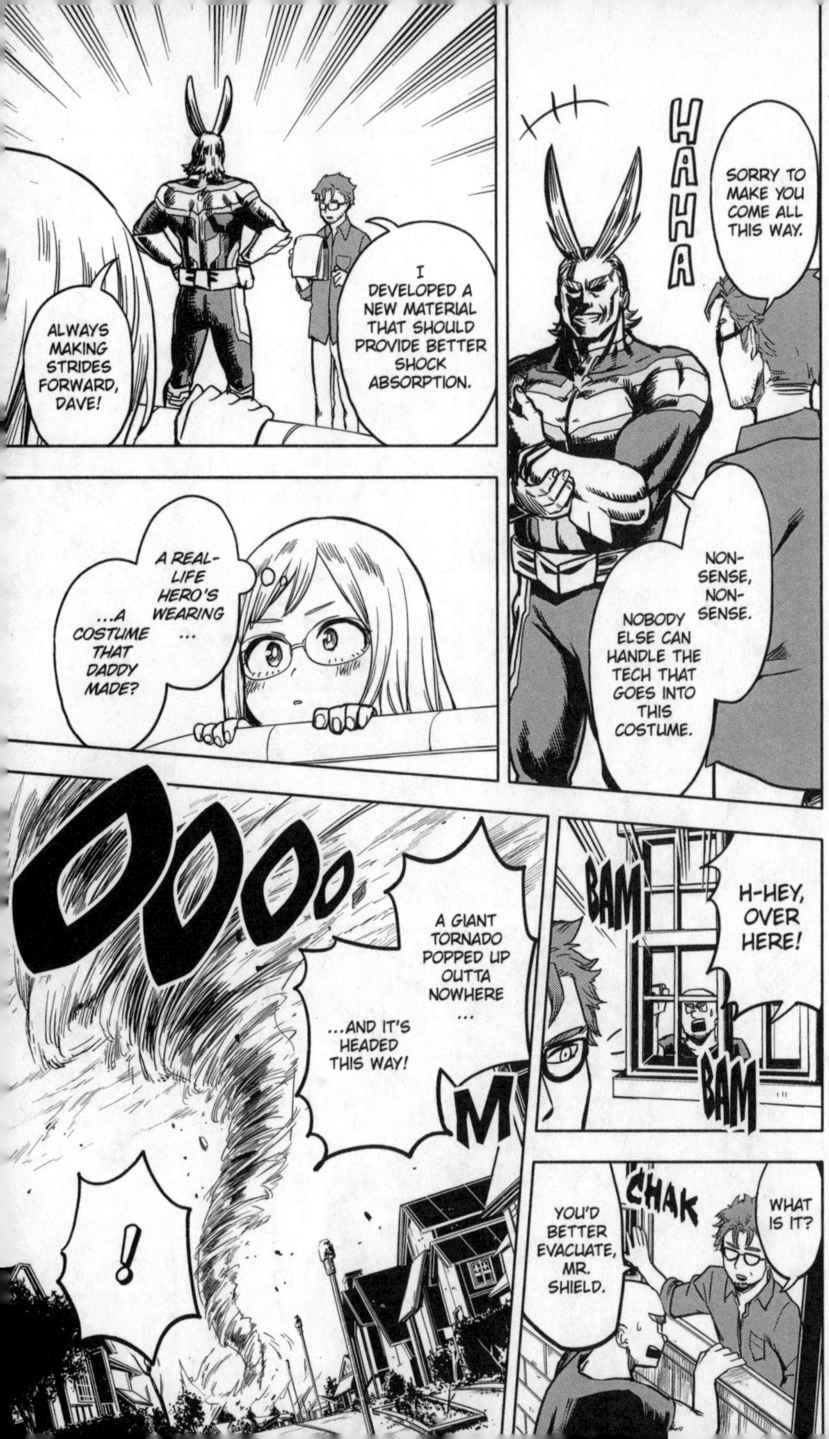
HAHAHA
SORRY TO MAKE YOU COME ALL THIS WAY.
NON-SENSE, NON-SENSE.
NOBODY ELSE CAN HANDLE THE TECH THAT GOES INTO THIS COSTUME.
I DEVELOPED A NEW MATERIAL THAT SHOULD PROVIDE BETTER SHOCK ABSORPTION.
ALWAYS MAKING STRIDES FORWARD, DAVE!
A REAL-LIFE HERO'S WEARING...
...A COSTUME THAT DADDY MADE?
BAM
H-HEY, OVER HERE!
BAM
CHAK
WHAT IS IT?
YOU'D BETTER EVACUATE, MR. SHIELD.
DOOO
A GIANT TORNADO POPPED UP OUTTA NOWHERE...
...AND IT'S HEADED THIS WAY!
M
!

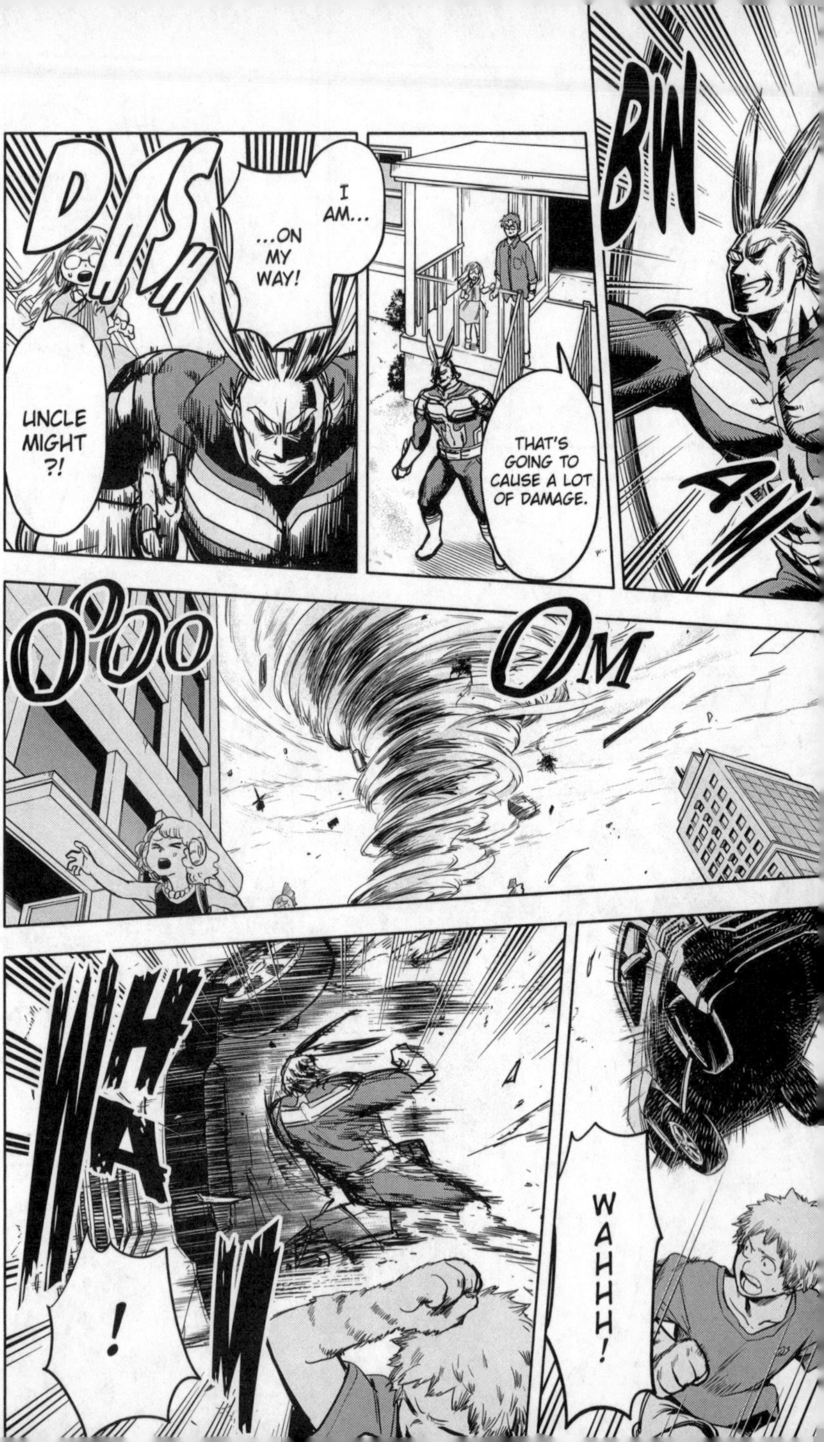

BWAN
THAT'S GOING TO CAUSE A LOT OF DAMAGE.
I AM...
...ON MY WAY!
DASH
UNCLE MIGHT?!
OOOOOOM
WAHHH!
WHAM
!

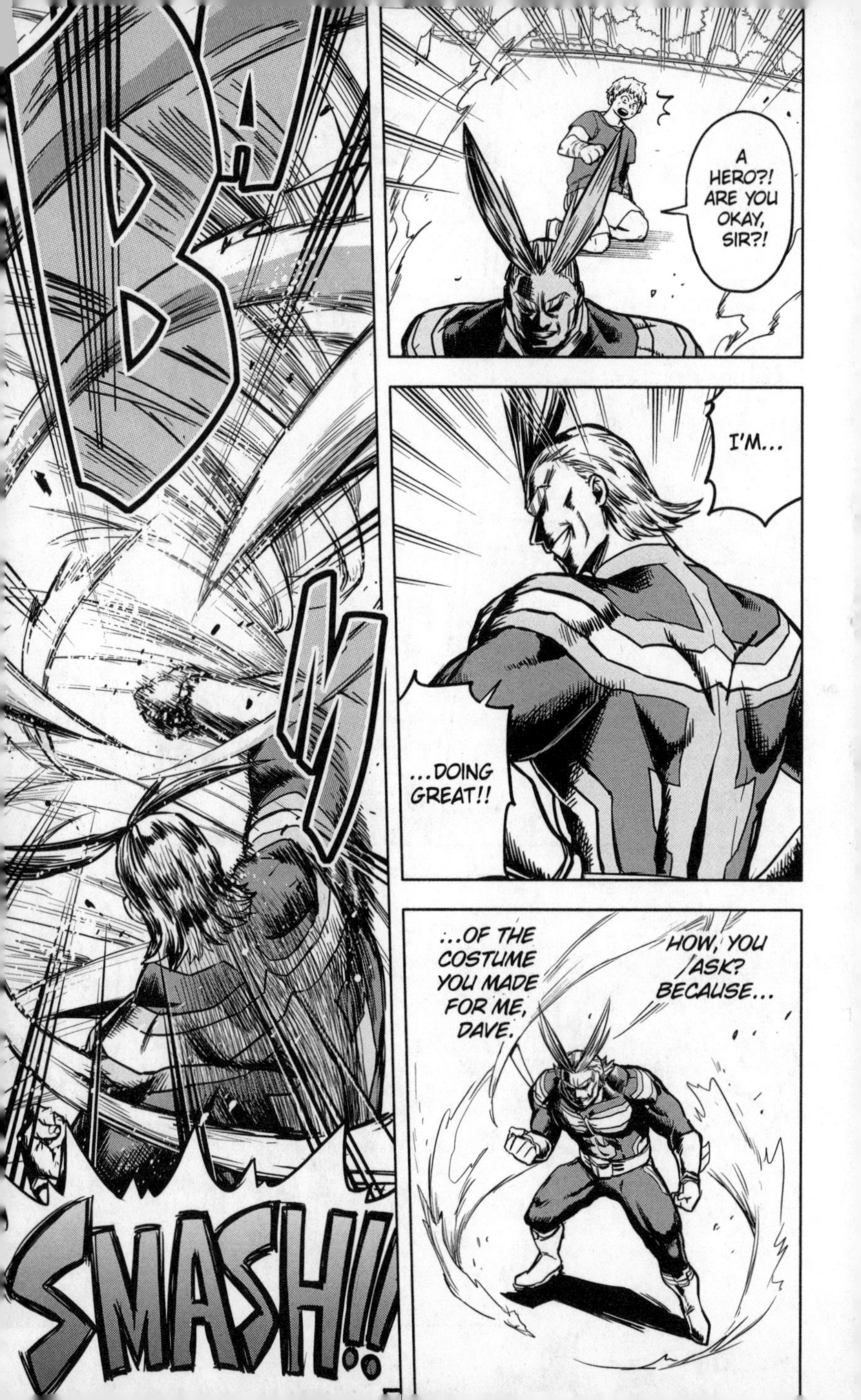
A HERO?! ARE YOU OKAY, SIR?!
I'M...
...DOING GREAT!!
HOW, YOU ASK? BECAUSE...
...OF THE COSTUME YOU MADE FOR ME, DAVE.
SMASH!!

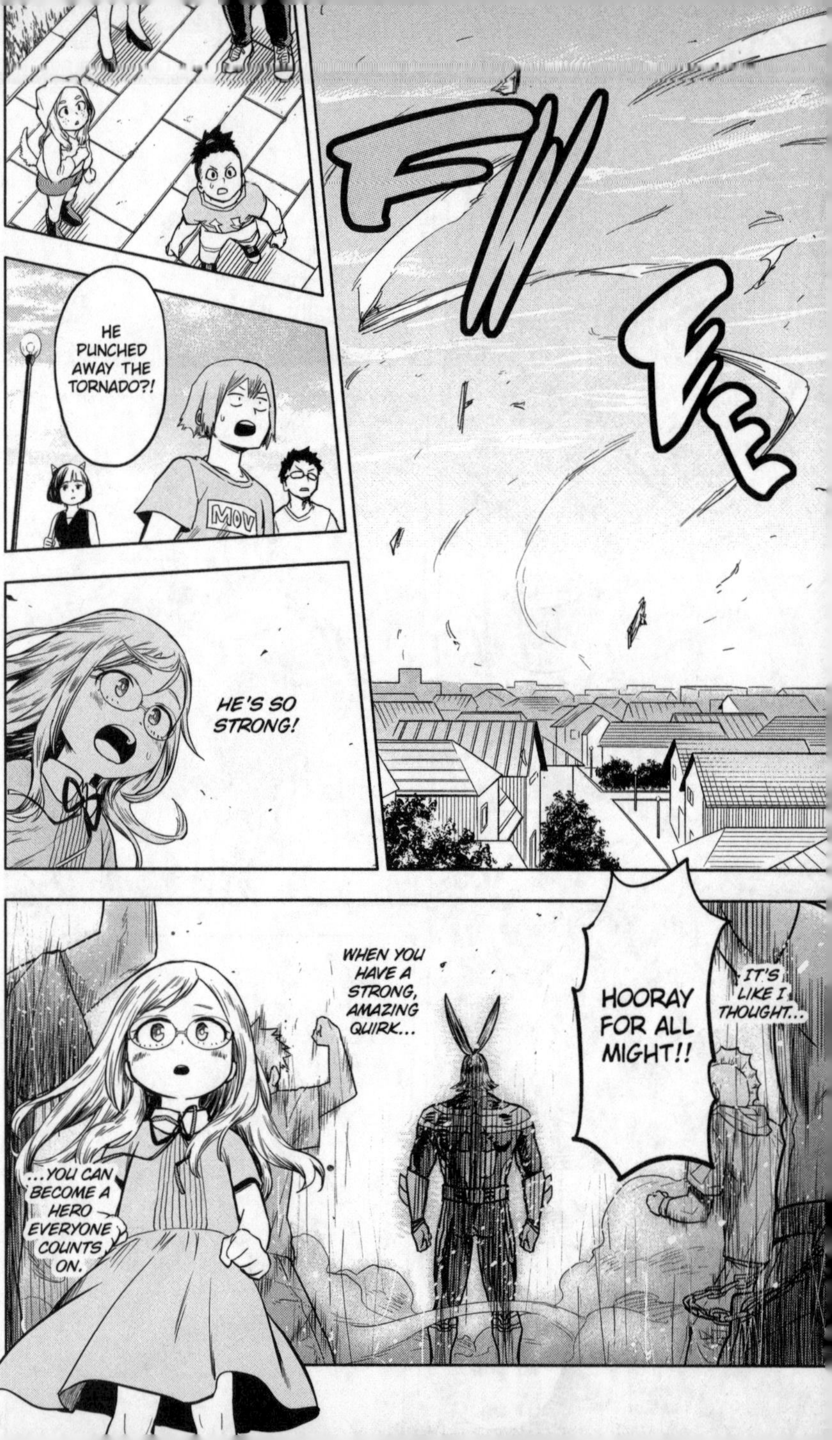
HE PUNCHED AWAY THE TORNADO?!
HE'S SO STRONG!
IT'S LIKE I THOUGHT...
HOORAY FOR ALL MIGHT!!
WHEN YOU HAVE A STRONG, AMAZING QUIRK...
...YOU CAN BECOME A HERO EVERYONE COUNTS ON.

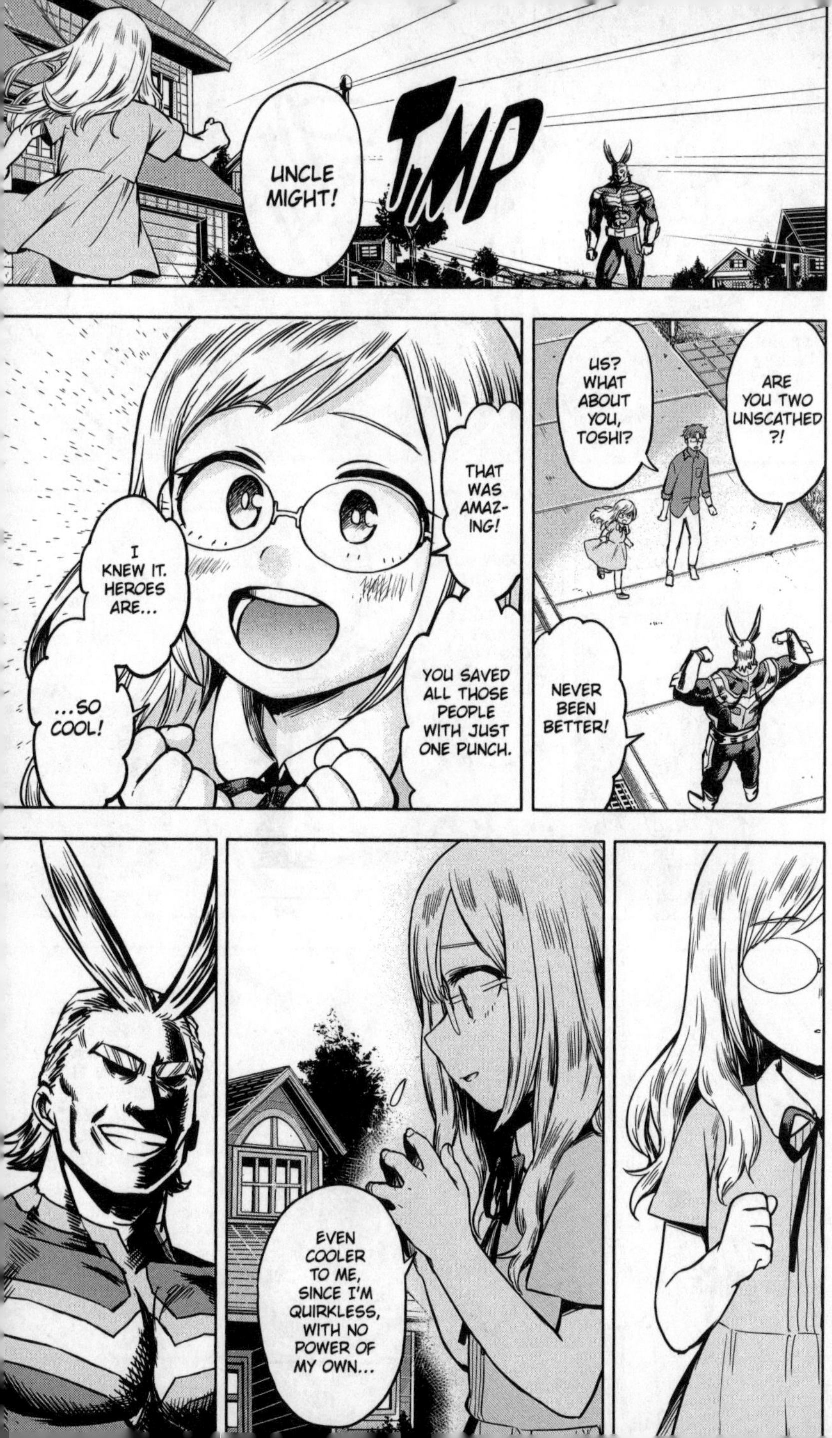
TMP
UNCLE MIGHT!
ARE YOU TWO UNSCATHED?!
US? WHAT ABOUT YOU, TOSHI?
NEVER BEEN BETTER!
THAT WAS AMAZ-ING!
YOU SAVED ALL THOSE PEOPLE WITH JUST ONE PUNCH.
I KNEW IT. HEROES ARE...
...SO COOL!
EVEN COOLER TO ME, SINCE I'M QUIRKLESS, WITH NO POWER OF MY OWN...

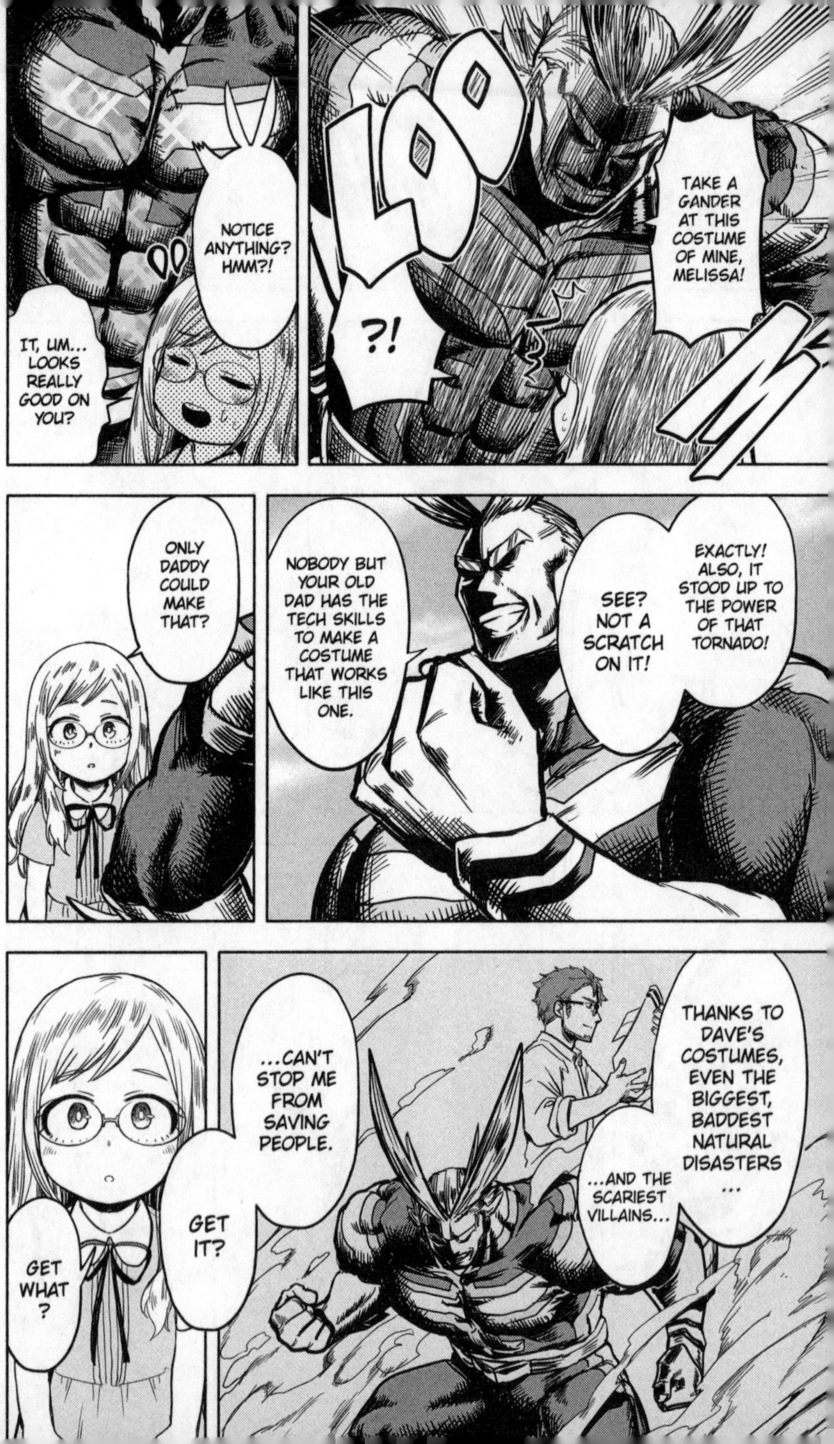
TAKE A GANDER AT THIS COSTUME OF MINE, MELISSA!
?!
NOTICE ANYTHING? HMM?!
IT, UM... LOOKS REALLY GOOD ON YOU?
EXACTLY! ALSO, IT STOOD UP TO THE POWER OF THAT TORNADO!
SEE? NOT A SCRATCH ON IT!
NOBODY BUT YOUR OLD DAD HAS THE TECH SKILLS TO MAKE A COSTUME THAT WORKS LIKE THIS ONE.
ONLY DADDY COULD MAKE THAT?
THANKS TO DAVE'S COSTUMES, EVEN THE BIGGEST, BADDEST NATURAL DISASTERS...
...AND THE SCARIEST VILLAINS...
...CAN'T STOP ME FROM SAVING PEOPLE.
GET IT?
GET WHAT?

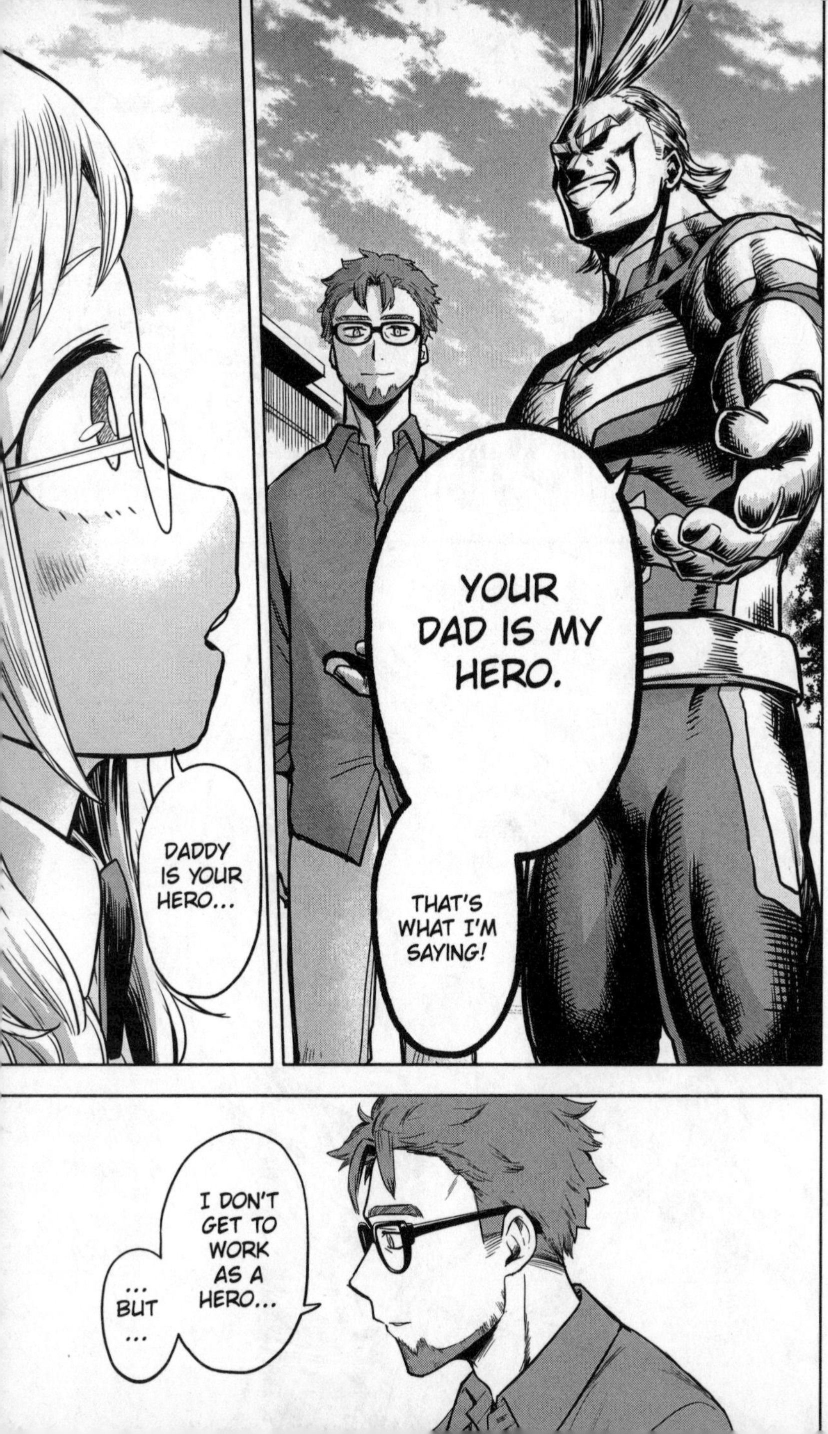
YOUR DAD IS MY HERO.
THAT'S WHAT I'M SAYING!
DADDY IS YOUR HERO...
I DON'T GET TO WORK AS A HERO...
...BUT...

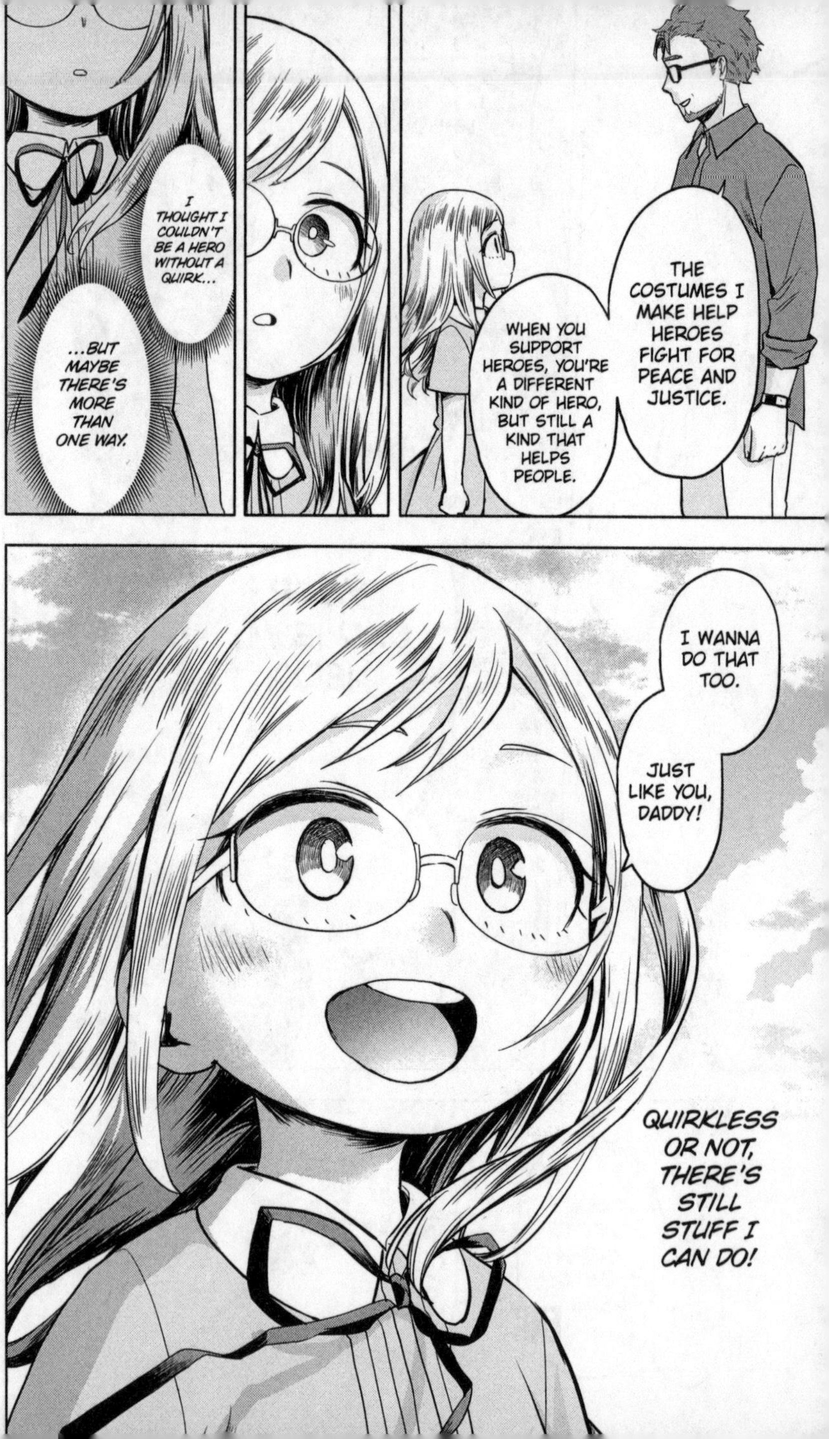
THE COSTUMES I MAKE HELP HEROES FIGHT FOR PEACE AND JUSTICE.
WHEN YOU SUPPORT HEROES, YOU'RE A DIFFERENT KIND OF HERO, BUT STILL A KIND THAT HELPS PEOPLE.
I THOUGHT I COULDN'T BE A HERO WITHOUT A QUIRK...
...BUT MAYBE THERE'S MORE THAN ONE WAY.
I WANNA DO THAT TOO.
JUST LIKE YOU, DADDY!
QUIRKLESS OR NOT, THERE'S STILL STUFF I CAN DO!

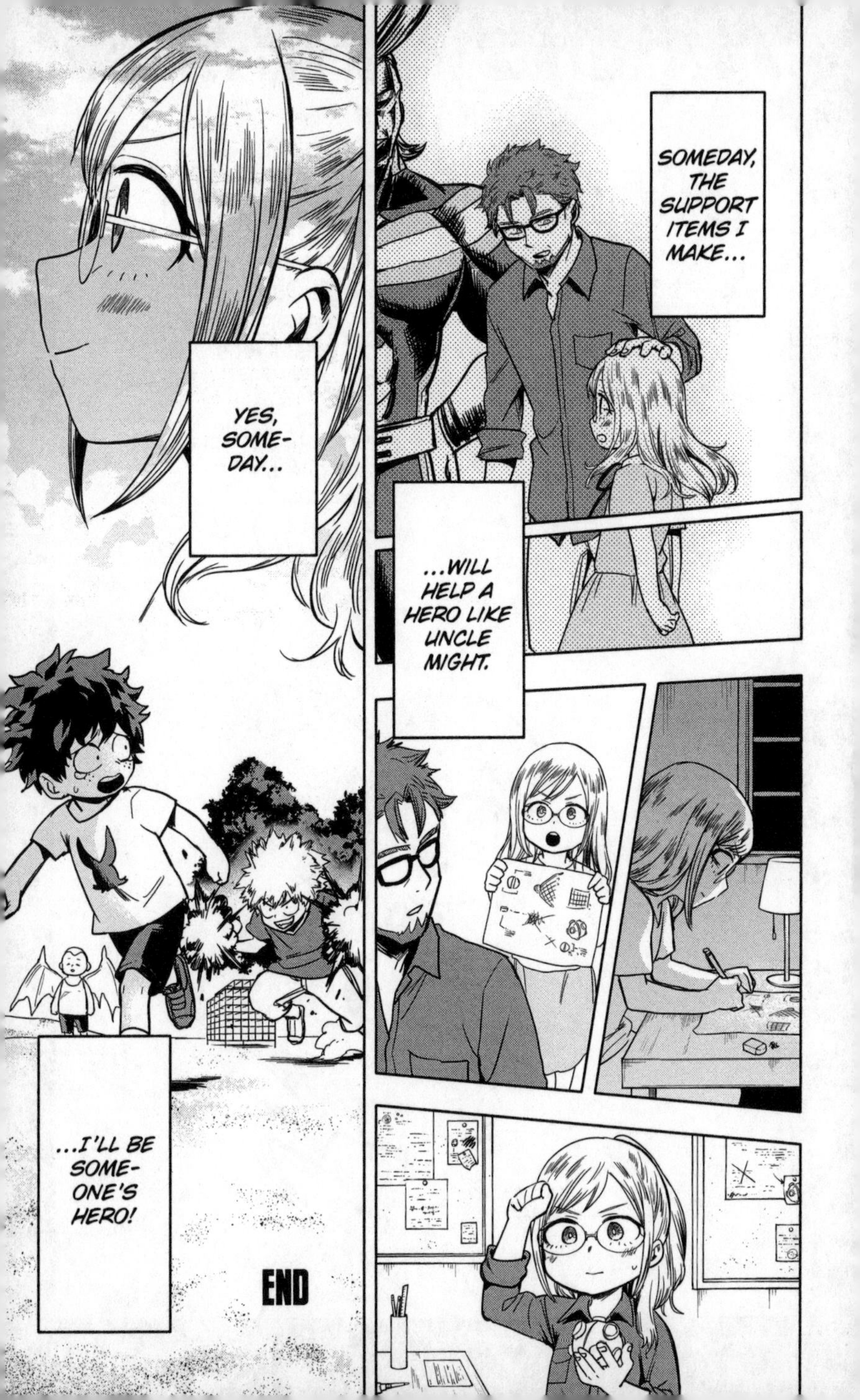
SOMEDAY, THE SUPPORT ITEMS I MAKE...
...WILL HELP A HERO LIKE UNCLE MIGHT.
YES, SOME-DAY...
...I'LL BE SOME-ONE'S HERO!
END

EVERYONE IS SOMEONE'S HERO

Melissa faces off against Hatsume in chapter 3, but this is her origin story. David's Quirk was never shown in the movie *My Hero Academia: Two Heroes*, so I got to decide what it was. Sorry if I made it a weird one!

I was so very happy when Horikoshi Sensei and many others said they liked this one-shot.

ILLUSTRATIONS FROM HORIKOSHI SENSEI
&
FOUR-PANEL COMICS: MY HERO(INE) ACADEMIA

When this spin-off first started, Horikoshi Sensei sent me some comments along with a pair of drawings.

And here they are for you to see! Across two whole pages! Thank you, Horikoshi Sensei!

AN ILLUS-TRATION OF THE *REAL* ME!

Message from
KOHEI HORIKOSHI

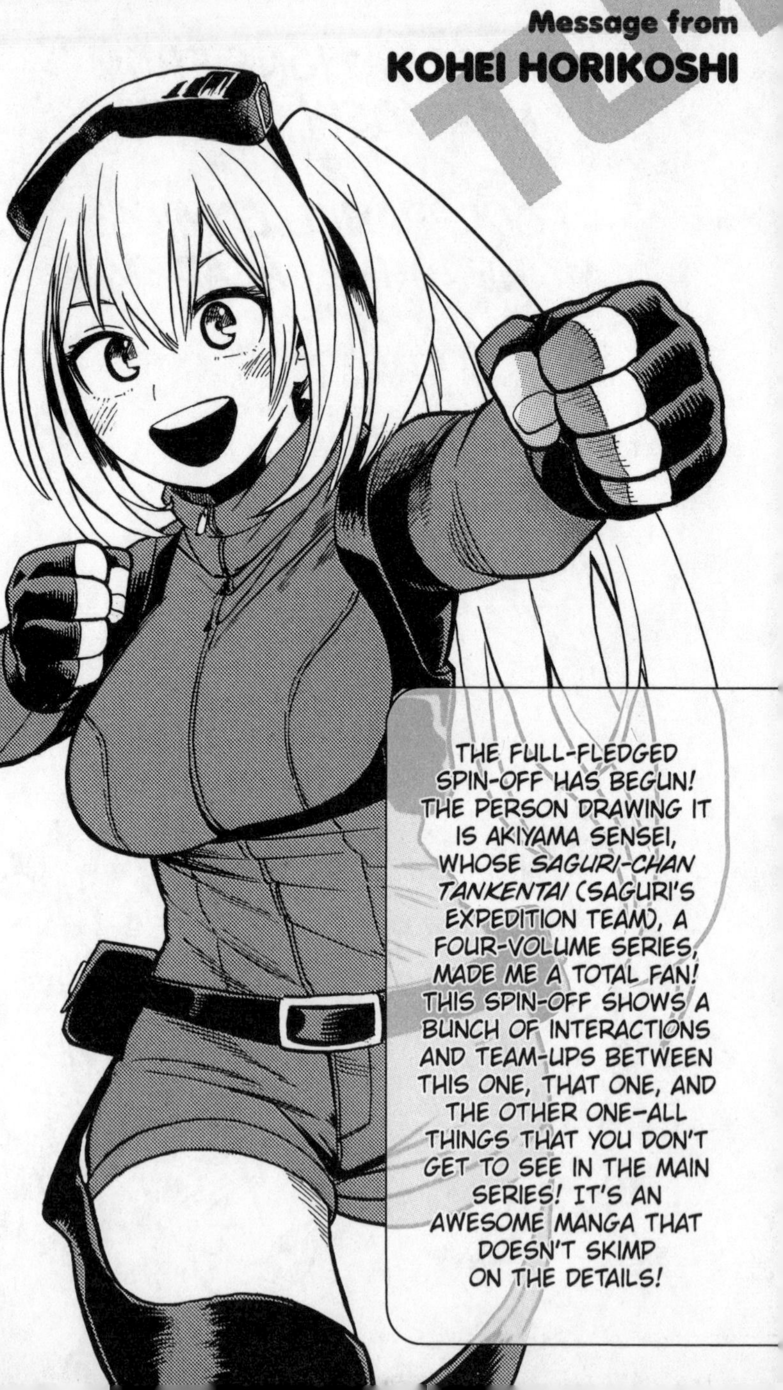

THE FULL-FLEDGED SPIN-OFF HAS BEGUN! THE PERSON DRAWING IT IS AKIYAMA SENSEI, WHOSE *SAGURI-CHAN TANKENTAI* (SAGURI'S EXPEDITION TEAM), A FOUR-VOLUME SERIES, MADE ME A TOTAL FAN! THIS SPIN-OFF SHOWS A BUNCH OF INTERACTIONS AND TEAM-UPS BETWEEN THIS ONE, THAT ONE, AND THE OTHER ONE—ALL THINGS THAT YOU DON'T GET TO SEE IN THE MAIN SERIES! IT'S AN AWESOME MANGA THAT DOESN'T SKIMP ON THE DETAILS!

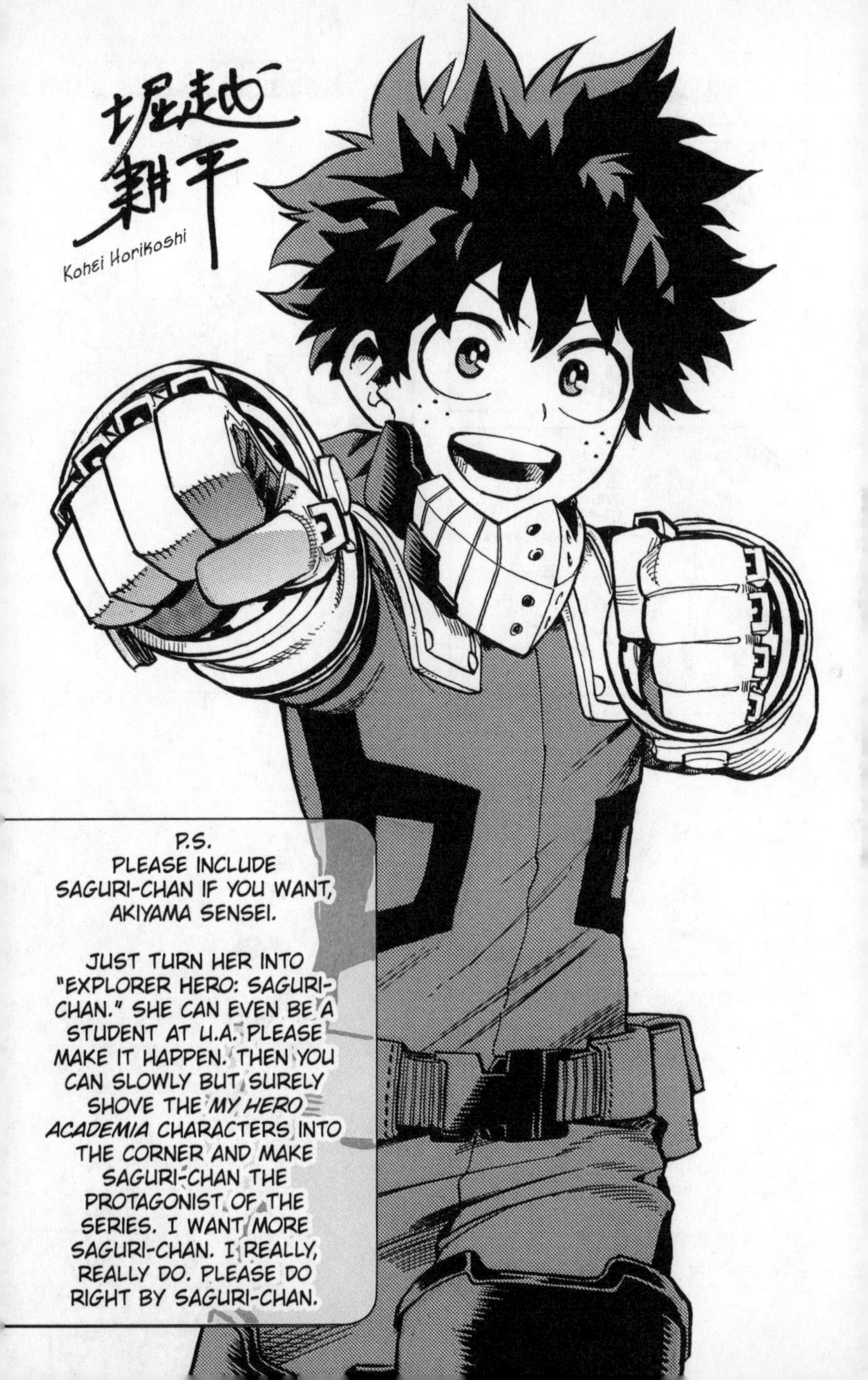
堀越耕平
Kohei Horikoshi
P.S.
PLEASE INCLUDE SAGURI-CHAN IF YOU WANT, AKIYAMA SENSEI.
JUST TURN HER INTO "EXPLORER HERO: SAGURI-CHAN." SHE CAN EVEN BE A STUDENT AT U.A. PLEASE MAKE IT HAPPEN. THEN YOU CAN SLOWLY BUT SURELY SHOVE THE *MY HERO ACADEMIA* CHARACTERS INTO THE CORNER AND MAKE SAGURI-CHAN THE PROTAGONIST OF THE SERIES. I WANT MORE SAGURI-CHAN. I REALLY, REALLY DO. PLEASE DO RIGHT BY SAGURI-CHAN.

MY HERO(INE) ACADEMIA

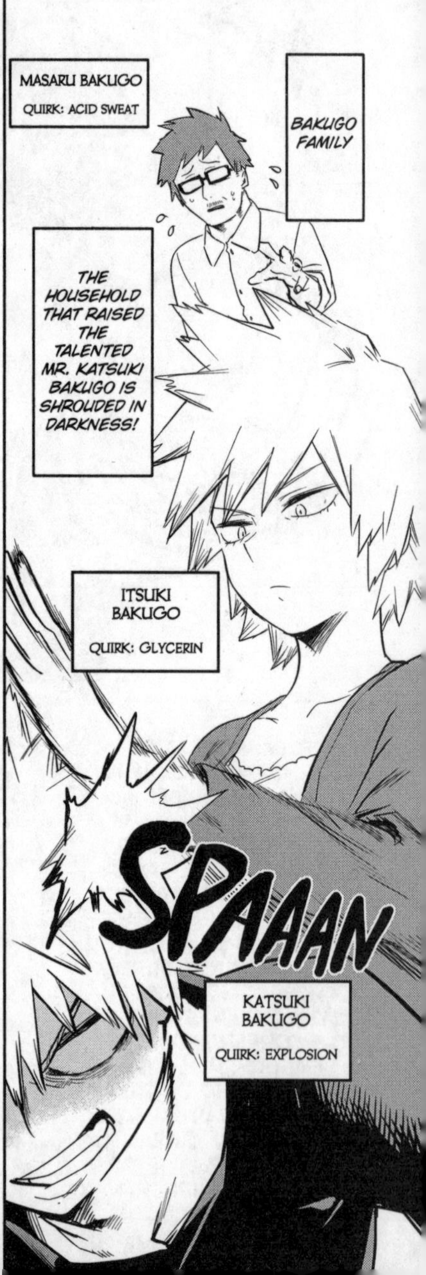
BAKUGO FAMILY
MASARU BAKUGO
QUIRK: ACID SWEAT
THE HOUSEHOLD THAT RAISED THE TALENTED MR. KATSUKI BAKUGO IS SHROUDED IN DARKNESS!
ITSUKI BAKUGO
QUIRK: GLYCERIN
SPAAAN
KATSUKI BAKUGO
QUIRK: EXPLOSION

THE BAKU CASTE SYSTEM

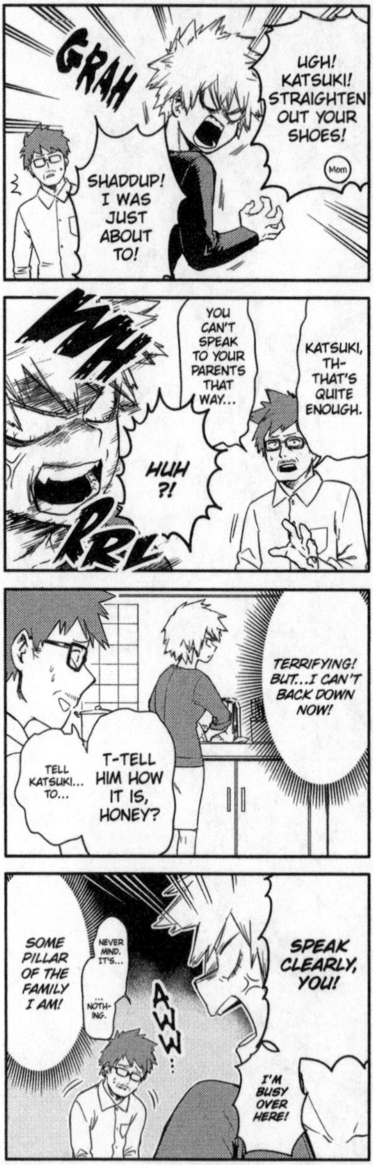
UGH! KATSUKI! STRAIGHTEN OUT YOUR SHOES!
Mom
GRAH
SHADDUP! I WAS JUST ABOUT TO!
KATSUKI, TH-THAT'S QUITE ENOUGH.
YOU CAN'T SPEAK TO YOUR PARENTS THAT WAY...
HUH ?!
TERRIFYING! BUT...I CAN'T BACK DOWN NOW!
T-TELL HIM HOW IT IS, HONEY?
TELL KATSUKI... TO...
SPEAK CLEARLY, YOU!
AWW...
NEVER MIND. IT'S... ...NOTHING.
SOME PILLAR OF THE FAMILY I AM!
I'M BUSY OVER HERE!

MOTHER-SON BATTLE

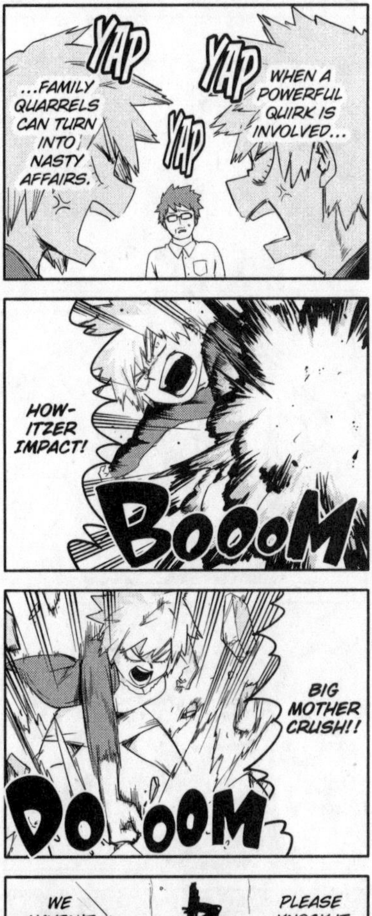
WHEN A POWERFUL QUIRK IS INVOLVED...
YAP
YAP
YAP
...FAMILY QUARRELS CAN TURN INTO NASTY AFFAIRS.
HOW-ITZER IMPACT!
BOOOM
BIG MOTHER CRUSH!!
DOOOM
PLEASE KNOCK IT OFF, YOU TWO...
BAM
KRK
WE HAVEN'T PAID OFF THE MORTGAGE YET!
KRK

BUDDING ROMANCE

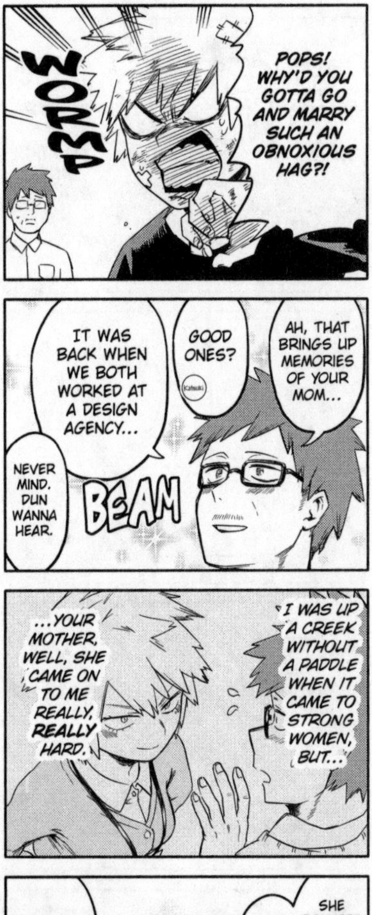
POPS! WHY'D YOU GOTTA GO AND MARRY SUCH AN OBNOXIOUS HAG?!
WORMP
AH, THAT BRINGS UP MEMORIES OF YOUR MOM...
GOOD ONES?
Katsuki
IT WAS BACK WHEN WE BOTH WORKED AT A DESIGN AGENCY...
BEAM
NEVER MIND. DUN WANNA HEAR.
I WAS UP A CREEK WITHOUT A PADDLE WHEN IT CAME TO STRONG WOMEN, BUT...
...YOUR MOTHER, WELL, SHE CAME ON TO ME REALLY, REALLY HARD.
SHE POUNCED LIKE SOME SORT OF BIG CAT...
...AND BEFORE I KNEW IT...
...WE WERE MARRIED...
SO YOU COULDN'T REFUSE HER.

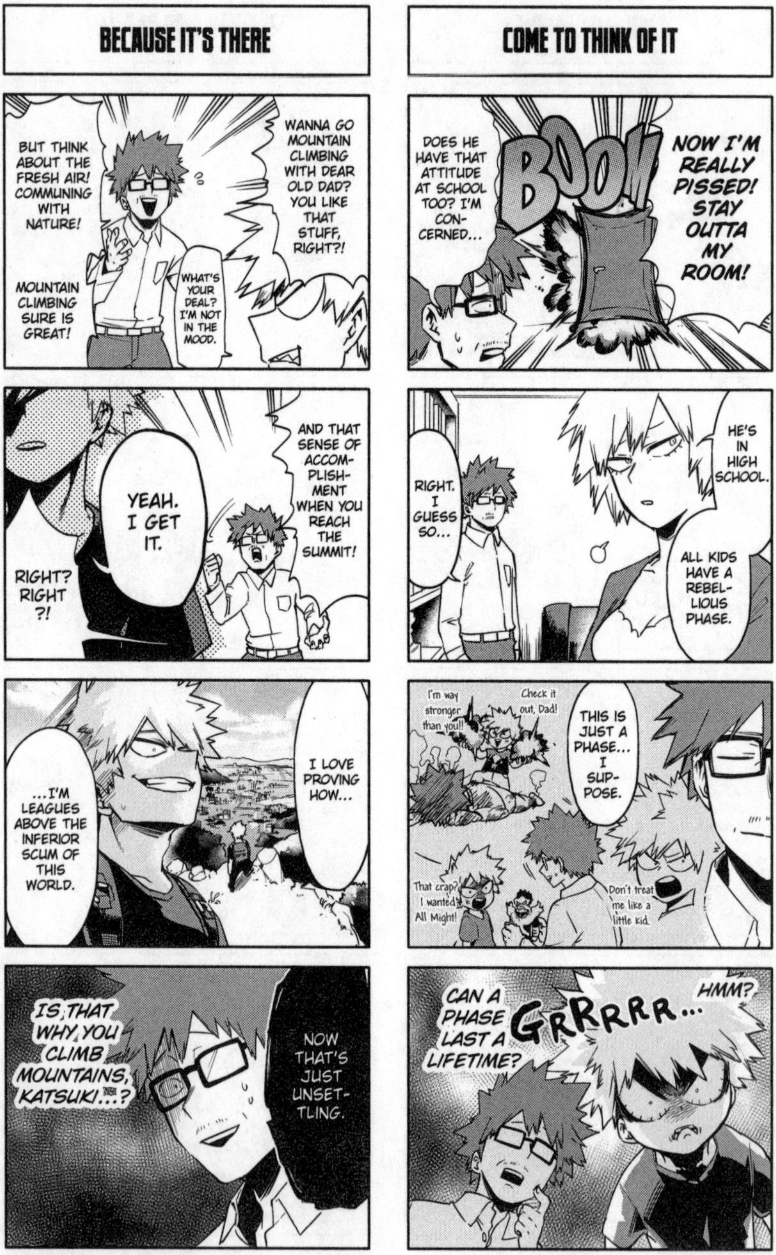
COME TO THINK OF IT
NOW I'M REALLY PISSED! STAY OUTTA MY ROOM!
BOOM
DOES HE HAVE THAT ATTITUDE AT SCHOOL TOO? I'M CONCERNED...
HE'S IN HIGH SCHOOL.
RIGHT. I GUESS SO...
ALL KIDS HAVE A REBELLIOUS PHASE.
THIS IS JUST A PHASE... I SUPPOSE.
Check it out, Dad!
I'm way stronger than you!!
Don't treat me like a little kid.
That crap? I wanted All Might!
HMM?
GRRRRR...
CAN A PHASE LAST A LIFETIME?
BECAUSE IT'S THERE
WANNA GO MOUNTAIN CLIMBING WITH DEAR OLD DAD? YOU LIKE THAT STUFF, RIGHT?!
BUT THINK ABOUT THE FRESH AIR! COMMUNING WITH NATURE!
WHAT'S YOUR DEAL? I'M NOT IN THE MOOD.
MOUNTAIN CLIMBING SURE IS GREAT!
AND THAT SENSE OF ACCOMPLISHMENT WHEN YOU REACH THE SUMMIT!
YEAH. I GET IT.
RIGHT? RIGHT?!
I LOVE PROVING HOW...
...I'M LEAGUES ABOVE THE INFERIOR SCUM OF THIS WORLD.
NOW THAT'S JUST UNSETTLING.
IS THAT WHY YOU CLIMB MOUNTAINS, KATSUKI...?
END

AFTERWORD

Thank you for reading this far.

Imagining how team-ups between different kids will turn out is exciting.

Going forward, I'm planning to feature the characters who didn't get much time in the spotlight in volume 1.

See you in volume 2!

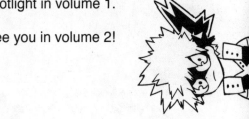

SAGURI-CHAN TANKENTAI IS A PREVIOUS SERIES OF MINE. THERE ARE FOUR VOLUMES TOTAL. PLEASE CHECK OUT SAGURI-CHAN IF YOU'RE INTERESTED.

Yoko Akiyama

YOU'RE READING THE WRONG WAY!

MY HERO ACADEMIA Team-Up Missions

My Hero Academia: Team-Up Missions reads from right to left, starting in the upper-right corner. Japanese is read from right to left, meaning that action, sound effects and word-balloon order are completely reversed from English order.

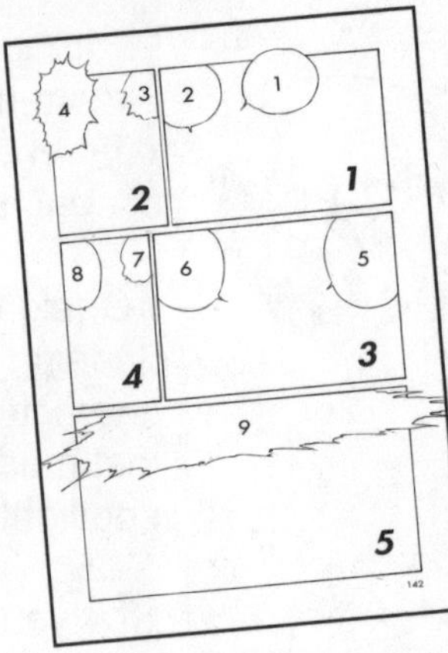
1
2
3
4
1
2
5
6
7
8
3
4
9
5
142

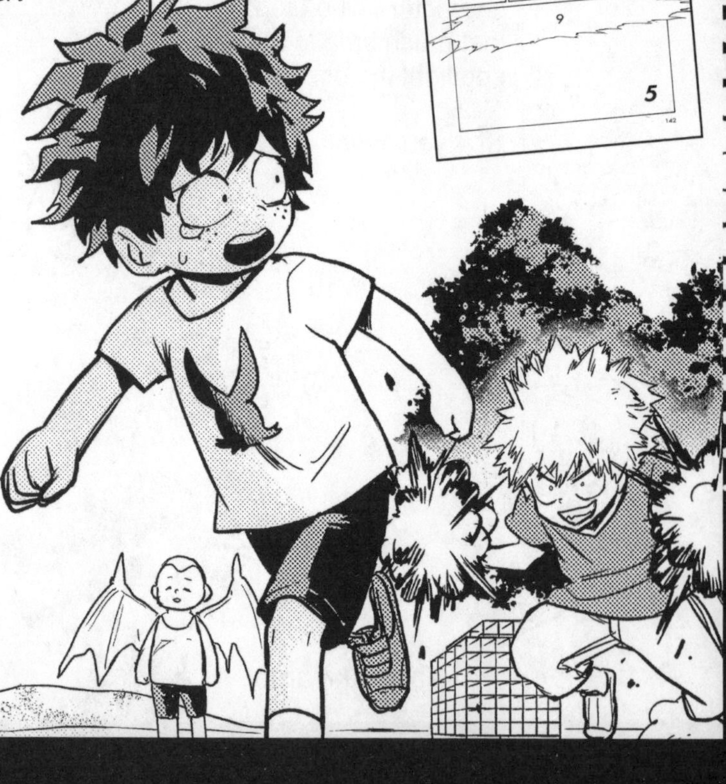